THE 33 1/3 B-SIDES

THE 33 1/3 B-SIDES

Edited by Will Stockton and D. Gilson

BLOOMSBURY ACADEMIC
NEW YORK · LONDON · OXFORD · NEW DELHI · SYDNEY

BLOOMSBURY ACADEMIC
Bloomsbury Publishing Inc
1385 Broadway, New York, NY 10018, USA
50 Bedford Square, London, WC1B 3DP, UK

BLOOMSBURY, BLOOMSBURY ACADEMIC and the Diana logo are
trademarks of Bloomsbury Publishing Plc

First published in the United States of America 2020
Reprinted 2020

Cover design by Louise Dugdale
Cover image © Paperkites/iStock

Library of Congress Cataloging-in-Publication Data
Names: Stockton, Will. | Gilson, D. (Duane)
Title: 33 1/3 B-sides / edited by Will Stockton and D. Gilson.
Description: New York, NY : Bloomsbury Academic, 2019. | Includes
bibliographical references and index.
Identifiers: LCCN 2019008330 (print) | LCCN 2019009950 (ebook) | ISBN 9781501342424
(ePDF) | ISBN 9781501342448 (ePub) | ISBN 9781501342455
(pbk. : alk. paper) | ISBN 9781501342943 (hardback : alk. paper)
Subjects: LCSH: Popular music–History and criticism.
Classification: LCC ML3470 (ebook) | LCC ML3470 .A16 2019 (print) | DDC
781.6409–dc23
LC record available at https://lccn.loc.gov/2019008330

ISBN: HB: 978-1-5013-4294-3
         PB: 978-1-5013-4245-5
         ePDF: 978-1-5013-4242-4
         ePub: 978-1-5013-4244-8

Typeset by Integra Software Services Pvt. Ltd.
Printed and bound in the United States of America

To find out more about our authors and books visit www.bloomsbury.com
and sign up for our newsletters.

CONTENTS

Contents

PREFACE

"I feel like B-sides are always better," Alicia Keys told *Rolling Stone* in 2005, "no matter whose record it is."[1] This anthology of crisp, compact chapters from previous 33 1/3 authors focuses on B-sides: albums these writers found better, best, bad, worth batting an eye over, or better yet, worth another spin. We asked the writers included here to think about a different future for their 33 1/3 contribution: an album they might have written about, but which didn't make the cut.

For our previous contribution to the 33 1/3 series, we wrote about a band—dc Talk—central to our young adulthood, and about a genre—contemporary Christian music—largely unexplored within the terrain of 1990s alternative rock criticism and the 33 1/3 series. Yet before we hit on writing *Jesus Freak*, we almost wrote separately on different albums. Will mapped out 30,000 words on Prince's multi-disc *Emancipation*, and D. brainstormed a pop-culture memoir that pivoted around Christina Aguilera's Spanish-language album *Mi Reflejo*. To us, these albums were B-sides: records that didn't distinguish their artist's careers, but which were important to Prince and Aguilera fanatics like us. In other words, these albums were superfluous to the rest of the world, but strangely essential to us as obsessive music consumers.

This collection brings together members of the 33 1/3 family who, like us, wanted to riff on albums they believe deserve a place in the series, albums that deserve a second glance. Charged with writing short chapters on their own B-sides, the authors here address the concept with an array of approaches reflecting the range and diversity of the 33 1/3 series itself. In keeping with the conventional notion of the B-side as an obscurity, something forgotten or appended, most of the albums found here have flown under the critical radar. But the use of the B-side itself expands outward from there to include albums of our adolescence refound ("Juvenilia"); albums relegated to the margins of a genre, a subculture, or an artist's catalog ("Marginalia"); and albums appended to or commemorating other events, like concerts or films ("Memorabilia"). Eschewing the generic organization of the albums discussed here, we honor our contributors' variety of perspectives through this three-part thematic organization. In turn, we hope the volume produces a notion of the B-side as capacious as the series itself.

In bringing this volume to print, we thank not only the authors, but also our dutiful Bloomsbury editor, Leah Babb-Rosenfeld. She challenged us to think deeply about the B-side, and gave us the breadth to do so. Thanks as well to Amy Martin, Deborah Maloney, and the anonymous copy editors and typesetters who made this sprawling volume possible. We surely tested their patience.

— Will Stockton & D. Gilson

INTRODUCTION: SUPERFLUOUS, REDUNDANT, ENDURING—PRINCE'S *EMANCIPATION* (1996)

Will Stockton

The Artist Formerly Known as Prince—hereafter referred to, for simplicity's sake, as Prince—released three albums in 1996. Or maybe two, if soundtracks don't count. Or maybe six, if a triple album counts as three. The soundtrack to the Spike Lee film *Girl 6* (itself a superfluity in Lee's catalog) appeared first in March. The inclusions are mostly vintage Prince: "Girls & Boys" (from 1986's *Parade*), "Erotic City" (the B-side to 1984's "Let's Go Crazy"), "How Come U Don't Call Me Anymore" (the B-side to 1982's "1999"), and "Adore," "Hot Thing," and "The Cross" (all from 1987's *Sign o' the Times*). The songs from Prince's side projects—The Family's "The Screams of Passion" (1985), Vanity 6's "Nasty Girl" (1982), and The New Power Generation's "Count the Days" (1995)—as well as newer songs like NPG's eponymous "Girl 6," "She Spoke 2 Me," and "Don't Talk 2 Strangers" (which Chaka Khan does better on her Prince-assisted 1998 album *Come 2 My House*)—nestle in as filler.

Featuring, by contrast, all new and previously unreleased material, *Chaos and Disorder* appeared a few months later in July. Relatively few people noticed. Prince popped up on the *Late Show with David Letterman* and NBC's *Today* to play "Dinner with Delores," the album's first and only single. But he otherwise refused to promote the album. *Chaos and Disorder* peaked at number twenty-six on the US *Billboard* charts, a notable decline from *The Gold Experience*'s number two peak in 1995. Reviews were also conflicted. Robert Christgau christened *Chaos and Disorder* "a guitar album for your earhole" and awarded it an A–.[1] *Rolling Stone*'s Ernest Hardy called the album "a collection of polished demos" from an artist with nothing left to say and awarded it two stars.[2]

Prince had his reasons for lying low and slipping *Chaos and Disorder* quietly onto music-store shelves. He wanted to move on—musically, yes (he was always trying to move on musically)—but more immediately from his record company, Warner Brothers, whom Prince rather audaciously claimed had turned him into a slave.[3] This claim smacked of the absurd for an artist who just one year previously, and despite declining sales in the late 1980s and early 1990s, had extended his contract with Warner Brothers to the tune of $100 million. But Warner Brothers refused to release music at the rate the notoriously prolific Prince demanded. Under the terms of the new contract, Warner Brothers also claimed ownership over all the music—the master tapes—Prince had produced for the label. Almost as soon as he'd signed the contract, Prince regretted it. He began performing with the word "slave" scrawled on his cheek. Abandoning the name

"Prince" as a Warner Brothers product, he bewildered the press by changing his name to a now infamous glyph. However misguided this maneuver was as a legal strategy—for the name change did not in fact free Prince from the terms of the contract—he began to focus all his energies on emancipation.[4]

When Ernest Hardy describes *Chaos and Disorder* as "a halfhearted transaction from a self-pitying artist,"[5] he is not entirely wrong. The packaging itself reads as an afterthought. A scant, bitter, three-page fold out, featuring images of a cash-stuffed syringe, a toilet, a vault lock, and the Bible, passes for the liner notes. Under the track listing, Prince appended a note legible as an apology for the album's shoddiness: "Originally intended 4 private use only, this compilation serves as the last original material recorded by [the Artist] 4 warner brothers records—may u live 2 see the dawn." Downgraded by its creator from a proper album to a "compilation" like the soundtrack for Spike Lee's flop comedy, *Chaos and Disorder* lands like a collection of B-sides delivered to Warner Brothers in coerced fulfillment of a contractual obligation.

Chaos and Disorder isn't awful for being that. My assessment leans more towards Christgau's than Hardy's. *Chaos and Disorder* is a respectable little rock record—brisk and gritty, deftly inflected with rap and hip-hop. The title track offers a garage-rock rewrite of the world-weary "Sign o' the Times." A blistering blues guitar drives "Zanalee." Prince seemed especially fond of the album's second track, "I Like It There," and performed the song often in the years that followed. Is *Chaos and Disorder* tossed off? Sure. Half-hearted? Only in terms of Prince's public disinterest in this Warner Brothers product. But the supposedly enslaved, self-pitying Prince remained a wicked musician. Consequently, even *Chaos and Disorder*'s lyrical missteps, like "I rock, therefore I am," arrive on earworm melodies.

Prince's delivery of *Chaos and Disorder*, as well as a second compilation called *The Vault: Old Friends 4 Sale* (not released until 1999), concluded the artist's contractual relationship with Warner Brothers. In November 1996, he celebrated this conclusion with the release of the triple-album *Emancipation*. The album constituted a labor of love in several senses. It commemorated not only his freedom from Warner Brothers, but also his marriage to Mayte Garcia and the impending arrival of their son Amiir (who would tragically die from Pfeiffer syndrome six days after his October 1996 birth). Whereas *Chaos and Disorder* ran a mere forty minutes, *Emancipation* extended to 180— each sixty-minute disc containing twelve songs. Whereas *Chaos and Disorder* tracked its songs as a "compilation," the meticulous cut of each *Emancipation* disc gave the appearance of expert album curation. And whereas the blue-and-black cover of *Chaos and Disorder* signaled its artist's angry subjugation to the label by planting a shoe print over a cut-out of Prince's eye, the sunny orange cover of *Emancipation* joyously boasted its creator's freedom with a pair of fists snapping apart shackles. Sitting side by side on the shelf with the summer release, *Emancipation* announced—as the far more robust liner note booklet confirms—that the listener had now lived "2 see the dawn."

If three albums seem excessive, superfluous, that was the point. Given the gradual dip in sales of new Prince records following the 1988 release of *Lovesexy*, Warner had worried about market oversaturation, about flooding the market with *too much*, and thereby diminishing the profitability and impact of any one product. With *Chaos and Disorder*, Prince's response to the label's request for restraint seemed deliberately perverse: he gave them a collection of songs he never intended to release.[6] The Artist coded *Emancipation*, however, as a pure expression of liberated artistic will. He spent a year recording the album—the longest he ever spent on a project. "This is my most important record," he told executives from EMI, the label he contracted to handle promotion and distribution. "I'm free, and my music is free."[7]

The problem with *Emancipation* itself is simply that it's not *that* good. The triple album contains some decent songs: the luxuriously lazy "Jam of the Year," the slow-build-to-searing "The Love We Make," and the crisp marriage hymn "The Holy River." But much of the album sounds rote, redundant. Prince does formulaic R&B: "Right Back Here in My Arms" and "Somebody's Somebody." Formulaic techno-pop: "Slave," "New World," and "Human Body." Formulaic hip-hop: "Mr. Happy" and "Da, Da, Da." All in all, the album sounds less ahead of its time (the accolade so frequently bestowed on Prince's past offerings), and more like a weak imitation of R. Kelly and Dr. Dre. Prince's choice of an unremarkable cover of the Stylistics' "Betcha By Golly Wow!" for the album's first single did not bode well for the other thirty-five tracks on Emancipation, not one of which would top Prince's last big chart success, 1994's "The Most Beautiful Girl in the World"

To be sure, *Emancipation* is not Prince's worst: that was to come in the early 2000s when he began releasing music through the online NPG Music Club and, in physical form, on CD singles sold at concerts. With some exceptions—like "When Eye Lay My Hands on U" and "U Make My Sun Shine"—the songs later collected on *The Slaughterhouse* (2004) and *The Chocolate Invasion* (2004) sound like *Emancipation* B-sides. In 1996, *Emancipation* foretold not so much the bright and bounteous dawn of awesome new music as the extreme variance in the quality of releases to come: the middling (1999's *Rave Un2 the Joy Fantastic*, 2001's *Rainbow Children*, 2002's *One Nite Alone*, 2004's *Musicology*, 2006's *3121*, 2014's *Art Official Age*, 2015's *HITnRUN Phase Two*) and the mostly bad (1998's *Newpower Soul*, 2003's *Xpectation, C-Note*, and *N-E-W-S*, 2009's *LOtUSFLOW3R* and *MPLSoUND*, 2010's *20Ten*, and 2014's *HITnRUN Phase One* and *PLECTRUMELECTRUM*).

I would be remiss in not pointing out that *Emancipation* has its defenders, including Robert Christgau, who called it "the book for the young turks of a reborn, historically hip R&B."[8] He awarded it, like *Chaos and Disorder*, an A–. Reviewing the album for *The Onion's* A.V. Club, Stephen Thompson declared "there are a hell of a lot of fates worse than having [Prince] crank out albums this good every three months—and the oft-excellent *Emancipation* is a whole lot better than the oft-mediocre Prince product that's flooded the market in the past few years."[9] Revisiting the album for *Billboard* in 2016, Dan Weiss argues: "The music on *Emancipation* is uniformly strong and varied, possibly Prince's most consistently good album of the 1990s."[10] (I would bestow that compliment on *The Gold Experience*, if not on 1992's *Love Symbol*.) Twenty years later, I find that *Emancipation* still makes a fine album for spring cleaning. It is upbeat, happy, and, yes, "free"—eclectic and jazzy. The propulsive anger of *Come* (1994), *The Gold Experience*, and *Chaos and Disorder* has vanished. A sense of relief and release infuses the whole effort. But forced to put something together fast to liberate himself from contractual oppression, Prince made a better album with *Chaos and Disorder*. As musically varied as it is sprawling, as uniformly strong as it is undistinguished, *Emancipation* ultimately comes off as both unchallenging and overworked.

Emancipation suggests, at least in hindsight, that Warner Brothers had been right. Prince wanted to release too much. He needed to edit himself—to slow down and hold back. However emancipatory, the ability to release whatever he wanted whenever he wanted didn't do the overall quality of Prince's work any favors. Of course, it's hard to underestimate today Prince's influence on modern methods of music distribution. Prior to the advent of Napster and streaming services, and the cratering of the compact disc market, Prince was uniquely poised to step off a major label and still make money. There are reasons other than his prescient changes in music distribution models, however, for Prince critics to so often divide his career into pre- and post-1995. The distinction registers the difference between a lot and too much, almost consistently brilliant and often dull. At his regular rate of production, Prince conceivably wrote or recorded over a hundred songs for *Emancipation*. And the thirty-six songs that survived number around twenty-four too many. *Emancipation* would have been better as a single album. "Jam of the Year" remains the lead track. "Curious Child" and "Emancipation" make the cut. I'm even partial to "Face Down," a Prince rap about the audacity of hearing "no" from the music industry. But "Damned If Eye Do" and "Style" become B-sides. "White Mansion" and "My Computer" never leave the vault.

For a triple album by Prince, *Emancipation* faired just okay, rising to number eleven on the *Billboard* 200. To date, it has sold north of one million copies.[11] For Prince's supposedly most important album, however, *Emancipation*'s sales landed far below *Purple Rain*'s twenty-one million or even *Sign o' the Times*' four million. One must always be cautious of judging quality in terms of sales, but, in Prince's case, the comparison is fair—a more or less accurate reflection of the changing cultural importance of Prince's music. *Emancipation* is today something of a lost Prince album. It's not an album anyone would use to introduce Prince's work. It lacks a track as memorable as later songs like "Musicology" (2004) or "Black Sweat" (2006). None of its songs appear on iTunes' list of the Essential Prince. *Emancipation* seems, in hindsight, like an album Prince needed to make in the moment but almost immediately move on from.

In this case, Prince moved on to the January 1998 release of *Crystal Ball*, another three albums of material from the vault, along with the acoustic album *The Truth* and the orchestral-ballet album *Kamasutra*. Again, there are gems in this five-disc bundle: the psychedelic "Crystal Ball," recorded alongside *Sign*'s "Starfish and Coffee" in 1986 and slotted for two ultimately abandoned albums *Dream Factory* and an unrelated triple-disc *Crystal Ball*; the insane "Cloreen Bacon Skin," a studio jam with Morris Day on drums and Prince on bass and vocals; and a thumping live version of "Days of Wild" (the studio version of which remains unreleased), in which Prince leads the audience in a chant of "free the slave." *The Truth*'s title track, "Don't Play Me," and "The Other Side of the Pillow" mark the best of Prince on acoustic guitar. But again, too, the package contains headscratchers. "Poom Poom" has to be one of Prince's least inspired terms for sex. *Kamasutra* bores. And what the hell is "Animal Kingdom?" An acoustic song espousing veganism, complete with dolphin chattering and an admonition to "leave your brothers and sisters in the sea." On Prince.org message boards, "Animal Kingdom" routinely ranks, along with *Emancipation*'s "Mr. Happy" and his 2010 song for the Minnesota Vikings "Purple and Gold," among Prince's worst.

If *Crystal Ball* and *The Truth* contain some of the best and worst of Prince, they, along with *Chaos and Disorder* and *Emancipation*, prove the artistic and career utility of a distinction Prince was arguably trying to escape in his feud with Warner Brothers: the distinction between an A-side and a B-side. Prince had released an album of B-sides before: the third disc on his 1993 *The Hits/The B-Sides* collection. Here, too, is some of the best of Prince: "Gotta Stop (Messin' Around)," "How Come U Don't Call Me Anymore," "Erotic City," "She's Always in My Hair," and "17 Days." But these B-sides are, for the most part, great, enduring tracks that hadn't found their own album. The slash between a hit and a B-side wears thin on that three-disc compilation. The same cannot be said of the album *and* non-album tracks released in and after 1996. The chart-toppers had vanished. And notwithstanding some minor flashes of his previous popularity in the two decades that followed (his ostensible "comeback" with 2004's *Musicology* and his twenty-one-night stand at London's O2 arena in 2007), the hits wouldn't return with the same frequency or force. Taken as a whole, Prince's post-1995 catalog provides the B-side to pre-1995's A-side.

***

Why, then, do I love *Emancipation*? Probably because I discovered Prince in the 1990s during my late adolescence, when music makes its most indelible impression. When music tangles itself up in the synapsis of emerging adult identity. When, as Gina Arnold writes in her chapter in this volume on R.E.M.'s EP *Chronic Town*, music leaves you feeling like you've been punched in the face.

The Prince who punched my acne-ridden teenage face was not the Prince of *1999* or *Purple Rain*, albums released when I was 3 and 4 years old, respectively. The first song of Prince's I remember hearing, or at least identifying as a song by that tiny black guy in high heels, was the aforementioned ballad "The Most Beautiful Girl in the World." On a loop with Elton John's "Blessed" and Hootie and the Blowfish's "Let Her Cry," the song played every couple of hours during my part-time shifts at Media Play, a long-defunct big-box retailer of music, books, and movies. The lyrics to "The Most Beautiful Girl in the World" sounded like the stuff of ordinary pop: "It's plain to see you're the reason that God made a girl." It could have been a line from the New Kids on the Block, whom I'd had the good social sense to stop liking several years prior. But this pop song was sexy, experienced, and sultry in a way the New Kids never were. I wanted to know what Prince knew about sex, about God.

To own "The Most Beautiful Girl in the World," I purchased 1995's *The Gold Experience*, as well as the 1994 EP *The Beautiful Experience*, which features the single and six remixes. (I was, and remain, a completist.) With the exception of bubblegum pop, most of the music I listened to as a young teenager fell into the genre of contemporary Christian music (CCM): dc Talk, for instance, about whom I wrote my 33 1/3 book in collaboration with my co-editor for this volume, D. Gilson. But I also listened to a lot of Michael W. Smith and Amy Grant. Some Twila Paris and too much Carmen. The minor-key grizzliness of so much grunge and alternative music scared me. The crime-, sex-, and bullet-ridden world portrayed in so much rap and hip-hop music remained entirely foreign to my rich suburban white boy experience. I had moral problems with the whole of the secular music industry and its championing of "worldly values," so even as I edged into the early-1990s mainstream, I remained safely on the adult contemporary margins with Sting, Rod Stewart, Bryan Adams, Elton John, and Billy Joel. In 1995, I had simply never heard anything as sexually aggressive as *The Gold Experience*'s "Eye Hate U": a mean slow burn built around the mock trial of a cheating girlfriend. Prince asks the court "to have the defendant place her hands behind her back / So [he] can tie her up tight and get into the act"—a form of sex I would later learn to call hate fucking. I had never envisioned the equation of female financial and sexual power espoused on "P Control." I did not know that music could be as throbbingly seductive as "Shhh" ("I wanna do you after school like some homework. / Am I getting you hot?") Or as gloriously wild as "Billy Jack Bitch," which culminates in a horn solo the likes of which I previously supposed the instrument incapable.

The literature on Prince swells with stories of discovering Prince: the punch, the moment of revelation, when the listener encounters a strange new world of sex and spirituality, of libidinous apocalypticism and virtuoso musicality.[12] My story is no different, however late my port of entry. I knew music, especially black music, could be dirty. I'd heard that 2 Live Crew produced an album so dirty it was illegal. My parents forbade me from buying Vanilla Ice's *To the Extreme* (1990). But Prince was too good to turn into my parents or the police. As a closeted gay Christian teen, I found Prince's music tantalizing and cathartic, brimming with jizz and Jesus alike. If he "sincerely want[ed] to fuck the taste out of your mouth" (*1999*'s "Let's Pretend We're Married"), he also wanted Delores to "introduce the carpet to something other than [her] knees" ("Dinner with Delores"). There wasn't much Christian goodness I could wrench from "Horny Toad" (the jump-blues B-side to "Little Red Corvette") or the incest-endorsing "Sister" (off 1980's *Dirty Mind*). But there was godliness aplenty in much of 1988's *Lovesexy*. "The Cross" (from *Sign*) was straight-up CCM, right? And the point of "Dinner with Delores" was clearly that Dolores *shouldn't* be whoring around.[13] When Prince sang, on "Chaos and Disorder," that if he "had fifteen women, he would only fuck with one," I nodded in approval of his inclination to monogamy.

Although I didn't predict Prince's conversion to the Jehovah's Witnesses (I hoped more for non-denominational Christian), *Emancipation* slotted easily into my narrative of Prince's awakening to Jesus. Compared to previous albums, Prince had cleaned up his lyrics. He sings about sex, of course, but less so, and he's not vulgar. The sex on *Emancipation* is mostly marital, chaste. He built "Sex in the Summer" around the sound of his unborn son's heartbeat. He invites his new wife to the bedroom for the purpose of procreation ("Let's Have a Baby"). He admonishes men to satisfy their wives (okay, their "babies") to keep them from straying ("Sleep Around"). "The Holy River" celebrates marriage as a spiritual and sexual transformation: "Relationships based on the physical are over and done / You'd rather have fun with only one." "Joint 2 Joint" strays slightly from the straight and narrow in its story of a one-night stand with a woman who thinks she's Prince's "soulmate," but we all make mistakes. I ultimately classified the song, along with the Song-of-Solomon-tinged "Soul Sanctuary" and the cover of Joan Osborne's "One of Us," as one of *Emancipation*'s songs about spiritual searching—for truth, for God.

I love *Emancipation* because I hear in it my adolescent sprawl—its poise as a moment of transition to something new. (For me, that would actually be to an out gay atheist, albeit several tumultuous years later.) I recognize now that the earlier albums, the albums of the 1980s, are better, more culturally enduring albums. But that recognition would only come with time, age, and musical exposure. Because, in 1996, my musical exposure was (severely) limited, Prince's catalog offered me a course in music history and genres: rock, pop, funk, dance, jazz, hip-hop, rap, even gospel. I followed along not only because *Emancipation* resonated with my Christian teen confusions about sex and spirituality, but also because it was sonically familiar *enough*. Much of *Emancipation* echoed the sounds I knew from their Christian music translators like dc Talk, and from popular Atlanta radio stations like Star 94: contemporary R&B and (radio-friendly) hip-hop. It took me a long time to understand how innovative, how pattern-setting, albums like *1999*, *Purple Rain*, and *Sign o' the Times* had been. How Prince fused rock guitar riffs with funk bass lines. How he at once embodied glam, punk, and soul sensibilities, male and female personas, and queerly exploded the notion of what it meant to be a "black artist." How everything that's great on *Emancipation* sounds like Prince imitating himself a decade previously. I had to listen. I had to be told.

***

My Prince collection now spans from 1978's *For You* CD to the 2018 vinyl release *Piano & a Microphone*, a collection of solo recordings from 1983. My husband finds this collection excessive; it's redundant now that almost all of Prince's music is available on streaming services. It's mere memorabilia. But I retain the hipster preference for anachronistic physical product. The collection also includes the unstreamable: for instance, *NYC Live 1/11/97*, a cassette single issued by NPG Records exclusively through the phone-order line 1–800-NEW-FUNK. This "cassingle" makes a distinction between its "Funky Side" and its "Funkier Side." But this distinction proves meaningless. The same live versions of two songs—"Jam of the Year" and "Face Down"—appear on both sides. When I bought the tape, I found this "joke" puzzling. I owned plenty of cassingles and CD singles, all of which I bought for their B-sides. I carried Elton John's "The One" to the checkout counter at Turtle's Records and Tapes because I wanted to hear "Suit of Wolves" and "Fat Boys and Ugly Girls." Sting's "Fields of Gold" single included excellent live versions of "King of Pain," "Fragile," and Jimi Hendrix's "Purple Haze" (all from the 1991 *Soul Cages* concert video). I have inexplicably strong memories of roller skating in my neighbor's carport to the instrumental version of Michael Jackson's "Black or White." The B-side was supposed to supply something extra, something not already on the album. Like the new songs tacked onto a compilation album, the B-side gave people who already owned the album a reason to buy the song again.

But to this demand—from labels, from consumers—Prince had also started saying no. Two other album tracks appeared on the single to "Dinner with Delores": "Right the Wrong" and "Had U." "Right Back Here in My Arms" appeared as the B-side to "Betcha By Golly Wow!" "The Holy River" appeared side-by-side with the radio edit of "Somebody's Somebody" (along with two remixes of the latter song and an already released remix of "The Most Beautiful Girl in the World"). Following the release of 1993's *The Hits/The B-Sides*, one could no longer expect to find a "17 Days" or "How Come U Don't Call Me Anymore" on the flip side of a new Prince cassingle or as track two on a thin-cased CD. Other album tracks and remixes padded these products out. Prince, we know, was now vaulting more music: holding onto it for another album, if not in perpetuity or "4 private use." The bonus tracks included on the 2017 re-release of *Purple Rain* confirm that he was capable of vaulting some of his strongest material: "The Dance Electric" (a song Prince gave to André Cymone) and "Electric Intercourse." Yet Prince's disinterest in releasing "proper" B-sides after 1993 proved prescient. In courting the disappearance of A-sides and B-sides, Prince was, as was so often the case previously, once again ahead of his time.

Since the invention of the vinyl record in 1948, the term "B-side" has referred, most literally, to the second side of the disc. On LPs, the B-side equates with the second side of the album—sometimes the place for filler, but not always, and less so as the idea of the album developed throughout the second half of the twentieth century. On singles issued to record stores, the B-side became a place to showcase non-album tracks, demos, and live recordings. The A-side featured the song the label wanted promoted to radio and consumers. The B-side housed something else, something presumably worth hearing, but also something generally considered lesser, and thus accorded secondary status. B-sides played to a fan's obsession: to our desire, as music listeners and completists, for something *more* that usually can't be satisfied.

This A/B distinction between album and non-album track, good and less-good, did not always hold. Plenty of singles featured only radio and album edits, remixes, and other album tracks. Some B-sides, like Elvis Presley's cover of "Hound Dog" (1956), The Rolling Stones' "You Can't Always Get What You Want" (1969), Gloria Gaynor's "I Will Survive" (1978), and The Smiths' "How Soon is Now" (1984), surpassed their A-sides in popularity. But ideally the consumer received something that hadn't made the album cut. If you wanted a sample of all the other material Prince recorded around *Purple Rain*, you had to buy the singles. If, in 1987, you wanted to hear the songs that didn't appear on U2's *The Joshua Tree* ("Luminous Times [Hold on to Love]" or "Spanish Eyes"), you had to purchase the singles (for "With or Without You" and "I Still Haven't Found What I'm Looking For," respectively). If you wanted to debate whether "Even in His Youth" should have been on Nirvana's *Nevermind*, you had to hear it on the single for "Smells Like Teen Spirit."

The decline of the cassette, and more recently the CD, has resulted in the diminished use of the term "B-side." Now merely figurative in the age of streaming music, the "B-side" sounds somewhat out of time. The album form, which *Emancipation* expanded to the point of explosion, has arguably outlived itself. The ease with which we sequence our digital playlists provides us as fans and consumers, rather than just the artist or the label, with the ability to privilege and subordinate tracks, to track our own "essentials" and "extras." For many of the writers in this collection, a B-side designates an extra. It means additional, leftover, supplemental, or excessive. Sometimes more is better. Sometimes not. Sometimes the B-side helps to illuminate the logic of the A-side—its sequencing, cohesiveness, and unity. Sometimes it outshines the A-side. Either way, B-sides help to flesh out our understanding of an album, an artist, a group, a genre, or a moment in time by asking us to focus on what gets relegated to the margins.

The 33 1/3 series focuses on albums, not songs, so perhaps titling this collection *33 1/3: The B-Sides* is misleading. Here, too, the focus lies on albums, although often on particular songs from those often-overlooked albums. We invited previous 33 1/3 authors to write short chapters on albums they chose not to write about originally: the ones that didn't make the cut. We asked, too, that these albums fall generally into the category of the forgotten or the neglected, whether justly or unjustly. Or if the album was popular (like Leonard Cohen's *Songs of Love and Hate* [1971]), or a breakthrough (like Sinéad O'Connor's *I Do Not Want What I Haven't Got* [1990], famous for its cover of Prince's "Nothing Compares 2 U"), what case remained for considering it a B-side? What about these albums consigns them to the outskirts of an artist's catalog or a historical moment? To the second side of a career or a cultural narrative? And what about the album endures: culturally, personally, sonically? Why write about it?

My lack of knowledge regarding Prince's previous catalog made *Emancipation* an important Prince album to me—one I took on face value as Prince's most important album. I effectively shoehorned it into the genre of CCM even as it anchored a catalog that helped me come to terms with my own queerness. In time, I realized that *Emancipation* was a B-side. I came to that realization sometime around 2000, perhaps the 170th time I heard *Sign o' the Times*. Prince seemed to realize it much more quickly, perhaps on the "Jam of the Year" tour (1997–1998). I saw all three shows Prince performed at the Fox Theatre in Atlanta (January 8–10, 1998). I wanted to hear "Face Down," sure, but the audience screamed for the hits that packed the set: "If I Was Your Girlfriend" or "Kiss" or "Purple Rain."

Prince would frequently chafe against the expectation that he tour with the hits and the hits alone. He said repeatedly, as the 1990s ended, that he would no longer perform "1999" in the new millennium. Then he performed it, a lot. On tour for *The Rainbow Children*, Prince stuck mostly to that album, captured on 2002's *One Night Alone ... Live!* box set. Then he followed it up in 2003 with a world tour of hits. It's as if Prince realized, by the mid-2000s, that his new albums were indeed the B-sides to the more enduring A-sides of his 1980s' catalog. Fans bought tickets to hear "Let's Go Crazy." If you played that, they might stick around for "Guitar" (from 2007's *Planet Earth*).

Prince's final two shows, also at the Fox Theater in Atlanta on April 16, 2016, themselves suggest an A/B distinction. Unfortunately, I did not attend either show. I live two hours away from Atlanta, and I was busy with work. The first show of the night was thick with crowd favorites: "Little Red Corvette," "Dirty Mind," "Baby I'm a Star," "Pop Life," "Kiss," and "Adore." It was only somewhat self-indulgent. Alone at the piano for this tour, Prince played "Linus and Lucy," his cover of Joni Mitchell's "A Case of You," *The Rainbow Children*'s "Muse 2 the Pharaoh," and even "Chopsticks." But Prince truly brought the strangeness in the second show of the night, what would prove to be his last live concert. He opened with The Staple Singers' "When Will We Be Paid," the *Love Symbol* deep-cut "The Max," "Black Sweat" (from 2006's *3121*), and "Girl" (a B-side to 1985's "America" [United States] and "Pop Life" [United Kingdom]). He played "Indifference," a song he'd recently written with 3RDEYEGIRL and released only as a live version online, and covered Bob Marley and the Wailers' "Waiting in Vain." He closed the night with a medley of "Purple Rain," "The Beautiful Ones," and "Diamonds and Pearls"—medleys having long been his preferred method of running through so many of the A-sides his audience demanded. "I got so many hits," he used to tell the crowd, "y'all can't handle me." But the April 16 shows, in their structure, suggest his heart was just as much in the B-sides. I should have been there.

Will Stockton is the co-author of Jesus Freak (#134). Find him at willstockton.com.

REINTRODUCTION: TRIVIAL, DERIVATIVE, TENACIOUS—CHRISTINA AGUILERA'S *MI REFLEJO* (2000)

D. Gilson

"I want to be an all-around entertainer. I want to act, make films, make albums, do whatever I can."

—Christina Aguilera

Between August 24, 1999, and October 26, 2002, Christina "The Voice" Aguilera released four studio albums: her self-titled debut (1999), *Mi Reflejo* (September 2000), *My Kind of Christmas* (October 2000), and *Stripped* (2002). Over this mere three-year, two-month, and two-day span, she sold over twenty-eight million of these albums; transformed her image from Disney child star to assless-chaps-wearing, sex-positive young feminist; and, it seems clear to me now, altered the state of the B-side from an undervalued album or song to an artistic identity in and of itself. Christina Aguilera is, herself, a B-side. And I love her for that.

Just as the MP3 digitized music—taking the art form from a physical enterprise to a series of ones and zeroes, likes and retweets—the B-side as a concept faced a peculiar conundrum in its cultural rotation. Initially a thing of necessity during the mid-twentieth century—the literal backside of a vinyl pressing—the B-side became a way for artists to include likely trivial tracks on otherwise sellable enterprises at the bequest of their record labels. As vinyl records became cassettes and then compact discs, the B-side didn't disappear, but became a powerful marketing tool to drive up overall sales. I didn't *need* to buy Amy Grant's 1991 single "Baby, Baby," as the song was her chart-topper off *Heart in Motion*. But I begged my sister Jennifer to buy the cassingle for me anyway, because on its B-side was "Lead Me On." With lyrics like "Bitter cold terrain / Echoes of a slamming door / In chambers made for sleeping, forever," the song *might* allude to slavery and the Holocaust—or so Grant told *CCM*, a magazine for contemporary Christian music that Jennifer and I read every month perched on her bed in our plain ranch house back in Aurora, Missouri. A budding poet, I found the metaphors she wrote (with Wayne Kirkpatrick and Michael W. Smith) intoxicating and "deep," but, had I looked back, I would have also realized the song appeared on her 1988 album. The "Baby, Baby" single was just an excuse for A&M to resell two songs they'd already been selling.

In his preceding introduction, Will points to songs like Prince's "17 Days" and "How Come U Don't Call Me Anymore" as superior B-sides in a pre-digital moment: non-album tracks, outtakes, exclusives, something extra. To this list I would add Madonna's "Act of Contrition," a B-side to 1989's "Like a Prayer," driven by Prince on guitar; and

Elliott Smith's "How to Take a Fall" (1998), a song with an unintentional manifesto on the B-side: "Make me a present and make it something sweet / Small enough to go unnoticed and big enough to compete."

The world, and certainly the world of popular music, turns on one's ability to be "big enough to compete." In the twenty-first century, many artists became lifestyle brands in order to secure their market share. "You a mom-and-pop, I'm a corporation," sang Mariah Carey on 2009's "Obsessed," a song supposedly dissing the hardly small-time rapper Eminem. Consequently, album B-sides became less about promoting singles, and more about artists promoting themselves to a hopefully expanding consumer base. This transformation, as well as this expansive concept of a B-side, had pre-digital precedence, of course. See the films of Elvis Presley, if not of Prince and Madonna, too. Music accompanied motion pictures to not only feed the appetites of music fans, but also to find new receptive listeners. (After seeing Madonna in *Evita* [1996] at the Wehrenberg 16 Theater in Springfield, Missouri, my 12-year-old queer self demanded my mother take me to our local FYE to buy the soundtrack. Years of me belting "Don't Cry for Me Argentina" alongside Madge from my bedroom subsequently ensued.) But, in the digital age, B-sides largely became something more tangible: pieces of memorabilia, perfumes, reality shows, tennis shoes, hair extensions, jeans, and Spanish-language translations.

***

Here is one of the many ways in which I am an American stereotype. Though I have spent weeks in Mexico, Argentina, Venezuela, and Nicaragua, and though I now live in Texas, I know only three Spanish phrases:

1. *Mi mariconcito* (My little faggot)
2. *Gloria a Dios* (Glory to God)
3. *Ven comingo* (Come on over [a mistranslation]).

The first is a more recent acquisition, from a friend taking Spanish lessons and taken to calling me *mi mariconcito* as a term of endearment. But the other two are distinct remnants, or ever-lingering spirits, from my evangelical childhood and, more specifically, holdovers from the missions trips I took as a Jesus-lovin' teenager. Listening to Christina Aguilera today, and to her perhaps laughable 2000 Spanish-language album *Mi Reflejo* in particular, inevitably transports me back to one of these missions trips: when I traveled with my youth group (Real Life Student Ministries of James River Assembly of God) to Venezuela in the summer of 2001.

Taylor, Aurora, and I occupy the back row of a Boeing 737 bound for Caracas from Miami, where we have flown via Dallas from Springfield. From our sleepy corner of Missouri to a Venezuela in upheaval, to a sprawling capital where Leftist revolutionary Hugo Rafael Chávez Frias has come to power just months before. We are newly 16, and will spend the week with local Pentecostal missionaries, devoting mornings to prayer in our suites at the Caracas Hilton; afternoons to volunteering in local orphanages or handing out tracts in plazas between towering, mirrored skyscrapers; and evenings to theatrical church services on the streets, performing skits in broken Spanish and giving testimonies through interpreters. *Gloria a Dios, Gloria a Dios*, we'll whisper to each other, and to God. Ours is a story typical of evangelical Christian culture at the beginning of the twenty-first century: we are white suburban teenagers here to save the brown urban Catholics.

Preparing for this trip back in the States, I have been consigned to minor roles in our skits because, it is quickly apparent, I have no tongue for Spanish. I spend two weeks perfecting the phrase *Gloria a Dios!* only to be relegated to a silent part in a skit which Taylor and I can't discern as comedic or tragic: I am just your everyday jock at an ordinary high-school party, bro'. As loud rock 'n' roll music fills our youth group auditorium—a stand-in for what will become a busy street corner in downtown Caracas—I pantomime shooting up heroin in my fleshy, white arm and eventually languish in the unseen fires of Hell.

I do not care. Taylor, Aurora, and I are silently realizing we're queer. Daily revelations are soundtracked by Whitney Houston, Selena, Matchbox 20, Michael Jackson, Britney Spears, The Goo Goo Dolls, Mariah Carey, Third Eye Blind, Madonna, and, of course, Christina Aguilera. On our first trip to South America, to a city more sprawling and more cosmopolitan than any we've ever visited, we skip out on prayer sessions and afternoon street canvasing to drink *café au laits* at coffee stands outside Best Buy or Macy's or Saks Fifth Avenue. (Chavez's government has yet to tank the then-flourishing Venezuelan economy.) In the world of our youth group, we three queers are relegated to the sidelines, so nobody notices us skipping out on prayer or witnessing. We are liked, but never the stars of the show that is evangelical Christianity in a youth-obsessed mega church at the dawn of the twenty-first century. Never the lead in a skit, never the solo in a performance, never the young person chosen to deliver a testimony or lead the group in prayer. In the world of our youth group, we're B-sides: superfluous, tangential, extra.

***

"I'm on a lonely road that leads to nowhere," Christina Aguilera crooned on Ed McMahon's Nielsen-topping *Star Search* on March 15, 1990. At just nine years old, it was instantly evident Aguilera could sing, belting out the jazz standard "A Sunday Kind of Love," a song that had last been made famous by Etta James on her 1960 album *At Last!* Watching Aguilera's performance on YouTube today, I'm struck by its novelty. She's belting impeccably, of course, a skill we've come to expect of her. But she's so young on that stage, and the song feels inappropriate for someone who has yet to turn ten. Not inappropriate in the sense of the performance's morals, but in the sense that Aguilera lacks a certain conviction. "Oh I'm hoping to discover," she pleads to the audience, riffing from a soft minor chord up to a vibrating major note she sustains in what will become her signature style, "a certain kind of lover who will show me the way." But her body, it's just too small to contain the gravitas, the lived experience, the song demands, rendering her performance a novelty, a schtick, and derivative.

But it doesn't matter, not really. Aguilera became a finalist that night in 1990, but she didn't win. She lost to a young African American named Christopher Eason. (He posts on social media sporadically now under the handle @TheKidWhoBeatChristina and is, last I can find, a barista in Oklahoma.) Eason, age twelve, dazzled in his interpretation of Patti LaBelle's 1986 song "There's a Winner in You." He appears completely comfortable in his young body, and it shows as he smiles at the audience: "There's a winner, there's a hero, there's a lover, too. Somewhere, there's a winner in you." For not the last time in her life, Aguilera was overshadowed. She was a living B-side.

***

This (in hindsight, lackluster) performance at age nine perhaps foretold a struggle Aguilera would face her entire career, a struggle to feel "at home" in that voice that so defined, and perhaps even defied her—or at least defied the body in which an overt sexuality, or plea to sexuality, would often feel more like a desperate commercial attempt as opposed to a "natural" expression, if such a thing is ever possible. And much of this desperation would come across as Christina being a reactionary to her supposed rival, Britney Spears. I don't want to dwell on this period, or to pit the two stars against each other, a strange (and gendered) pitting we, the listening and viewing public, have long insisted upon. But it is important to a discussion of Aguilera herself as a B-side. Whereas Britney started off as a mid-riff-bearing Catholic schoolgirl, a sexual spectacle and archetype if ever there was one, with her 1999 *Billboard*-topping single "… Baby One More Time," Christina offered herself (or RCA offered her, depending on whose account you believe) as a flirty but family-friendly alternative with "Genie in a Bottle," and then her self-titled debut as well as the hasty follow-up commercial albums *Mi Reflejo* and *My Kind of Christmas*. I mean, a Christmas album! This was more in the trajectory of Amy Grant, queen of the holiday compilation, than Madonna or Cher.

Thus, it was shocking, to say the least, when Aguilera largely disappeared for two years and returned with 2002's *Stripped*. I still remember the afternoon of October 4, 2002, when I plopped on the couch after school and watched MTV's *TRL* (*Total Request Live*) as my mother bent over her sewing machine nearby. Although Aguilera's handlers wanted to release the ballad "Beautiful" as the lead single from *Stripped*, Christina insisted on "Dirrty"—yes, with two "r"s!—as an assertion of her sexual liberation. A collaboration with hip-hop's Redman, the video opens with a tight shot of a woman's butt. Barely encased in tiny red panties with a black "X" below assless leather chaps stitched with "Xtina," Christina walks forward and her cheeks bounce free. The shot widens and we find her, hair filthy and face bearing several new piercings, in a dark, wet, Thai warehouse. She eventually finds herself in a boxing ring, fighting or dancing or *something* with a group of similarly-dressed women. She half-sings, half-spits lines like "you can just put your butt to the maximum." And I don't want to slut-shame Christina, but none of it feels like *her*. It feels forced. Like a plea, not for sex—I'm totally fine with that—but for attention, i.e., for sales. It certainly didn't help that Christina can't dance or act, and the song hides what she can do, which is flat-out sing. As the video played that afternoon, my mother stopped sewing and looked up at the television. "Huh," she sighed, "When I was young we had to pay a nickel to see that."

But again, Christina was too late, a reactionary in a marketplace that largely rewards early adapters. Prince had made the assless pants famous as far back as 1991, when he appeared on the MTV Video Music Awards to perform the also double-consonanted "Gett Off." Only months prior, Britney Spears had released *Britney*. Its lead single, "I'm a Slave 4 U" (here again, Prince script), featured Spears in her own bikini top, sweating in a Latin American club as dancers—male and female alike—lick the sweat off her body. The song and video are iconic, positioning Spears as the heiress apparent to Madonna's and Prince's kingdoms of sex in public. And watching it today, it feels sexy as fuck, still, and, unlike Christina's "Dirrty," somehow unforced, organic, and natural. Watching it renders Aguilera imitative, juvenile, a B-side.

***

It is a muggy afternoon in Caracas when we should be at an underground train station, smiling wide on the platform and inviting people to street church that evening. (From my experience, commuters don't want to be bothered by teenagers trying to proselytize. We stood in that metro station, as Ezra Pound writes, smiling dumbly at the "apparition of these faces in the crowd" rushing to pass us and board their train.) But Aurora and I don't stay underground long. We sneak off to the Museo de Arte Contemporáneo, where we stand before a giant print of Andres Serrano's 1987 photograph "Piss Christ," the rough crucifix floating in a glass jar of the artist's own urine. Aurora and I wear matching green T-shirts bearing *James River Assembly Missions 2000* on the front, *Gloria a Dios!* in huge, tacky, white font across our backs. "It's beautiful," she says of the portrait, and I nod my head.

Technically, *Gloria a Dios!* was the second Spanish phrase I mastered. That summer, Taylor and I drove around the Ozarks every day in my gold Saturn sedan. We drove to the mall or to get cashew chicken at Hong Kong Inn or to Barnes & Noble, where we sat for hours in the *café* with a stack of magazines, each reading *Out* or *XY* or *The Advocate* behind a screen of *The New Yorker* or *U.S. News & World Report* or *ESPN*. Taylor was taking Spanish lessons and I was taking a class in HTML coding at the local community college, and every day as we drove around town we listened to Christina Aguilera's second studio album, *Mi Reflejo* (2000), on repeat. The album, which somehow won the Best Female Pop Vocal Album at the 2001 Latin Grammy Awards, is mostly known for its Spanish translations of Aguilera's self-titled, *Billboard*-topping 1999 debut. Track five, "Ven Conmigo (Solamente Tú)" ("Come On Over Baby [All I Want Is You]"), was by far our favorite and, in the Ozarks humidity—my AC had broken that summer—we'd drive from wherever to church to practice for our upcoming missions trip, the windows down and our 16-year-old queer tenors belting, *Ven conmigo, ven conmigo baby, ven conmigo, ven conmigo baby*, out of the open windows as Christina, herself not fluent, struggled on the stereo.

Like me, and despite the suggestion of the surname Aguilera, Christina did not speak Spanish before (during, or after) recording a Spanish-language album. This did not daunt her producer, Cuban-American Rudy Pérez, who was used to working with artists seeking reverse crossover into the Spanish-language market from mainstream

(English-centric) American pop: itself a type of missions work in the name of capitalism, if not Christ. Before Christina, he brought Mexican-American Christian pop star Jaci Velasquez to the top of the *Billboard* Hot Latin Tracks with the single "Llegar a Tí" ("Get to You"), the first Christian song to reach that status; but, unlike Christina, Velasquez grew up speaking Spanish along the US-Mexico border in south Texas. When it came to preparing Christina for the studio, *Billboard* reports: "Pérez wrote out all of Aguilera's lyrics phonetically and devised a system to help her roll her 'r's."[1] On the track "Falsas Esperanzas" ("False Expectations"), Christina avoids the rolling "r" of the repeating *corazón* by trilling in her signature vibrato. This is true not only of "Falsas Esperanzas," but also of *Mi Reflejo* as a whole, a technique of avoidance that leaves the album feeling chaotic, other-worldly, but from a world to which few want to travel. In the arc of her career, the album is a B-side, but a telling one: it doesn't matter that her Spanish translation of hits like "Come On Over Baby (All I Want Is You)" ("Ven Conmigo (Solamente Tú)"), "Genie in a Bottle" ("Genio Atrapado"), "I Turn to You" ("Por Siempre Tú"), and "What a Girl Wants" ("Una Mujer") are not, aesthetically speaking, *good*. It matters that they poised the pop starlet to expand her selling power with minimal effort on her part or the part of producers and her record label.

In his chapter on commercialism and J-pop for this volume, Jordan Ferguson argues that the women of the group Perfume, whom he loves, "aren't artists per se, they're sales people. Every Perfume single is tied to a fizzy drink or an automobile or a line of supplements, because in Japan 'selling out' isn't something to be avoided, it's necessary for survival." I want to extend his thesis *avant la letre*: in any crowded marketplace, "selling out" is necessary for survival. And if ever there was a crowded marketplace in contemporary American pop, it was the group of young white women vying for bubblegum royalties in the late 1990s and early 2000s following Madonna's foray into electronic dance music with 1999's *Ray of Light*.

***

The original title for *Mi Reflejo* was *Latin Lover Girl*, although marketing agents decided to cash in on the earlier success of Aguilera's 1998 single "Reflection," which had garnered her original record deal with RCA. Aguilera made a music video for "Reflection" to accompany the DVD release of Disney's *Mulan*, an animated "interpretation" of a legendary Chinese woman warrior who disguised herself as a man in the Northern Wei province sometime during the fifth or sixth century C.E.

Of course, race brings complexity to the B-side at every turn. In his superlative chapter herein on De La Soul's *De La Soul is Dead* (1991), Shawn Taylor explains how "black whimsy is about being playfully odd. It's about mapping your inner joy and curiosity over the mundanity of your everyday existence. It's about looking into the shadows without fear, possibly even venturing into them, just to see if anything is there." This is true, but what happens when a white girl with the surname Aguilera records in a non-native language? Is she venturing into some shadow of her past—real or imaginary—just to see if anything is there? Or is she, like the Walt Disney Company that largely created her, a white mass media colonizer?

***

Following her thwarted win on *Star Search*, Christina traveled to Orlando in 1991 to audition for a reboot of Disney's 1950s' *The Mickey Mouse Club* (*MMC*). Billed as a variety show to include musical and dance performances as well as sketch comedy, *MMC* producers loved Aguilera's audition, but couldn't find a way around union rules; Christina was two years too young to be cast. An 11-year-old Christina Aguilera was sent packing back to Pittsburgh.

When she turned 13, Aguilera immediately joined *MMC* in 1993 for the show's final two seasons. Her cast-mates—including Britney Spears, Justin Timberlake, Ryan Gosling, and Keri Russell—lovingly nicknamed their kid sister Christina "The Diva" for her vocal prowess. (I say "lovingly," but in an unattributed interview I watched on YouTube, a young Spears, who would quickly become Aguilera's biggest competition in the marketplace of early-twenty-first century pop music, explained that the nickname arose from Christina's demanding and over-the-top behavior on set.) And although she had the voice to earn this moniker, the die was already cast, and Aguilera was, by necessity, in the shadow of her *MMC* co-stars, who could not only sing, but also dance and act. By the time Aguilera released her debut album, Keri Russell and Ryan Gosling were staring in their own hit television series, *Felicity* and *Breaker High*, respectively; Justin Timberlake was fronting the explosive boyband N*Sync; and Britney Spears was not only touring the world with Timberlake and the boys, but also releasing her own debut seven months before Christina, a debut that would go on to become the biggest selling album by a teenage artist ever.

***

Mi Reflejo was a relative flop, selling less than three million copies worldwide (and less than half a million in the United States) during an era when Aguilera sold fourteen million of her self-titled 1999 debut and ten million of 2002's *Stripped*. Something was lost in translation, even if I can't stop listening to the lead single, "Ven Conmigo," over and over still today.

Ven conmigo translates not as "come on over baby," as Aguilera might have us, the English-language listeners of her Spanish-language album, believe. Instead, *ven conmigo* means literally "come with me." Song lyrics often change, slightly or significantly, in the process of translation. Meter, meaning, rhyme: these require adjustment from one tongue to another. Michael Jackson's 1987 single "I Just Can't Stop Loving You," to take just one example, became "Todo Mi Amor Eres Tú"—literally, "You Are All My Love"—when Jackson re-recorded it, using a similar phonetic rendering system, as a single for Latin audiences. Considering, however, the nakedly commercial marketing push behind Aguilera's endeavor here, a paranoid reading of Aguilera's "Ven Conmigo" might have us believe that this translation, a technical mistranslation, is best understood as an act of white American appropriation under late neoliberal capitalism—or an expression, at the very least, of American exceptionalism. To this end, as George Steiner explains in his book *After Babel: Aspects of Language and Translation*, "bad translations communicate too much."[2] I hazard that this paranoid reading is one almost any progressive scholar in the humanities is trained and ready to give: it's an easy argument to make when music is re-recorded in non-native, or not even second, languages for the express purpose of increasing sales. And yet, I don't believe this is the only, let alone the best, reading.

What is the very queer possibility in a (let's face it, white) American teen mistranslation of a simple Spanish phrase? And further, what is the queer possibility of two budding queers like Taylor and me belting out this mistranslation in a late-model Saturn sedan as we traverse the hills and valleys of the Missouri Ozarks? "Come on over baby" cum "Come with me." So much depends on the collective preposition *with*. Sometimes, as Philip Shaw argues here in his chapter on 1980's *The Return of the Durutti Column*, the love of a B-side is "a solitary affair." But sometimes, thank god, that solitary affair becomes a cult obsession, particularly for marginalized or niche groups, like queer teenagers in the backwoods of Missouri in love with both pop music and the seeming cosmopolitanism of "speaking" a second language.

Our listening to this odd B-side constituted a type of micro-collectivity. Odd, too, at a time when queers were (as if they are not still) so often rejected from the national collective. So much of modern socio-political life has been organized on the biblical principle of exclusive or illusive collectivity. "So," the writer of Matthew teaches us, "do not worry, saying, 'What shall we eat?' or 'What shall we drink?' or 'What shall we wear?' For the pagans run after all these things, and your heavenly Father knows that you need them. But seek first his kingdom and his righteousness, and all these things will be given to you as well."[3] That's great, in theory. But queers—like so many other groups throughout our nation's history—have so often been refused entry to the kingdom of heaven, and to the kingdom collective of the state, that queer theory, for a moment, refused the call to come together with the outside world, urging us instead to seek out first our own pleasures. Forever and ever, amen.

***

This anthology represents another type of collective: a group of distinct and diverse writers geeking out about the B-sides they love. And like the queerness I talk about above, the chapters collected here are promiscuous. Promiscuous, I mean, in a few key ways. Here we've been lucky to bring together many different types of writers, including academics, music journalists, and musicians themselves. They write promiscuously, too, across a variety of forms. Here you'll find music criticism fused with memoir, such as Walter Biggins's chapter on the Digable Planets or Jovana Babovic on the Smashing Pumpkins. Pete Astor writes an abecedarium on Bob Dylan's *Love and Theft*. Rebecca Wallwork writes a manifesto on disco transformation through the soundtrack to *Can't Stop the Music*. And Drew Daniel writes a treatise on suicidal ideation via an examination of Leonard Cohen's *Songs of Love and Hate*. Our writers come from a wide variety of backgrounds—racial, class, sexual, and gender—to discuss a wide variety of albums—from jazz and R&B, to folk and Jpop—beginning with 1961 and released as late as 2015. And even though we have asked them all to write under the signpost of the "B-side," that very term has taken here as many forms as there are writers and albums in these pages.

For me, a B-side means something you love—or, as evidenced here, something you can geek out about with a chosen few. Taylor and I loved this Christina Aguilera album despite the fact that we knew, even at age 16, it was not "good." We are not alone. "As critical standards go," David Smay writes in his chapter on The New York Dolls, "you may think that judging everything by the pleasure you got out of your favorite album at age 16 is a flimsy foundation. But you would be wrong. In fact, for rock criticism, it is the very best standard." It's hard to compare The New York Dolls to Christina Aguilera, sure. But, as I've said, the B-side is relative. What The New York Dolls' *Too Much, Too Soon* was to Smay, a suburban disgruntled teen in South Florida in the 1970s, might not be all that unlike what Prince's *Emancipation* was to Will or Christina's *Mi Reflejo* was to me, both of us closeted queers at the end of the millennium.

The B-side, unlike the A-side, is sometimes more about the listener—about us—than it is about the artist. The chapters we have collected here under the rubric of "juvenilia" testify to the enduring, shaping power of the music we encountered as teenagers: good music and bad, popular and unpopular; the music that introduced us to what music is and could be. Sometimes our juvenilia is a band's or an artist's too. Sometimes not. In any case, it's the music of youth: of pleasure and possibility.

***

The collective potential of pop divas in the marketplace stretches the limits of such a market. Christina was part of a late 1990s and early 2000s slew of hypersexualized young white women over-saturating that marketplace, a group also including Britney Spears, Jessica Simpson, and Mandy Moore. Britney, a decidedly more entertaining if also less vocally talented singer than Christina, was the only one to retain major selling power; today she joins the ranks of Madonna, Mariah Carey, Whitney Houston, Celine Dion, and Janet Jackson as one of the best-selling female artists of all time. Christina is the second-best selling of the millennial group, the materialized B-side. While Britney recently signed a contract to make $500,000 per show for a residency at The Park MGM on Las Vegas's Strip, Christina left NBC's *The Voice* over "contractual disagreements" and released *Liberation* in the summer of 2018. After spending so many years on non-recording projects like *The Voice*, Aguilera told *Billboard*: "I was longing for freedom."[4]

Liberation compares almost too easily to Prince's *Emancipation*, although where Prince's frustrations lay with his record label, Aguilera's centered on the lack of music in the industry formerly known as music. On "Accelerate," the lead single from *Liberation*, Aguilera gloriously fails to address that problem, however. "All my boss ladies," she sings, "Go get your Mercedes," and the B-grade rapper 2Chainz follows quickly with a signature spin out of "skrt skrt skrt skrt." It's not horrible—it's blandly fun, in fact—but it's also not *good*. It's a return to that Christina too young to sing the song she's crooning on *Star Search*, but inverted. She's nearing 40 now and faces competition from a new crop of white pop starlets, like Lady Gaga, Katy Perry, Miley Cyrus, and Kesha. In comparison, Aguilera looks silly singing a song with lines like "Sex drive Nascar crash it like the Nasdaq." And not silly because a woman her age (which is just a few years older than me) shouldn't sing about taking drugs at the club and staying out all night with her ladies.

(After all, Madonna embraced such a lifestyle on her own seventh studio album, *Ray of Light*, released at the dawn of the artist's 40th birthday. But unlike Christina, Madonna had always flaunted the club life and sex in public, so her embrace of electronic dance music did not read as an uncharacteristic and desperate grab for commercial success, but rather as an evolution.) Aguilera comes across as silly on *Liberation* because she can actually *sing*, and she doesn't here, not really. She's finally ready for the lived gravitas "A Sunday Kind of Love" makes requisite, but she's, like she's always had to, reaching for that thing that's just out of reach.

One could argue that Christina has always been an artist of the B-side. Her 1999 self-titled debut sold the most of any album in her career—well over nine million in the United States alone—and cemented her as a young pop powerhouse with the singles "Genie in a Bottle," "What a Girl Wants," "I Turn to You," and, of course, "Come on Over Baby (All I Want is You)." But despite the success of this album, it was publicly received as the B-side to an album released three months prior: … *Baby One More Time* by Britney Spears, which would go on to sell nearly double *Christina Aguilera* and cement Spears as the contemporary auteur of pop, albeit of the bubblegum, radio-friendly variety. Commercial and for the most part critical success were all downhill for Christina following 1999, with a few exceptions. Her single "Beautiful," from 2002's *Stripped*, provided Aguilera with a formula for success: heartfelt ballads paired with market campaigns addressing social issues, such as LGBT youth suicide and eating disorders. Her 2001 collaboration with Pink, Lil' Kim, and Mya on a cover of Patti LaBelle's 1974 hit "Lady Marmalade" became the center of a genius marketing campaign for the indie-film-cum-blockbuster *Moulin Rouge*. But her record sales and largely her critical reception, where there was any reception at all, fell thereafter. And it didn't help that Britney Spears remained a cultural force with a parallel rate of album output. By the time Aguilera attempted a reinvention comeback with 2010's *Bionic*, Spears had just released her most critically-acclaimed albums to date: the club smash *Blackout* (2007) and the radio-ready *Circus* (2008), which spawned the number one singles "Womanizer" and "Circus" and paved the way for her first Las Vegas residency at the Planet Hollywood Resort & Casino.

Liberation debuted at a respectable sixth on *Billboard* the week of its June 15, 2018, release. The following week, however, the album fell to the ninety-eighth position, one of the largest downward falls in *Billboard* history, and it has yet to rise higher. It, like many of Christina's albums, was immediately relegated to the margins.

Most artists have such marginalia in their catalogs. That is why the majority of the chapters collected here fall under the category of "marginalia." These chapters explore everything from the relatively diminished (see Clare Nina Norelli on The Doors' *Strange Days*) to the cobbled together and minimally distributed (see Marvin Lin on Daniel Lopatin's *Chuck Person's Eccojams Vol. 1*). These chapters take these B-sides outside of the margins and recenter them as important to an artist's trajectory: to the course of music over time, as it develops from the juvenile to the mature, or to the late.

***

We might have seen *Liberation* coming if we'd been paying more critical attention to Aguilera's earlier appeal to a market she mostly fails to reach through the recording of a B-side. By all accounts, Aguilera had few connections to Latin audiences despite her name. She was, after all, a white girl from the Pittsburgh suburbs. But she capitalized on her name and voice to reach the fastest-growing population of the western hemisphere: Spanish speakers. And, for them, she translated the hits from her 1999 debut and mixed them with a few songs rejected by Latina pop stars. I don't blame her for this. It is not entirely unlike Elton John's 1997 re-release of his hit "Candle in the Wind," which he performed at his friend Princess Diana of Wales's funeral earlier that year. Looking back, I would hazard that Aguilera's *Mi Reflejo* and John's re-recorded "Candle in the Wind" are best understood as acts of queer reinvention within the constraints of market capitalism. I saved up my allowance for weeks to buy every copy of the re-release of "Candle in the Wind" that our local Best Buy had in stock. Although I kept two for myself—still shrink-wrapped and stored in my parents' fireproof safe—the others I took to school and sold as collectables, no matter how derivative. At a premium, of course. All of us, every last one of us, is beholden to opportunity, and the B-side in all its forms provides Exhibit A for this opportunism in the music industry today.

"Candle in the Wind" was the B-side as memorabilia *par excellence*: music attached to, recorded for, something else, another event; something always tied to something else. Although often continuous with juvenilia—music that reminds us of our youth—the chapters we gather under "memorabilia" privilege the album's status as an accompaniment or memento. See here the writers taking on soundtracks and concert recordings, such as Bruce Eaton's *Bruce Springsteen and the E Street Band Live at the Geneva Theater* and Cyrus R. K. Patell's *American Idiot: The Original Broadway Cast Recording*. B-sides as "memorabilia" may also memorialize a certain time in a listener's post-adolescent life. Although often continuous here with "marginalia," the emphasis in these chapters, such as Hayden Child's piece on the Silver Jews' *Bright Flight*, resides in memory itself.

***

Looking back again and again: when Christina Aguilera pleads *ven conmigo, ven conmigo, come with me, come with me*, over and over, perhaps it is not just an act of mistranslation, but one of possibility. And when Taylor, in his good Spanish, and I, in my poor Spanish, belt out the generative mistranslation, perhaps the possibility found there takes on a specifically queer turn of sociality, of collectivity. And when Taylor, Aurora, and I skip out on our missions work to sit on a balcony thirty-something stories up at the Caracas Hilton and listen to Christina's *Mi Reflejo* on an early generation MP3 player (before iPods cum iPhones and their ubiquity), when we eat Doritos and stifle our laughter, lest the prayer group inside hear us, perhaps we form our own family, our own culture, our own society. And Christina, you're no superfluous, unnecessary B-side songstress to us.

"Contigo quiero estar, ser tuya, nada mas," Aguilera later stammers on the track, never quite landing that ultimate *-ar* on *estar*, her Pittsburgh accent showing through like rust on the Roberto Clemente Bridge on Sixth Street downtown. *With you I want to be, be yours, nothing else.* Queers understand this desire, not necessarily romantic, to be with you, to become an our, to be *with*, even if it means being second best, a B-side. A mistranslation of the individual that renders one anew, re-born, not in the biblical sense (who needs that?) but in the sense of the here and now. "Ven Conmigo," like all the songs on *Mi Reflejo* and later *Liberation*, is pure camp. But when Taylor and I drive down a two-lane highway outside Springfield, Missouri, singing and signing, learning the words and hitting repeat, and, unbeknownst, mistranslating, we're saying that nothing, not a song this bad, not a life of queer rejection, is beyond transformation. We are boys on the B-side, and I wish you could hear us.

D. Gilson is the co-author of Jesus Freak (#134). Find him at dgilson.com.

PART ONE
JUVENILIA

CHAPTER 1
LEONARD COHEN'S *SONGS OF LOVE AND HATE* (1971)
Drew Daniel

I came upon this most famous of albums from behind. My friend Rat had a black T-shirt on the back of which he had painted in white block capital letters:

THEY LOCKED UP A MAN
WHO WANTED TO RULE THE WORLD
THE FOOLS
THEY LOCKED UP THE WRONG MAN

Rat, aka Sean Garrison, singer for Louisville, Kentucky's angriest hardcore band Maurice (who would himself go on to be a scene-stealer in the 33 1/3 devoted to Slint), told me "It's from the back of Leonard Cohen's *Songs of Love and Hate* album and you should stop bothering me and go listen to it." I tried to do everything that Sean said back in those days, or everything that wouldn't get me killed or arrested. So I found a vinyl copy.

Given the matrix of my tastes at the time, it didn't seem promising: a Canadian singer-songwriter accompanied by acoustic guitar and moody string arrangements moaning about love and diamonds and raincoats? Really? I might well have reacted as Ryley Walker did when *Noisey* provided him with his first listen to *Songs of Love and Hate* in 2018: "I appreciate good lyricism but I don't relate to this shit."[1] Too coiffed. A Dylan B-side. But Leonard Cohen arrived blessed by not only the fandom of my own local hardcore teenage idol but other bands I liked too: Coil had covered "Who By Fire" and Nick Cave and the Bad Seeds had covered "Avalanche" from this very album. Apparently, this particular whiny Canadian guy with an acoustic guitar who was not Neil Young not only got a hipster pass but inspired the kind of devotion that warranted making T-shirts in his honor. My stepfather, a Jewish Canadian from Montreal with a droll sense of humor and tastes that were sophisticated beyond the Louisvillian norm, noticed and approved of my purchase too, with a cautious thumbs up that the record in question was "dark but great."

"Avalanche" begins with a description of private torment that also stands in for the experience of the listener's sudden immersion in Cohen's tortured inscape:

I stepped into an avalanche,
it covered up my soul.

When I am not this hunchback that you see,
I sleep beneath the golden hill.[2]

Nervous fingers scythe through chords as a low voice declaims lyrics whose highly wrought turns of phrase plunge aggressive affect into an ice bath of witty inversions and disclaimers. There's plenty of hate to go around: the speaker is abject, misanthropic and insolent, pre-emptively hating themselves while proclaiming an indifference to judgment. At the time I was reading Par Lagerkvist's "The Dwarf" and the song seemed to align eerily with that narrative of existential angst draped across a cold-medieval setting.

When I am on a pedestal, you did not raise me there
Your laws do not compel me to kneel grotesque and bare
I myself am the pedestal for this ugly hump at which you stare

Cohen's lyrics reward the kind of close reading typically reserved for poetry, and they solicit this attention even as Cohen's delivery lands with an uncomfortable, sleeve-tugging immediacy—as when he slurs and drags out the "a" in "stare" in the lines quoted above. Performance upstages planning. By the time I arrived at the lyrics "Do not dress in those rags for me, I know you are not poor," I was stung with a blush of recognition. I was attending a posh private high school situated in downtown Louisville, but I wore shoes so worn out that they had to be held together with duct tape, a punk-by-numbers sartorial choice that prompted some kind soul to offer me spare change under the assumption that I was homeless. I was barely through the first song and Leonard Cohen had already read me to filth.

I didn't love it all. Upon first listen, I found the dowdy amble of "Diamonds in the Mine" repellent, and the songs struck me then as formally repetitive and tonally monotonous, with Cohen cycling through the same choppy little phrases over and over. However poetically elaborate, Cohen's jeremiads felt twice as long to ears accustomed to thirty-second punk spasms. To be fair, the horn lines were occasionally doubled with a chirpy and quite unexpected citrus burst of synthesizer, but all the same, it was and remains a deeply dour affair. As a singer, Cohen seems willfully unaware of his own voice's restrictions, slurring into quasi-laughter and braying and powering through the incantatory restatements of these songs with a "fuck it" energy that is uglier than punk. As in the sonnets of Sir Thomas Wyatt, Leonard Cohen's women, invoked but unnamed, summoned and repelled, seem like ciphers and sphinxes, proxies more than presences. Lyrically, many of the erotic countercurrents around dalliances with unnamed "girls with chestnut hair" that busy Cohen's attention were far beyond my ken as a closeted gay teenager in the shadow of AIDS. Upon repeat listens, the emotional currents of world-weary fatigue, cocksure braggadocio, and guilt-ridden self-recrimination on offer sounded like grandiose, poetic versions of my own everyday discomfort and longing.

But the album has one song that clicked into tight focus for me, a wound of a song that still won't quite heal. That song is "Dress Rehearsal Rag," a searching excavation of what psychiatrists and counselors clinically diagnose as suicidal ideation, but which has gone by other names over the centuries: melancholy, weltschmerz, saudade, the blues. Written early in his career, Judy Collins had recorded the tune in 1966, but it's Cohen's version that hit me then and it remains harrowing listening even now. Joining the album's rogue gallery alongside its hunchbacks and saints and would-be Scientologists, its speaker starts low ("4 o'clock in the afternoon and I didn't feel like very much") and heads down from there:

A bitter voice in the mirror cries hey prince you need a shave
Now if you can manage to get your trembling fingers to behave
Why don't you try unwrapping a stainless steel razorblade

The set up for this agony of collapsed masculinity in defeat is simple and everyday: you are looking at your face in the mirror covered in shaving cream and realize that you could always use your razor to kill yourself. It's a theme as old as Seneca: the freedom to die is always present. It's in our hands. When the song pivots from self-hatred to the possibility of action, Cohen's speaker shivers and stammers as he keeps double-checking and re-announcing intentions on the brink of an ending:

That's right it's come to this
Yes it's come to this
And wasn't it a long way down
Wasn't it a strange way down

The face in the mirror is a tragic mask, but also a comic one: Cohen's speaker sees himself as both a Hamlet-esque failed prince and as a ludicrously white-bearded Santa Claus. Cue the children's choir! Into the mix they creep on tiny feet, singing along with Cohen "wasn't it a long way down" with a hushed sort of horror. However much the decision to use a children's choir to intone "Wasn't it a long way down" follows logically from the Santa image, those children's voices have always struck me as both deeply perverse and damning (and it's a move that Yo La Tengo revisit in their cover of Sun Ra's "Nuclear War" to similar effect).

Cohen's lonely despair and hopelessness feel compounded by the plurality of voices rather than consoled, and the song keeps upping the ante of self-laceration:

Now Santa Claus comes forward, that's a razor in his mitt
And he puts on his dark glasses and he shows you where to hit
And then the cameras pan, the stand-in stuntman
Dress rehearsal rag
It's just the dress rehearsal rag
You know this dress rehearsal rag

This is the mockery of the self that cannot bring itself to die but doesn't want to live. We are not in the space of a suicidal climax, but in the bad faith of a loose attachment to life that fantasizes about death but suffers a sort of showy, pseudo-hapless impotence about the capacity to truly act. The dress rehearsal is not the real performance, it's a practice before the real thing to come, so it lacks the courage of its suicidal conviction, and it hatefully knows its own falsehood. One feels soiled by the intimacy of Cohen's disclosure. We squirm alongside the will to die, but never make it to the finish line.

While listening again to this song I visited Beachy Head, the moody and beautiful cliff-side which forms the site of the cover photograph of Throbbing Gristle's *20 Jazz Funk Greats*, the album I wrote about for the 33 1/3 series. It is also the most notorious site for suicides in Great Britain. The day I went was sunny, and there were little clusters of German and Japanese tourists, schoolkids, and British families dotted upon the green lawns that extend to the dizzying edge of the cliff. Lying upon my stomach, I crawled slowly towards the rim of the land, only briefly allowing myself a short but nauseating stare downwards to the fatal ground below. In that moment, I felt what is called "l'appel du vide" (the call of the void), the sense of vertiginous freedom unto death offered by the possibility of self-killing, but also a writhing inward sense of aversion, of attachment to life in the midst of that possibility. Leonard Cohen's "Dress Rehearsal Rag" takes that feeling and rotates it ninety degrees, turning every mirror we pass into an opportunity to sound out ourselves and see if we want, or can bear, to stay attached to life.

In its self-mockery and its humor, "Dress Rehearsal Rag" also let me know that I could survive my own feelings of despair and self-hatred. As a gay teenager who found the closet both suffocating and inescapable, I had been sent by my frightened parents to see a psychiatrist because of some para-suicidal behavior, including bragging and threats about self-harm. "Dress Rehearsal Rag" showed me that other people rode these waves of feeling, walked through them and out the other side. When I heard *Songs of Love and Hate* at the age of 16, I knew more about hate than love. More about the B-side than the A-side. Just as my stepfather had promised, Cohen's "dark but great" album offered handholds towards the abyss, but it also offered guard rails that kept me from tipping over. Rat's T-shirt may be frayed or lost, the famous blue raincoat may be torn at the shoulder, but the album that inspired it still stands, and scares, and endures. I'm glad it stood in my way.

Drew Daniel is the author of *20 Jazz Funk Greats* (#54).

CHAPTER 2
THE NEW YORK DOLLS' *TOO MUCH, TOO SOON* (1974)
David Smay

You could sense the pressure building first as a distant howl. Then the rattle turned into a roar and it exploded into the station with the shriek of steel on steel. And because it was the 70s, a disorienting smear of color resolved into a leering Mickey Mouse graffito entangled in cryptic bubble letters. People shoved in, hips and asses grinding out a space, strap-hangers airing out a bit of funk: Chanel No. 5 and Hai Karate, Right Guard, nicotine, sweat, and Aquanet. The train rolled out, rocking bodies side to side. And that was The New York Dolls—the band that was a city that was a band.

It's misleading, though, to simply classify The Dolls as a New York band. They were something much more specific and compelling—an East Village band. The Velvet Underground carved out that corner of Manhattan for art, rock and roll, noise, outrage, androgyny, and drugs. When The Velvet Underground played their last show at Max's Kansas City in 1970, The Dolls followed close behind with their own residency at Max's in 1972. The Dolls passed it on, creating a direct lineage to country bluegrass blues (CBGB): Patti Smith read poetry before one of their gigs at the Mercer Arts Center, and Debbie Harry sang backup on stage with them with the Stilettos. Joey's pre-Ramone glam band, Sniper, opened for The Dolls out in Queens, and Television was on the bill at the Little Hippodrome at the very end, a few weeks before Richard Hell hooked up with Johnny Thunders to create the Heartbreakers.

That subterranean influence didn't emerge until decades after The Dolls' flash, crash, and burn. The Dolls' immediate impact on the 1970s was less than negligible, derided as "mock rock" on *The Old Grey Whistle Test*, dismissed as a camp novelty, a joke band without sales or radio play. Like a true B-side they weren't appreciated until the entire decade had been flipped over and the novelty revealed as a lipstick killer with a dirty laugh.

The Dolls certainly cracked wise but that's not what fans and critics mean when they refer to their sense of humor. No, it's the pure glee The Dolls took at everything falling apart. It's no coincidence that The Dolls collapsed around the same time that New York City went bankrupt. The center could not hold, mere anarchy let loose on the Lower East Side, and The Dolls celebrated with "Seven Day Weekend." You almost have to go back to Harpo Marx to find that sensibility, and it's the gift The Dolls gave to The Replacements, that cackle of delight in a car wreck.

That is the complicated thing about The Dolls' legacy; every band could break off a little chunk and make it their own. Kiss copied the makeup. The Sex Pistols stole the riffs and the outrage. The Ramones took their New York velocity. Guns N' Roses walked off with their swaggering sleaze (and every hair metal band of the 1980s copied their look). The Strokes kept the five-man twin-guitar lineup and the Manhattan hangover. (Last Night they were in Babylon, boys.) The Cramps picked up their mantle as supreme rock and roll archeologists, unearthing chunks of raw id embedded in forgotten 45s.

When Johnny Marr knocked on Morrissey's door for the first time he won Moz over by playing a Marvelettes B-side. Morrissey was President of the New York Dolls Fanclub and The Dolls obsessed about girl groups like the Shangri-Las and Marvelettes. It was a secret handshake disguised as a B-side.

The New York Dolls weren't the only girl group fans in the 1970s. The composer of "Will You Still Love Me Tomorrow" herself was dominating the charts in the year The Dolls formed, Ronnie Spector cut cool singles with George Harrison and Bruce Springsteen, Andy Kim took "Baby, I Love You" into the top ten, and even Grand Funk had a hit with "Locomotion."

But what The Dolls did was bequeath it to punk. They built it right into the foundation so that Blondie could step into that space with a knowing wink, and decades later indie poppers could tease out that same girl group strand and say, "Yes, this is punk. Vulnerability is punk as fuck." When Jeff Magnum covers the Paris Sisters, he does that in part with a permission granted by The Dolls. When he sang "I Love How You Love Me" he meant LUV, L-U-V.

That is the virtue of The Dolls' brand of anarchy. As Patti Smith sang it, "Anything's allowed." The Dolls' genderfucking what-the-fuckery offered a very radical kind of permission. Their androgyny gets misconstrued or devalued or filed without context under "Shocking!" Perhaps because they don't neatly slot with the current edition of the Diagnostic and Statistical Manual of Mental Disorders (DSM). Perhaps because they purposefully muddied every distinction.

They weren't gay (well, by 1970s rock-star standards—what's a little blow job among friends?), but they did play gigs at the Continental Baths while gay men were screwing in the shadows. They weren't drag queens, but they did play in women's dresses at a famous drag venue, Club 82 (not to mention their first album cover). They weren't transexual, but they were very definitely trans-something. Transgressive. Transplendent. Prince would sing about trading clothes with his girlfriend, but The Dolls were obviously putting that into practice a decade earlier.

Nothing was forbidden. Nothing was shameful. Maybe you were born that way, but maybe—the way The Dolls saw it—gender was a form of play. That's the way they made it look. Neither locked into law, nor biological destiny. You could strap on a kid's set of cowboy guns *and* tease up your hair. You could go down to the beauty shop and get your hair styled *and* rock a blues harp. Throw a hockey jersey over white tights, look like Eddie Cochran raided his sister's closet, or rouge up your cheeks with Liza Minelli poppet realness. Lots of people sang about freedom, but The Dolls showed you how that might actually apply in the world. And they made it look *so* fun.

I bought *Too Much Too Soon* at the Thunderbird Drive-In Swap Meet in 1977, aged 16 and ready to be perplexed. I'd just read *Rolling Stone* magazine's tenth anniversary issue. They polled critics to name the ten best albums of the last decade and two writers, Robert Christgau and Paul Nelson, picked The New York Dolls. So when I dug it out of a cardboard box I was happy to turn over all my lawnmower money and eager to play it.

I loved the album cover, the back cover, and Bob Gruen's gorgeous photography on the inner sleeve. Their look was so potent and alluring. Just the coolest looking band ever. I don't know what I expected when I put it on, but it didn't sound right to my teenage ears. This wasn't like Led Zeppelin and Deep Purple, the default rock settings in the hinterlands of South Florida. It wasn't heavy, it was fast. And not just the tempos, but the way the guitars played off each other, ricocheting and careening, and the way the lyrics went whipping past your head, a rapid-fire enfilade of pop cultural references about Charlie Chan and Buck Rogers and Diana Dors.

I kept listening and looking at the pictures and song by song I learned it. Or rather, it taught me. It rewired me so completely that the very tone of Johnny Thunders's guitar—that miracle of filth—defined rock. All other bands would henceforth be judged by whatever tiny scintilla of Dolls-y pleasure they could generate. Were their lyrics as funny as David Johansen's? Was their front man as charmingly charismatic? Were the backing vocals as bratty? Did the drummer accelerate and drive like Jerry? Were the songs organically arranged give-and-go pleasure machines? Did they have the telepathy of Syl and Johnny guitar interplay? Did anybody anywhere have cooler guitar moves than Johnny Thunders? (Answer: Nobody ever.) Why was it so staggeringly perfect to see Lumpen Arthur staggering about on his platforms? I can't tell you, but it was clearly so.

As critical standards go you may think that judging everything by the pleasure you got out of your favorite album at age 16 is a flimsy foundation. But you would be wrong. In fact, for rock criticism, it is the very best standard. I'm not saying that's the end of all aesthetic inquiry, but I am saying that sensing and seeking out the depth of play the creator put into their work has proven a sophisticated strategy.

The New York Dolls made a kind of promise to me at age 16 about sex and rock and roll, what I could and should expect from art, what freedom and pleasure and joy might look like in the world. Forty years on, it is curious that a band that was decried as degenerate, a mockery, a shambling calamitous ineptitude, has proven to be so lastingly true.

David Smay is the author of *Swordfishtrombones* (#53). He tweets @Hecubot99.

CHAPTER 3

THE ROLLING STONES' *IT'S ONLY ROCK 'N ROLL* (1974)

David Masciotra

My grandfather was dying in my parents' bed. Every morning when I left for school, rather than taking pride in my status of senior and anticipating the emancipation mere months away, I feared that, when the final dismissal bell rang, I would drive home to the inevitable and imminent devastation: my mother crying, my father already home from work, my grandfather's heart suddenly and eternally quiet.

Nick Bruich, my mom's dad, managed to accomplish the most daunting and inspiring coalescence in his character. He was both the strongest and sweetest man I knew. A Second World War veteran who cut stone in a quarry for nearly forty years, he carried and conducted himself with an impenetrable and formidable bravado of masculinity. He also acquired a neighborhood reputation, in our small town of Northern Illinois, as a generous benefactor—attending the softball games for an orphan who lived down the block so that she would not feel alone and unappreciated as she hit a home run or stole a base; collecting cans and bottles for the town drunk who turned in bags of empties for sustenance; driving a developmentally disabled man to the grocery store once a week and slipping him a twenty to supplement his food stamps.

When I first needed a haircut, I experienced an unnatural terror of a stranger with scissors. I would shout and protest until my mother relented, ordered the barber to stand down, and took me home. My grandfather offered to take me to his barber, and promised me that everything would work out alright. I knew the crying had to end, because I knew that I had to demonstrate toughness for my grandfather. With him sitting near the entrance, periodically flashing me a smile, I survived the haircut in silence. He had always been there when I needed him, but soon he wouldn't be.

The clock on the wall in my old high school was creeping towards three o'clock. I dreaded returning home, and risking the finality of a death announcement. If my grandfather has died, I thought, it isn't real until I go home, and find out for myself. I desperately scrambled to delay my return home. First, I asked a pretty girl I was casually dating if she would like to go out after school. She had to work. Then, I began inquiring with friends. As unlikely as it seemed, they all had plans. All alone and aspiring to distract myself from the weight of loss pressing down on my mind and back, I drove to the record store. Scanning through the selection of the CD aisle, I settled on an album about which I knew little except for the title track. I made my purchase, drove to the nearest park, and slid the disc into the slot in the dashboard. With the window rolled down and the cool October air biting my face, I lit a cigarette. As the first inhale of smoke invaded my lungs, the opening notes of my new CD filled the compact space of my car and, with more power than the engine idling a few feet in front of where I sat, transported me to a hedonistic and peaceful oasis far removed from the troubles of my mind.

The album was *It's Only Rock 'n Roll* by the Rolling Stones. Released in 1974, the Stones were midway into the second decade of a career that now spans fifty years. The band's members had already slowed down with experimentation and exploration of new sounds and styles, and had proudly accepted the title of elder statesmen of rock and roll. No better ambassadors for the musical genre exist to this day, and the title track was not only a declaration of supremacy, but also a well-delivered slap in the face to critics who, in the words of Mick Jagger, would greet each new Stones release with the ridicule, "oh, it's not as good as the last one." "An anti-journalistic thing," according to the Stones' lyricist and charismatic front man, the song acts as dismissive gesticulation—a shrug and elevation of the middle finger—to writers increasingly hostile to the Stones for not writing more songs of social consciousness or displaying the creative adventurousness of *Sticky Fingers* and *Exile on Main Street*.

It's Only Rock 'n Roll is an essential B-side because the critics are partially correct—it does not belong in the same category as the Stones' best work—but it is an outstanding record of signature rock and roll from the genre's best practitioners, and it represents a shift when the band, for good and bad, settled into a role that it helped to create. Or in the words of its unforgettable tag-line lyrics: "I know it's only rock 'n roll but I like it."

The title track of *It's Only Rock 'n Roll* remains one of the Stones' most popular songs, and a live-set staple, for good reason. Immediately after completing its composition, Jagger insisted that the record company release it as a single. "The song is a classic,"[1] he said, and he was right. Its groove embeds itself in your mind, threatening to never leave. The interplay between acoustic and electric guitars is a feast for the ears, and the chorus, with its unforgettable lyrics, is as intoxicating as a secret elixir. The lead singer of the biggest band in the world wrote most of the song with Ronnie Wood, while David Bowie sang back-up vocals, at Wood's house in London.

It's Only Rock 'n Roll would prove monumental in Stones' history, not because most consider it one of their greatest records, but because it was the last album featuring Mick Taylor on guitar. Ronnie Wood, the former Faces guitarist who remains a Rolling Stone, would replace Taylor full time following the record's release. Taylor's most dazzling moment on the record comes in one of the most underrated, and oddly enough, never performed songs in the Stones' canon: "Time Waits for No One." His closing solo is dynamic and, as its power swells over a Latin-infused jazzy beat and rhythm section, it acts as a metaphor for the force of the song's subject matter: mortality. "The dreams of the night time vanish by dawn / And time waits for no one ... " Mick sings with particularly effectual delivery.

The cruel indifference and impatience of time hovered over my vehicle like a bloodthirsty hawk, but my focus was not on the song's eerie resonance with my own moment of grief. I was simply enjoying the experience of hearing Rolling Stones songs that, to me, were new. Mick Jagger's growl in the title track was in the exact frequency of my spirit, and it facilitated a direct conversation between me and the gift of escapism that music can so often provide.

It's Only Rock 'n Roll begins with a beautifully lusty serving of swagger. An irresistible rock riff opens the song and record with propulsive rhythm, while a lead guitar cries over the top. Mick Jagger, in full throat and at full mast, addresses several unnamed women, inviting them to "thrills and spills." Their answers are largely irrelevant. "If you can't rock me, somebody will," Mick announces with unshakable confidence. "If You Can't Rock Me" is a ribald and rollicking exercise of familiarity—a song that the immortal team of Jagger and Richards could probably write in a coma, but that no other rock band among the countless Stones acolytes can quite pull off with the same joy and gusto.

When "If You Can't Rock Me" concludes, there is a second of silence. Jagger's voice comes crashing through with a battering ram—"I know you wanna leave me … " The energy remains high, the music remains aggressive, and the concentration remains carnal when the Rolling Stones tear through a raucous cover of the Temptations hit, "Ain't Too Proud to Beg." The rendition does not rise to the level of achievement the Stones scored when the band reimagined "Just My Imagination" as a spunky rock song fit for the dance floor, but it does serve as a reminder of the Stones' versatility and utility in the cross section of rock and roll and rhythm and blues.

"If You Can't Rock Me" and "Ain't Too Proud to Beg" coalesce to offer all the evidence necessary to animate the words of "It's Only Rock 'n Roll," coming third in the album's sequence. And, with all that vigor and vitality—strength of sound and rebellious certainty of sentiment—who wouldn't like it?

The entirety of *It's Only Rock 'n Roll* allowed me to experience forty minutes and twenty-six seconds of unmitigated pleasure. Smoking cigarettes, singing along, whooping at the guitar solos, playing drums on the steering wheel, and swinging my hips in my seat, I learned a lesson in the joyousness of good music, and, while my automobile acted as the private world of a rock and roll reverie, the Rolling Stones showed how, in an essential spiritual sense, art and love can have momentary victory over death.

The ballads, most especially "Till the Next Goodbye," sounded beautiful in their romantic sweep, and the funky protest song against the FBI's violation of Americans' right to privacy, "Fingerprint File," closed the record with a delightful contradiction of Jagger's thesis statement in the title track. Rock and roll is fun, but it can also employ its artistic capacities for the exploration of topics of sociopolitical consequence. It was the opening three songs that I needed most, however, along with the raver that comes on the record's second half, "Dance Little Sister." The physicality of those songs emphasized the sensuality of life, just as I wrestled with the fear and pain that accompanies its extinguishment.

The great essayist and novelist, Albert Murray,[2] titled one of his extraordinary books on blues music "Stomping the Blues." The shuffling of feet on the dance floor, Murray explains, is the attempt to stomp the blues into the ground—to get over them by walking on them. The Rolling Stones, as everyone knows, entered the emporium of rock and roll with the usher of the blues and, in many ways, remains a blues band at heart. The band's music is medicine for the blues. My grandfather died a couple of weeks later and, throughout my mourning, I would often return to music for comfort and escape.

The Rolling Stones originally conceived *It's Only Rock 'n Roll* as an album with one side of R&B covers and the other side of original compositions. "Ain't Too Proud to Beg" is the only song that survived the elimination of the cover songs. Another cover that the band recorded during the *It's Only Rock 'n Roll* sessions is the imperishable classic, "Drift Away." The Stones' rendition has gained popularity among committed fans, who, long before the internet made everything instantly accessible, treasured the track on cassette and CD bootlegs. Songwriter mentor Ralph Williams's immortal words not only summarize the service that the Rolling Stones provided for a 17-year-old afraid to face the death of his boyhood hero, but also became my hymn of gratitude to all of the legends of rock and roll and rhythm and blues who manage to inject color into our lives when we find ourselves shrouded in darkness:

Oh, give me the beat boys and free my soul
I want to get lost in your rock and roll and drift away.

David Masciotra is the author of *Metallica* (#108).

CHAPTER 4
THE DURUTTI COLUMN'S *THE RETURN OF THE DURUTTI COLUMN* (1980)
Philip Shaw

On a sunny day in June 1980 I sat alone in my Mum's car, staring at a picture of Ian Curtis on the cover of the *NME*. I remember the sound of the exhaust ticking over in the heat. Until that moment death had been an entirely abstract affair, and I had certainly never experienced any form of grief, but Curtis's death affected me deeply, and in ways that I could not explain.

A few days later I was flipping through the racks in Nottingham's Selectadisc on Bridlesmith Gate, cued by Joy Division's *Unknown Pleasures* (FACT 10) to seek out LP covers that gave nothing away. I was on the look-out for something black, textured, wordless, and preferably with a FACT number on the spine. In the autumn I would find the black embossed sleeve of Joy Division's posthumous 12-in. single "Transmission," but on this day I discovered the reissue of *The Return of the Durutti Column*: FACT 14, black with small reproductions of three naïve-looking paintings, textured and, but for the enigmatic title—who were the Durutti Column and where had they been?—almost wordless.

Being a kid from the sticks I wasn't cool enough to have known about the original pressing of the LP with its coarse sandpaper sleeve, reputedly glued together by Curtis on a per-piece pay rate while his band mates watched a porn film in the same room. Nor was I savvy enough to pick up on the allusions to Guy Debord, the Situationists, May 1968, and Spanish Civil War anarchism. That would come in time. But I wonder, now, what it must have been like to be one of the first to own the version with the sandpaper cover; to have appreciated the link with Debord and Asher Jorn's autodestructive *Mémoires* (1959)—a book that would literally wear away whatever object it came into contact with—and then to have experienced the sweet irony of listening to the record's pure, unabashed beauty. To some extent the Raoul Dufy paintings on the sleeve of the reissue had prepared me for the chiming, pastoral sound of Vini Reilly's solo guitar-based instrumentals, the only fixed point in the Durutti Column's protean line up. Even so, this was music of a different order, far removed from the dark, industrial menace of Joy Division.

What the record did share with *Unknown Pleasures* was the sonic ingenuity of Factory in-house producer Martin Hannett. On Joy Division's LP Hannett had used delay, compression, and reverb to place the voice and instruments in strange, unsettling surroundings, interspersing and sometimes overlaying the tracks with bizarre electronic effects and found sounds. With *The Return of the Durutti Column*, Hannett experimented still further, adding synthetic bird song to "Sketch for Summer," providing a cavernous, hammering pulse to "Requiem for a Father" while filtering Reilly's multi-tracked Les Paul through digital delay and reverb to create an impression of airy expansiveness. The guitarist, for his part, explained in an interview that he used these effects as a form of "musical private joke," adding echo to a piece like "Conduct," "which uses fourths and fifths against the principle of harmony" in order to "sink one interval into the next," thereby creating "other harmonies so you get an archetypally pretty sound."[1] This statement gives a clue to Reilly's instinctive grasp of counter-cultural aesthetics. While the Sex Pistols manager Malcolm McLaren had boasted of making "cash from chaos," Reilly took the punk dialectic a stage further by making harmony from chaos. In so doing, the Durutti Column offered a glimpse of artistic modes and states of being that punk, out of a need to present itself as hard, unflinching, and confrontational, had been forced to repress: beauty, transience, innocence, melancholy, and yearning.[2]

To the few who may have been familiar with Reilly's previous work as guitar player in the Manchester punk band Ed Banger and the Nosebleeds, *The Return of the Durutti Column* represented a bold departure. Here, instead of three-chord thrash and anti-art diatribe, the listener encounters minor key poignancy, tone poetry, and virtuoso delicacy. Classically trained, but from a proud northern working-class background, Reilly's new music defied categorization, being neither punk nor prog, populist or recognizably avant-garde. In this sense, the anarchist and situationist trappings—most likely informed by the leftist leanings of Tony Wilson, Factory's charismatic and quixotic co-founder—seemed entirely appropriate: no less than the Sex Pistols, the Durutti Column sought to confound expectations only, in this case, not through overt shock tactics but by deploying nuance, vagueness, and ambiguity. Beauty can be abrasive too.

Like the relationship between William Blake's "The Tiger" (1794) and its sister poem "The Lamb" (1789), *The Return of the Durutti Column* could be regarded as the B-side to *Unknown Pleasures*; that is, as an album bound in "fearful symmetry" with its better-known A-side.[3] And just as Joy Division's record, stalking through the jungle like Blake's "Tiger," sought to forge a terrifying and corrosive vision of imaginative power, so Vini Reilly's record offered that vision's counterpart: a vision of sadness, to be sure, but sweetened by echoes of harmony and delight. Born out of the guitarist's struggle with physical illness and depression, I understand now that it was *The Return of the Durutti Column* that helped me to come to terms with Curtis's death.[4]

My love of this record was, initially, a solitary affair. But a year or so later I became friendly with an older lad named Andrew, who shared my enthusiasm and who taped selections for me from the Durutti Column's later records. I still have this tape in my collection. Some of this music filtered into the songs that my friend John and I composed in a very early incarnation of our band, Alberteen. Then, in 1984 I met Jeff. Jeff and I were students at the University of Liverpool. We lived in adjacent rooms and I knew I'd found a friend when I heard him playing New Order's "Your Silent Face." Jeff was keen on the Durutti Column too, so when we heard that Vini was going to play live at the Stanley Theatre in support of a new album called *Without Mercy* (FACT 84) we were determined to go along. No longer a solo act, the Durutti Column now included the affable "Mr.

Manchester" Bruce Mitchell on drums and a small string and brass section led by the viola player John Metcalfe. Afterwards I got to meet Vini; his blue eyes sparkled as I gushed about how much we'd enjoyed the gig.

It was around this time I met Jeff's old school friend Julian, another fan. By now, with the addition of my best friend Adrian, we were four. I don't know how many times over the subsequent decades we've seen the Durutti Column, but on each occasion the music has acted as a kind of emotional cement, allowing us to inhabit and share feelings that might otherwise remain black, textured, and wordless.

The last time was in the summer of 2014 at a church in Chorlton, South Manchester. We'd heard that Vini had recently suffered a series of strokes but that he'd recovered enough to take part in an interview and to play some guitar. We sat in the pews and listened to Vini speaking about his guitar teacher and "second mother" Miriam, a holocaust survivor who told him that many of the stars we see at night have already died. Vini's words flowed, but he seemed to be struggling, like a swimmer battling against the tide. When, finally, he knelt down to play, we became aware of just how badly his illness had affected him. The piece ended and Vini burst into tears.

Since that performance I've spoken only briefly with my friends. Perhaps we've been worn down, but then I place the record on the turntable, the music returns and, for a time, the world is renewed.

The world returns, the world is renewed and we've been worn away.

Philip Shaw is the author of *Horses* (#55).

CHAPTER 5
R.E.M.'S *CHRONIC TOWN* (1982)
Gina Arnold

Isabelle texted me from the airport to say that the elderly-looking woman in the seat next to her on her flight had "Gardening at Night" as her ringtone, but was too technically challenged to make it stop ringing. The flight attendants had to come over to help her hush it. The ringtone, Isabelle added, was making her sad. "It's distressing to think that I will never see R.E.M. play 'Gardening at Night' again," she said. And yet she can. Well … sort of. Because just the other night someone posted a video of R.E.M. on YouTube from a performance they gave in Athens in 1982 and I accidentally clicked on it. I say "accidentally" because doing so caused an actual accident. Before I clicked, all was well. After, I was a goner. I stayed up until the wee hours of the morning, reliving my beauteous youth.

More often than not when you look back at the bands you loved when you were little, it turns out they were silly and sophomoric or are now just so dated that you can no longer look at them without laughing. Even the good ones tend to sound thin and wavery from this distance; seldom do you get that punched-in-the-face feeling that you got from hearing them at the time. But the "you are there" quality of this video performance was entirely different. The minute it began it was like I was grabbed by G-forces and smacked into the wall of the past. Flattened. It was so evocative.

When you click on it, the first thing you hear, though the screen is black, is a disembodied voice. "Thanks Peter Holsapple. Ghengis Khan. Let's Active." Then: "*Mirror,*" it mutters. "*Flower.*" And suddenly the scene appears before you, smelling strongly of stale beer, and it took my breath away. There is Michael Stipe, in all his youthful beauty, bee-stung lips, curly hair flopped over his forehead, and that particular way of dancing: swinging his arms like an ape, hunching over and backing almost fearfully away from the mic stand. The first time I saw it, I and everyone else I knew immediately began to mimic this. I had forgotten the origin of the move. Then he begins singing. "*Suspicion yourself suspicion yourself suspicion yourself don't get caught.*"[1] Oh yeah. "*Wilder, lower, wolves,*"[2] he continues, and then on and on through the rest of the four songs from the *Chronic Town* EP, plus a few tracks from the soon-to-be-released album *Murmur* and a couple of unreleased tracks (which we will all hear many years later on *Dead Letter Office*, but not until then).

Presumably your level of interest in this video is dependent entirely on your interest in R.E.M. back then (not now), but me, I loved everything about it, including the cuts away to the album cover of *Chronic Town*, which presumably masked moments on the tape that the videographer didn't want seen. What I liked about those shots was that, in 1982, I was so obsessed with that record that I would often stare at this cover while I listened to the music on it, completely absorbed by the image of the gargoyle, and I did the same thing with *Murmur* as well. It was different then, of course—since we didn't have videos, we didn't really know what the band looked like except for maybe a blurry photo or two; we only had the album cover to think about. But that cover in particular captured the mystique that R.E.M. cast over my musical world of the moment. The shadow it cast was a long one, too, since the majority of my wardrobe has been in those colors or colors like them ever since—as have my linens, my towels, my bathing suits, even my bathroom tiles.

Chronic Town was barely twenty minutes long, but those twenty minutes changed my life.[3] Today your iPod can keep track of how many times you play something. Back then there was no such form of measurement, but *Chronic Town* definitely tops anything else I've heard before or since. In part this is because it was so damn short. In those days, bored by suburban life, we used to drive to San Francisco almost every night in Isabelle's old VW bug, with this music recorded on a C-30 cassette tape and it would play three times through before we got there and three times through on the way home: six times per trip, four or five times a week, and that's not even including the times we listened to it on shorter journeys.

What was it that captivated me so? Well, to begin, the stream of consciousness lyrics, the impressions they gave, the jagged snippets, the phraseology … they made me understand so much about language, poetry, and even authors like James Joyce and Thomas Pynchon, who, prior to hearing R.E.M., I just dismissed as being "too hard" or "gobbledygook." It was only after hearing R.E.M. that I could read *The Crying of Lot 49*, without which my life would be a poorer place.

So there's that. But beyond lyrics, of course, driving them onward and into my head, there was the music, the twelve-string jangly guitar, the speedy arpeggios, the hollow, droney voice of Stipe, harmonizing with Mills's pretty sing-song, the snare. To me, their sound was so complete, so fully realized, so in and of itself that I couldn't even connect it to the music it clearly sprang from, like Hera out of Zeus' head. One day Peter Buck came to the college radio station where Isabelle and I both worked and said on air that there were bands like his in every town in America, and he was right. Gone was our obsession with gothy-looking boys and romantic-sounding English bands; we started to look at small-town America for music put out on singles and from independent labels, and it was like Dorothy finding home in her own backyard. There was a there there after all.

He also said he was influenced by The Velvet Underground and Big Star and the Byrds, but you know, although I made a point of listening to all that music immediately, I couldn't hear it at all. To me they came straight out of nowhere, and immediately filled the vacuum that was my mind. Of course back then I was easy to impress, but I still think they made something new out of what they had heard, something that felt like it was mine in a way that those old bands surely didn't. For my era, they were my Beatles, and seeing them live was my equivalent of going to the Cavern Club, or the Reeperbahn—and then going over and over again.

The first time I saw R.E.M. was in 1983, in June, about six months or so after the YouTube video was shot and, incidentally, after I had bought *Chronic Town*, and I remember that Isabelle and I had simply waited and waited and WAITED for them to come to our area, and then when they finally came we saw them a whole ton of times in a huge rush that basically laid waste to every other show we'd seen prior to it and shaped the way we experienced music ever after. I used to think I was imagining that blissful week, but no: according to Wikipedia, R.E.M. played the Bay Area five times between June 14 and June 22 of 1983. Isn't that fantastic? Well, fantastic or pathetic, since nowadays when I get into this state about a piece of music, it doesn't even feel like I've really seen a band until I've seen them five times on the same tour. That week is surely what laid the groundwork for a lifetime of concert idiocy, like up and flying to Paris to see the Replacements in 1986, or more recently, to Vienna to see the Afghan Whigs. It's fun, yeah. But it's also, frankly, a bit impoverishing.

Anyway, given what an impact seeing R.E.M. play five times in one week in June of 1983 had on my life, it is certainly heartening to see from this videotape that yeah, they were pretty damn good. More importantly—and I don't think this can be captured in the hearts or minds of any except those who were there—they were so incredibly different. To understand that jolt, you have to recall what was big on the radio at that time. I knew it was all horrid, and that R.E.M. were not, but a quick look at the charts for 1982 shows that the situation was far more dire than I even remember. The number one song of the year was "Let's Get Physical" by Olivia Newton John; other non-stop hits included "Eye of the Tiger" (Survivor), "Abracadabra" by Steve Miller, and "Hard to Say I'm Sorry" by the deathless band Chicago. Air Supply, Vangelis, REO Speedwagon, Asia, Foreigner, Journey, Loverboy, the Little River Band, Christopher Cross … what more needs to be said about a year when the only tolerable song in the entire *Billboard* Top Fifty is … um, wait, there IS no tolerable song in the top fifty, if, like me, you don't care for Joan Jett. These acts, with their vapid lyrics, overproduction, and super soft centers, like the worst possible chocolates in the box of a very, very cheap bad brand, overlaid the atmosphere at the time.

Hearing R.E.M. just wiped that shit out. Clean slate. Brand new. From then on music was dark blue and turquoise, like the cover of *Chronic Town*. It shone in my ears. It was gilt.

It was more attractive, inside that moral kiosk.

But time changes everything, right? And now "Gardening at Night" comes out of old ladies' cell phones, and those of us who once proclaimed "I *am* R.E.M." as if we were Spartacus or something, hunker down with embarrassment when we hear it. The flickering light of a YouTube video notwithstanding, there seems to be no link between 1982 and now, no way to draw those experiences together. "You had to be there" has become the motto of our age. But there is this: I was, and thank heaven for that. I was.

Gina Arnold is the author of *Exile in Guyville* (#96).

CHAPTER 6
RITES OF SPRING'S *RITES OF SPRING* (1985)
Will Fulton

Singer Guy Picciotto begins Rites of Spring's "For Want Of" like an orator making an impassioned speech: "I, I believed memory might mirror no reflections on me / I, I believed that in forgetting I might set myself free / but I woke up in the morning with a piece of past stuck in my throat / and then I choked." As is the case with all of the songs on the twelve-song album *Rites of Spring*,[1] "For Want Of" is somehow both intimate and public, intensely personal to the singer and yet still resonant with the listener as if reflecting their own experience. The doubled "I" that opens each line in the first verse functions as a doubling of the subjective. "*I! I* believed!" As if to say, *me*, right here, this raw nerve, just-on-the-edge-of-tears voice, with all of the internal conflicts of youth laid bare: a cocktail of fraternal and romantic love, frustrations nameless and nameable, embarrassments, fuck-yous, lusts, regrets, angers, and sadnesses.

Picciotto reflects on the lyrics:

> I think they were incredibly, maybe weirdly honest, cause I really feel at that age you're in this very solipsistic, fraught headspace. It's pretty intense. There was always like, this burr that was in my head of trying to find something that was a new way of—something that just felt realer or more different. So I think I was just trying to write the way I thought in my head.[2]

In 1985, *Rites of Spring* was like nothing I'd ever heard before, and yet so incredibly familiar. It was Brian Baker (Minor Threat, Dag Nasty, Bad Religion) who, in a 1985 interview, somewhat derisively coined the mid-1980s shift in the ethos of DC bands as "emotional hardcore" or "emo-core." Although Picciotto, album producer and Dischord Records co-founder Ian MacKaye (Minor Threat, Fugazi), and many others in the DC punk scene thought this moniker was "the stupidest thing we had ever heard,"[3] nationally distributed 'zines like *Flipside* and *Maximum Rock 'n' Roll* ran stories about the "emo-core" scene in DC, with *Rites of Spring* touted as its flagship album. Over thirty years later, music genres and record labels have tagged "emo" to a range of music from pop-punk to hip-hop. For the original bands involved, however, "emo" as a subgenre had nothing to do with what was going on in DC in 1985. Rites of Spring just thought of themselves as a punk rock band that was trying to push punk rock forward.

It's strange in retrospect that the emotional content in the lyrics was seen as so abrupt a shift from earlier DC punk rock. Minor Threat's "Little Friend" from *Out of Step* (1983) featured verses examining different emotional states. In the same year, The Faith's *Subject to Change* had shifted the focus of feeling toward introspection. And local DC heroes Marginal Man's Pete Murray couldn't get through a performance of "Forever Gone" (a tribute to a friend who committed suicide) without breaking down. Perhaps the exaggerated lore of DC "Straight Edge" and the "12XU" hardcore sound (evident on the Dischord Records *Flex Your Head* compilation) had created a false image of a monochromatic DC style with a long, rigid, anger-is-the-only-emotion straight-edge tradition. But when Rites of Spring formed in late 1983 and early 1984, the DC punk scene was only 5 years old, and had been in a near-constant state of change.

Picciotto describes the Cramps' Georgetown University show in 1979 as a "watershed event" for the scene.[4] In the crowd, Picciotto first saw MacKaye, members of the Bad Brains, and other key participants in the burgeoning DC punk scene. Most of them were high-school students at the time, and they all recognized that something important was happening. For Picciotto, the fervent energy in DC punk rock had a clear source: "The sheer excellence of the Bad Brains had this liberating effect on kids there. It opened this door, and inspired bands like Minor Threat, and that in turn inspired us … So it was kind of a passing of the torch that happened that was based on that."[5] And then, by late 1983, there was a lull. Minor Threat, Faith (a band that included later-ROS guitarist Eddie Janney), and a number of other bands broke up. The year 1984, the year in which Rites of Spring wrote their only album, proved to be a year of change and new ideas.

Rites of Spring represents, first and foremost, a moment in four teenagers' lives—middle-class white kids who were weaving through a fabric of creative encounters and artistic endeavors. They were boys who were in Deadline, Insurrection, and Faith a year before ROS, and then in One Last Wish, Happy Go Licky, and Fugazi within a year after, as well as making experimental tapes at home in various incarnations. ROS hardly played outside of the DC area, had only a few dozen shows, were barely together for two years, and didn't sell a lot of records. The era within the DC scene is more famous for bands breaking up, often before their record was released, and for the transcendental element in music that was (for the most part) made without career goals. It's the element that keeps me coming back to *Rites of Spring*.

Inspiration came from everywhere. Picciotto and ROS drummer Brendan Canty worked with Ian MacKaye at the *Yesterday and Today* record store, and their ears were open to a multi-faceted, international punk rock scene that influenced their new directions. "If I had to name one band musically that influenced Rites of Spring, it was the Buzzcocks," Canty recalls, "Buzzcocks and Wire, but we were also listening to the Church."[6] Guy adds:

We were really into the Adverts and the Saints, and there was also stuff that was coming out, like the first Meat Puppets seven-inch and Rudimentary Peni from England that were way weirder and way more psychedelic and strange in the guitar playing. We'd seen the Birthday Party, and we'd seen stuff that was different, and we wanted to do stuff that was different too.[7]

Canty, Picciotto, and Mike Fellows had been playing in Insurrection in 1982 and 1983, which Picciotto describes as a "really, kind of straight up, English influenced, Discharge type band." But with their new band, they wanted to incorporate more of their disparate influences: "We wanted to make a statement. In Rites of Spring, all four of us wrote riffs. [Bassist] Mike Fellows—he wrote a lot of the riffs that were really important to that band, but so did Brendan and Eddie, and so did I."[8]

Picciotto had never sung in a band before, but had been writing lyrics. As he was too shy at practices, no one had heard him sing until they recorded their demo in May 1984. The reaction was instantaneous, recalls MacKaye, who produced both the demo session and the album: "That session was so intense, 'cause nobody had heard Guy sing before, he'd never sung. So when he went to do vocals it was mind-blowing. Absolutely spine-tingling."[9] All six of the demoed songs ("End on End," "Remainder," "Persistent Vision," "Hain's Point," "All There Is," and "By Design") would end up on the album. Six more ("Drink Deep," "Theme," "For Want Of," "Deeper Than Inside," "Spring," and "Nudes") were written in the summer and fall of 1984. The band would have their first show in late July 1984, but would break up only eighteen months later.

Like many punk scenes in the country, the DC scene in 1984 was being taken over by racist skinheads. Hardcore shows were becoming increasingly bad scenes for many who had embraced them a few years earlier. MacKaye and others aimed to "make a new scene" in which they could carry DC punk rock forward. However, Picciotto rejects the historical narrative that Rites of Spring "was just a reaction to a few morons," and stresses that they were far from enlightened saints themselves.[10] The band's activity preceded the "Revolution Summer" cultural movement in 1985, but they were key participants. Performances from Beefeater, Embrace, Gray Matter, ROS, and others were promoted on flyers under the moniker, which signified the new progressive political engagement of the scene (including protests against Apartheid and activism in local issues), as well as the new ethos of the music.

In January 1985, Rites of Spring returned to Inner Ear studio to record *Rites of Spring* on eight-track reel-to-reel. Picciotto recalls: "we just recorded it live in a day, we had the lights all off, strobe light going, just played it really quickly, sang all the songs in one go, and that was it."[11] Canty remembers that Picciotto's profoundly intimate words and delivery instilled in the band a drive to match his intensity: "I always was astounded by his lyrics, and his singing, his commitment to the whole thing. You don't just bring lyrics like that and have a very gentle [sound]. If he was going to put himself out there, he needed that level of volume, to put himself out there that way."[12]

The album recording captured the live energy of the band, and the arc of a great live performance. "Spring," the set opener, is as close to straight-up hardcore as the album gets, the second track "Deeper Than Inside" begins to draw the listener toward the emotional chasm of the album's core. "For Want Of," (perhaps) a love song narrative, slows just slightly to a mid-tempo pace. "Hain's Point," named for a favorite hangout in East Potomac Park, furthers the lost love intensity of "For Want Of." The aptly-named "All There Is" is a raw nerve. Finally, *almost* in a release, the first side ends with the dirge-powerhouse "Drink Deep" (probably the best-known ROS track). "Theme," the opening of the LP's Side Two, shows the band's extraordinary intimacy. "By Design" and "Remainder" expand on Picciotto's poetry. "Persistent Vision" is a brooding pair to "All There Is." "Nudes" is heavy and intimate. Finally, "End on End" brings Side Two and the album to an end. Like "Drink Deep," "End on End" is expansive and explosive. During Rites of Spring shows, their instruments were often smashed to pieces by the end of the song. When the show, and album, finished, there was nothing left to give.

Rites of Spring's lasting influence would seem to go hand in hand with its success in capturing the ethos of friends coming of age, without exterior motives. MacKaye recalls: "The Washington music scene was super tribal … it was almost more of a family thing. We were just doing it for each other, in a way. But it was mostly to be a family."[13] Picciotto agrees, although with some regret:

> Looking back on it, we didn't really have an ethic of going out and touring. I wish I could go back and make it different, 'cause I really think it was a huge mistake. Maybe the bands were just too fragile to actually go out and do it. We were young, really young, and I was in five or six bands before I was twenty-two. We didn't have any kind of vision outside of a very small circle of people, we weren't ambitious for it in any kind of way.[14]

As Picciotto sings: "all there is, is in the knowing / this never has to end." He speaks of course to his core group of beloved friends, and the musical life they shared. But his words resound with many who have experienced the intense maelstrom of emotion that is coming of age.

Will Fulton is the co-author of *Uptown Saturday Night* (#125).

CHAPTER 7
JANE'S ADDICTION'S
NOTHING'S SHOCKING (1988)
Rolf Potts

I was riding in the passenger seat of Hadley's red Honda CRX when I heard Jane's Addiction's *Nothing's Shocking* for the first time. It must have been a Saturday, since that's the only day of the week we ever had off from our summer jobs at Eagle Lake Camp, where we were tasked with taking adolescents into the Rocky Mountain backcountry and telling them about Jesus.

Hadley was from California. She was blonde, leggy, doggedly cheerful, and a tad clumsy when she shouldered her backpack and led campers into the Colorado wilderness. She had a goofball sense of humor, a jolly inability to show up on time for staff meetings, and a tendency to drive too fast on the pine-hemmed curves of Rampart Range Road, the gravel track that linked our summer camp to Woodland Park, the nearest town, thirty-five minutes away. Hadley kept the CRX sunroof open as she drove, and the car swirled with the summery chill of mountain air and the vanilla smell of ponderosa. I had recently graduated from high school in Kansas, and my two months in Colorado amounted to the longest I'd ever spent away from home. I was in love with Hadley in the passive, uncomplicated way all 18-year-old boys fall in love with 21-year-old women who pay attention to them.

Hadley liked to talk when she was driving—usually about people she knew or places she wanted to visit. When she tired of talking she would snatch one of the dozen or so unsheathed cassette tapes that slid around on the CRX's floorboards and blast tunes. Apart from U2, which all young Christians were obligated to enjoy (or at least acknowledge) in 1989, I didn't recognize any of Hadley's music. I had suggested we play *The Joshua Tree* at the outset of our drive to Woodland Park, but—halfway through Bono's emotive rendering of "Running to Stand Still"—Hadley frowned at the sunlight slanting through the pine trees all around us, as if something wasn't quite right. Ejecting U2, she brandished a gray Maxell dub-cassette and slid it into the tape deck. "Jane's Addiction," she announced, cranking the volume as a slurry, roiling bass groove shook the car.

"Up the Beach," the ethereal, muscular, faintly psychedelic anthem that swelled over the bass-line as Hadley's car sped through the pines, was like nothing I'd heard in all my years of listening to pop and classic-rock radio in Wichita. When the singer's voice shrieked up over the opening groove, it didn't form words so much as weave its way into the cascading guitar notes, swirling out and echoing back in on itself. The effect was magical, incoherent, mesmerizing. Time, it felt, was decelerating, spooling out in slow motion. The song's only discernible lyric was "home," which the singer intoned with a plaintive, almost tender sense of urgency as the song's final chords rang out, pulsed, and faded away.

In the span of just three minutes, "Up the Beach" had filled me with a haunted sense of longing. I might have asked Hadley to rewind the tape and play it again had we not at that moment been speeding toward my favorite stretch of Rampart Range Road—a spectacular, two-mile span of grassy, treeless plateau with the elegant hulk of Pikes Peak dominating the westward horizon. The echoing silence after "Up the Beach" melded into a new texture—the shiny, almost classical-sounding chime of guitar threaded with a falsetto coo that built up, stretched out, then softened as Hadley drove us up from the trees into the sun-dazzled alpine meadow. Glancing over at me with a sideways grin, she shouted, "One, *two!*" and, before I could figure out what she was getting at, a banshee voice screamed "three, *fooouuurr!*" and the little world inside the car exploded into a thunderous clamor, a hammering swell of guitar, bass, and drums, a sound too powerful and thrilling for me to ever put into words. "Wish I was *ocean size*," the vocalist howled, sounding like there was a thousand of him calling to me from a thousand miles away, "no one moves you, man, *no one tries!*"

As Hadley's CRX crested the grassy rise and Pike's Peak came into view above the rocky sprawl of Colorado's Front Range, I felt like I was gazing out at a whole new universe.

***

In retrospect, I think Hadley was a bit startled by my fixation with Jane's Addiction after that heady Saturday-morning drive. I've come to realize that Hadley has, in my memories, become a kind of Manic Pixie Dream Girl—a stock narrative character (often seen in movies) whose eccentric tastes and quirky enthusiasm for life ultimately serve to shepherd the young male protagonist on a journey of self-discovery. Hadley was indeed quirky and ebullient, but her decision to play *Nothing's Shocking* that day hadn't been a symbolically charged ploy to change my life. In real-time, with the sun filtering through the pines on Rampart Range Road, I reckon she'd simply felt the blissed-up urge to hear it. In the days and weeks after our drive I grilled her for more information about Jane's Addiction, but she didn't seem to know a lot about the band. She was pretty sure they'd emerged from the post-punk glam scene in Los Angeles, and that their bewitchingly powerful sound was the result of them blending gothic rock with heavy metal. I recall nodding along as she said this, though the only phrases that had any meaning for me at the time were "heavy metal" and "Los Angeles."

Unlike Hadley, I wasn't a full-on counselor at Eagle Lake Camp. As the youngest member of the staff I'd been given the apprentice-level job of trip outfitter, which meant I spent a good deal of my time preparing food for the other counselors to use when they took kids into the backcountry. The trip outfitter's office had a battered Panasonic boom box, and the fact that I worked alone meant that I didn't have to endure the syrupy Christian praise-pop favored by my coworkers. After my first flirtation with Jane's Addiction, I'd begged the dub-cassette off Hadley, and I wound up listening to

Nothing's Shocking as many as three times a day for the rest of the summer. The tape's B-side featured the new debut album by the Stone Roses, an English band whose songs proved consistently catchy, but for the most part I just rewound the tape and listened to Jane's Addiction again. (To this day I can't hear a Stone Roses song without thinking of *Nothing's Shocking*.) My affinity for "Up the Beach" and "Ocean Size"—the opening tracks that had so beguiled me that day up on Rampart Range Road—was so strong that sometimes I'd stop the tape when the final strains of "Ocean Size" faded, rewind it, and listen to them both again.

My relationship with all of the music on *Nothing's Shocking*, as it played out on the boom box each day, was very much constrained by the pre-internet era. As I listened to the songs on that gray plastic dub-cassette I had no idea who the members of Jane's Addiction were, what they looked like, or even the names of the songs. (Hadley had, as it happened, misplaced the cassette-case J-card that bore the penciled-in titles.) The first few times I listened to the album all the way through I was drawn to the heavier tunes, particularly the stomping fuzz-riffs of what I later learned was called "Mountain Song." The album's closing track, "Pigs in Zen," was even heavier and edgier—unhinged and menacing and uncomfortably electrifying. It also culminated in a demented spoken-word pre-coda that included swearwords, which meant I rarely listened to it all the way through for fear some earnest Christian might walk in and overhear it.

The more I listened to *Nothing's Shocking*, however, the more I began to appreciate its less-bombastic songs. The punk-riff lyrics of "Had a Dad" bewailed the seeming absence of God, for example, yet I found it oddly hopeful (no doubt because I misheard "He's not there at all" as "He's not dead at all"). "Jane Says," a sweet, sad, steel-drum-driven pop number, told the story of the band's drug-addicted namesake through a progression of lyrical, telling details; it was catchy enough to sing along to, and felt ready for rotation on American rock radio. (Unbeknownst to me, this had already happened.) Over time, however, I came to most anticipate the middle of *Nothing's Shocking*, when the thunder of the album's early songs eased into the psychedelic euphoria of "Summertime Rolls." Anchored by a sleepy, bouncing bass-line, its lyrics recount a sun-blissed day spent in the company of a loopy, faintly clumsy girlfriend. At the time it made me think of Hadley; now it just reminds me of being young and alive in the summer of 1989.

For the most part I listened to these songs in secret, since the religious atmosphere of the camp tended to view all secular enthusiasms as potentially idolatrous. As it happened, Jane's Addiction had indeed found a way into my soul, just not the part of my soul that plumbed the divine; it had occupied that raw, 18-year-old part of my being that was hungry for new music, new experiences, new ideas. It spoke to an inchoate part of me that wanted to be different, to pay closer attention to what I might have been missing, to commune with as-yet-unseen versions of myself. *Nothing's Shocking* hadn't moved me because it filled me with numinous purpose; it had moved me because it filled me with an exhilarated, inarticulate feeling of *possibility*—a sense that the world was wider and wilder than I had previously assumed.

***

Two years after my first encounter with *Nothing's Shocking* I saw Jane's Addiction live in concert for the first time. I was back home in Kansas that summer, working the graveyard shift at a supermarket in Wichita. I took a day off work and drove three hours to Kansas City's Sandstone Amphitheater, where I proffered my $20 ticket and settled in for a sweltering day-long show that also featured acts like Siouxsie and the Banshees, Nine Inch Nails, Ice-T, Rollins Band, and the Butthole Surfers. I've since come to refer to that summer—the summer of 1991—as "the year I cut off my mullet and went to Lollapalooza."

In the popular imagination, 1991 has come to be remembered as a turning-point year in that *fin de siècle* moment before the internet upended the way we consume culture. Prior to 1991, the story goes, bloated pop and hair-metal acts ruled the airwaves, before the meteoric success of Nirvana's *Nevermind* revolutionized the notion of what could be popular, knocked Michael Jackson's *Dangerous* off the top of the Billboard charts, and ushered "alternative culture" into the mainstream. Jane's Addiction plays a de facto supporting role in this fable, since the popularity of Lollapalooza—the itinerant music festival founded that summer by Jane's front man Perry Farrell—is commonly acknowledged as a harbinger of what was to come. In this sense, *Nothing's Shocking* could be seen as a revelatory B-side to *Nevermind*'s messianic moment—a voice crying in the desert, as it were, prophetically anticipating a sea-change in the way we would all come to hear music.

But for me, at that time in my life, the songs on that album weren't about zeitgeist or historical cause-and-effect so much as the way they made me feel when I listened to them.

Jane's Addiction was the last band to play that day at Sandstone Amphitheater, and they took the stage in the darkened cool of the late-July evening. They opened with "Up the Beach," closed with "Ocean Size," and played "Summertime Rolls" during the encore. I watched, enraptured, from a fenced-off general-admission lawn 150 yards away from the stage. To this day it remains the most affecting rock performance I've ever witnessed in person—less for its artistic virtuosity than for the way it made me yearn for everything in my life that was about to happen.

Rolf Potts is the author of *The Geto Boys* (#114). Find him at rolfpotts.com.

CHAPTER 8
DEL AMITRI'S *WAKING HOURS* (1989)
Alex Green

At Passover dinner in April 1990, our Seder came to the pivotal symbolic moment where we poured a cup of wine and opened the door for the Prophet Elijah. As if on cue, in walked a guy wearing ripped jeans and a black mask, holding a shotgun. It wasn't exactly how I'd pictured him. I'd always thought skinny, long hair, a beard, maybe a robe …

"Sorry to barge in like this," the guy said, "but we're going to be taking some shit." Then he whistled out the door and in walked an identical masked intruder with an equally menacing shotgun. The two of them tied my family up and then proceeded to ransack the house right in front of us, pulling out drawers, throwing around dishes, and kicking over plants as they searched for anything of value.

"This is the second worst Passover dinner I've ever had," my grandfather said. Later, he told me the first, but because this was for sure *my* worst Passover ever, I'm going to focus on this one for now.

The thieves went upstairs and from where we sat all we could hear was a rolling and violent wave of beds being moved, dressers upended, closets pillaged. The home invasion went on for about an hour and they didn't take *some* shit, they took a lot of it: jewelry, money, cameras, watches, stereos, and CDs. While the sounds of plundering and destroying things upstairs went on directly above our Seder table, my grandfather looked up at the ceiling and delivered a fulminating verbal assault in their general direction.

"Fucking motherfucking asshole fuckers," he said. "If I had just one hand free I'd beat the shit out of both of them." He wasn't joking. Known as "The Hebrew Henchman," my grandfather had been a boxer back in the 1930s and not only was he 14–0 with nine knockouts, one time he had broken his wrist mid-fight, but still sent his opponent to the floor with just one operative hand. But the Hebrew Henchman didn't have one hand free and there was nothing he could do.

"Fucking motherfucking cocksuckers," he said, as they left the house with our stuff. "Degenerate fucking asshole fuckers."

Opening the door for the Prophet Elijah is supposed to be a gesture to show trust in God's protection and I'm not sure how much my grandfather was into that before we were robbed, but he sure wasn't into it anymore.

"Fuck Passover," he said, trying to wriggle free from the ropes they'd tied us up with. "Fuck the Haggadah, fuck Elijah, and fuck fucking gefilte fish." "Hey, I worked a long time on that," my mom protested. "You can work on gefilte fish as long as you want," my grandfather said. "It'll always taste like shit."

A jogging neighbor wearing a Peter Gabriel shirt saw the predicament we were in and in minutes we were untied, the police had arrived, and the surveying of the damage had begun. Our house was a mess and even long after the thieves were gone it still vibrated with violation. Everything they had left us didn't feel like ours anymore. My parents lost their class rings, a few thousand dollars in cash, a stereo and a camera, my sister had a bunch of jewelry taken, and I had lost a few stacks of CDs and my Sony Walkman.

All the violence they had in them seemed to have been really taken out on my room. They had emptied every drawer, overturned my bed, ripped the posters from the walls, and although they weren't interested in taking my records, they were quite interested in destroying them. They took the albums from their sleeves and whipped them against the walls, where they shattered into pieces. My room was filled with shards of *Surfer Rosa*, remnants of *Reckoning*, fragments of *Flip Your Wig*, and halves of *Hallowed Ground*. Even the ones that remained whole had grooves no longer fit for a needle to find them.

The only album left alive was my copy of Del Amitri's *Waking Hours*. A #6 album in the United Kingdom, it hadn't been out in America for long, but because I was the Music Director at my university's radio station, A&M Records had sent me an advance copy a few weeks earlier than its US March release date and it hadn't left my stereo since.

"Put on some music and I'll help you clean up," my grandfather said. And so I did. And *Waking Hours*, which begins with the sheer pop gallop of "Kiss This Thing Goodbye" soundtracked out the reassembly of my room. Looking back at it now, it's funny that we were putting things back together while listening to an album about how they fall apart.

As an album opener, I always thought nothing could top R.E.M.'s "Begin the Begin," but the leaping "Kiss This Thing Goodbye" proved me wrong; it's a stone-cold classic whose catchy right hook is backed by an equally potent left. It's no wonder my pugilist grandfather liked it immediately. "I like this guy's voice," he said as singer Justin Currie's vocals wrapped magically around guitarist Iain Harvie's melodic slide opening. "Who doesn't like a crooner with bite?"

Only the second album from the Glasgow band, *Waking Hours* is a monster of a record that positively surges from start to finish. For the purpose of time and space I'm going to focus on the way it opens and closes, but for the uninitiated, in-between there are wrenching ballads ("Move Away Jimmy Blue"), crunchy rueful pop ("When I Want You"), and winning, jangly folk ("This Side of the Morning"). Not only that, but it's also got scorching rockers ("Opposite View"), rootsy stomp ("Hatful of Rain") and, thanks to the prowling bassline of "Stone Cold Sober," the cry of "We are the dead life / So come on / Come on" is both denunciatory and urging.

Produced in part by Mark Freegard, Gil Norton, and Hugh Jones, thirty years later *Waking Hours* still sounds as crisp, fresh, and urgent as ever—it's one of those rare albums that will always keep obsolescence at bay. The album's first single, "Kiss This Thing Goodbye," is about a relationship going sour, just about to jump the track completely and add to the wreckage in the romantic ravine. It's as accusatory as it is retiring, and it finds Currie pleading not only for a mutual euthanasia, but also for someone to make the merciful first move. Not only that, but the realization that love is dead finds Currie seeing the world as a metaphorical conspiratorial pollutant. Looking out at the cars driving by his window, he sings: "Now I'm watching the fumes foul up the sunrise/I'm watching the light fade away."

Currie has always been able to strike a perfect balance between the caustic and the poetic, the cynical and the hopeful, the darkness and the light. My grandfather was right—his bite is undeniable, but so is his ability to write with literary elegance and poetic finesse. *Waking Hours'* world of struck matches, nervous laughs, scheming smiles, and jackpot philosophy demonstrates his philosophical dexterity, linguistic gymnastics, and unreasonable gift for metrical command.

Two months after the Passover disaster, I watched Del Amitri make their network debut on *Letterman* with "Kiss This Thing Goodbye" and it crackled with immediacy. Letterman seemed knocked out. Walking over to the band after their performance he gave Currie a long handshake and, as NBC cut to the commercials, he was clearly under the influence of an unexpected pop daze. Putting it in baseball terms, if Rickey Henderson is the greatest lead-off hitter of all time, then "Kiss This Thing Goodbye" is the Rickey Henderson of rock and roll; it pounces on the first pitch and lines it right over the fence.

If "Kiss This Thing Goodbye" is exactly how an album should start, "Nothing Ever Happens" is exactly how one should end. With its padlocking janitors, standoffish postal clerks, and closing-time secretaries, it's a Kafka-esque look at daily working life, sure, but on a deeper level it's perhaps the most accurate depiction of our unwillingness to change our lives no matter how bleak or dire, for no other reason than the bleak and the dire are so familiar. The band's biggest hit in the United Kingdom (#11), "Nothing Ever Happens" is a crushing collage of quotidian life; a battered anthem of heartbreaking beauty and loss whose wrenching roll call serves as a reminder that, while the world burns around us, we'll just keep doing nothing about it over and over until our inaction tricks us into thinking it's the opposite. Or, as Currie puts it: "The needle returns to the start of the song and we all sing along like before."

I've seen both Del Amitri and Justin Currie play live several times and the fact is fans are always positively *thirsty* for this song. It's a thrilling thing to hear fans sing along to a cherished number in a band's songbook—think Oasis's "Don't Look Back in Anger" or Bowie's "Heroes"—it's a transcendent instant where the song floats above the crowd like an idea about the world or an accepted truth about ourselves that everyone agrees on for just under four minutes. I have to admit, to hear a crowd of people so enthusiastically singing the album's last line—"We'll all be lonely tonight and lonely tomorrow"—is both oddly comforting and slightly disturbing.

But the song knows that from Sandy Hook to Charlottesville to the burning down of synagogues, all we ever do about disaster is pretty much nothing because we're cowards and, if silence really is a form of approval, then that's the worst kind of complicity I can think of. And what many tend to forget is that the punishment for this kind of behavior is we're doomed to live alongside our cowardice for the rest of our lives. And cowardice, as we all know, is awful company. It may take years, but it will slowly destroy us, piece by piece, until all the blood is drained from our useless and hopeless hearts.

Waking Hours is an album that always holds me together when things are falling apart. It's rousing, it's painful, it's stirring, and it's rife with the kind of brutal beauty I love. It transports me back to my bedroom after getting robbed by the Prophet Elijah on Passover, but it constantly reminds me that you can always put things back together even after they have been ripped to pieces.

Because they will.

And you'll have to.

The late novelist Robert Bolano once wrote: "So everything lets us down, including curiosity and honesty and what we love best. *Yes, said the voice, but cheer up, it's fun in the end.*"[1] That may be so, but sometimes the end is just a retired boxer by himself plagued by the instinct to keep hitting things.

My grandfather boxed well into his eighties. He'd go late at night to the gym just before closing, and he always dressed in slacks and a long-sleeve button-down shirt. He looked like he was going to work at an accounting firm. He rejected the electric spandex that was in fashion at the time and favored a more low-key sartorial approach to fitness. When I asked him why he'd say: "I don't need to dress up like a Vegas magician to hit a bag hanging from a ceiling."

If I was the one who was supposed to pick him up, I'd stand outside the room without announcing myself and watch him peppering that bag with shot after shot, his Star of David necklace clicking against his chest not so much like it was keeping time as it was counting it down: how many minutes before closing, how many punches still in the hands of the Hebrew Henchman, how many hours left to live in this useless, stupid world.

Del Amitri's *Waking Hours* is an album that had two jobs—end the 1980s and kick off the 1990s—an in-betweenness that renders it a B-side forever. Offering a prescient indictment of the consequences of living in a world run by infidels and popstars, *Waking Hours* is an underappreciated masterwork that left a decade crumbling in the rearview mirror and the band's musical contemporaries gasping at the sound their tires made as they crunched over the glass.

Alex Green is the author of *The Stone Roses* (#33).

CHAPTER 9
SINÉAD O'CONNOR'S *I DO NOT WANT WHAT I HAVEN'T GOT* (1990)
Tara Murtha

Every song is a prayer pulled from her throat.

Sinéad O'Connor's breakthrough record *I Do Not Want What I Haven't Got* opens with a recitation of the Serenity Prayer and ends with the titular poem, performed as a chant, about walking through the desert alone but unafraid. Released in 1990, *I Do Not Want What I Haven't Got* is a transformational record, meaning it charts the artist surviving a failed relationship, and its critical and commercial success transformed the Irish singer into an international star. The album spent six weeks atop the US charts and earned O'Connor four Grammy Awards. Sinéad was invited to perform at the ceremony. Instead, she became the first musician to protest against it. In a letter to the National Academy of Recording Arts & Sciences, O'Connor wrote: "As artists I believe our function is to ... always speak the truth and never keep it hidden even though we are operating in a world which does not like the sound of the truth."[1]

The opening track, "Feel So Different," is an orchestral dirge wherein O'Connor laments how different she feels after a bad experience. O'Connor seems shocked that the world she intended to change had instead managed to change her—an endearing glimpse of *naiveté* in a young artist wise beyond her years. At 23 years old, O'Connor already understands that the primal pain of loss isn't the beloved's departure, it's the loss of the person you got to be while you were with them.

O'Connor also knew that a world that does not like the sound of truth is particularly disinterested in women's stories. Back in 1990, pop stars definitely did not talk publicly about reproductive trauma, but O'Connor sang about her miscarriages in "Three Babies," the third track on the album.

She looks outward, also. "Black Boys on Mopeds" is a powerful anthem protesting against police brutality and racism. At least eight artists including The Nields and Amanda Palmer (with her father Jack) have covered the song, but it wasn't a hit.

Ironically, the biggest hit on *I Do Not Want What I Haven't Got* was the only cover. Written and originally recorded by Prince, O'Connor's searing interpretation of "Nothing Compares 2 U" was bolstered by an innovative music video that relentlessly focused on O'Connor's face. "Nothing Compares 2 U" is a feral cry, an anthem for the abandoned. It is the opposite of the album's title track, in which O'Connor expresses a commitment to remain brave within the solitude she sensed was her destiny.

It is difficult to think of O'Connor's album as a B-side, especially given the momentous success of its hit single. And although *I Do Not Want What I Haven't Got* showcases O'Connor's profound songwriting talent, ability to seamlessly knit together many musical styles, and commitment to truth-telling, it qualifies as a B-side because the firestorm surrounding its release ultimately produced her commercial downfall. Here the B-side is a phoenix that flies high, but does not rise from the ashes. As a prophetic *Rolling Stone* review observed, *I Do Not Want What I Haven't Got* "is less about O'Connor's ambitions than the cost of those ambitions."[2]

It's the fall of 1990, and 23-year-old O'Connor is performing at the Amnesty International Concert in Santiago, Chile. The opening note of "Nothing Compares 2 U" rings out and O'Connor takes the stage, her head shaved and feet bare. She's wearing a black motorcycle jacket with the Virgin Mary emblazoned on the back. She steps up to the microphone. *It's been seven hours and fifteen days since you took your love away.* The audience responds by singing the back-up melody line, and she powers through the rest of the song with the devotion of an artist willing to molt right there in the light, explode into aura. After the chorus, O'Connor tilts her face to the sky and wails for twelve seconds—an eternity—wet animal sounds escaping from her throat as she bends backward, flailing her arms as if falling off a very high ledge.

Two years after the concert in Santiago, O'Connor was the musical guest on a now-notorious episode of *Saturday Night Live*. She sang an *a cappella* version of Bob Marley's "War," updating the lyrics to address *child abuse, ye-AH*. At the end of the song, O'Connor holds up a photograph of Pope John Paul II, rips it up, and then tosses the pieces at the camera and says, "Fight the real enemy!"

The backlash was swift and brutal. Frank Sinatra called her a "stupid broad" and said he'd kick her ass if she was a guy. Actor Joe Pesci, who hosted *SNL* the following week, joked about smacking O'Connor in the face, and the audience laughed. A Catholic cardinal was pretty sure it was "voodoo." Even Madonna was aghast, or pretended to be.

In 1992, most Americans were not yet aware of the Roman Catholic Church sex-abuse scandal, but the story was already out in Ireland. Americans didn't begin to reckon with the depth and breadth of the church's systemic abuse and cover-up until the *Boston Globe* published a series of reports in 2002—a full decade after O'Connor's *SNL* stunt. But O'Connor, a victim of child abuse herself, knew. She has said she was violently beaten by her mother, locked in her room, deprived of food and clothes, verbally abused, thrown out of her home, and sometimes forced to sleep alone outside in the garden. She traced her abuse to the Catholic Church. "What happened to me is a direct result of what happened to my mother and what happened to her in her house and in school," she's explained.[3] "I'm one of millions of people who grew up in the same situation," she said. "Who grew up terrified constantly."[4]

O'Connor tried to quell the hysterical reaction to her stunt. She repeatedly explained that reports about the church's scandal were already out in Ireland and that her attack was on the institution, not one man.

It's two weeks after the *Saturday Night Live* incident, and O'Connor walks onstage at Madison Square Garden to perform at a concert celebrating Bob Dylan's thirty years in music. The audience is screaming a chaotic mix of boos and cheers. The band repeatedly attempts to start the performance, but the crowd won't settle down enough to let her sing. She stands alone in the spotlight and clasps her hands behind her back, scanning the crowd like a sea captain searching for her coordinates. Finally, she motions for the band to stop, grabs the microphone and launches into "War," doubling down on her *SNL* performance. She finishes the song, calmly walks off-stage, and curls into Kris Kristofferson's arms. She's crying. *Everywhere is war.*

Almost three decades later, I still picture O'Connor standing there, immured in the crowd's roar, the sound of blood rushing, of 20,000 arrows in the air. O'Connor has said she thought people, especially musicians, were enraged by her actions "because I'm a girl, for a start." As she put it, she is not, after all, Neil Young.

Now 52, O'Connor is no longer known mostly for her music or voice, despite the brilliance of *I Do Not Want What I Haven't Got*, despite releasing ten studio albums over the course of more than three decades. A common theme in reviews of O'Connor's records is that the quality could or should be enough to redeem her so that she may once again be primarily recognized, and celebrated, as one of the most talented artists of the twentieth century. But so far that hasn't happened. Instead, Sinéad O'Connor has become our lady of perpetual redemption. She most often appears in headlines as a stock character in a well-worn media storyline, starring as (yet another) gifted female star unraveling in slow motion through a zoetrope of clickbait stories exploiting her personal struggles: O'Connor disappeared and was found in a hospital. O'Connor is engaged in a custody battle. O'Connor attempted suicide, again.

In August 2017 a video appeared on Sinéad O'Connor's Facebook page. She recorded it amid an apparent breakdown while hiding out at a New Jersey motel. She is crying. A tattoo of Jesus Christ blooms from her chest. Once again, she talks about suicide. "I shouldn't be here," she says. Later, she'll say she thought she had to be dead to be heard. After the video went viral, someone posted a Facebook update on her behalf assuring fans O'Connor was no longer suicidal and receiving care.

As for the audience, we never apologized for our grotesque overreaction to hearing what we now know to be true. The era of #MeToo has been a tipping point for the Catholic Church. In July 2018, the highest official yet stepped down due to alleged sexual abuse. In August 2018, Pennsylvania's attorney general released a massive grand jury report detailing seven decades of systemic child sex abuse and cover-up in six archdioceses. New Jersey, New York, Missouri, Nebraska, and Illinois have all launched their own sweeping investigations, with more states surely to follow. In Chile, where O'Connor performed for human rights decades ago, all thirty-one active Catholic bishops offered to resign after it was revealed that church officials destroyed evidence that children were sexually abused by priests. "We showed no care for the little ones," Pope Francis admitted. "We abandoned them."[5]

O'Connor's full birth name is Sinéad Marie Bernadette O'Connor, in honor of Saint Bernadette of Lourdes. In 1858, when Bernadette was 14, she encountered a vision of the Virgin Mary. Five years after Bernadette's visions, the church confirmed the apparition and officially designated the grounds a miracle. But, at the time, townsfolk didn't believe her. They harassed, repeatedly interrogated, and ultimately shunned Bernadette, who escaped to a convent where she lived the rest of her life in virtual seclusion.

In September 2018, O'Connor released a song called "Milestones" under a new moniker, Magda Davitt. Like "I Do Not Want What I Haven't Got," the new song is essentially a prayer. This time, instead of looking ahead to a life walking through the desert alone, she envisions her death. She imagines sitting with her critics before God to discuss: "Which one of you and me was braver / Which one of us was a truth soldier."

A month after the hotel video was posted, O'Connor was invited to share her most intimate pain and thoughts on the *Dr. Phil Show* for a segment teased as "Sinéad O'Connor Speaks Out After Hotel Breakdown." Dr. Phil asked her about her abuse, about her mother, her suicide attempts, and, of course, *Saturday Night Live*. "That's when it became acceptable and it became the norm, that I was treated by everyone I knew from family to everyone like I was an absolutely insane crazy person," she says. Throughout the interview, O'Connor looks pained. She seems so different from the young woman with the breakthrough record, the bald-headed rebel that radiated serene defiance. Then Dr. Phil asks her to recall the moment she ripped up the photo and she smiles calmly, as if lit from within. "Silence," she says. O'Connor glides her arms out in front of her, palms up, gesturing toward Dr. Phil. She spreads them further to include the studio set, the camera people, the microphones, the production people, the audience watching on television and computer screens, splintering her image and words into hundreds of headlines. "Silence everywhere," she says. "It was fantastic."

Tara Murtha is the author of *Ode to Billie Joe* (#102). She tweets at @taramurtha.

CHAPTER 10
DE LA SOUL'S *DE LA SOUL IS DEAD* (1991)
Shawn Taylor

Lived blackness can be exhausting. Are you walking correctly? Talking correctly? The laces of your sneakers tied in the most current fashion? Do you have the right sneakers? How is your bravado? Can you walk into a room and have all eyes on you? How cool are you? Are you the right kind of black for your fellow black folks? Are you safe enough so other POC (and white folks) accept you without fear? Are you willing to be twice as good, for a third of the respect and a fifth of the rewards? Questions and negotiations abound. In 1991, this was my crisis. Layer this with an undulating wave of depression and I was, not suicidal, but pretty ambivalent to what happened to me.

I had barely completed a disastrous first year at a predominately white university. Dyslexia, poverty, strife with family, and racial identity crisis all conspired to bring me to my lowest. I was in the kitchen of my mother's apartment—not having lived with her in years—getting my hair cut by Derek Turner (Spawn from the original incarnation of the indie hip-hop group, Atmosphere), before going to the club. I didn't want to go, but had no good reason not to. Things seemed alright, until I heard a subdued "oops" and the clippers made an unfamiliar noise. Derek handed me a mirror and allowed me to see the new pattern he had shaved into the side of my head. In that remarkably charming way he had, he laughed: "Yo. Just say it's some De La Soul shit."

The more I considered his mistake—it was awful—the more I took his words to heart. Yeah. I would De La the hell out of this look. A half-hearted joke implying De La Soul was anything goes helped to lift me out of my funk. I got out of the chair, changed into a *dashiki*, put on a few leather African medallions, and went to the club. I had the time of my life. The last song I danced to was "A Roller Skatin' Jam Named 'Saturdays.'" *Now is the time / To act a fool tonight.* Never in my relationship with popular culture had I needed a message more than that, at that time. This wasn't the first time De La Soul gave me the lift I needed.

In the spring of my junior year in high school, I was pretty much a brawler by default. Routinely shuttling back and forth from Fort Green, Brooklyn and Minneapolis, Minnesota, I regularly found myself in situations where a quick mouth or quicker fists had to be deployed. I'd be too "white talking" for Brooklyn and too black for Minneapolis, and folks around me would make damn sure I knew I didn't fit into their preconceptions. I stood firmly at the four-way intersection of Dana Dane, The Cure, the Rude Boys from my mom's Jamaican heritage, and science fiction—folks did not know what to make of me. I was just figuring it out myself.

I had one foot down a very slippery slope, in danger of not being able to recover my footing. After a particularly bad week my uncle, Maurice (R.I.P.), came by and dropped off a cassette tape. "This is all you, nephew. I hope you can see it." The j-card was all yellow and purple and orange and green and pink day-glo with three black men on it. One of them even had glasses. Not Cazals, but regular-ass, I-need-these-to-see glasses. I played the tape and was damn near instantly transformed. *3 Feet High and Rising* got me through the remainder of high school. I played it almost every day, for a year. De La showed me that another black world, another (real) me was possible. I was brawling over my identity because I never owned it. I was trying to be too many things to too many people, and I was lashing out because of my lack of *isness*. I had no anchor. De La Soul helped me to see how I could be all things at once; no need to be a (poor) chameleon any longer. *Proud, I'm proud of what I am / Poems I speak the plug two type.*

If *3 Feet* was a window into a new black world, allowing us to see all the fascinating ways to be black, their follow-up, *De La Soul is Dead*, was an invitation to live in that world. *Dead* is the ultimate B-side to *3 Feet*. Not only does it show De La in the full spectrum of their sonic possibility, it sneaks up on you and forces you to reckon with it on its own terms.

The greatest trick De La pulled was in fooling us all into believing that their second album was a refutation of their first. *Dead*'s cover showed a smashed daisy filled flower pot, seemingly declaring that the D.A.I.S.Y. (Da Inner Sound Ya'll) was dead—their non-existent "hippies of hip-hop" (reverse shout out to Arsenio Hall) personas exorcised. In fact, *De La Soul is Dead* is a magnification of all the ideas espoused on *3 Feet High and Rising*. It is a reification of their ethos of "black whimsy."

Simply put, black whimsy is about being playfully odd. It's about mapping your inner joy and curiosity over the mundanity of your everyday existence. It's about looking into the shadows without fear, possibly even venturing into them, just to see if anything is there. It's the opposite of a deficit model. It is also an intervention. Black whimsy has allowed De La Soul to talk about some very serious subjects, while never betraying their sense of wonder.

While De La's production (courtesy of Prince Paul—my vote for most underrated producer in hip-hop history) stayed fanciful, whimsical, and left of their contemporaries, their lyrical content matured. There is still the scatological humor, exemplified by the *beep* turn-the-page children's book framing of *Dead*. There are songs that exist as exercises of the imagination—pushing the boundaries of what rap could (should?) be. But then there is also "Millie Pulled a Pistol on Santa" and "My Brother's a Basehead."

"Millie," driven by Patrice Rushen, Funkadelic, and Melvin Bliss samples, tells the tragic tale of Millie, a De La classmate, who is molested by her father. The song concludes with her shooting her father, who is dressed as a department-store Santa. This song is directly responsible for my working in juvenile justice and adolescent mental health for two decades. As a kid who grew up in an abusive home, this song forced me to confront my abuse and also spurred me to provide the help and support I didn't get to kids in similar situations. When I train clinicians, I have them listen to this song as part of their training. It roughly punctuates the gravity of the work they do.

No one I know, from my generation and cultural circumstances, escaped crack. Either you did it, saw people do it, saw people get rich selling it, witnessed people being robbed and killed for it, or watched as it decimated entire communities. These things overlapped for many people. *Told me you needed a stronger fix / Stepped to the crack scene in '86.*

"My Brother's a Basehead" is both a love letter to Posdnous's brother and an almost cartography of trying to help someone with addiction. Dougie Fresh and Slick Rick, N.W.A., The Doors, and Wayne Fontana and The Mindbenders are used to create a 1960s' beat to underscore Pos's (and his brother's) struggles. The beat seems almost too happy to soundtrack the pain. The jangly, loose-limbed beat is near antithetical to the message of the tune. And this is why De La Soul as a band, but *De La Soul is Dead* in particular, is so vital to who I am.

With *Dead*, De La delivered on many levels. They stressed specificity without the burden of uniqueness. They mapped joy over the crooked and pitted paths of young black life. Their black cultural multi-speak allows us to dance in pain, to find our collective humanity in horror, and to be ourselves, our full and beautiful and flawed selves: *I was John Doe / Now I'm Mr. Jolicoeur*. Not so much demanding or earning respect, but being respected on our strength, respect as our default setting—until we are disrespected—then it is *time for some heads to be flown*.

Shawn Taylor is the author of *People's Instinctive Travels and the Paths of Rhythm* (#47).

CHAPTER 11
DIGABLE PLANETS' *REACHIN' (A NEW REFUTATION OF TIME AND SPACE)* (1993)
Walter Biggins

When I was 17, I thought of myself as a record. It was 1994, so I didn't even have a turntable at the time, but a record seemed cooler, and coolness is essential at that age. Teenagers define themselves by their tastes, because they have neither the financial independence nor the emotional clarity to have the power to define themselves otherwise. Kids get into fistfights over their aesthetics and make friends because of them, too, for their aesthetics *are* their ethics, in a way that doesn't happen once they're in their 30s. Or, if they still do that, we call them arrested adolescents, teenagers who never grew up. At that age, our tastes in books, movies, music, and clothes broadcast who we are and who we're not.

I was as music-struck as I was girl-dizzy. (A lot.) Aaron Waldkoetter and I became good friends, despite being opposite in almost every way, because we loved music. We loved sharing it with our friends, to the point of foisting it on them. Somehow, sometime during my junior year of high school, Aaron and I became the unofficial DJs of our small Dallas high school. We spun CDs and cassettes at chaperoned dances held in a downtown school-district administration building, unchaperoned parties at friends' houses, backyards, and poolsides. Probably, it happened simply because we were the only ones who had bothered to get good speakers and a crossfader. Collectively, we had what was apparently thought of as good taste and an eclectic, oddball, and just-weird-enough music collection. People *stayed* on those sticky linoleum dance floors when we were spinning, even after we'd periodically fuck up by hitting the wrong button, wiring the wrong equipment together, or blowing fuses.

As records go, Aaron was the shiny "A"-side—six feet tall, blonde, blue-eyed, slim, Greek statue-cheeked, cocky. Meanwhile, I was the "B"-side—black, nerdy, awkward in gesture and statement. I failed to fit in with my fellow black students, a few of whom called me an "Oreo"—black on the outside, white on the inside.

Outside of DJing, I mostly felt less like I was a side than like a bootleg demo— unfinished, poorly made, castoff, lost. Being a B-side would have been an improvement, socially speaking. It's no wonder my musical tastes gravitated, yes, toward popular genres (hip-hop, rock, techno—the 1990s A-sides that I longed to join), but the underground, oddball, ironic ends of those genres. That end of the pool, the B-side deep end, felt right to me.

The first time I heard Digable Planets' "Rebirth of Slick (Cool Like Dat)," I was riding in a van full of black teens on our way to a high-school baseball game. We were the L.G.

Pinkston Vikings, and we were terrible. There I was, a mediocre utility outfielder at best, listening to 100.3 JAMZ with everybody else when that rolling acoustic bass and finger-snap percussion came on. So casual, so understated, so fucking cool. Then the breakbeat kicked in, somehow even deeper than the jazz bass. Then the sly horns kicked in—not a blast so much as an insinuation. I was just getting into jazz, and this jazz-rap fusion hit me right between the ears. I was grinning ear-to-ear before Butterfly even started rapping, relaxed, low-volume, sing-songy. I didn't understand half of what he was saying but what I *did* get was seductive, filled with double entendres ("She frequents the fattest joints caught underground / Our funk zooms like you hit the Mary Jane"[1]), cool but not flashy about it. I dug the flow, and wanted to find out more about what I wasn't getting, because I wanted to be a part of whatever story this group was telling.

Hip-hop was the genre supposedly telling the story of my life better than any other at the time. But I wasn't hearing the story of my middle-class blackness in N.W.A.'s tales of Los Angeles strife—if we met in real life, I was pretty sure those guys would beat my ass and call me a faggot—and the perpetual boasts of Biggie, Run DMC, and so many others rang false to a boy who thought so lowly of himself that he hardly asked a girl out on a date until college. Whether it was the flashy glamour of Big Daddy Kane or the grit-and-gold of Tupac, rap's "A" game seemed unattainable.

Digable Planets, though, seemed like the B-side avatars of my dreams. They joined such heroes as De La Soul, A Tribe Called Quest, Del the Funkee Homosapien, and Black Sheep in my personal pantheon. We played that dismal baseball game (we lost; we always lost), we slung ourselves back to school, and I whipped my way to the closest record store to buy the Digable Planets album.

Reachin' (A New Refutation of Time and Space) was so dense (to me) that it made sense that its title essentially featured a subtitle. There, I heard a story of blackness that I could fit inside, that allowed for "black *and* _____" rather than "black *or* _____." As in, I could be black *and* love *Star Trek*, and I could be black *and* rock out to R.E.M., and I could be black *and* have white (and Asian, and Latinx) friends, rather than having to choose one (and only one) or risk having my black card revoked. I could be black and, as I did, love both the hip-hop I played at parties *and* the jazz I was just discovering for myself.

The album's entire production evoked the dimly lit, intimate camaraderie of what I imagined a jazz club to be. I had never been in one, of course. Jazz's story, as told by smoke-accented black-and-white photos, abstract-art record covers, and handsomely detached black men in crisp suits, was a narrative of adult coolness to me. It was adult, in that being cool was a given rather than an adolescent posturing. Jazz was voluptuous; hip-hop was, as rappers told us constantly, *hard*.

Jazz was and is the quintessential B-side of the black musical experience, the crazy genius granddad who's necessary to convey versions of black life that get otherwise missed by poppier variants. I needed both sides, and here one album combined them. *Reachin'* taught me, as I played it over and over and over, that maybe there was a place in the story of blackness for *me*.

At parties, I forced "Rebirth of Slick" and other songs from *Reachin'* upon partygoers. It entered the regular Biggins/Waldkoetter rotation along with: They Might Be Giants'

"No One Knows My Plan" (which got kids to make an impromptu conga line); Prodigy's "Fire" (which got kids raging); R.E.M.'s "It's the End of the World as We Know It" (which got everyone yelping in unison); Sugar's "Helpless" (which got kids singing alone in corners by themselves, not even caring); The Breeders' "Cannonball" (which made kids roll their eyes because we played it every dance); Arrested Development's "Mama's Always on Stage" (which got kids back on the floor after I'd cleared it with a ballad, always, and with no exception); and two or three dozen other regular songs. "Rebirth of Slick," "Nickel Bags," "Pacifics," and "Escapism (Gettin' Free)" became part of that narrative.

It was a narrative, after all. We listen to music largely because music either tells us stories or provides atmosphere for the stories in our mind. As DJs, Aaron and I learned on the fly how to choose songs that told the night's story, ebbing high and low, fast and slow, loud to quiet, to keep the crowd on the same page. We failed as often as we succeeded. We were stubborn, insisting that some songs were great despite the lack of reaction from the crowd, because they spoke to us, projected our desires out into the world. I foisted *Reachin'* onto crowds, as if to say: "Here's *my* story, here's *my* blackness, here, it can belong to you, too."

It both was and wasn't my story. Digable Planets hailed from New York City (NYC), and *Reachin'* is so NYC-specific in its lyrics that I, a Dallas native who had never been to that city, couldn't hope to understand it all without CliffsNotes. I was getting into jazz but wasn't knowledgeable enough to know all the musicians that they alluded to in their lyrics or to hear those cats in the beats that the Planets were sampling.

Looking back, it's obvious why the album's mystery was so appealing to me. In it, the Digable Planets cast themselves as aliens coming down to Earth from a more enlightened world. What 17-year-old doesn't feel like an alien? At the time, the story I told myself was that I was more alien than most, but I know now that millions of black kids were telling themselves versions of that very same story. *Reachin'*'s first song, "It's Good to Be Here," tells the listener explicitly that the Digable Planets are outsider visionaries, come down to our world to essentially save hip-hop: "Left my mom's a note with these quotes on a trunk / It says 'I split to Earth to resurrect the funk.'"[2]

The whole album is intended to be seen as the Digable Planets playing a concert at the "Cocoon Club" (a play on Harlem's famed Cotton Club), debuting their funky new vision. Throughout *Reachin'* there are interludes that bring the listener back to the narrative of that interstellar jazz club. A chant throughout the record evokes the astral planes of Sun Ra: "The mind is time, the mind is space ..."

Emphasizing their alternative nature even more, they envision themselves as insects. The bug metaphors trip through every song on the record and, of course, the three MCs are Butterfly (Ishmael Butler), Ladybug Mecca (Mariana Vieira), and Doodlebug (Craig Irving); Silkworm (King Britt) is the producer. As the Cocoon Club's MC puts it in that first song, "They're some weird motherfuckers but they *do* jazz it up."[3] There are no guest MCs on the album, and the album's psychedelic packaging highlights their outsider status even more.

At the same time, though, they tell the story of themselves as the hippest *insiders* around. In "Pacifics (N.Y. Is Red Hot)," Butterfly raps a tale of his typical relaxed Sunday in New York, and it's so lived-in and naturally flowing that he seems like a city native, expressly willing to show you around. The cultural allusions and obscure jazz samples pile up on *Reachin'*, as if the Planets feel the need to remind you how plugged in they are to the scene. One song, "Jimmi Digging Cats," is basically an excuse for the Digable Planets to posit the idea that Jimi Hendrix (a hero of the album) would have loved them, repeatedly using a sample from an old interview with Hendrix and setting it up as if it's about them. In other words, the Digable Planets are within the natural continuum of African American popular music *and* they're pushing it forward. They come from the masters but are also masters themselves. It's a tricky narrative conceit, playing as both consummate *insiders* (the A-side) and weirdo *outsiders* (the B-side).

All of this carefully articulated distance from hip-hop culture was, of course, a story—a cock-and-bull one, to be exact. Even I kinda knew it in 1993. *Reachin'* carries on in the jazz-rap tradition that includes A Tribe Called Quest's *The Low End Theory* (1991), the Dream Warriors' *And Now the Legacy Begins* (1991), Guru's *Jazzmatazz* collaborations between jazz artists and hip-hop stars (1993–1997), and De La Soul's *Buhloone Mindstate* (1993). It's both brassy and silly for the Planets to presume that they were inventing this, or that they were alone in doing so.

Indeed, in the very next year, the Planets seemed eager to flip the record over, and show a different version of themselves. Their second (and final) album, *Blowout Comb*, starts with rhymes that align the Planets with two black political prisoners—Mumia Abu Jamal and Sekou Odinga—and situate themselves not just in NYC, but in *Brooklyn*.[4] They are no longer aliens, and no longer detached from their world. *Blowout Comb* (1994) is not spacey or filled with black bourgeois versions of hippiedom, as was *Reachin'*. Brooklyn's streets, corners, and blocks reign supreme here. And this particular Brooklyn is black— Spike Lee's Bedford-Stuyvesant of *Do the Right Thing* more than Jonathan Ames's *Bored to Death*. Revolutionaries and their ideas come up often in *Blowout Comb*, from George Jackson to the Five Percent Nation, from Leonard Peltier to the Nation of Islam, from Nikki Giovanni to Steve Biko. They're casting themselves again as outcasts but this time not in a way that makes them hip (B-siders), but instead makes them dissident (bootlegs, and proud of it).

Mostly, *Blowout Comb* is concerned with connecting with its community rather than being set apart from it. There are way less samples here than on *Reachin'* and way more musical collaborators. Guru and Jeru the Damaja, both Brooklyn natives, provide key guest raps on "Borough Check" and "Graffiti," respectively. Live musicians build most of the tracks, with minimal samples woven in rather than serving as the foundations for songs. The album is thus grounded in a *social* space as well. This album wasn't created in a flying saucer, but in a 'hood.

If the alien dreamers of that album landed on Brooklyn in 2019 they wouldn't recognize that borough—with its Whole Foods Markets, boutique dog-food stores, and those annoying rental scooters—as belonging to them. Now, there's a part of me that concedes that *Blowout Comb* is musically, technically, superior to *Reachin'*. But, as good as it is, *Blowout Comb* feels sonically and lyrically like a time capsule, while *Reachin'* feels timeless. *Reachin'*'s themes of alienness and striving for coolness will be universal so long as black adolescence exists. The record taught me that there were fresher, more open, and consciously oddball narratives out there about what blackness and Americanness could be. It was a teacher, a mentor that showed me that it was okay to retell my story, to imagine my blackness for myself. Digable Planets taught me that all of that was fine, and even gave me a model for living on the B-side of life, and being happy—no, grateful—for that.

Walter Biggins is, with Daniel Couch, the co-author of *Workbook* (#124).
He tweets @walter_biggins.

CHAPTER 12
BILLY IDOL'S *CYBERPUNK* (1993)
Sean L. Maloney

Plucked from the Blendo Stream

Somewhere out there, buried in the all-seeing all-searching Cloud next to a spam folder full of dick pill scams and the desperate marketing emails, there is a fiery, fuck-you-for-existing take on Billy Idol's 1993 album *Cyberpunk*, the fifth and mostly forgotten album from the New Wave poster boy.[1] This is not that take. That take has been chopped up, mellowed out, echoes amplified and psychological space widened. The vicious attack on its career-stalling mediocrity and strange similarities to horrors of 2018 has been repurposed and rejigged to reflect reality: it ain't *that* bad. There's plenty of awfulness in both Idol's B-side sci-fi concept album and our current socio-political climate, but if we tweak a few knobs and tune out the most caustic elements, there's still joy buried deep in the mix.

Truth be told, *Cyberpunk* had always been a joke within my small circle of nerdy friends, shorthand for the underwhelming side of the cutting edge in the pre-meme era. The album reads like fan-fiction, a collection of genre tropes held together by sheer enthusiasm. The near-future tech, the psychedelic drugs, and pop-culture worship were all there but with a Golan-Globus level of narrative incohesion. We thought we were getting *Jurassic Park* but instead we got *Carnosaur*. We had pooled our lawnmower money to buy the deluxe edition, splitting the cost of the CD and floppy disc combo pack that promised next-level entertainment adventure: a "digital magazine." The set cost almost double the amount of a usual CD and, frankly, only one person in our extended circle had a computer with enough processing power to handle that much digital art. (My family was still months away from upgrading our tan-and-brown Apple IIe to the still sorta shitty pre-/post-Steve Jobs Apple Performa.) But we weren't about to let a shortage of funds and a lack of RAM prevent us from mainlining a dose of heavily pixelated pop-futurism from one of the world's biggest rockstars.

From the Adrenalin Channel …

We were nerds and we were desperate. It was the era of the sulking art kid and geek culture was at a low ebb. The *Star Wars* franchise was frozen in carbonite, *Star Trek* was still recovering from the save-the-whales silliness of the 1980s, and Roger Corman's Fantastic Four (F4) was the closest thing to a big-budget superhero we could imagine. (We also couldn't imagine how bad Corman's F4 would actually be, but that's a discussion for another essay.) Cool sci-fi fanzines weren't making it to our sleepy little suburbs, cable TV was pretty much limited to the dystopian rollerskate flick *Solarbabies* and the occasional screening of *Scanners 3*. And *Krull*, a lot of *Krull*. A weekly trip to the comic-book store and the rare Saturday night when we could tie up the landline to dial up the local Bulletin Board System were our only source of nerd-stuff news. Being a hyper-consumer of all things science fictional was hard work and involved consuming a lot of low-budget crap to hold us over (hello, *Hell Comes to Frogtown!*).

So when one of the biggest stars of the MTV era announced that he was going to be working in our weird little wheelhouse *of course* we started saving our allowance. His 1980s output had been permanently etched into our brains, the kind of pop mega-hits that would be branded into our collective consciousness. Although our Junior Grunge Scout instincts may have bristled at the idea of a glossy, big budget album, the nerdy-ass nerds were first and foremost. We were already obsessed with genre-defining *Neuromancer* author William Gibson and the genre-distilling roleplaying game *Cyberpunk 2020*. All we needed was a soundtrack. Clearly, Billy Idol was making this record for us. Clearly, we were idiots.

VR Shangrila

It is tough to say who Idol was actually making this record for: at least part of the reason for its commercial and artistic failure is that it just didn't know what audience it was looking for. For every cool, edgy idea you can almost hear an A&R guy in the back of the room mumbling "*don't forget, the kids loved 'Mony Mony,'*" trying to retain some sense of commercial appeal as Idol expands his musical palette beyond the black-leather bubblegum pop that had been his bread and butter since his first-wave punk band Generation X. For every moment of pure fury—like the chorus to lead single "Shock to the System"—there's some ham-fisted rich-white-dude hot-take on current events that fucks the whole vibe up (everything else about "Shock to the System"). For every cool drumbeat there's some dreadful New Age noodling and all of it is served up as a gross, bloated misread of the cultural climate. It may have "punk" in the title but the reality of *Cyberpunk* was just not punk. Not punk at all. That there was nary a hook as good as "White Wedding" certified the album's ignominious fate.

Who knows how many times the tape dub of the community CD made it to the stereo but it couldn't have been more than a handful of times. The floppy disc, with its cutting-edge digital magazine, probably never spun up a second time. My friends and I would move on to other things, like actual punk rock, underground electronica, and AOL chat rooms. Time would march on and cutting-edge technology of the literary genre—Computers! Cellular phones! Computers with cellular phones!—would become commonplace consumer goods. Evil corporations were taking over the government.

Endless war was *de rigueur*. Militarized police forces would be found in every big city and small town. Music would become severed from its corporeal form and, alongside journalism, be smashed underneath the boot heel of corporatist technophilia. And with each new push forward, each new format, and each new freak out, I'd go back to my old gag: "Y'all remember *Cyberpunk*?"

Scream.tiff

After nine months of politics-fueled, internet-stoked freakouts—and a sinking feeling that a decade in entertainment media made me complicit in the whole monstrous affair—*Cyberpunk* seemed like the perfect record for an analytical deep dive. Technology was very clearly tearing the culture apart. We had weaponized computer graphics. The 'bots were turning grandpa and grandma into rabid, hate-spewing monsters. There was an *internet of things* and hackers *knew how to control it*. There were packs of hippies roaming the country consuming research chemicals for kicks. The bad guys were winning and things were getting weird. My wife had a miscarriage and I wasn't prepared for the emotional tailspin it caused. Our latest attempt at parenthood was still unconfirmed. *And worst of all:* I had a lot of time to think about it. My decade-long writing career was a casualty of the "pivot to video," arts journalism's sudden and ruthless shift of resources from text to those damn videos that are always auto-playing at the worst possible time. The all-consuming brain-eating social network had swallowed my career too. I had given up writing, had started slinging booze around the corner from my house. "LOL, *Cyberpunk*" seemed like the right fit for dark times. This was the future Billy Idol was singing about.

Zigzag.tiff

I ordered a copy of the CD from the All-Consuming Mega Corporation. I didn't spend the extra money for the minty OG-complete-with-floppy-disc version. Twenty-five years later I still don't have a computer that could run the thing. On the other hand, I am able to dial up a two-decade-old video of psychedelic philosopher/cartoon Timothy Leary interviewing Idol or the clip of Idol on The Arsenio Hall Show replete with bleach-blonde dreadlocks. I can tell the robot in my handheld device to bring up the "Shock to the System" music video and laugh at its *Freejack*-meets-*Tetsuo: The Iron Man* riff on the L.A. Riots. The All-Knowing Search Engine serves me up long-forgotten record reviews—reviewers talking about "art-disco" like that's a bad thing![2]—and I supplement them with constant streams of the worst H. W. Bush era sci-fi films the All-Consuming Mega Corporation and its competitor The Broadcast Destroyer can beam into my living room. Vintage paperbacks of cyberpunk classics like Bruce Sterling's *Mirrorshades* begin showing up on my doorstep, the result of late-night anxiety-stoked click fits. Strung out on internet conspiracies and non-stop, jaw-dropping acts of horror it became easier to hate *Cyberpunk* and this damn dumb future that we were living.

… To the Endorphin Channel

I began to resent the sixteen-bit shitshow take on the future that Idol had assembled like a well-engineered, well-financed but ultimately bumbling cyborg. Grafting Mad Max imagery to narcissistic messianic atheism and letting it marinate in old-dudes-on-ecstasy sexuality just doesn't make for a fun repeat listen. The joke wears thin real quick. And that point is driven further into your skull when in 2018 you can't leave the house without hearing Billy Idol. His biggest songs are omnipresent. And not just omnipresent but goddamn perfect. "Dancing With Myself"! "Rebel Yell"! "White Wedding"! "Cradle of Love" is super-creepy but otherwise he had cranked out an entire decade's worth of killer pop. He had been on the cutting edge of studio technology since Generation X's dub-mix B-sides and his savvy image manipulation at the beginning of the MTV era fit perfectly within the cyberpunk aesthetic, bleeding-edge tech fetishization, and pop-culture obsession. But by *Cyberpunk* he'd become cartoonish, clueless, pitiable. I was pissed at myself for wanting to engage with this record in depth as the world burned around us.

And then my son was born, surrounded by incredibly smart people making kind decisions with some *Star Trek* looking med-tech around him, and it became nigh-impossible to focus my rage on such an undeserving target. Idol's only real offense was being out of touch with the next generation of cool kids. He was in his mid-thirties, comfortable, and successful. That's a terrible recipe for relevant art in a youth-focused market. Having just been tossed aside by the pivot to video, I could sympathize. He made an ambitious record at a time when ambition was really unfashionable. The rock aesthetic had a hard-reset in the wake of Nirvana's breakout, and the rejection of corporate opulence in the recording booth ensured that *Cyberpunk* was dead on arrival. But you can't blame Idol for trying. Or at least I couldn't but I was high on baby hormones, wired from sleep deprivation, and propelled by the peculiar endorphin rush of love caused by reactions on the all-consuming brain-eating social network to pictures of my adorable little newborn. It's not unlike the final hours of an acid trip: everything is shiney and I'm sure I will never, ever sleep again. It's a weird little evolutionary glitch.

My brain had been rewired, I re-examined the very acts of reading, writing, and listening. Rethought the whole "living in the dystopian future" thing. *Cyberpunk* is a quaint, cultural artifact rather than a reflection of everyday horrors. The act of disengagement— blocking anxiety-inducing aunts on social media, uninstalling notification-crazed apps, deleting that damned LinkedIn page that never did me any good anyway—became easier, less traumatic. It made it easier to see *Cyberpunk* in a nostalgic light, a warts-and-all encapsulation of the best and worst of speculative art in the mid-1990s, rather than a reflection of the outside world. *Cyberpunk* and its low-res CliffsNotes take on the future of the future capture an unconnected world yearning to plug in, unable to know how predictably dire the downsides would be. Its impact was minimal, its harm negligible. Idol still tours and still records and someone, somewhere in your neighborhood, is listening to "White Wedding" right now. *Cyberpunk*, it seems, was just a momentary glitch in a short-circuiting system. There might just be hope for us yet.

Sean L. Maloney is the author of *The Modern Lovers* (#119). You can send him dad jokes at facebook.com/SeanLMaloney.

CHAPTER 13
GUIDED BY VOICES' *MAG EARWHIG!* (1997)
Matt LeMay

"Shove it cuz I'll just stay / Like an ugly unwanted stray." These lyrics, from the Guided by Voices song "Choking Tara," are among many scrawled on the cover of the diary I kept throughout junior high. They are written and rewritten several times over in varying shades of blue and black, carving a channel in the book's cardboard cover that is still perceptible twenty years later. For two very awkward and uncomfortable years, these words rarely left my head or my headphones, forging a life-long connection with a band I would go on to obsessively idolize, then smugly betray.

By the middle of seventh grade, my social identity was beginning to crystallize at the intersection of "weird kid" and "music kid." At the time, my musical diet consisted largely of parentally sanctioned classic rock. But if I was to embrace my destiny and become "weird music kid," I needed to find some *weird music*. A bunch of seventh graders who happily yielded the "music kid" mantle to a spaz with a few Led Zeppelin CDs were clearly not going to be much help. And besides, if a band was well-known enough for somebody *else* to recommend them, how *weird* could their music really be? Armed with an explorer's zeal and a 13-year-old's ignorance, I turned to the weirdest place I knew: *the internet*.

Through a series of Dogpile and Alta Vista searches, I found my way to a page on the now-defunct ecommerce site cdnow.com that listed a bunch of bands I had never heard of before: Pavement, Sleater-Kinney, Modest Mouse, and ... whoa, "Guided by Voices?" Now *that*, it seemed to me, was a suitably *weird* band name. I saved up a few weeks' allowance, made an after-school visit to Tower Records, and was shocked to discover that they actually had *Mag Earwhig!*, clearly the weirdest album in the world by the weirdest band in the world that *nobody else knew about*, for sale. I purchased the CD, unwrapped it, and placed it in my Discman—where it stayed for the better part of two years.

At first, my obsession with *Mag Earwhig!* was less a matter of the album itself and more a matter of what it represented. Self-styled "weirdness" is one of very few brands of social armor available to unpopular teenagers, and the simple fact of *Mag Earwhig!* was enough for me to feel safe behind the persona of "weird music kid." But as the customary indignities of junior high unfolded before me, *Mag Earwhig!* always seemed to have an answer. When I had to disrobe for eighth-grade swimming—an experience that one classmate remarked "must be difficult for somebody with your body type"—there was "Bulldog Skin," a swaggering ode to resilience that I would listen to on repeat the second

I left the locker room. When my first real group of junior high friends turned insular and mean, there was the social anxiety ballad "Now to War." And when the girl I was madly in love with told me "you're so ugly that nobody will ever love you," there were those dejected-yet-defiant lyrics from "Choking Tara."

In a discography marked by defiant anthems, those words—and *Mag Earwhig!* at large—suggest a different kind of defiance. Not the defiance that comes from proving everybody else wrong, which Pollard deftly articulated in the *Alien Lanes* single "Motor Away." But the deeper, realer defiance that comes from realizing that, in your quest to prove everybody else wrong, you may have lost sight of yourself. There's an open, raw, and self-questioning quality to *Mag Earwhig!* that makes it unique and special among the band's many masterpieces, and has perhaps contributed to its status as a relatively minor or "B-side" record in the band's vaunted catalog. But *Mag Earwhig!*'s lack of anthemic certainty spoke directly to the messy and complicated questions I was grappling with the most during those oft-unbearable teenage years: how do you figure out who you really are when you're used to defining yourself in opposition to others? Where is the line between self-preservation and paranoia? And how do you play Doug Gillard's note-for-note perfect guitar solo on *Mag Earwhig!*'s standout "I Am a Tree?" (The answer, it turns out, is to put a capo on the seventh fret, a fact I only learned years later after spending countless afternoons forcing my left hand into impossible-seeming contortions.)

Slowly but surely, I began to learn more about this mysterious band called Guided by Voices. I learned that they were from Dayton, Ohio, and that their singer Robert Pollard used to be a school teacher. I devoured their back catalog, and scrawled "GBV rules" in the margins of my class notebooks. I convinced my best friend's dad to chaperone us to a show at Irving Plaza, where I stood in the very front row and requested the relatively deep cut "Over the Neptune/Mesh Gear Fox," prompting Pollard to call me a "good kid" and pour a beer out over my head. At one point, while driving past Dayton, New Jersey, on the way to visit my grandparents, I closed my eyes and imagined that I was on my way to the mythical and surely wondrous land of Dayton, *Ohio*—the place where *my favorite band in the world* was from.

Having a favorite band in the world that was neither defunct nor deceased also provided my first occasion to anticipate a new release. I got into the habit of checking Guided by Voices' website daily for any new scraps of information about their forthcoming album *Do the Collapse*. To my amazement, many of these scraps came from publications that were actually writing about bands like Guided by Voices—publications with names like *Magnet* and *Pitchfork*. It had barely even occurred to me that anybody else knew or cared about these bands, let alone that there were entire publications devoted to them. Finally, it seemed, I had found my people.

One Sunday afternoon during my sophomore year of high school, I responded to a call for new writers on *Pitchfork* with a review of the Bevis Frond's *Live at the Great American Music Hall*. It was, in retrospect, a piece that reads a lot like it was written by a teenage boy in the year 2000. It drips with unearned arrogance and is riddled with cheap shots, most notably a series of entirely off-topic digs directed at the Backstreet Boys. Perhaps I inadvertently captured the "us vs. them" zeitgeist of that "pre-poptimism" moment in indie rock because, somehow, I got the job. And one of my first assignments was to review *Hold On Hope*, an EP anchored by a single from the new Guided by Voices album *Do the Collapse*.

My initial reaction to *Do the Collapse* had been mixed. Some of the songs, like the grooving "Surgical Focus" and the soaring "Teenage FBI," were among Pollard's best. But the album's production, provided by none other than Ric Ocasek, felt both flat and cold. My genuine feelings towards the record could be described as those of a mildly disappointed fanboy. But, in my insecure and self-serious brain, "critic" and "fanboy" were mutually exclusive categories. And, more importantly, "genuine feelings" were the very last thing I wanted to express in my first review of a relatively high-profile release. This was a chance to display complete mastery and zero vulnerability, a total inversion of how I felt in my day-to-day life as a teenage boy who spent his afternoons listening to CDs, playing guitar, crying, and writing in his lyric-adorned diary.

Determined to show the world that I was not afraid to kill the thing I loved—or, even better, that I never loved *anything* in the first place—I wrote up the most dismissive and scathing review I could conjure. This review ended with a zinger of which I was cringingly proud at the time: "If Pollard's recent output is any indication, he'd better hold on hope that the elementary school he used to work at will take him back."

With those words, I had shown the world that I had the cool detachment and witty barbs necessary to be a *real* critic. And, better still, I had symbolically killed off my younger self—the kid who probably would have cried upon reading something so mean written about a band he loved so much. I was no longer that powerless, awkward kid buried in his headphones—at least, not as far as the internet was concerned. Was I still listening obsessively to Guided by Voices at home, shouting along to the chorus of *Do the Collapse*'s deep cut "Picture Me Big Time" and letting myself be completely overwhelmed by the pop music perfection of *Alien Lanes*' standout "Game of Pricks?" Nah, you must have me confused with somebody else.

At the time, it did not occur to me for even a second that my smug and shitty words would ever make their way to Pollard himself. After all, I was just some teenager writing record reviews on the internet—Bob Pollard was a brilliant songwriter and successful career musician. But, a decade or so after the review ran, a sound clip from a March 3, 2000, Guided by Voices show appeared in my inbox. In this clip, Pollard issues an emphatic and well-deserved "fuck you" to "a rock critic named Matt LeMay." My review-ending zinger, it turns out, had made an impression.

When I first heard this recording, I did my best to play it off as a funny bit of personal history. "Haha, that dumb review I wrote when I was 16 was actually really hurtful towards the person whose music *meant the most to me out of anyone in the world*." But it wasn't particularly funny, and it isn't particularly funny now. I lost sleep over it, and I still sometimes lose sleep over it. To whatever extent I forgive myself, it is under the banner of "forgiving oneself for being an idiot at 16," not "forgiving oneself for doing something that is actually kinda funny in retrospect."

None of which is to say that one cannot write an honest, transparent, and thoughtful negative review of a work by a beloved artist. But I did no such thing; instead, I unleashed a bit of eighth-grade-style cruelty on the very artist that had helped me survive such cruelty. I thought of the meanest thing I could say and then said it—a strategy that scratches the same insecure itch whether you're telling a boy who likes you that he's ugly, or a musician you admire that his career should be over. And Pollard's response was, in so many words, "Shove it cuz I'll just stay."

After another near-decade of suffering over this whole situation, I had the pleasure of watching Guided by Voices perform at Underground Arts in Philadelphia in late 2016. Underground Arts is a relatively low-key venue, and I was able to secure a position directly to the side of the stage. The music started, fists were raised, lyrics were shouted, tears were shed. It was a cathartic experience and one which, to be perfectly honest, I still felt a little bit guilty about enjoying as much as I did. As the band launched into "I am a Tree," my left hand began making shapes that it still instinctively remembered nearly two decades later. I had spent so many after-school afternoons trying to untangle that song, to hear it and feel it from every angle, to make it a part of myself. It still is, it always will be, I'm sorry, and thank you.

Matt LeMay is the author of *XO* (#63). Find him at mattlemay.com.

CHAPTER 14
THE SMASHING PUMPKINS' *ADORE* (1998)
Jovana Babovic

I saw the Smashing Pumpkins play in 1996 as they toured in support of their third studio album *Mellon Collie and the Infinite Sadness*. It's difficult to articulate exactly what I liked about the band's music at the time beyond that it resonated with my general teenage angst, but I do remember that I jumped around, sang along, and nearly experienced euphoria during the show. I continued to follow the Pumpkins for several more years. I bought their two subsequent records as well as some B-sides and live recordings. My enthusiasm, however, gradually waned. The more time passed, the less likely it seemed that I would ever revisit my favorite bands from the 1990s like the Smashing Pumpkins, let alone their less popular albums like 1998's *Adore* and 2000's *Machina/The Machines of God*.

I wasn't the only one who lost interest in the Smashing Pumpkins by the end of the 1990s. Album sales plunged, and the group eventually disbanded. In the years that followed, primary songwriter and frontman Billy Corgan reformed the Pumpkins in several different incarnations and released four more albums under the band's name. Corgan also performed under different monikers, published a book of poetry, and opened a tea shop and art space in Chicago, while the other original members similarly remained active with new projects. Although the Smashing Pumpkins never left the public eye, they did not accrue many new listeners after the mid-1990s. Instead, most fans retrospectively cite *Mellon Collie* and its predecessor, 1993's *Siamese Dream*, as the band's cornerstone outputs. When *Rolling Stone* conducted a readers' poll of the best Pumpkins songs in 2012, only one of the twenty tracks voted onto the list ("Ava Adore" from *Adore*) had been released on an album proceeding *Mellon Collie*.[1] Critics tend to agree with this hierarchization. When *Stereogum* writer and 33 1/3 author Ryan Laes ranked the Pumpkins' ten best songs in 2018, only one (again "Ava Adore") was not from the mid-1990s. "There's a lot to love about Corgan's work after his peak years," Laes conceded, "but nothing matches the weight and impact of what he did when he was young and furious."[2] Others were more forthcoming. *New York Times* music critic Joe Coscarelli suggested that Corgan "has never again sniffed the creative or commercial success of the band's heyday."[3] By all estimations, that heyday ended with the release of *Adore*.

It was never going to be easy to follow up *Mellon Collie*, a double album that sold ten million copies, but the Pumpkins also faced additional setbacks. They had fired their powerhouse percussionist Jimmy Chamberlin on the grounds of his drug addiction after the band's touring keyboardist Jonathan Melvoin fatally overdosed in 1996. Corgan, often described as having an abrasive personality, continued to engage in tabloid-grade spats with other celebrities. And as the band wrote and recorded its follow-up to *Mellon Collie*, it experimented with sound instead of reproducing the template that had propelled it to fame.

In interviews from the early 1990s and onward, Corgan repeatedly articulated that he felt as if he was "publicly committing suicide" with every new record. That is to say that he experienced writing and recording as a process of reinvention. But his choice of metaphor also hinted at his exasperation with fans, critics, and fellow musicians who complained that each new Pumpkins album sounded different than the last—and that that was a bad thing. When *Siamese Dream* was released, for instance, it elicited snide comments from indie circles. Stephen Malkmus of Pavement, Bob Mould of Hüsker Dü, and producer Steve Albini (who also played in Shellac at the time) separately criticized the record and claimed that it made musical compromises in the interest of commercial success. The Smashing Pumpkins had "sold out," these naysayers implied, because *Siamese Dream* had sold four million copies, which was a lot more than the band's 1991 debut *Gish*. That album had moved only 100,000 copies in its first year, but it had been an underground hit and peaked at number one on the *College Music Journal* radio charts. With *Mellon Collie*, the band was similarly taken to task for changing too much or, alternatively, not changing enough. In a review for *Spin*, the critic Ann Powers wrote that the record was "not quite the masterwork it [was] meant to be,"[4] while Jim Derogatis declared that it was a reflection of Corgan's "lyrical rut."[5] When *Adore* was released in 1998, three years after *Mellon Collie*, it earned the band a stronger backlash than ever.

Adore is dark and brooding, and it is often described as the Pumpkins' "goth" album. Songs like "Shame," "Crestfallen," and "Blank Page" make it the truly melancholy entry in the group's discography. Although Corgan and guitarist James Iha had previously expressed interest in moving away from the drums-and-guitars rock formula and toyed with an electronic foundation on tracks like "1979" and "We Only Come Out at Night," the loss of Chamberlin cornered the band into using a drum machine on *Adore*. As a result, the overall sound is less punchy and monumental at the same time as it is more mechanical and stripped down. Some songs are nearly acoustic. But the band's musical pivot away from *Mellon Collie* was also intentional. During the *Adore* sessions, the Pumpkins recorded songs like "Let Me Give the World to You" that were flagged as obvious singles, but Corgan pulled them at the last moment and left the new record devoid of the sound the group had come to be known for. In the weeks after *Adore*'s release, the album was met with lukewarm reviews and sluggish sales. For those who never quite took to Corgan's personality, the new record became a renewed excuse to berate the band's primary songwriter. "The lyrics are generally on the wrong side of the line between deeply personal and deeply meaningless," Douglas Wolk wrote in *Spin*.[6] In a review for *Rolling Stone*, Greg Kot, an early champion of the band, suggested that *Adore* was "a weird little album that turns its back on the band's previous strengths and shrinks the Pumpkins' sound."[7] While Kot was dismissive in his remark, he hit upon the core reason why the record did not replicate the success of *Mellon Collie*: it did not replicate its sound.

Most bands, if they are lucky, have several well-received and well-respected albums. For the Pumpkins, those were *Siamese Dream*, *Mellon Collie*, and, to a lesser extent, *Gish*. In part, this success is attributable to the fact that they were most prolific in the mid-1990s. In 1994, just a year after the release of *Siamese Dream*, the Pumpkins put out the fourteen-track compilation of B-sides and outtakes *Pisces Iscariot*. *Mellon Collie* followed in 1995 with another twenty-eight songs. *The Aeroplane Flies High*, a six-disc compilation box set with thirty-three tracks, came out a year later. Additionally, the band contributed to movie soundtracks, released live recordings, and made award-winning music videos. Another reason that *Siamese Dream* and *Mellon Collie* have remained the band's most prominent outputs is that these albums—ironically, unlike 2007's *Zeitgeist*—captured the zeitgeist. Like grunge half a decade earlier, the Pumpkins' music in the mid-1990s resonated with a general sense of societal dissatisfaction and a feeling of entrapment in American capitalism. It also had a whimsical dimension that reflected the simultaneous excitement and anxiety GenX listeners felt toward technology. In the "Tonight, Tonight" video, the Pumpkins invited fans to imagine a pseudo-world full of new possibilities akin to the time of early industrialization. Others, like "Today" and "1979," romanticized the innocence of the post-war period and enveloped it in nostalgia. Several years before the Y2K panic in which a minor computer glitch was feared to precipitate a global meltdown, the Pumpkins articulated the skepticism and hope a generation of listeners felt toward the changing world around them.

Some twenty years after *Siamese Dream* and *Mellon Collie*, the Smashing Pumpkins have been firmly historicized into the 1990s. They are sometimes grouped as part of the grunge movement, sometimes as "grunge-adjacent," and sometimes as alternative rock. Corgan pushed back against these comparisons in the 1990s, and he continued to resist the periodization well after. As he wrote, recorded, and toured in support of new material, he also consistently voiced resentment of audiences who clamored for renditions of 1990s songs. "Fans think you're there to be a jukebox," he complained in a 2012 interview. "When you're older … you're supposed to become the museum version of yourself."[8] Corgan expected fans to request the hits at shows, but he was increasingly frustrated that they demanded nothing but the Pumpkins' mid-1990s hits. For a musician who never stopped evolving, Corgan felt pigeonholed into a single sound from his own past. Surprisingly—or perhaps mockingly—only months after he released a piano-based album as William Patrick Corgan, he also announced that the original Smashing Pumpkins minus bassist D'Arcy Wretzky had reunited and planned a tour on which they would only play songs from the first few albums rather than new material recorded for a forthcoming release. The 2018 "Shiny and Oh So Bright" tour can be read as either a concession or a blatant attempt to recapture the band's narrative and take part in shaping its legacy. If fans and critics were well on their way to codifying the band's music, Corgan may have reasoned, then the reunion tour was a way to reintegrate his voice into the conversation.

All the attention given to the Pumpkins' mid-1990s music means that their less popular albums have become underrated B-sides of their discography for many listeners. I have few recollections of how I experienced *Adore* and *Machina* when they were released, likely because I found them lackluster at the time. When I recently revisited these records, I recognized the songs, but I couldn't associate them with a moment or a memory, I couldn't visualize any videos, and I initially had a hard time telling the albums apart. As I continued to listen, however, I began to hear the evolution in the Pumpkins' sound. This is what makes it exciting to rediscover the band nearly twenty years after its peak commercial popularity. *Adore*, in particular, resonates. As I listened to it in the late 2010s, it didn't evoke the late 1990s like *Siamese Dream* and *Mellon Collie* do. Neither did it bring back the feeling of being a teenager. Instead, I experienced *Adore* anew. I listened to it on a long and unexpected weather-related layover in Chicago when I was travelling to a job interview. The lonely piano chords on "Blank Page" and Corgan's chilling vocals on "Tear" haunted me as I played them on a loop. The album tapped into the hopelessness I felt in the face of a winter storm, and it matched my despair at the prospect of seemingly endless limbo in an airport terminal. I eventually arrived, but I forfeited all ambitions of getting the job since the delay had caused me to miss an entire day of planned presentations and meetings. In the week after, I continued to listen to *Adore* as I moped around and contemplated my bad luck. It sounded as resigned as I felt. It also sounded as present as my predicament.

I started listening to *Machina* a few weeks after that—around the time I heard that I had gotten the job after all. The record could match my celebratory mood because, like *Adore*, it was not loaded with old emotions and memories. It was then that I began to hear the Smashing Pumpkins for the band they had always been: flexible and dynamic. Their discography is vast enough to capture what it felt like to be a teenager in the 1990s, and it was equally accommodating to capture what it feels like to be an adult in the 2010s. Although the Pumpkins certainly did not plan to scale back their commercial success, their declining popularity in the late 1990s disassociated their later albums like *Adore* from that era. Revisiting them two decades later allows us to engage with these records on their own terms as music that has not so much aged as much as it has matured.

Jovana Babovic is the author of *Dig Me Out* (#115). Find her at jovanababovic.com.

CHAPTER 15
THE WEAKERTHANS' *LEFT AND LEAVING* (2000)
Daniel Couch

At the end of the summer of 2001, I joined the Peace Corps. I was 24 and full of good intentions, but as I filed past first class and into coach, my confidence gave way to doubt and doubt to panic. I adjusted the straps on my new backpack, a gift from the owners of the school where I'd worked. They had orchestrated a hero's send-off, equipping me with everything I could possibly need for my two years in Senegal. By the time I found my seat and began to rummage through their goodwill, however, I felt unprepared and utterly alone.

"I guess I'm with you." She extended her hand and added, "I'm Sandi." Beneath a white baseball cap, she offered a tight smile I recognized. It's the one you wear when you are trying to summon your own bravery by being strong for someone else. She had looked on in the terminal as my family took turns hugging me and taking pictures and telling me how proud they were. I had been wearing that same tight smile for them only a few minutes earlier.

Sandi and I chatted over an empty middle seat for most of the flight, swapping stories about jobs and schools and why we decided to join. When we got to the lives we were leaving behind, our enthusiasm faltered, and we shaded our answers with distance. Eventually we fell into our own thoughts, and the headphones came out. She put on the Beastie Boys and turned toward the window. I disappeared into The Weakerthans' 2000 album, *Left and Leaving*.

In 1997, John K. Samson left the polemical thrash-punk band Propagandhi and formed The Weakerthans. Their debut, *Fallow*, was similarly filtered through punk's power chords and alienation, but the album also made room for a broader musical and emotional range. By *Left and Leaving*, the band's second full-length album, the songs had grown even more expressive as they experimented subtly with focal points and textures, expanding their instrumentation to include the occasional lap steel, Rhodes, and even, on one song, a whirly-wind.

The Weakerthans' lyrics were no less progressive than Samson's former band, but they came by their political action differently. Whereas Propagandhi were confrontational in their championing of the rights of the marginalized and exploited, The Weakerthans acknowledged the experiences of those same groups indirectly, telling their stories in "small fictions"[1] that drew their power from their own lack of certainty. There is a service worker and a deaf girl, an ignored activist and a dropout who gives in to the struggle of today. Out of step with their own time or place and unable to adequately communicate with others, they are resigned to "imperfect offering[s]"[2] or, more often, silence.

I suspect I brought *Left and Leaving* along with me because it had anticipated much of my last year. I had been living with one foot out the door, ever conscious of a looming appointment with a responsible, respectable future abroad. In two places at once, I belonged to neither. The album had understood this, and in its stories of self-deception, where hope was often a way of hiding and change a way of keeping things the same, I recognized more than I cared to admit.

⁎⁎⁎

It was late when the bus pulled up to the training center, a waning moon providing just enough light to make out the word "Bienvenue" on the wall of an expectant classroom. Jetlagged and overwhelmed, I headed straight to bed. The next morning I was jarred awake by the call to prayer from a nearby mosque. I threw off the mosquito net and listened, unsure if this was one of the vivid dreams my antimalarial medication had promised. I don't know what I thought was going to happen or how I was going to feel when I finally arrived in Senegal to the life I had been anticipating for so long, but I laid there and thought about the faithful on their mats in the predawn darkness, facing Mecca, and wondered which direction was west.

I listened to *Left and Leaving* every day during my first week in the country. Resignation mingled with regret, the present with the past. The familiar songs traced the contours of my absence and closed the distance by degrees. In my spare time, I wrote letters and sent eager, searching emails at an internet café that crackled with syncopated talking drums and balafon. On the afternoon of September 11th, I placed an indulgent phone call to catch up with a friend back home. It was a shorter conversation than I had expected, full of questions neither of us could answer and emotions neither of us could name, the 5,176 miles between us made suddenly unpassable.

The lunch break was nearly over when I returned to the center. I tried to compose myself. Surprise, especially an intense and unwelcome one, sometimes manifests as laughter in me. I explained to my fellow trainees what I knew and what I didn't, grinning broadly despite myself. Classes were canceled for the rest of the day. We pored over CNN reports and heard the distant drums of retaliation that moved within them. Someone suggested that we, serving in a predominantly Muslim country, might be evacuated. I smiled again, this time genuinely. I was going home. I was sure of it.

Left and Leaving's title track is a lament to the push and pull of home, contradictory impulses wound together with a patient finger-picked guitar and cymbals that sizzle like a long-lingering sigh. Initially, I had heard my long year spent waiting to depart. Now the song seemed to ask the question I grappled with on a near-daily basis.

Wait for the year to drown
Spring forward, fall back down
I'm trying not to wonder where you are
All this time

Lingers, undefined
Someone choose
Who's left and who's leaving[3]

Sandi was asking herself the same question, and we each leaned into the other for support. As it became clear we were not going to be evacuated, she tried to explain why she needed to go. I refused to listen. In plying her with reasons to stay, I had been attempting to convince myself as well. I shrugged off her anxieties because not doing so would have meant confronting my own. Nevertheless, one Monday morning in October, I arrived at breakfast to find an instructor waiting for me, an envelope in hand. I immediately knew what it contained. In the past few days Sandi had drifted away from me, her isolation the final steeling of her resolve. Over the weekend, she had made her choice. Sandi had left, and I would, in turn, be leaving.

***

"Watermark" was the de facto single from *Left and Leaving*. The song is lyrically through-composed, relying on dynamic shifts rather than structured repetition to signal emphasis. It's only near the end of the second chorus as the song risks slipping into its own dark musings that it snaps back to the present and a final, climactic stanza surges to the forefront:

Hold on to the corners of today
And we'll fold it up to save until it's needed
Stand still, let me scrub that brackish line
That you got when something rose and then receded.[4]

In the booklet, these lines are enclosed in parentheses, presenting them as a tender aside. It's a gracious gesture for an album that more typically withholds direct words of comfort. In Senegal, I dwelled on *Left and Leaving*'s themes of loss but, back home in the States, I looked for the way songs like "Watermark," reached toward recovery and offered a way to scrub clean my own brackish line.

In those three short months so much had changed. I was fifteen pounds underweight and had a scraggly beard that reached my protruding collar bone. The country was nearly as unrecognizable, and my friends and family, though glad to have me back, had understandably moved on with their lives. Staring off into the middle distance, I recited for them my stories about death threats scrawled on the training center's wall and the guy who followed me home one afternoon, but I was hiding under the same banner of fear that politicians of the day were exploiting. The things I needed to say out loud— about my shame, my guilt—I couldn't bring myself to admit to anyone but Sandi.

She and I have managed to stay in touch, but after we overcame the initial shock of uprooting ourselves from the lives we'd expected to live for the next two years, we needed space to figure out what would come next. She turned to graduate school. An old friend suggested I do the same, but I wasn't capable of another year of applications and waiting for life to begin any more than I could stand to relive the past. I needed to find a way to unpack the present tense I had so carefully folded up to save.

Doing so has meant returning to *Left and Leaving* again and again throughout the years. Rather than turning away from the painful memories, I have assembled a B-side of new ones that I hear alongside them: joyous ones, funny ones, somber ones, most of which have nothing to do with the Peace Corps at all. I have found the album to be capable of carrying much more than I ever expected. At this point, the songs are so crammed with personal associations that the specifics of its storytelling belong solely to me. The soldered wire is mine. The duct tape is mine. The stray cymbal hit in the second verse of "This Is a Fire Door Never Leave Open" is mine. The album has become a place where my past and future circle back on each other, both responding to where I've been and announcing where I'm headed. And in those moments, when the volume is up and I'm singing along, there's no space left for shame.

Daniel Couch is a co-author of *Workbook* (#124). Find him at noicegoice.com.

PART TWO
MARGINALIA

CHAPTER 16
HANK THOMPSON'S *SMOKY THE BAR* (1969)
Joe Bonomo

Born in Waco, Texas, in 1925, Henry Williams Thompson served in the Second World War as a radioman in the Navy and studied electrical engineering at Princeton University. After the war he returned to the Lone Star State assuming that he'd follow the career in electronics for which he'd been trained. Instead he indulged his life-long love of music, and began writing and recording songs, eventually scoring regional hits in Dallas with "Whoa Sailor" (Globe Records) and "California Women" (Blue Bonnet), before enjoying a number one single, "The Wild Side of Life," in 1952. He sang in a gentle baritone, and his band, the Brazos Valley Boys (in various iterations), played honky tonk softened by the commercial balm of Western Swing, an irresistible blend that would ensure his decades-long success and enormous influence in country music. You know Hank Thompson's voice even if you can't summon it right now; like George Jones's or Loretta Lynn's, it's come to define a certain legitimate, iconic sound of country, a twang that feels reassuringly familiar even as it's narrating from the darker corners.

In 1966, Thompson issued *A Six Pack to Go* (Capitol), a collection of songs about bars and drinking that reached #19 on *Billboard* Country; the album featured a re-recording of the title track, which had been a Top 10 Country hit for Thompson back in 1960. A handful of albums followed, but a through-line of sorts was established with two more albums of songs about serious drinking, *On Tap, in the Can, or in the Bottle* (Dot, 1968) and *Smoky the Bar* (1969).

On Tap, in the Can, or in the Bottle features several strong tracks (plus a killer, thirsty close-up of a frosty glass of beer on the cover) but, of the two albums that complete Thompson's tavern triumvirate, *Smoky the Bar* best captures the singer's blend of bar-room romance, tipsy lightheartedness, and hangover remorse. Ten of the dozen songs were culled from a two-day session over February 4 and 5, 1969 at Woodland Sound Studios, in Nashville. Joe Allison produced, and Thompson sang and played acoustic guitar, accompanied by Harold Ray Bradley and Pete Wade on electric guitars and Bob L. Moore on bass. The title track and "I See Them Everywhere" were recorded three years earlier on May 18 and 19, 1966 at Capital Tower, in Hollywood. Thompson re-cut three songs for *Smoky the Bar*: "Girl in the Night" was first released in 1957 on *Most of All*, and versions of "Cocaine Blues" and "Drunkard's Blues" were first issued in 1959 on *Songs for Rounders*.

Smoky the Bar moves effortlessly between pleasure and melancholy, and, with geniality and the nimble swing of the band, Thompson's songs score what I think of as the "drinker's sweet spot"—between, say, beers two and three, or shots three and four, whatever your tolerance—before the bonhomie becomes edgy and the high gets complicated. For the most part, darkness is kept at bay. The mellifluousness in the singer's voice might suggest that he's been on the outside of the local tavern looking in—there's little bourbon gruffness or hungover timbre to it—but listen to the album enough and that timeless, reverb-laden voice grows ironic, starting to sound like the inner pep talk of the hang-dog regular at the end of the bar, kept at a necessary if desperate goodtime pitch. It's the melody of denial, and forgetfulness. Stroll past any backstreet bar and peer in with Thompson playing on your inner soundtrack: the paradox of his mild tone, the strings, and the Nashville Sound female backing vocals serenading the glum inertia of the low-rent joint create a David Lynch-esque place where humor and pleasure mask pain and despondency.

The title song, "Ace in the Hole," "Let's Get Drunk and Be Somebody," "My Rough and Rowdy Ways," "Cocaine Blues," "I See Them Everywhere," "What's Made Milwaukee Famous (Has Made a Loser Out of Me)," and "Pop a Top" are upbeat, Thompson and the Boys grinning and well-oiled, their wallets still fat, the night young. "New Records on the Jukebox," "Drunkard's Blues," "Girl in the Night," and "Bright Lights and Blonde Haired Women" are downbeat, mid-paced, letting in despair and regret. Thompson's interested in maintaining this balance of fun and dejection, and song sequencing is key. The album kicks off with the title track and "Ace in the Hole" and closes with "Bright Lights and Blonde Haired Women" and "Pop a Top." The opening songs brightly demonstrate how a bar can feel cheery even as it cloaks dysfunction, and might offer a pulpit for the boozily righteous. "Smoky the Bar," written by Thompson with William Penix, is a pun-filled tribute to a favorite joint, the album's theme song, really, in that it narrates suffering in jolly tones, both musically and lyrically. After all, what's sprightly word play but deflection, in this case a drinker's misdirection from genuine lament to bemused punning. But a few beers in, the blues are pushed aside in favor of an old-timer's pastime: putting down the younger generation. The jaunty "Ace in the Hole" is the one song on *Smoky the Bar* that's time- and date-stamped; references abound to sandals- and beads-wearing hippies, demonstrators, and draft-dodgers whose ace in the hole is the welfare line. Thompson wrote the jeering tune with his producer and Merle Travis ("Sixteen Tons"), and he's clearly preaching to the choir, basking not only in booze but in the recent election of President Richard "Law and Order" Nixon. Here's to the Greatest Generation. Drink up, boys.

The album's closers evoke the bittersweet intersection of redemption and self-sabotage. In Eddie Kirk's "Bright Lights and Blonde Haired Women," the singer, exhausted with drinking and the bar lifestyle, pleads with his woman to let him come home, as roamin' around and the shiny things in the title no longer entice him. Yet this contrition, slow-paced and knowing, is followed by the happy-go-lucky "Pop a Top" (written by Nat Stuckey, a hit for Jim Ed Brown in 1967). The singer's still at the bar and he's still got a story to tell; he's got time for one more, then he'll go. Where? Back home to the woman he's beseeched in the previous song? The song ends with the singer ordering one more round, and then promising to go so that "some other fool" can take his place. As the album ends, he's yet to leave the joint.

In-between these bookends, Thompson runs the gauntlet of exuberance and sorrow, containing chaos, burden, and violence in traditional forms. Side Two kicks off with the grinning "I See Them Everywhere," a novelty tune co-written with Tommy Higgins, delivered by the regular who holds forth with a bizarre yet endlessly entertaining sense of humor, the one folks worry about but who's too funny, or too pathetic, to confront. It's a ditty about the hallucinations brought upon by staying away from the bottle—a nine-foot spider chasing a thirty-pound fly, a striped ape in a black cape, a grizzly bear in a rocking chair, and so on—each maddeningly vanishing and metamorphosing into a bottle of wine when the singer tries to grab it. Delusion as dark comedy, a queasy tension made explicit in the lurid drama of T. J. "Red" Arnall's "Cocaine Blues," also narrated with a wink and a *bottoms up*. The speed-fueled tale of the man who shoots his woman because she's with other men earns grimly knowing head-nods up and down the bar with its concluding advice to shun the whiskey and lay off the cocaine, but its carefree vibe of tossed-off violence and misogyny is unsettling, to say the least. Jimmie Rodgers and Elsie McWilliams's "My Rough and Rowdy Ways," Glenn Sutton's "What's Made Milwaukee Famous," and "Let's Get Drunk and Be Somebody," co-written by Thompson with Chuck Hall, are also played upbeat, the guitarists and the pianist chuckling atop Thompson's dry acoustic, shaking their heads bemusedly at the singer's shrugs as yet another round materializes, and at his tumbles down the inviting road and through those swinging doors where everyone's their happiest, where three drinks in everybody's a somebody, and yet where nothing good can happen.

Three bleak songs add more dimension and gravitas to *Smoky the Bar*, elevating the album to something greater. The cinematic "Drunkard's Blues"—a traditional folk blues arranged by Thompson—and "Girl in the Night"—an original—each traces the limits of the bar, the former telling a harrowing story of a man who learns his woman is gone, views her body at the infirmary, and endures her funeral; the stark title phrase mourned by a searching fiddle that powerfully admits his sorrow, loss, and feebleness. "Girl in the Night" is a rarity, a song with its lens turned on a female regular. Although she's composed entirely of the singer's gaze, the portrait's a respectfully sympathetic one; atop a twinkling piano and a pedal steel, he wonders what she's thinking about as she lights her cigarette: a lost love, heartache, desire? She remains alone at the song's end—the singer doesn't desire her, or he prefers to watch and mythologize from afar, that old tavern sport—and one wonders what she, absent a voice in his song, might sing about from her own perch in the smoky bar. Who or what is she regarding? She, too, is alone in the crowd.

"New Records on the Jukebox" should be a standard. Co-written with William Penix, the song describes an aching reality: the newer the songs on the jukebox, the older the stories that they sing. The singer wants the barkeep to stock some recent 45s because the old tunes remind him too much of her, yet the dawning epiphany—it rises with the bubbles in his glass—is too durable to avoid, and with it Thompson makes the album's greatest discovery: "New records on the jukebox, but nothing else has changed at all." The band plays beautifully, restrained yet in touch with the desperation in the words, and it's the prettiest melody on the album, a song that in its timeless lamentation will remind someone of his or her heartache sometime, somewhere else, in the future, the cycle as sure as any record spins.

Harlan Howard has said that the ingredients of a great country song are "three chords and the truth." As with any pithy statement, there's some candor there, and some deflection. What Howard means is that a great country song is simple, and truths are best related clearly. But every truth is dimensional, complicated, and messy. Country music has never shied away from songs about bar rooms and drinking; if you're a country singer, you face the bottle in song at least once, and some artists have made careers out of writing and singing about alcohol and those who suffer for it. If you're a traditional country artist, you trust the old songs that are handed down to you and the old truths embodied in them; you aspire to make them new again, and mine the form for your own songs that are at once fresh and ancient.

Smoky the Bar hasn't been reissued on CD or onto streaming platforms, and remains criminally obscure. Anyone wanting to track it down needs to go down the used record store or online marketplace route. On the back of the album, Hank Thompson is heralded as "The Poet Laureate of Beer Drinkers," an honorable title if ever there was one. With these mid- and late-1960s drinking songs, he joins Eddie Noack, Jerry Lee Lewis, Del Reeves, Johnny Bond, Porter Wagoner, Merle Haggard, Gary Stewart, Moe Bandy, and many others who sing—some darkly, some painfully, some humorously—in twanging tribute and sober regret to the smoke-filled bar, the half-full glass, and the regular. Thompson's songs make contact with the complexities of alcoholism, but with a wry half grin, a formal distance that's both romantic and incongruous, the pretty surface lie of the drink that blurs the depths below.

Joe Bonomo is the author of *Highway to Hell* (#73). Find him at nosuchthingaswas.com.

CHAPTER 17
ROBERT JOHNSON'S *KING OF THE DELTA BLUES SINGERS* (1961)
Jeffrey T. Roesgen

When the sun goes down on the Delta, the mists from the Mississippi and Yazoo rivers set upon the expanse. It's within this misty darkness that Hoodoo spirits, Jim Crow oppression, and Christian devotion merge with hardship to yield a land of angst and unresolved mystery. Sometime around the year 1900 this convergence spawned a new musical expression: the blues. Transforming slavery-era call and response field hollers into pentatonic figures played on a piano, guitar, or didley bow and sung, it quickly became a popular form of entertainment gaining prominence with stars like Bessie Smith and Ma Rainey. With impassioned vocal delivery, plaintive lyrics, and gyrating polyrhythm the blues reached its listeners, both emotionally and culturally. As such it became the music of conjuring, eliciting, in a single performance, moods of sadness, elation, and sexuality.

With the Great Depression, the blues sank back into the locales from whence it came. The Southern blues singer began to occupy smaller stages at labor camps, and juke joints, most often serving as respite from exhausting field labor and an oppressive racial caste system.

Within this short span between the Depression and the Second World War Robert Johnson performed, recorded, and died. Through the scant, inconsistent memories of those who knew him and the lyrical mystery of his best-known songs, history is largely blind to his movements along the country roads and rails of the deep South (and occasionally beyond). Staying in no one place with no one person for long, Johnson is defined by his conjuring prowess as a blues singer. He's remembered by fellow blues singers for his brooding demeanor and friendly yet detached attitudes. The women with whom he stayed recall waking in the night to find him in an open window, fingering at his guitar strings so gently he hardly made a sound. Under the mentorship of Ike Zinnerman, he rehearsed in Beauregard Cemetery, in Hazelhurst, Mississippi alone at night, sitting upon the gravestones.

The King of the Delta Blues Singers is not a proper album, having been compiled twenty-three years after Johnson's death. Recorded in San Antonio and Dallas in November 1936 and June 1937, the sessions produced twenty-nine songs over forty-one takes. Some of the songs were printed during his lifetime while others were either released posthumously or remained unreleased in the years following his death. The recordings drew mild interest amongst listeners of his era. The enthralling "Terraplane Blues" even scored a regional "hit." Overwhelmingly, however, neither his recordings nor his murder a little over a year following his final recording session evoked much concern.

Yet, as seemingly defeated as he was by his vices and environs, Robert Johnson also transcended them. Contemporary fascination with his life remains avid. His music has served as the gateway to virtually every derivation of rock music. His songs have been covered by fellow musicians (and US presidents) in blues, folk, jazz, and rock traditions since the 1950s. His life, and the mythology surrounding it, have been portrayed in major motion pictures. *King of the Delta Blues Singers*—released as Volume I (1961) and II (1962)—is a staple of music collections the world over. The myths of Robert Johnson have eclipsed the power of his music. Blues enthusiasts aside, the songs of *King of the Delta Blues Singers* are largely unknown to contemporary music listeners, rendering it a B-side. Instead, he is renowned as a highly mysterious and influential artist from an era that lacks modern, cultural touchstones.

Music scholars and fans alike have sought, with some success, to retrace his life and movements. Through these efforts we now know which of Johnson's three gravestones mark his true, final resting place. His siblings and grandchildren have been identified and interviewed. Childhood recollections of a "Little Robert Dusty," the youngest of eleven, have been collected from the plantations where he lived, bouncing from his mother to his stepfather's care, failing to show any interest in field labor. Still the narrative arc of his short life remains largely unknown. Aside from his death and marriage certificates and just two certified photographs bearing his image, his songs are the sole documents of his existence. The story they reveal is of a young man bearing exceptional talent and heartbreaking conflict. His repertoire is broad with loose, vaudeville songs like "They're Red Hot" and complex, desperate ones like "Hell Hound on My Trail," the latter enabling the listener to feel the angst ingrained into his existence, as if his survival as a Delta bluesman itself was a burden.

Stylistically he often plays both a bass rhythm and a melody. While not unique to Johnson, his melodies and abrupt triplet strums are often a counterpoint to his vocals. He was adept at generating boogie beats, delighting audiences with the reaction it elicited: lidding eyes, arcing the head heavenward, passionately rotating the shoulders, waist, and pelvis. Although it has influenced guitarists like Clapton, Page, and Richards, his guitar alone was not the source of his conjuring. Rather, its interplay with his voice created not only great entertainment but deep, soulful art. His voice's expressive ability remains singular in its range and phrasing. In "Come On in My Kitchen," a rendition of the popular blues song "Things About Comin' Way," he coaxes a woman inside from the howling wind with a lustful whisper while he strokes a soft, alluring rhythm. Lighter songs like "They're Red Hot" and "Terraplane Blues" find him shifting his voice in comic role play. In "Me and the Devil Blues" his voice is sullen, haunted with regret and death fantasy.

Into this void of scant biographical data and enigmatic, expressive compositions wander the Hoodoo deity Legba, blood-thirsty hounds, jealous, pistol-whipping husbands, cryptic lyrics about a Christian God that cannot deliver him, and a pursuing Devil who every day draws closer. In this sense Robert Johnson will remain obscured in the dark Delta haze, his spirit yearning to transcend the Mississippi Delta, and his heart pulling him to stay. His image will forever be merged with night.

He sings in "Cross Road Blues":

Standin' at the crossroad, baby, eee-eee, risin' sun goin' down
I believe to my soul, now, poor Bob is sinkin' down

Metaphorically the crossroads has many meanings. In blues culture it signals a choice in life's path. Vice or virtue: should the bluesman surrender his guitar, bless the abundant cotton crop, and pray for better fortune? Should he drink whiskey, and conjure trysts with women? For others, the Delta crossroads may either lead away to fairer places, most notably Chicago, or deeper into the fields and swamps; closer to kin who have lived there since slave times. Bluesman Son House, full of deep timbre, sings of the crossroads, as does Elmore James with his exuberant slide guitar style. Both present their narrative as if they have been to the crossroads, suffered their choice, and survived. Robert Johnson's crossroads is different. The choice he makes haunts him. His choice is a desperate one, and he falls to his knees, cursing and embracing nightfall at the same time. His voice yearns, his guitar weeps. Does he regret the vices of a life in the blues? Does he fear a lynch mob will find him there alone? Even as the recording whispers to its conclusion, his survival is uncertain. His crossroads choices shadow his thoughts to the end.

With "Hell Hound on My Trail" the plot deepens. Being the only one of his recorded songs to use an open E tuning (most others use open G, "Spanish"), it's clear the song had special significance to Johnson. Once more, it's night and he's on the road, alone, along the impossibly flat Delta floodplain. The wind howls and he whispers to himself to break the loneliness. Stray wisps of the newly-harvested cotton crop stir at his feet. Back in town the husbands have run him off. He is some distance away when he sees the headlights approaching. Chances are it's a farmer hauling for the storehouse across, managing his own Depression-era existence. Fear sets in regardless. Lynch mobs and joy killings happen in Coahoma, Sunflower, and Tallahatchie counties with some regularity and without much attention. So, he stops for a moment, sets down his case, and lowers the brim of his fedora. Despite the wind, he feels the mist holding around him. As the headlights pass, they resolve the details of his image for a moment: long, adroit fingers gripping the handle of the guitar case, the fine creases in his suit cutting into the dust. He glares downward and away, holding a smirk tight enough to reveal the desperation behind. He is being chased and knows it's a matter of time.

I got a kind hearted woman, do anything in the world for me.

Keeping him sheltered as he wandered from place to place were a trail of women. While renowned for living the life of an itinerant and sexually promiscuous musician, his seductive prowess also ensured his survival. Sent away by his mother as a child to live with his stepfather, and later with the passing of his wife at 19, Robert Johnson expresses as much a desire for feminine nurture as he does for sex. While "Come On in

My Kitchen" is provocative with whispers and lust, it's also dressed with vulnerability. Johnson's artistry conveys this complexity where all other great blues singers, save perhaps Skip James, cannot. The women he encountered, only temporarily, kept him from the hell hounds that prowled the country roads at night. Then, on other nights he'd meet the wrong woman, whose husband or father thrust him back into the night.

In the summer of 1938 Robert Johnson turned south from Memphis and returned to the Delta. It was cotton layby season, a time when the crop is left alone to blossom. The money during layby was good, with sharecroppers and laborers converging on cities like Greenwood to celebrate the month-long wait before the harvest. Johnson found himself a standing gig at Three Forks Grocery, a juke near Greenwood. There the pursuit ended. In the most accepted telling, Johnson had established relations with a married woman during his stand at Three Forks. One night her husband laced Johnson's whiskey bottle with strychnine, and he died of the poisoning a few days later.

As he sullenly requests in "Me and the Devil Blues," he was buried by the roadside between the towns of Money and Greenwood under the heavy shade of a pecan tree. Beyond the road the Delta fields stretch into each direction. Fans who visit leave pennies, guitar picks, even crushed beer cans on his grave. In visiting it's impossible not to feel his tragic presence, to think of his bones encased, defeated by the Delta world that haunted him so. Yet, the ubiquity of his influence on music, film, and folk culture causes him to transcend this world at the same time.

I prefer to regard him differently. When I listen to Robert Johnson's music I imagine his lonely footsteps, guitar case in hand, traversing the fields and swamps. With his heart yearning for lost love and a mother's gentleness, he's pulled into a world he cannot escape. He turns his collar up against the wind, rejects salvation, and keeps moving and playing on, guitar and voice, symbiotic. They express the urge of a budding entertainer and a man carrying profound loneliness and fear. But before I can truly grasp these, his steps quicken along the road. He hums quietly as he goes away into the dark, eager to keep his appointment with midnight.

Jeffrey T. Roesgen is the author of *Rum, Sodomy, and the Lash* (#60).

CHAPTER 18
THE DOORS' *STRANGE DAYS* (1967)
Clare Nina Norelli

I remember clearly my first visit to Le cimetière du Père Lachaise, Paris's largest and most famous cemetery-cum-green space. It was a gray February afternoon and the air was crisp and cool and hazy, the clouds overhead so thick that the sun was barely able to penetrate the layer of gauze that kept the distant blue at bay. I was alone and on vacation and was thus afforded the freedom to take my time as I wandered the cemetery's charming cobblestone paths and striking gardens. I stopped here and there to admire tombs that resembled miniature cathedrals, observed the numerous decaying angels that presided over the dead, and watched in amusement as the cemetery cats preened and played atop the solemn graves—a little flicker of life eschewing the customary silence that is usually expected when traversing amongst the dead. As crows conversed with one another across the tops of the trembling maple trees—a suitably gothic soundtrack for a cemetery excursion—I sought out the graves of such cultural luminaries as Oscar Wilde, Édith Piaf, Colette, Frédéric Chopin, and Marcel Proust, artists who at one time or another had been, or continued to be, sources of inspiration for me. There was one artist, however, whom I consciously left until last. I knew his grave would not be hard to find; I would just need to follow the numerous tourists, fellow fans, and "beautiful friends" tracing their own version of one of rock and roll's most lauded, albeit *clichéd*, pilgrimages: a visit to the final resting place of James Douglas Morrison, American poet and lead singer of The Doors.

***

My discovery of The Doors was precipitated by the death of a loved one. I was barely 14 years old and she was only a couple of months shy of turning 11—her death signaled to me the end of childish things. Everything that had mattered before her demise now appeared frivolous in comparison to my meditations on the impermanence of life. It seemed unthinkable and inhumane to me that someone could die so young, and I grappled for meaning, some reason for her death amidst the confusion and pain that lay in the wake of her passing. I had so many questions, but I was surrounded only by sorrowful adults struggling to cope with the loss, their own hearts so hurt and heavy with tragedy that they had no answers for my childish inquiries as to why she had to die. And really, is there ever a suitable explanation for the death of a child? It always seems so improbable. So, as a young musician, I turned to what I understood best in order to make sense of it all: music.

I am not quite sure when it was that I first heard Jim Morrison's alternately languorous and raucous baritone, the eerie "liquid night" of Robby Krieger's finger-picked guitar, John Densmore's jazz-informed rhythms, and Ray Manzarek's brooding electric organ: the strange confluence of sonorities that constitute The Doors' distinct psyche-blues sound. But I do recall the moment their music truly caused my ears to prick up and my head to spin. It was a balmy evening several months after she had died, the sort of Australian summer night in which the heat is so suffocating that sleep is near impossible. Listless and uncomfortable, my father and I decided to stay up and watch a rerun of Oliver Stone's overwrought, but nonetheless enjoyable, 1991 biopic about The Doors that was screening on television. Almost an hour into the film and now fully immersed in Stone's mythologizing, I watched wide-eyed as The Doors attended one of Andy Warhol's Factory parties in New York City. Jim Morrison (Val Kilmer) passes through the scene "stoned, immaculate," as various Factory decadents (including Warhol himself, played to campy extremes by Crispin Glover) vie for the attractive singer's attention. Morrison's Orphic journey into the New York underworld is heightened through flashing camera bulbs, hallucinogenic projections, the droning dirges of The Velvet Underground, and the slow lilt of cinematographer Robert Richardson's camerawork. The onscreen atmosphere is so dizzying that the viewer almost feels as disorientated as the drug-addled Morrison. Then, Morrison is summoned by the legendary Nico (Christina Fulton) to engage in further debauchery and The Velvet Underground's "Heroin" is suddenly supplanted on the soundtrack by "Strange Days," the arresting opener of The Doors' 1967 album of the same name.

I was sent to bed before the film finished, my parents concerned that it was all getting decidedly too "adult" for me. But it was too late, a spell had been cast. The psychedelic stimuli onscreen, the erotic implications of Nico purring "*Mooorrrison*," the destabilizing spookiness of "Strange Days," so unlike anything I'd ever heard before: my young mind was both terrified and excited by the promise of it all. There was something in The Doors' haunting music and the tragedy surrounding Jim Morrison's death that offered me solace, and "Strange Days" seemed to crystalize sonically the thoughts born of months of confused contemplation.

***

In January 1967 The Doors released their self-titled debut album, a record teeming with sex, death, calculated chaos, and the occasional Weimar Republic drinking song. A product of many nights of experimentation during their infamous run of live shows on LA's Sunset Strip, *The Doors* features some of the band's most recognizable songs, most notably their signature hit "Light My Fire." With their nightmarish imagery and diverse musical and literary influences, The Doors had proven to be a band that sounded quite unlike any of their rock and roll contemporaries. They were angry, depressed, and fixated with death, eschewing life-affirming sunshine in favor of "endless night"—even their love songs were morbid. Where other bands sang about the healing properties of coming together and loving one another, and declared that all you needed was love, The Doors likened the burn of romantic desire to the intensity of a funeral pyre, to self-immolation; a moonlight tryst by the beach ends not with lovemaking but drowning. This is to say nothing of the dangerous energy of their live shows where, with the highly unpredictable, incredibly intoxicated, and sexually charged Morrison calling the shots, anything could happen, and almost everything did.

As "Light My Fire" began climbing the charts and their popularity grew, The Doors commenced recording their follow-up LP *Strange Days*, beginning in May 1967 with a release in September. For an album recorded during the much idealized "Summer of Love," *Strange Days* is a decidedly wintry, melancholic affair. The album builds on the darkly enigmatic sound world established on *The Doors*, but it is a more refined effort, the mark of a band now treating the studio as a second home. Using Sunset Sound's newly acquired eight-track recording capabilities, The Doors were able to experiment with the four extra tracks for overdubs. Manzarek especially capitalized on this development, contributing, in addition to his usual funereal electric organ (arguably the crux of The Doors' sound), Moog-generated harmonies on "Strange Days," a reverse piano track on "Unhappy Girl" (he actually performed the whole piano track backward, and it was then played forward in the final mix), and marimba on "I Can't See Your Face in My Mind." The spirit of experimentation reaches its peak midway through the record with "Horse Latitudes," an unnerving spoken-word piece concerning a jettisoned horse drowning at sea. Morrison's vehement oration becomes more and more incensed over the course of the piece, vying to be heard over a chorus of ghoulish voices that moan and shriek with agonized abandon. In addition to the tortured vocalizations, a cacophony of other sounds contributes to the chaos, including the insides of a grand piano being brutalized by drum mallets, coconut shells being slammed against the ground in imitation of a horse's hooves upon a ship's deck, and electronic effects that evoke the howling winds of a storm at sea.

Over the course of *Strange Days*' tight thirty-four-minute run time, a mood of detached alienation prevails that allows each song to feed seamlessly into the next. From its cover artwork, which depicts a group of carnival folk cavorting in a gray New York alleyway, to its lyrical content and weird timbres, it is clear that *Strange Days* is an album dedicated to outcasts, to those who are lost, unhappy, and at odds with the world around them. Nowhere is this sentiment clearer than on "People Are Strange," an ode to outsiderdom in which Morrison bemoans his world-weariness atop Manzarek's dive-bar honky-tonk piano, Krieger's guitar sobs, and the Weill-ian oom-pah of Densmore's percussion and studio musician Doug Lubahn's bass. But for all its gloom *Strange Days* ends with a consolatory message for its despondent listeners, albeit a death-laden one. As the final strains of the album's closing epic "When the Music's Over" ring out, Morrison cries, "Music is your only friend … until the end," repeating "until the end" as his bandmates climax in support of his final bloodcurdling iteration of the word "end." Music, Morrison assures the listener, is all you need when the rest of humankind has turned its back on you, it's got you till the end.

Strange Days sold well upon its release but ultimately its achievements were diminished by the overwhelming success of "Light My Fire" and, by association, The Doors' self-titled LP. The band was despondent that the record did not have the impact of its predecessor; *Strange Days* seemingly disappeared from public and critical consciousness as soon as it arrived. In the fifty-plus years that have passed since The Doors' primal rock first commanded attention, it is usually *The Doors* or their final release before Morrison's death, 1971's *L.A. Woman*, that are cited as the band's strongest records. *Strange Days*, however, has not garnered quite the same adulation, and its more well-known songs ("Love Me Two Times"; "People Are Strange") are usually discovered via the multitude of commercially lucrative "best of" compilations that have been issued since the early 1980s. To my mind, *Strange Days* is the band's most solid and evocative offering. My interest in Jim Morrison and The Doors may have diminished somewhat in the years since their music soundtracked my lonely teenage reveries, but the moody *Strange Days* has remained a favorite record.

***

When I finally arrived at Jim Morrison's grave, I was met by a few fellow tourists taking photographs of his gravestone. There was very little talk, just quiet observation, and I was immediately struck by how small Morrison's plot was in comparison to the immensity of his myth. It was weirdly humbling. As I leaned against the fence that had been erected around his grave to deter overenthusiastic fans, observing the wilted flowers and notes by his gravestone, and waiting for who knows what to happen, an energetic young woman approached me. "Could you take my photograph? I will take yours too!" I agreed, took her camera, and watched as she clambered over the fence, utterly indifferent to the cemetery's attempt to keep her passion at bay. As I took her photo I remembered fondly how I had once been that girl, so brazen and intense in her fandom. When it was my turn to have my photograph taken I was not so bold as to breach the space beyond the fence, but I reveled in the comradery of it all nonetheless, and as the girl returned the favor I posed politely by Morrison's grave with a wistful smile.

Clare Nina Norelli is the author of *Soundtrack from Twin Peaks* (#120). Find her at clareninanorelli.com.

CHAPTER 19
THE DELLS' *THERE IS* (1968)
Joe Bucciero

On November 21, 1958, The Dells were riding in a station wagon on the Ohio Turnpike en route to their next gig. The five Dells had been singing together since the early 1950s while students at Thornton High in Harvey, Illinois, a south suburb of Chicago. The group found modest success early on, recording for Vee Jay and Chess Records, and playing gigs at the clubs that had opened on Chicago's South Side to accommodate the city's R&B boom. And it wasn't long before The Dells found success beyond their hometown: their 1956 hit "Oh What a Nite" reached number four on the national R&B charts, setting them on a path toward stardom.[1]

But on November 21, 1958, The Dells got into a car accident. Everyone survived, but the shaken members decided to call it quits amid their rise to fame. When they eventually reunited in 1961, they had trouble reclaiming their mid-1950s success, for the country's R&B preferences had changed. Instead of the doo-wop of "Oh What a Nite," early-1960s audiences wanted *soul* music—the kinds proffered by Motown, Stax, or Chess's Etta James, the kinds played on WVON, Chicago's first all-black-music radio station, started in 1963 by the Chess brothers. So The Dells, despite intermittent success, struggled into the second half of the 1960s.

That is, until 1968. Recording for Cadet, Chess's jazz- and rock-oriented subsidiary, The Dells teamed up with producer Bobby Miller and arranger Charles Stepney, who would help both radicalize the group's sound and put them back on the charts. The first album they made together, *There Is*, found The Dells experimenting with new genres and recording techniques; the LP also charted well and produced six singles.[2] Yet for all its innovation and career-rehabilitating success, *There Is*, like most of The Dells' catalog, has drifted into the margins of music history over the past fifty years. Released in the same year that their hometown would host historic riots—in April, following Martin Luther King Jr.'s assassination, and in August at the Democratic National Convention—*There Is* is hardly marginal. Rather, it's a landmark of Chicago soul's heyday, an empowering sonic portrait of a group, a genre, a city trying to survive.

***

The resonant snare hit that begins the opening title track acts like the gunshot at the start of a race. As it echoes, the band, like a mid-distance runner, sinks into its task. Keys, bass, and drums assemble in a descending pattern: an aural bending of the knees. But rather than continue apace, another shot sounds after about ten seconds—this time, a reverberant fill—and the band pushes forward with an ecstatic energy that never quite dissipates.

"There Is" introduces many of the traits that make the same-titled album difficult to pin down, even within 1968's expansive soul music landscape. When the five Dells come in after that second snare shot, their voices are stitched together in an unresolving refrain of the song's two-word title phrase. It isn't until almost forty seconds in that the group vocals separate, allowing lead baritone Marvin Junior to show off his mountainous shout: "Girl!" Then he softens to a croon, in harmony with the other Dells: "Why won't you let me love you?" Backed by swirling strings, Junior's opening salvo forecasts not only the precise interplay of The Dells' voices that marks *There Is*, but also the album's lyrical content. While some of the twelve tracks celebrate harmonious love, many present situations like "There Is": a precarious romance that The Dells hope to solidify. Today the sentiments strike a possessive note, yet perhaps The Dells sang so passionately about saving doomed relationships because they entered the recording sessions with their career—their tight, musical relationships—against the ropes.

Like many local peers, The Dells recorded on Record Row, a strip of South Michigan Avenue that housed numerous labels and distributors, and opened onto the city's segregated Black Belt. The basic ingredients of *There Is* were, accordingly, common in Chicago R&B, employed by groups like The Radiants and The Impressions: close harmonies, melisma, and call-and-response from the singers; horns, clean guitars, and heavy rhythm sections from the band. But *There Is* spreads out too, summoning Norman Whitfield's psychedelic soul with its echo and droning strings, and contemporary Chicago jazz—Ramsey Lewis's fusion, Roscoe Mitchell's free jazz—with its eclectic arrangements and underlying swing. These affinities filtered through Charles Stepney, a veteran of the local jazz scene. Indeed, if Bobby Miller's new songs helped The Dells find their voice, Stepney's interventions—like the crescendoing coda in "Wear It on Our Face," reminiscent of The Beatles' "A Day in the Life"—pushed *There Is* far out.

The LP contains a blurb from DJ Hy Lit: "Something old, something new, something borrowed, something blue," he writes. "No more fitting words can be found to describe … THE DELLS." Indeed, the Motown bounce of "Show Me," the dissonant melodrama of "The Change We Go Thru (For Love)," the Spectorian reverb on "Love Is So Simple," the Northern Soul of "When I'm in Your Arms": *There Is* nods to the music of its time, but it never copies, and Miller and Stepney's ingenuity coupled with the immediacy of The Dells' voices effuses "something new."

***

The opening seconds of "Wear It on Our Face" and "Please Don't Change Me Now" are definitely *new*. Each song employs what sounds like prepared piano, a technique attributed to the composer John Cage, in which objects are placed on the piano strings to give the instrument an unpredictable, percussive sound. In "Wear It on Our Face," a driving, atonal run of piano plunks leads quickly into full orchestration. "Please Don't Change Me Now" features slower piano clusters; the bass then takes over, introducing a sedate ballad. The piano is perplexing, invigorating, an avant-garde touch that seems to expose each song's skeleton.

The intermingling of musical styles on *There Is* resonates with the artistic model proffered by Chicago's Association for the Advancement of Creative Musicians (AACM). Formed on the South Side in 1965 by pianist and composer Muhal Richard Abrams, the AACM established a network of artists and ideas that, in the words of member George Lewis, stressed "the importance of asserting the agency, identity, and survival of the African-American artist."[3] With black Chicagoans facing segregation, cultural appropriation, and police brutality, the AACM sought to create music that celebrated the black roots of American music while breaking new ground artistically and commercially. "Black creative artists must survive and persevere in spite of the oppressive forces which prevent black people from reaching the goals attained by other Americans," wrote Abrams and fellow member John Shenoy Jackson. "We must continue to add copiously to an already vast reservoir of artistic richness handed down through the ages. Black artists must control and be paid for what they produce, as well as own and control the means of distribution."[4] Their principles echoed down Record Row, a thriving ecosystem of primarily black music production and distribution. Stepney himself provided another link from the AACM to Chicago soul, having played with Abrams's Experimental Band in the early 1960s.

John Cage saw the unpredictability of prepared piano as resisting the structures of prior Western composition. Unpredictability runs throughout *There Is*, too, not only in Stepney's unconventional arrangements, but also in The Dells' vocals, whether Marvin Junior's extended wail at the end of "Stay in My Corner"—which surprised even the other Dells during recording—or the way Johnny Carter's tenor slithers underneath Junior's lead in "Close Your Eyes," an improvisation that disrupts the straightforward harmonic motion.

While Stepney was knowledgeable about the avant-garde, he and The Dells were by no means *following* Cage. As George Lewis has noted, Cage's interest in unpredictability (or "indeterminacy") attributes Euro-American roots to a black musical tradition: improvisation. Lewis has traced improvisation through what he terms Afrological and Eurological perspectives, showing how black artists have established new musical devices within their own lineage, often before the advent of similar developments in Euro-American music. Stepney and The Dells came to their sound not through Cage, but Chicago's jazz and R&B scenes: South Side venues and Record Row studios.

"One important aspect of Afrological improvisation," writes Lewis, "is the notion of the importance of personal narrative, or 'telling your own story' ... Part of telling your own story is developing your own 'sound.'"[5] In 1966, on similar grounds, Amiri Baraka drew a connection between free jazz (like the AACM's) and R&B—two members of "the same family," in his view, "looking at different things."[6] Like the AACM's, The Dells' new, eclectic sound was a sonic timeline of their ongoing story—of striving together for agency, for survival.

***

"It's time for us to try uniting. We gotta make a whole new scene. Maybe then we'll understand what freedom means." So ends the spoken introduction to The Dells' 1971 LP *Freedom Means*. It articulates the group's political and musical M.O.—a call for unity, for making something new—evident throughout their career. The post-accident line up remained united from 1961 until 2009, when Johnny Carter died; throughout those decades they experimented with new musical styles, exploring contemporary techniques of black popular music, from cosmic funk to new jack swing.

When the five Dells were born in the mid-1930s, Chicago's population was under 10 percent black; by 1968, after the Great Migration, it was around 25 percent. But black life in Chicago remained largely confined to the South Side, with worsening conditions. Music-wise, Record Row began to crumble in the late 1960s, with black-owned labels like Vee Jay running out of business. In April 1968, as *There Is* climbed the charts, South Side clashes with the National Guard resulted in eleven dead, over 2,000 arrested, and lasting damage. Even if The Dells didn't discuss these conditions on record, *There Is*, with its dynamic emotional palette and stylistic freedom, summons Brian Ward's notion that R&B "absorbed changes in mass black consciousness and reflected them primarily by means of certain musical devices and performance techniques, rather than in the form of neat narrative expositions."[7]

Yet one song on *There Is* does stand out lyrically: the rocking, rolling "Run for Cover." Instead of love, the song speaks of "suffering," "fatigue," and The Dells' "need to be free," a need that Marvin Junior shouts to fulfill as they "run for cover." Freedom is a fraught concept, but it has long been a central theme in black music—in blues, jazz, disco, hip-hop, and other genres. And while in 1971 The Dells pondered what freedom meant, three years earlier they had enacted it musically. Their new 1968 sound absorbed its surroundings, projecting personal and cultural histories and cultivating a "whole new scene." *There Is* traces life's extremes ("Wild Joy—Deep Hurt"), running across grounds of experience toward a type of freedom, a freedom that The Dells, voices woven in harmony, "wear on [their] face."[8]

Joe Bucciero is the co-author, with Michael Blair, of *Colossal Youth* (#121). Find him at joebucciero.website.

CHAPTER 20
SHIRLEY AND DOLLY COLLINS' *ANTHEMS IN EDEN* (1969)
Sam Inglis

Launched in 1969, EMI's Harvest subsidiary quickly became *the* prog rock record label, striking the motherlode four years later with *Dark Side of the Moon*. Yet the success of Pink Floyd and Deep Purple inevitably relegated to B-side status those Harvest albums that did not fit the prog pigeonhole. Among them was one of the first releases on the label, and one of vanishingly few by female artists. Neither psychedelic nor progressive, and in no sense rock and roll, *Anthems in Eden* is one of the most extraordinary fusion records ever made.

At its center is a voice. Not a great voice, in the way that Aretha Franklin or Carl Wilson or Kate Bush had great voices; not a trained voice; not a voice with a particularly wide range, nor one capable of much dynamic contrast; neither a versatile voice nor yet a character voice in the tradition of Lou Reed or Mark E. Smith. A limited voice, in fact, but what makes Shirley Collins so compelling is the very fact that she never sounds like a professional vocalist.

The folk revival of the 1960s produced many fine singers, but none with the same determination to serve the song rather than her own ego. Even now, Shirley Collins gets exercised about the right way to sing English folk music:

> You not only have to do your best for the songs, but you have to trust them as well. You can't, in my opinion, dramatize the songs vocally, because you'd lose their special quality then. I think a lot of people don't trust the songs enough to be able to sing them straightforwardly. They feel they've got to double up the rhythm, or push it in some way, and that drives me nuts, because that's not how the English have done it over centuries and I like the way it's been done. I think that's the proper way to do it.[1]

The "proper way to do it" can sound jarring at first listen. Shirley's delivery is almost entirely unornamented, never striving to be heard for its own sake, only to serve as a conduit for the song and the tradition behind the song. It can seem detached, almost flat, but once you're familiar with it, other singers sound affected and false in comparison. Never has the art of artlessness been practiced to such devastating effect.

***

Shirley Collins's singing is inseparable from Shirley Collins's material, much of it learned at first hand from "source singers" such as Sussex's legendary Copper family. Like all her records, *Anthems in Eden* is a collection of songs that come primarily from the English tradition, with two obvious exceptions. "Ca' the Yowes" is one of Robert Burns's best-known compositions, while "God Dog" was written by the Incredible String Band's Robin Williamson.

The collectors who noted down English folk songs from source singers invariably heard them sung unaccompanied. If the contents of *Anthems in Eden* were presented thus, it would be a fine collection of traditional folk music. What makes it a great album without qualification, and a unique one, are the ways in which it departs from this tradition, and the contributions of the other people involved in its making.

Principal among these was Shirley's older sister, Dolly Collins. Sharing a Sussex childhood with Shirley, Dolly likewise acquired a lifelong love of English folk music; but rather than channeling her creative energies into performance, she chose instead to learn composition and music theory, studying with the radical Communist composer Alan Bush and his Workers' Music Association. From the mid-1960s onwards, Dolly began to contribute keyboard parts to Shirley's records, usually performed on an archaic instrument known as the "portative organ" or "flute organ."

Dolly Collins rarely sang on record, but her voice as a composer is unmistakable. Alan Bush, like Ralph Vaughan Williams, was interested in early counterpoint, and the influence is apparent in Dolly's work. Austere and frequently minimal, yet confident and direct, her arrangements underscore the melody with ruthless economy. By the time Dolly and Shirley recorded *Anthems in Eden*, her style had crystallized, and with Harvest supplying a generous budget for a folk album, she was able to give that style its fullest expression yet. Like Michael Nyman, another Bush pupil, Dolly often begins with simple motifs that suggest music of the past, but organizes them in new ways to create a whole that is clearly modern. On Side One of *Anthems in Eden* she took this process even further, assembling a selection of well-known traditional songs and tunes into a continuous suite with a loose narrative theme.

***

EMI's money also made possible the other key elements that make the album unique. Just as English composers of the time were championing antecedents such as Purcell, so too were performers exploring the instruments and techniques of the baroque period. Dolly's arrangements for *Anthems in Eden* were realized by an ensemble of the brightest stars in this "early music" movement, including harpsichordist Christopher Hogwood and wind virtuoso David Munrow. Munrow, who acted as musical director, is credited with playing soprano and alto crumhorn, bass racket, tenor sordun, and treble recorder, set against a gleeful riot of rebecs, cornets, viols, and sackbuts from the other contributors.

When "classical" instruments are employed in a folk or rock context, their role is usually to ice the cake, prettifying and adding the illusion of depth. *Anthems in Eden* is the very antithesis of this approach. There is nothing pretty about it, nor any false sophistication. Nor are there any guitars or drum kits for bewildered rock fans to cling to in the hope of orienting their perceptions. *Anthems in Eden* plunges us forcibly into a new sound world that is pungent, earthy, abrasive, and frequently discordant, and keeps us immersed fully for forty wonderful, baffling minutes.

Properly capturing this difficult racket on tape would probably have been beyond the specialist folk labels of the time, which were shoestring affairs. The Harvest connection meant that *Anthems in Eden* was recorded at EMI's Abbey Road Studios in London: then, as now, the most famous recording studio in the world, and one of the most technologically advanced. Engineer Peter Mew saw to it that the force and vitality of the performances came through unscathed.

***

Hearing a great album for the first time is exciting. Hearing a great album for the hundredth time is fulfilling. But the magical listening experiences are the ones in-between, the ones that happen on the way to loving an album. You're intrigued, startled, perhaps even slightly repelled. You press "Play" as much with apprehension as anticipation. Not yet familiar enough to be experienced as the background to some other activity, it demands your attention, offers itself up proudly to judgment, and defies your attempts to impose a musical logic on it.

The beauty of "difficult" music is that it prolongs this process. An album that gives up all its treasures on the first couple of listens might be easy to like, but you can't fall in love with it. Great music offers a challenge to the listener. It doesn't rush out to fulfil our preconceptions like an expectant puppy, it stands firm against those preconceptions. Great music demands that we ourselves change in order to understand it, and rewards us the more for doing so. *Anthems in Eden* is a case in point.

Musical fusion projects fail more often than they work. Over the years, traditional music has fallen prey to such unhappy marriages as "chamber folk" and "techno-folk," not to mention innumerable pointless mash-ups of different countries' musical cultures. Shirley and Dolly Collins's masterpiece stands aloof outside this process. For fifty years it has been sending the same message to every new generation of listeners: this is what it is, and if you find it strange or difficult or shocking, well, that's your problem. The people who created this particular fusion were not dilettantes or fading stars, bored and looking around for something new to dabble in. They were musicians at their creative peak, young enough to have extraordinary ambitions, yet sufficiently experienced and talented to carry them through. *Anthems in Eden* draws deeply on music of the past, yet it sounds like no other music that has been made before or since.

Actually, that's not quite true, because, in this case, lightning struck twice. *Anthems in Eden* was no *Dark Side of the Moon*, but it did well enough that Harvest encouraged Shirley and Dolly Collins to repeat the experiment. This they did the following year, working with many of the same musicians to produce a follow-up called *Love, Death and the Lady* which, remarkably, is even better. Along with a handful of rarities, both albums are now available on a single CD release called *The Harvest Years*. Deeper, richer, and stranger than any prog rock, it might just be the best thing the label ever released.

Sam Inglis is the author of *Harvest* (#3).

CHAPTER 21
VON FREEMAN'S *DOIN' IT RIGHT NOW* (1972)
Aaron Cohen

I must have been 20 years old and making a regular visit to Chicago's Jazz Record Mart when I bought a copy of saxophonist Von Freeman's 1972 album *Doin' It Right Now* (Atlantic). The cover art stood out, maybe because it attempted to look downscale. At that time the jazz musicians I knew of dressed in suits and pop artists cultivated their own fashion statements. But Freeman half-stood/half-sat wearing a tank top in a building that looked way past abandoned. The picture also emphasized his physical strength, and his sound backed it up.

Growing up just north of the city in Evanston, I knew Freeman and his work before I encountered that album because he played on the 1983 *Hyde Park after Dark* (from Bee Hive, a label that my neighbors owned). So I sought out his appearances at free events, like the Chicago Jazz Festival, and slipped in to see him at bars where IDs were not rigorously checked. I kept on devotedly attending his gigs until his death, at age 88, on August 12, 2012. Since he was the only great jazz musician I knew as a teen, I assumed that they were all like him. When I became an adult, I realized that, actually, there was none other like him. While I cannot count the numerous times and places I saw him perform, his most memorable show was on May 11, 2008, at the city's Garfield Park Conservatory. That gig was my wedding.

Freeman performed jazz as well as its continuum—blues, soul, and gospel. I interviewed him just once, and that was for my college newspaper in Madison, WI, when he played on campus in 1990. For the next twenty-two years, the nights I spent listening to his music, stories, and usually hilarious observations about life and people proved more rewarding than if we had sat down and followed usual magazine article guidelines and protocols. None of this means my time with Freeman made me special. He was just as open with legions of musicians, students, and everyday fans.

Even in the years before Freeman received his designation as a Jazz Master from the National Endowment for the Arts, everyone in the saxophonist's orbit knew his biography. He lived his entire life on Chicago's South Side. As a child, he met such jazz legends as Louis Armstrong and Fats Waller when his music-fan father, a policeman, brought them home for visits. His musical family included his guitarist brother George, whom he saluted through the tune "Brother George," the closer on *Doin' It Right Now*. Also, as Freeman's drummer Michael Raynor reminded me, the music of the Sanctified Church surrounded the family and may have contributed to the ecstatic cries of

Freeman's saxophone shouts. He attended DuSable High School, where his teacher, Captain Walter Dyett, also guided such future jazz stars as saxophonist Gene Ammons and bassist Richard Davis. After serving in the Navy, he played in the house band at the Pershing Ballroom and alongside such innovative bandleaders as Andrew Hill and Sun Ra. He also worked as an arranger for Vee-Jay Records, particularly for blues legend Jimmy Reed. (He told me about meeting Curtis Mayfield when the soul star jammed with Reed.) While he turned down Miles Davis's invitation to replace John Coltrane in his group, he may have influenced more musicians through holding court at Chicago's Enterprise Lounge and New Apartment Lounge than he would have if he joined the ranks of the famous names outside the Midwest.

That influence was evident since so many musicians from around the world came to Freeman, rather than the other way around. The brilliant multi-reedist Rahsaan Roland Kirk produced *Doin' It Right Now*. This was Freeman's first LP, released as he turned 50. *Doin' It Right Now* did not become a smash hit, but it did spark a series of solid recordings that continued up until his final years. During the 1970s, the valuable indie company Nessa released his albums *Have No Fear* (1975) and *Serenade & Blues* (1979). Toward his final decade, he remained strong and inspirational on *The Improvisor* (Premonition, 2001) and *Good Forever* (Premonition, 2006). Freeman's unmistakable musical identity runs throughout all of them; just as he drove through constantly startling tempo shifts on the bandstand, he powered through whatever one might surmise of what it means to grow older.

Those fleet changes were just part of what made Freeman's tenor so extraordinary. His repertoire stuck close to ballads, American Songbook standards, or rhythm changes on blues that he composed. And he'd often tell of trying to combine the heavy approach of saxophonist Coleman Hawkins with the airiness of Lester Young. But Freeman's own chord changes and extended lines became as daring as the generations of jazz revolutionaries who admired him. Furthermore, he made all of these leaps and dives flow beautifully; his individual pitch made his playing seem as close as an acoustic instrument could get to the human voice. He enraptured jazz musicians and jazz fans while his unbridled warmth on the ballads enveloped everyone.

One such ballad, "The First Time I Ever Saw Your Face," opens *Doin' It Right Now*. At the time, the song was a hit for Freeman's Atlantic label mate Roberta Flack. There's no mistaking the two versions. After starting the melody with a warm vibrato, he unveils his distinctive tone in surprising leaps while his long-time sparring partner, pianist John Young, responds with strong bluesy chord changes. It's a bracing beginning to an album that's filled with such a sense of drive in clear and subtle ways. On Freeman's composition, "White Sand," the saxophonist's fast-paced extensions come especially alive in combination with drummer Jimmy Cobb's velocity. The title track, another Freeman original, features his impeccable timing through quick short notes responding to Cobb's seemingly light touch on cymbals. This piece conveys the excitement of watching Freeman count off a bandstand jam session. But the most striking song on the album is a performance of the standard "Sweet and Lovely" that includes just Freeman and bassist Sam Jones. I had not heard this saxophone/bass duo format much (if at all) before picking up this album, and I've heard no teams perform as expertly in this context in the thirty years since then. Jones's lines change gradually and mainly serve to frame the bandleader's explorations. For every note Freeman plays, he infuses pauses with just as much depth.

He achieved all of this within relatively succinct statements on the album. Each track runs between four and eight minutes. This brevity contrasts with his tracks from later in the 1970s and his typical concerts, when he unleashed chorus after chorus on extensive takes on a song like Gershwin's "Summertime." His concision likely had a deep impact on my outlook as a budding newspaper journalist, a medium where space constraints are ever present. So did hearing his singular pitch within this context—essentially, it should not take long to make your own voice ring out, no matter what it is. While other saxophonists whose work I knew at the time—Charlie Parker, John Coltrane—had already been absorbed within jazz, Freeman's sidelong way of approaching notes struck me as something that exclusively he could do.

If *Doin' It Right Now* did not provide Freeman with the immediate jazz stardom that it should have, during the almost thirty years I knew him, I never heard him utter any words of regret or resentment, nor did commercial apathy dim his exuberance. This example taught me a lot, not just regarding the artists I encountered as a writer but about all people. He also spent these years inspiring and reflecting on the musical changes in Chicago. His longer harmonies on "Have No Fear" and "Serenade & Blues" could be considered his answers to the experiments going on among the Association for the Advancement of Creative Musicians, an organization that he partially inspired. Turning further inward, he brought lovely self-reflection to "Good Forever." On the live sessions that comprise *The Improvisor*, his local group of Raynor and guitarist Mike Allemana joined up with New York pianist Jason Moran and drummer Nasheet Waits—similar to the combined talents on *Doin' It Right Now*. I attended those recording dates at Chicago's Green Mill, and everyone was equally in awe of the master.

Alongside Freeman's music, *Doin' It Right Now* fed into my imagination of what Atlantic Records itself was like in the early 1970s. It seemed to me back then rather incredible that a major company—with a track record of hits in R&B, rock, and jazz—allowed for such risk taking as bringing Freeman and Young from Chicago into New York to record with such session vets as Jones and Cobb. Producer Kirk was a popular artist at the time, and this album led me to seek out more of his music. I wondered about how much Atlantic's soul stars influenced its jazz recordings and how its jazz players shaped its soul expansions at this time. All of which led me to my growing fascination with Aretha Franklin's own album for the company, *Amazing Grace*, which came out in 1972. Doubling back, perhaps it was the sanctified sound in Freeman's saxophone that helped steer me toward gospel and Franklin's return to the church recording.

Not that such community-building emphasis actually existed in Atlantic's boardrooms, but it truly did in Freeman's Chicago. As musicians like saxophonist Steve Coleman came up through those jam sessions, he took his mentor's lessons to international acclaim, as did another saxophonist, Freeman's son Chico. Staying here in Chicago, Allemana frequently performs around town (often with George Freeman), while also describing his bandleader's work for a PhD dissertation. This communal embrace is the image that should last as long as Freeman's music, as Moran and I discussed shortly after his 2012 passing. The pianist said that what he remembered about the live sessions was the way Freeman used implied harmonies and played ballads that would, in his words, "take you into the stratosphere." But just as much, Moran remembered how at breaks the elder saxophonist just sat on the stage and hung out with his adoring public. That multitude stretched beyond any single room.

Aaron Cohen is author of *Amazing Grace* (#84). He tweets @aaroncohenwords.

CHAPTER 22
JOHN CALE'S *PARIS 1919* (1973)
Mark Polizzotti

Paris 1919 was released in 1973 and went straight to obscurity. By the time I'd learned of it, only a few years later, it was already hard to find, a B-side anomaly lost (for a while, at least) between its experimental predecessor and its hard-rock follow-ups. Even my discovery of it was obscure: a brief mention in the liner notes to Nick Drake's initiates-only *Five Leaves Left*, to the effect that John Cale's album, "the epitome of the Neo-Romantic Ethos," was "thoroughly inspired" by Drake. I was obsessed with *Five Leaves Left*. If there was a similar record out there, I wanted to hear it.

In the event, while I liked *Paris 1919* well enough at first (nice, but no "River Man"), I was soon seduced away by the concentrated burst of paranoia-tinged rock noir that was Cale's newest release, *Guts*—a 180-degree swing from any ethos that might conceivably be labeled Neo-Romantic. The song titles alone ("Guts," "Gun," "Dirty Ass Rock and Roll") were a whole program, a pure shot of zeitgeist-appropriate nihilism. Cale to me became the hockey-masked, Flying V-wielding terrorist of his proto-punk phase, rather than the seated, white-flannel gentleman who graces the cover of *Paris 1919*.

But passions are curious things, and I've since come to appreciate the particular staying power of *Paris*. In part, it has to do with the sound: mostly understated, controlled, yet emotionally resonant; in part, with the playful, wistful surrealism of the lyrics. Most of all, *Paris 1919* is one of those rare albums that is entirely of a piece. Like *Tumbleweed Connection*, Elton John's 1970 fantasia on post-Civil War America, it lives in its own space, self-contained, sui generis. Neither a simple collection of songs nor a "concept album" in the overblown, Pink Floyd sense, *Paris 1919* creates an aura, a setting in which each piece fits perfectly after the one before it and helps create the proverbial sum that is larger than its parts.

This is where sequencing enters the picture, an art that was crucial when albums dominated, less so in the age of shuffle-play. As we spin our way through *Paris 1919*, we realize how skillfully Cale has orchestrated its shifting tones. There is nothing extraneous, nothing that could drop out or wedge in without causing the delicate structure to collapse.

It begins on a note of grandeur and yearning, the triumphal piano ascent that opens "Child's Christmas in Wales" simultaneously undercut and prolonged by Lowell George's aching, straining slide note—the figure immediately repeated like a double-take before Cale begins his Thomasian reminiscence of a childhood that might never have existed, but is nonetheless keenly missed. And just as memory reaches a crescendo, then finishes with the solemnity of a church hymn, a downward cascade ushers us into the soft pastoral haze of "Hanky Panky Nohow," with its lovely, seesawing guitar arpeggios, lilting melody, and humorously baffling words ("Elephants that sing to keep / The cows that agriculture won't allow"—lyrics that used to annoy me no end). A fade, and suddenly the mood darkens, muddies, and we're slogging through "The Endless Plain of Fortune": English pastures yield to a turn-of-the-century battlefield, the Boer War, perhaps, a time just before the Modern World crashed the party. Then comes the gentle love-lost ballad "Andalucia," a cradling, shuffling vibe straight out of Lou Reed's "Walk on the Wild Side," its breathy mood shattered by the incongruous thump and crash of the raucous Side One closer, "Macbeth," just to shake things up a bit.

Side Two dives back into early-century mode with the title song, an impressionistic scherzo for piano and orchestra about the Paris Peace Conference and the Treaty of Versailles. An unlikely basis for a pop song, granted, but Cale wasn't the only one mining European history for his material (Al Stewart's *Past, Present and Future* came out the same year as *Paris 1919*). More to the point, all these references—childhood in a province threatened with absorption into the English mainstream, an agricultural past coping with modernization, transformative military and political upheavals, and murderous ambition—form a tapestry that weaves together nostalgia for a world gone by, the cavalcade of human error, and cataclysmic loss on both a personal and global scale.

Cale has called this album "an example of the nicest ways of saying something ugly,"[1] which I take to mean not only the Versailles Treaty and its disastrous sequels (fascism, the Second World War, Potsdam), but also, more generally, the endless plain of our misfortune. A daub of Great War, a splotch of Elizabethan regicide, a dash of faded Hollywood glory (the "paranoid great movie queen," shades of Norma Desmond, in "Antarctica Starts Here"), a smear of post-war racism (the reference in "Graham Greene" to Enoch Powell, author of the anti-immigration "rivers of blood" speech—as well as to the anti-Semitic Greene himself), and pretty soon the canvas encompasses centuries of man-made tragedy, our whole sorry saga.

Getting back to sequencing: one of the revelations of the 2006 CD reissue of *Paris 1919*, after years of listening to the original vinyl, was the confirmation of just how choate the album is. I'd had an inkling of this at Cale's live performance of it at BAM in 2013, when he displaced "Macbeth" to the end—good showmanship, in the context, yet entirely different in tone. The 2006 disc features a full, alternate version of *Paris 1919*, including "Child's Christmas" without George's slide, a guitarless "drone mix" of "Hanky Panky Nohow," arrangements of "Paris 1919" with only piano or only orchestra, "Half Past France" minus the gently rocking guitar fills … fascinating as sketches, and oh so incomplete.

In his 1999 autobiography, *What's Welsh for Zen*, Cale draws a distinction between this album and the more "abrasive" mid-1970s trilogy of *Fear, Slow Dazzle*, and *Helen of Troy*: "The reason *Paris 1919* stands out among my solo albums is that the songs had time to percolate. Everything else I've done has been off the cuff, but on *Paris 1919* I went into the studio with complete pieces … I wrote arrangements in the Wordsworth way: emotion recollected in tranquility."[2] As it happens, *Paris 1919* was written and recorded during a period of Cale's life that was anything but tranquil: he was seeking an artistic direction after his first, inconclusive solo efforts (from the scattershot *Vintage Violence* to the avant-classical *The Academy in Peril*) had failed to advance his post-Velvet Underground profile; paying corporate dues as a record producer and A&R man for Warner Bros. (the same label that issued *Paris 1919*); and navigating a turbulent marriage that would soon end in divorce ("She knew it all / And made you see things all her way," he chides in "Macbeth"). But perhaps because of that percolation, the vintage violence on *this* record is muffled, softened by nostalgia and humor, its darkness barely visible—much like the quartet of photos on the sleeve's back cover that show our hero decked out in white suit, white shirt, and white tie, placidly keeling over in a sun-bleached room.

Still, if you listen carefully, you can hear the storm inside the calm. The wonder-eyed neighborliness of "Child's Christmas" includes "ten murdered oranges" and a reference to another Dylan Thomas poem, "The Ballad of the Long Legged Bait," which begins with an angler tossing "a girl alive with hooks through her lips" into the sea. The genteel tea party of "Graham Greene" is rife with personal humiliation and social distortion. And so on.

You can also pick up a dark motif that recurs throughout *Paris 1919* in seemingly disparate ways. "Nothing frightens me more / Than religion at my door," Cale intones in "Hanky Panky Nohow." Religion infuses the album, often with an ominous cast: "You're a ghost, la la la la la la la la la / I'm the church and I've come to claim you with my iron drum" ("Paris 1919"); "So shocking to see the old Church of E / Looking down on you and me" ("Graham Greene"); "If they're alive then I am dead / Pray God and eat your daily bread" ("Half Past France"). Religion, of course, has been a primary driver of the social and political hanky panky alluded to in these songs, and anyone attuned to the ills of the twentieth century has good reason to fear it at the door.

But Cale might be exorcising a more personal darkness. In his autobiography, he relates how he was molested as a preadolescent by two men, one of them the organist at his local church. "It was distasteful and difficult to deal with," he writes, "and it certainly took care of my religious sensibility."[3] Unable to turn to anyone for help or guidance, the boy endured the abuse for the better part of a year, finally managing to extricate himself. But the feeling that "there was something wrong somewhere" persisted. "I never came to terms with the problem. It always haunted me,"[4] he writes, and his albums from that period seem to bear this out. Before *Paris 1919* came *Church of Anthrax*, which says it all. A few years later, on *Helen of Troy*, he again revisited the scene of the crime, sometimes with a plea: "Save us from the House of God" ("Save Us"), sometimes in full frenzy: "I got something locked up inside me ... / Wanna find out what that something that's driving me out of my mind is" ("Engine"). I don't know how much if anything has changed since those years. "I'm not afraid now of the dark, anymore," he informs us on *Paris 1919*, but he might be whistling past the graveyard. I can all too easily imagine that the sense of helplessness and inconsequence, of enforced silence, must threaten to reduce anyone who has survived such a terror to feeling like a wraith. Insubstantial and ghostly. La la la.

The blend of stark shadow and soft sunlight, of the personal and the historical, the private and the mythic, the (in Cale's phrase) "dense musical texture"[5] of it, is no doubt what keeps me listening to *Paris 1919* after all this time, what makes it resonate, what tugs at my ear when I try to craft phrases of my own. That, and the fact that it all fits so marvelously in a mere thirty-one minutes and thirty seconds of music, brief even by 1973 standards. With its encyclopedic juxtapositions and fleeting evocations, it seems to present the whole panorama of Western history—musical as well as political—in a few spare strokes, like a master class in expressive economy.

Moreover, as Matthew Specktor notes in his booklet essay for the CD, *Paris 1919* is probably Cale's most "humane" effort. After his later albums, when the rage grew more explicit, this record would come to feel unseasonably mild; but to my mind, one of its lasting strengths is precisely that the parade of human folly and horror is viewed, not with contempt, but with compassion. The record is unsentimental (at any rate, less sentimental than many releases in that year of *Goodbye Yellow Brick Road* and *Band on the Run*), but unlike its successors, it doesn't play rough. It is bleak, but at the same time, aspirational. Stephen Holden, reviewing the original LP for *Rolling Stone*, wrote that Cale "employs imagery that is fundamentally cohesive in an impressionistic way and further unified by its elegiac spirit … Wit, humor and irony are here in abundance. So too are metaphysical contemplation and sadness."[6] That's a tall order, for the creator as for the listener. But why aspire to anything less?

Mark Polizzotti is the author of *Highway 61 Revisited* (#35).

CHAPTER 23
BERT JANSCH'S *L.A. TURNAROUND* (1974)
John Perry

Bert Jansch is, to my mind, the most interesting acoustic guitarist to come out of twentieth-century Britain. Building on the legacy of Davey Graham, he devised a unique method of accompanying traditional ballads then applied it to his own compositions. Although the comparison is somewhat hackneyed, he became a stylist every bit as influential as his peer Jimi Hendrix.

Jansch's mystique rests in part on the speed at which he developed. Within a couple of years of picking up the instrument, he was dazzling audiences and fellow musicians. Hamish Imlach tells a tale of the young Jansch playing for Brownie McGhee at the Howff. "How long you been playing?" asks an impressed McGhee. "Six weeks," says Jansch.[1] In 1965 Anne Briggs taught him the traditional Irish song "Black Waterside"—a ballad she preferred to sing unaccompanied since the busy three-chord strum favored by most folk guitarists left little room for vocal subtlety.[2] Over several nights, Jansch evolved a sparse accompaniment that eschewed chords; top lines and bass parts moved independently and the melody, constantly mobile, might be carried by either. Martin Carthy called it "contrapuntal blues."[3] The whole had considerable rhythmic "drive," a feel Jansch picked up from Bill Broonzy and Brownie McGhee.

A Jansch cult developed. Electric guitarists were as fascinated as folkies. Neil Young and Jimmy Page both attest to being "obsessed" by Jansch, while others, including Paul Simon and Ralph McTell, tried their best to work him out. Early Donovan records contain at least two songs in praise of Jansch.[4] Rory Gallagher was set to record an album with him. Tales circulated of his casual brilliance. Bert seemed to favor "difficult" guitars with high actions and old, dull-sounding strings and frequently performed with whatever instrument was lying around. If he couldn't find a thumb-pick he'd bend an old teaspoon into shape. In performance he never entirely lost the air of a man who'd hitchhiked to the venue, had a few beers, and borrowed a guitar.

***

L.A. Turnaround is Bert Jansch's first solo LP following the break up of his band Pentangle and came almost a decade into his career. A clutch of songs recorded at the Sussex country house of Charisma Records boss Tony Stratton-Smith are joined with sessions from Sound City in Van Nuys and a pair of instrumentals recorded the previous year in Paris—including the definitive Jansch piece, "Chambertin." Well-suited to its era,

L.A. Turnaround might have sold by the truckload but instead remained obscure. For decades it was one of the last Jansch albums to be reissued on CD; Bert himself didn't own the record till Johnny Marr gave him his. (If that doesn't qualify the album as a B-side, I don't know what does!)

A soloist's individuality can become diluted during years with a regular band— especially a musician as singular as Jansch. His facility, his unusual inversions and his idiosyncratic diction and vocal timing could throw accompanying players; the rhythm of his vocals can seem strangely at odds with his guitar phrasing. In fact, his timing is just fine but his way of phrasing around the beat can be disconcerting. Of his old pal John Renbourne, Jansch simply said: "[his] timing and mine are two different things."[5]

Away from Pentangle and newly signed to a supportive record label, Jansch regained much of the musical freedom of his early solo days. Tony Stratton-Smith—proprietor of Charisma Records, former Bonzo Dog Band manager, and as much Patron of the Arts as Label Boss—was noted for signings considered eccentric by straighter parts of the music business. Flourishing on sales of Genesis and Lindisfarne albums, Smith's 1973 signings included the poet laureate John Betjeman and Bert Jansch.

Both Jansch and Pentangle had a long association with Transatlantic Records, widely perceived as a specialist folk music label (despite a catalog that included The Fugs). Left to his own devices, Jansch would almost certainly have continued to draw from that same pool of folk revival musicians, but Stratton-Smith looked elsewhere. He planned to reposition Jansch, moving him out of the folk ghetto into the lucrative singer/songwriter market. Bert could only ever be Bert, but *L.A. Turnaround* represents a deliberate break with the Pentangle era.

Finding a sympathetic "name" producer was crucial. Stratton-Smith asked Jimmy Page, a noted Jansch devotee; Page, busy at the time with his own band, said "yes" but failed to find time. Smith's next choice was ex-Monkee Mike Nesmith who brought along his steel guitar chum, Red Rhodes. An ex-boxer with a lovely melodic sense, Rhodes's pedal steel is high in the mix throughout and gives the record much of its character, although, as film from the Sussex sessions shows, Jansch had little idea who either of them was.

The felicity of Stratton-Smith's choices is evident from the opening track, "Fresh as a Sweet Sunday Morning." Written in Montmartre and recorded in Sussex it includes the sound of birdsong from the garden. Rhodes's pedal-steel locks in tight with Jansch's acoustic guitar in a satisfying blend of English pastoral and Californian country-rock— Laurel Canyon meets the High Weald. It sounds like a natural single. A minor key waltz that modulates briefly to the major on the word "fresh," the arrangement derives much of its temper from the rising crests of steel guitar that accompany the modulation. The song pivots there, its emotional center reinforced by the strong major chord and the swelling pedal steel, before resolving back to the minor for each new verse. Beneath the pedal-steel intro—E minor and A7 arpeggios[6]—you can hear the acoustic guitar, low in the mix, connecting the chords with a hammered-on run down the bass strings—brief but definitively Janschean.

A bluesy song about Watergate sits beside "Stone Monkey" (drawn from the sixteenth-century Chinese novel *Journey to the West*) and a re-recording of "Needle of Death" (a gentler reading of Jansch's 1965 eulogy for friend Buck Polly). "Cluck Old Hen" could be a Townes Van Zandt song. All feature The Beatles' pal Klaus Voorman on electric bass. "One for Jo" can seem merely pleasant—until you try playing it—but it's the two instrumental tracks recorded in Paris, "Chambertin" and "Lady Nothing," that represent the mature sound of Jansch. "Lady Nothing" is a reworking of John Renbourne's baroque standard "Ladye Nothinge's Toy Puffe." Taken at a slower tempo, it illustrates the differences between Renbourne's masterly, controlled style and Jansch's diverse and more improvised voicings. Its distinctive D/A minor/C major 7 progression turns up a decade later at the front of The Smiths' song "Unhappy Birthday," Johnny Marr signaling that he's a serious Jansch fan.

The album's crowning glory is "Chambertin," a four-minute piece celebrating Jansch's favorite Burgundy. A wonderfully complex composition, its intricate layers sound more like two guitars than a single instrument. The full extent of his technique and his individuality as player and composer are on show here. He rarely attempted the piece live. I first saw him play in 1968, a relaxed figure who shambled onto the stage, sat down, and spent several silent minutes going slowly through his pockets before asking the audience for a pick. If he got bored he'd stop mid-song and play something else. He worked with his head down or his eyes closed, yet he was riveting to watch, possessing a sort of anti-charisma as potent as more orthodox varieties. I last saw him play in 2007 in Spitalfields and, in the sort of dangling conversation that often typified chats with Jansch, I spoke of the impression made by his 1960s shows—but *he* wasn't impressed. No longer a man whose days were spent in pubs, he replied: "I prefer it these days—I can remember what I've played." When I asked about a 1974 performance of "Chambertin" he was skeptical—"I don't think I ever played it live." I showed him the newish *River Sessions* album, "It's on this, Bert." His surprise was genuine.

Archie Fisher (who, along with Davey Graham's half-sister Jill, taught the young Jansch the rudiments) explained how a typical Jansch piece "would start with an extended guitar intro that set the mood and tempo and a song would break out almost seamlessly from that … he often composed the tune around a set of guitar motifs—building a symbiotic parallel run of words and guitar music."[7] He might have been describing "Chambertin." The piece starts and ends with a vamp in A major—reminiscent of the 1966 duets album *Bert and John* (Renbourne) and the Mingus and Miles compositions they loved as jump-off points for improvisation. An initial melody develops and layers of sound start to build. The first technically astonishing phrases come at the one-minute mark, where descending bass runs accompany syncopated top lines—kind of staggered octaves. The theme is restated and then, just before the four-minute mark, a slight softening and a faint *rallentando* signal the tune's end. Some suggest comparisons with the French school, Ravel, Debussy etc., and there is something of Impressionism about "Chambertin," but I doubt it's anything Jansch ever considered. He never consciously worked at a "style." When asked about it, he said, "Sorry … it's a mystery to me how it developed like this,"[8] and there's only so far you can go in identifying forebears and influences.

The problem decades later—when a style is established, copied, and widely accepted as "standard"—is conveying the impact it made when new. We've become so accustomed to every sort of guitar virtuosity it's almost impossible to comprehend the effect that Jansch's arrival made on the scene. There was nothing like him. Those who saw him in 1965 or 1966 describe him as "arriving fully-formed" or "coming from nowhere." The orthodox folk scene struggled to follow what he was doing; some were reminded of the young Bob Dylan's one-off appearance at Ewan MacColl's deeply traditional Singers Club in 1962.

At a time when most acoustic guitarists were strumming simple chords or fingerpicking basic claw-hammer style, Jansch used the whole guitar. His left hand wandered the neck, producing sounds more polyphonic than chord-based. He never used barre chords. He rarely stayed long in any one register; he voiced high notes against low open strings, hammered on with great force, and pulled and snapped the strings in a manner we associate more with funky bassists. One can *start* by comparing his method to orthodox classical playing but classical guitarists don't use those bends and pulls, those percussive snaps and slurs that Jansch took from country blues. Nor do they hit the strings so hard their instrument needs retuning after every number. Jansch's playing, often subtly modal, is instantly recognizable for its unusual voicings, syncopated timing, and general sense of motion. On or offstage he created his own space, although the nonchalant, uncommunicative exterior concealed a dry wit. Songwriter Martin Stephenson remembers touring with Bert in the 1990s: "In the dressing room, he'd get all these high-end luthiers trying to get him to play their guitars—then he'd wink at me and pull out his old bog standard Yamaha party guitar."[9]

The album title *L.A. Turnaround* has several derivations. In blues and jazz, a turnaround signals the end of a chorus. In post-war country music circles the term was a nickname for Obedrin, an amphetamine that enabled musicians to drive from Nashville—and back again—without sleep. Flight crews also use the term to signify a brief stopover, so possibly it's a pun on all these and on Jansch's own brief migration to Laurel Canyon.

Bert Jansch has influenced generations of acoustic players, but no acoustic guitarist ever inspired so many *electric* guitarists. More than Davey Graham, more than John Fahey, or Sandy Bull—and more like jazz guitarists Charlie Christian and Wes Montgomery—Jansch has made an oblique but powerful mark on mainstream rock 'n' roll. He stands alongside Maybelle Carter and Sister Rosetta Tharpe both as a stylist and a legend.

John Perry is the author of *Electric Ladyland* (#8).

CHAPTER 24
THE CARS' *CANDY-O* (1979)
Susan Fast

In the Beach Boys' 1964 song "Fun, Fun, Fun," a kick-ass, adventure-seeking girl borrows her Daddy's T-Bird on the promise she's going to the library, and instead takes a spin through the local hamburger joint with the radio blasting. She "walks, looks and drives like an ace," which makes other girls hate her and boys "try to catch her" (to no avail). It's all super fun, but her Daddy eventually takes the keys away and all she's left with is the offer of a rescue by one of the guys she presumably rejected.

Fast forward a decade and a half to The Cars' second album *Candy-O* (1979). The Cars were the band that brought American new wave into the mainstream, breaking into the Top 40 singles chart in 1978 with "Just What I Needed," and going on to multi-platinum sales of both their first self-titled album and *Candy-O*, although, upon its release, the latter was considered by many critics a pale comparison—a B-side—next to the extraordinary debut.[1] Among the spate of remarkable bands that began to define new wave in the late 1970s (Talking Heads, Blondie, The B-52's, The Knack, XTC, Joe Jackson, and Patti Smith, to name just a few that shaped my personal musical journey at the time), The Cars offered perhaps the most balanced combination of what was considered *avant-garde* and straight-ahead rock.[2] Taking their cue from punk, these bands rejected rock excess and embraced early rock 'n' roll, but, unlike punk, reveled in the craft of songwriting and skilled musicianship, to varying degrees infusing the music with new sounds made possible by recording and instrument technology (especially synthesizers) and the dark, art-house musings of artists like Kraftwerk and Bowie, and lacing it with a healthy dose of irony that was mostly conveyed through a stilted, emotionally-detached delivery. The Cars were comprised of veteran musicians—Ric Ocasek and Benjamin Orr, co-founders of the group, were into their 30s by the time the first Cars' album was released—all of them ace technicians. Driven by Ocasek's quirky songwriting, Elliott Easton's pristine, compact guitar solos, Greg Hawkes's Barnum and Bailey synthesizers weaving in and out of the texture, David Robinson's metronomic drumming, and Benjamin Orr's inventive bass lines and beautiful baritone ("the perfect combination of fire and ice" as one commentator on YouTube describes it), the group crafted spectacularly fresh-sounding music. They updated and twisted around old rock 'n' roll tropes like the one in "Fun, Fun, Fun" for a new era that had new views of women's empowerment, *sans* Daddy, *sans* male rescue, driven forward by the second wave of feminism that blossomed between the release of "Fun, Fun, Fun" and *Candy-O*.

OK: bringing up "women's empowerment" in the same breath as The Cars might seem like a stretch, but, among other reasons, it was the confidence and agency of the woman depicted on *Candy-O* that made me love this album when it first came out and what draws me to it even more powerfully now—more than the "A-side" debut album, which critics and many fans have often preferred. The debut album offers a collection of mostly unrelated songs—it's sometimes referred to as a "greatest hits" record—while *Candy-O* offers not only more refined production values and songwriting, but a narrative thread. I've always understood the Alberto Vargas album cover image, the name of the record, and the woman in the lyrics as one and the same, her songs ("Let's Go," "Candy-O," "Night Spots," and "Dangerous Type," in particular) framed by muscular, guitar-driven, up-tempo music that drives her "lust for kicks," her flippancy, freedom, and pursuit of pleasure, sexual and otherwise. Although a character drawn by men, she has more than a little in common with Madonna, who would appear on the scene only a few years later and revolutionize the public expression of sexual power, pleasure, and freedom for women.

I suspect that the album covers for *Candy-O* and *The Cars* were created as part of the band's ironic, new-wave appropriation of rock 'n' roll's blueprint (fast cars + chicks), even as their name is such an appropriation (it has been noted that the name is not of *a particular* car, like a Corvette, Thunderbird, or "little deuce coupe," but of cars, generically, because after all, what does it matter?). But it's always fascinated me that the elements of the blueprint were conflated, so that the *girl* takes the wheel and is in the driver's seat, not a boy with a hot car and hot chick; hence my comparison to "Fun, Fun, Fun," which, despite the controlling presence of Daddy, does the same. The first Cars album cover has the woman at the helm of the wheel—I can almost hear the lyrics to the Beach Boys' song when I look at this photo. She's mischievous, fun-loving, while she simultaneously mocks rock 'n' roll convention. On the Vargas cover to *Candy-O*, the narrative is turned on its head. The girl *possesses* the car, which is reduced to a mere outline so that, in Vargas's characteristic style, nothing competes with her presence, "[a]ll the action t[aking] place in a surreal void that seemed the result of the women's refusal to accept anything on the page that might detract from the viewer's undivided attention to their person."[3] It's worth pausing to reflect on the choice of Vargas—lured out of retirement by drummer David Robinson to create this image. His Candy-O is part of a long lineage of pin-up girls, a genre that has produced "silly caricatures of women that mean to construct their humiliation and passivity as turnons," but that has also "represented the sexualized woman as self-aware, assertive, strong, and independent."[4] The latter is especially true of Vargas's pin-up girls during the time he worked for *Esquire* magazine, before and during the Second World War, and I think Candy-O is an extension of those images.[5] As Maria Buszek has written, his "Vargas girls" during this time "were sexualized yet pointedly active women usurping and clothed in the accoutrements of male power."[6] "Their hypersexual physique and prosaic innuendo shaped them into creatures whose sexuality tended to be more than a little fearsome ... in image and prose, the Vargas Girls were remarkably aggressive about their sexual desire and prowess."[7] Buszek also notes that women comprised a large percentage of *Esquire*'s readership, and that women who read the magazine were regularly featured in its Letter to the Editor section, commenting on the Vargas girls. Similarly, as I have often argued, pop music produced by men is regularly enjoyed by women, the images, lyrics, and music adapted to suit our own purposes.

While the imagery of girls and cars doesn't carry over into the concept or lyrics of the first Cars record, it most certainly does on *Candy-O*, starting, of course, with the title. Candy-O is, again, intended as irony, a reductive, one-dimensional send-up of the beautiful, vacuous girls that rock stars are supposed to desire. But, in fact, she is as kick-ass as the girl in "Fun, Fun, Fun," but, in keeping with the cultural moment, with a more independent sense of rebelliousness. The car is ever-present on this record, a symbol of Candy-O's public presence and dynamism. ("It takes a fast car lady / to lead a double life"; "You ride around in your cadmium car"; "A silly driver kinda of the wall"; for years I also heard "razor lights, assorted cards" as "assorted cars," which in the context of the album seems to make more sense.) In "Let's Go," Candy-O recklessly "drives away with her dim lights on," "doesn't wear her shoes," and "doesn't like to choose." Rather than being offered continued fun only if she goes along with the boy, the boy caves in to *her* whimsy, relenting to *her* mantra, "I like the night life, baby: let's go." She's in control of her sex life, too, telling the boy that she's "holding out," a marvelously archaic expression. In-between songs in which a nearly unglued protagonist yearns for her are those that further depict her as the one with agency, a woman who craves the public sphere, who "keeps her lovers in a penny jar," cries "without blinking a lash," and who'd "like to come in colors," wielding her power over men with a wink and a nod.

Among the many brilliant musical choices made to tell Candy-O's story on this record, the title track, "Candy-O," "Night Spots," and "Dangerous Type" stand out. "Candy-O" and "Night Spots" are busy, driving, with chromatically-inflected riffs that offer a whiff of the exotic in the first and lend to the sense of agitation and unrest in the second. "Candy-O" appears midway through the record (it closed Side A of the vinyl version) and is relentless in its repeated riff, shimmering, dark synthesizer arpeggios, and downbeat articulation of the groove by bass guitar. The busy texture of "Night Spots," including the active bass lines and staccato synthesizer arpeggiations, evokes a risky, wildly exciting dance floor, where Candy-O plays with her hair while guys crawl up to her on their knees. The energy, vibrancy, and chaos, both emotional and physical, of these songs capture Candy-O's allure and power. And despite evoking the classic femme fatale image, the really interesting thing about the T. Rex-inspired "Dangerous Type" is the ultimate elusiveness and fluidity of the object of desire: someone who is known but has never been met; who can be addressed directly, but has no specificity; who is both "you" and "she." Slippery. The outro to this song is about half its total length, repeating the minor-mode chorus over and over in a final lament that eventually engulfs the singer. One gets the sense that, while he fades away, Candy-O carries on, unscathed.

In his review of the reissue of another Cars album (1981's *Shake It Up*), Alfred Soto writes that "Ocasek uses irony for poignancy: the more detached his performance, the more moving the scenario."[8] This so beautifully captures not only Ocasek's, but co-lead singer Orr's style of vocal performance (indeed Orr is often more captivating, more subtle, in this respect) and, indeed, the band's whole aesthetic. One could say the same about The Cars' lyrical and visual minimalism. The detachment and reductiveness distill pop convention down to its essence, as only really skilled musicians with the pop/rock canon at their fingertips could do: think of the clockwork precision of the music—that ultra-crisp drum groove on "Let's Go," the composed guitar solos, packed to the rafters with the whole history of tasty licks, the clipped phrasing of the vocal delivery. Perhaps because of the reductiveness, this scaffolding managed to harbor real emotional vibrancy and was able to convey something meaningful, about romance, pleasure, and women at the dawn of the new wave.

Susan Fast is the author of *Dangerous* (#100). Find her on Twitter @SusanFast3.

CHAPTER 25
IAN DURY AND THE BLOCKHEADS'
LAUGHTER (1980)
Terry Edwards

Ah—that "difficult" third album. It's a funny old record. Funny ha-ha, funny peculiar. The "Scottish" album to use a Julian Cope-ism, coined to describe his own *My Nation Underground* LP when he deemed it as doomed as Macbeth. *Laughter* is riddled with the same self-effacing black humor, consigning it to history as an album without a hit and without even a mother's love, which is totally unmerited and unfair. The problem is that it simply isn't an easy listen, but if you can steel yourself against the stench of much of the subject matter and the band-busting circumstances under which it was written and recorded, you'll be rewarded with getting to know and love a truly exceptional record.

It had me from the off as it features a lot of Davey Payne's excellent left-field sax solos, some supreme wordplay, and plenty of industrial language. The latter often masks the seriousness within, treating life as a joke. Many a true word spoken in jest. Album closer "Fucking Ada" displays this best with its "moments of sadness, moments of guilt—stains on the memory, stains on the quilt" where regret is piled upon regret, but the refrain of "Fucking Ada" is belted out at the top of the Blockheads' voices to drown out the voices in Dury's head. In fact, it's belted out seventy-two times in the entire song. Go ahead, count them. "Can't seem to wash the blood off your hands however hard you try. We're all whistling past the graveyard."

The Blockheads are an exceptionally funky band and this explains the uplifting atmosphere permeating this album of love and regret, optimism and wistfulness. Opener "Sueperman's Big Sister"—willfully misspelt to head off any heavy-handed litigious behavior by DC Comics—is a joyous love song, complete with soaring strings arranged by maestro Ivor Raymonde (father of Simon Raymonde, head honcho of Bella Union Records and member of Cocteau Twins) who, along with Ray Cooper's prominent percussion, gets hands clapping and toes tapping. Raymonde's strings bookend the album, by the way, the good cop to the aforementioned bad cop known as Ada. Although I play *Laughter* on heavy rotation regularly, it wasn't until I did some truly intensive listening that I noticed a particular aspect to the groove. There are almost no drum fills on the entire record. Aside from a roll or upbeat at the top of songs, Charlie Charles hardly touches a tom-tom—not to signal a move from verse to chorus nor to telegraph the end of a song. On paper this would appear to be a blueprint for motorik/krautrock beats (amusing, given that one song on the album ironically suggests that we "invite the

Germans home for tea," hinting that it would go against the grain), yet the overall effect isn't of a drum machine as you might expect—it simply grooves. Wonderful.

Side Two's opener is equally positive, but the good vibes are tempered with silliness to mask the embarrassment of an unabashed love-lyric—"You're a darling and I love you"—followed by the refrain "Take your elbow out of the soup, you're sitting on the kittens," but when it's so damn catchy and fun who cares? To be simple and wise, indeed. But no sooner has Dury cuddled you with his charm, he's crippled with nerves again. It's "Delusions of Grandeur" on Side One and "Uncoolahol" on Side Two. Let's take the latter first. It's no great secret that Dury was partial to a drink and other recreational asides. The non-album single precursing *Laughter* was *I Want to Be Straight*, a tongue-in-cheek manifesto in praise of all things wholesome as an antidote to a life of self-medication. "Uncoolahol" seems to rant about others' behavior as those losing all sense of reason, humor, and style aren't specified. Dury doesn't own up to splashing noxious liquids everywhere, but, given that the song is in good company with others here where self-loathing and regret are largely the order of the day, you twig pretty soon that the finger-pointing is homebased.

Given that the album was written in the wake of punk rock in a climate of anti-pop stardom in the left-field/independent quarter, "Delusions of Grandeur" is a timely self-effacing dig at public notoriety, something Dury seemed to both crave and despise. He wrote exceptional material most of the time, naturally wanted recognition for it, but also needed to keep his feet on the ground and be "normal"—whatever that means—something that is difficult enough for a non-disabled person, but also an aspiration for a polio survivor, whatever their chosen job and lifestyle. With no lyric sheet provided with the LP, I misheard a couple of lines on this tune. I always thought he was "polite to the punters and sweet to the press," but according to Jemima Dury's wonderful and exhaustive book of her father's lyrics, *Hello Sausages*, it's "street to the press."[1] And I always thought there was a dig at the record label, too—"Stiff may hype me up the charts." It's "stiff me, hype up the charts." Still, I can always sing my own version in my head.

Given that the band's greatest hits were what's known as "Shopping List Songs," that genre is in short supply on *Laughter*. The closest we get is "Dance of the Crackpots," containing the delightful tongue-twister "from Rosemary Clooney to Jerry Lee Looney, from Debussy to Thelonious Monk," swiftly followed by "Over the Points," a spoken-word paean to rail travel narrated from the locomotives' point of view. The driving rhythms are a natural progression from the previous "dance" track—featuring a remarkable performance by tap-dance virtuoso Will Gaines (reminding me of my grandmother's 78s of Fred and Adele Astaire)—both tunes co-written by guitarist Johnny Turnbull, bringing us neatly onto how *Laughter* neatly comprises two well-matched sides of six tunes. The subject matter pulls and pushes, Dury's co-writers chop and change and the moods and tempi ebb and flow, yet the album remains homogenous throughout, which I attribute to the mastery of The Blockheads and the way in which they overcame the challenges of Chaz Jankel's departure, Wilko Johnson's arrival, and Dury's temperament.

A band swiftly becomes a gang, one way or another. The Blockheads were the union of several camps that became a single force to be reckoned with. Dury and saxophonist

Davey Payne played together for years in Kilburn and The High Roads. Co-writer of much of Dury's solo material, Chaz Jankel met Dury just as the Kilburns reached the end of the road. The remaining members—Charlie Charles, Mickey Gallagher, Johnny Turnbull, and Norman Watt-Roy—comprised Loving Awareness, a studio-based outfit who'd become a brotherhood. These three strands became enmeshed after initial tours promoting *New Boots and Panties* and the chart successes of "Hit Me with Your Rhythm Stick" and "Reasons to Be Cheerful Pt. 3." Follow-up album *Do It Yourself* was relentlessly toured, too, after which Dury went on sabbatical and the tightest, funkiest gang of musicians in the United Kingdom decided to pen an album in their own right.

Will Birch, erstwhile member of Essex-based band The Kursaal Flyers, wrote the sleeve notes for the 2004 reissue of *Laughter*, documenting the way Dury usurped The Blockheads' recording sessions, turning their collective efforts into a cohesive Ian Dury and The Blockheads album. Disc Two of the reissue contains the pre-Dury versions of most of the tunes on the final album. It's an interesting gander into the creative process. Most of the material was fully formed, some tunes needed a "short back and sides," and some were left by the wayside, but for once it's great to have bonus material which isn't make-weight or "previously unreleasable" as it were. Dury distributed lyrics amongst the individuals in the band to fashion into new songs—the same method as he'd used for *Do It Yourself*—and the sessions took shape. Mickey Gallagher has the most co-writes on the record plus a mysterious omission from one song, "Oh Mr. Peanut," which started life as "Duff 'Em Up & Do 'Em Again (Boogie Woogie)." It's clearly a Gallagher tune, but ends up on the album as a Dury/Johnson song. Mickey told me the song got "Wilko-ized" and became a different entity with only the chords and structure remaining, gallantly allowing the credit to pass to Wilko.

Which brings us neatly to the difference between Blockheads mark 1 and mark 2. Chaz Jankel took a sabbatical after *Do It Yourself* to pursue his career in America and signed a deal with A&M Records, which spawned the Quincy Jones hit *Ai No Corrida*. He was replaced by ex-Dr. Feelgood guitarist Wilko Johnson, who stepped in as covering fire with his trademark machine-gun guitar antics. Well, not so much stepped in as steam-rolled in by Dury who was calling the shots. The resulting overall sound has a different kind of energy: more punk-funk than jazz-funk. The album artwork reflects this, too. *Laughter* has straightforward monochrome photos of the band members (plus soundman Ian Horne), contrasting with the Barney Bubbles cover concepts for *Do It Yourself*, which included black-and-white photos of the touring retinue with wallpaper designs and post-punk graphics. It's a subtler difference than I've intimated, though. The intelligence in the songs is reinforced by the guest appearance of Ornette Coleman sideman Don Cherry on pocket trumpet. Don joined the band for the occasional gig, too. I vividly remember seeing this legend perform with them in London, wearing a Blockheads T-shirt (fitted with blinking lights) and singing along lustily on "Fucking Ada," having played blistering solos throughout the set.

The songs that haunt longest and deepest on this album are the ones that lay open Dury's physical and mental states. "Yes and No (Paula)" relies on troubled repetition indicating a bi-polar mind, muttering away at itself/selves: "You think I'm wrong,

I think / I think you're right." On the face of it an argument between Paul and Paula, but maybe Paul and Paula are the same person. "Hey, Hey Take Me Away" and "Manic Depression (Jimi)" sit side-by-side in the middle of Side Two, representing the album in microcosm. The former recreates Dury's time at Chailey Heritage School, an institution for "crippled" children. A bleak picture, but delivered humorously, swiftly becoming obvious that the wordplay is a veneer—"There's nutters in here who whistle and cheer when they're watching the one-legged race." "Manic Depression (Jimi)" opens with "The mind is a very precious flower, that finds itself a-strangling 'mongst the weeds."

So, the laughter became hollow, reverberating around the minds of band and fans alike. Ian Dury and The Blockheads retired themselves and weren't quite the same again. Tragically it was cancer that reunited them, first to play benefit concerts for drummer Charlie Charles who succumbed in 1990, then six years later when Dury was diagnosed with terminal cancer himself. The Blockheads still play to this day—I count myself blessed to be a deputy for the saxman when he's not available—but they rarely touch upon the subject of *Laughter*. By the way, Dury christened the album *Laughter* when it was a work in progress, to cheer himself up as he was in a really dark place. You know the saying: laughter is the best medicine.

Terry Edwards is the author of *One Step Beyond ...* (#66). Find him at www.terryedwards.co.uk.

CHAPTER 26
FRANKIE ARMSTRONG, BRIAN PEARSON, BLOWZABELLA, AND JON GILLASPIE'S
TAM LIN (1984)
Allan F. Moore

When Ewan MacColl and Bert Lloyd accidentally, it seems, sparked the second English Folk Revival in the 1950s, the motive was less one of simple rescue of the tradition than of its re-employment.[1] MacColl's new songs and Lloyd's revisioning of old scraps were a world away from the activities of the Edwardian and Victorian collectors. And the ideology was reversed: for the First Revival's romantic conservation read the Second's earnest socialism.

Frankie Armstrong and Brian Pearson cut their teeth as singers and thinkers amid MacColl's *Critics Group* of the 1960s and 1970s. While their material extended beyond the rural and maritime mainstays, into the songs of the industrial heartlands, the power of what a song could do in committed hands and voices meant that the extended ballads, many of which were first collected on the Anglo-Scottish border, retained for the revivalists their pedigree as the crowning glory of the tradition. To hear live such a song whose course was familiar, but whose details were ever subject to change, made listening a matter of active engagement rather than passive consumption. And just as the presentation of the song had been rethought, so too would be the presentation of dance, come the 1970s. Blowzabella approached the playing of English traditional dance music with new ears and newly unearthed (initially self-built) instruments. No chording guitars, no jaunty violins, but varieties of wind, percussion, and drone instruments and a penchant for Flemish, Balkan, and French tunes and soundworlds. The collaboration that produced *Tam Lin* was early, unsettled, and unsettling, a risky venture that has spawned nothing, and that vanished like its record label,[2] yet to be unearthed in digital format. Unloved, perhaps unlovely, and ignored: a prime candidate for a mere B-side if ever there was one. Of course, the ballad "Tam Lin," arguably the most potent of the Border Ballads, with its shapeshifting, its Queen of Elfland, its medieval court, and its selfish anti-hero won over by a woman's passion, has no place in contemporary society. Its time is long gone. We have other concerns now.

As if to rub it in, who, at the height of Thatcher's depredations (1984), would dare/would be as commercially inept as to open a vinyl album with nine minutes of unaccompanied solo singing as the outlandish tale of Tam and the Lady Margaret is recounted (and that in abbreviated form), before the entry of some brash nasal whining from a set of grotesque instruments? Embattled the British folk scene may have been by the 1980s, but remnants of the political tone of the revival still surfaced occasionally, although to call Frankie Armstrong a remnant downplays her still commanding contemporary presence.

Tam Lin is effectively a concept album, but of a sort rarely attempted. Eleven new songs, mainly by Pearson and Armstrong, follow the old ballad, each expanding or encircling moments of the ballad's plot and taking them elsewhere, often to matters of very contemporary concern if you can only hear them. What comes across so strongly in these vignettes is sheer unadulterated *commitment* to matters beyond the material; this too has no place in contemporary society ... There's the vitriol of Armstrong's "... I ask whose world we live in where we women are but guests," #MeToo *avant la lettre*, perhaps ("Song of the Second Serving Maid"). There's the deep green unconcern of nature over human affairs ("The Four Seasons," "Earth, Air, Fire, Water"). There's the *jouissant* thrill of immersion in a tale beyond explanation ("The Ride," "In the Garden"). And there's what at first sounds like "entertainment" too, such as the reassuring echoes of Brecht and Weill ("Christmas Lady"). Of course, it's common(-ish) practice now to take old folk songs and rewrite them (can't let that revenue stream go to waste, you know), but this album does so much more than comparable musicians attempt, and with rare potency of vision. For these ears, though, all is held together by two sets of experiences.

Frankie Armstrong's voice ("knock you flat at a hundred paces," as an old mate once said) is angry, impassioned, and not singing for your pleasure. In "The Owl," a paean to the simple quiddity of the natural world and its proceeding, there's the sheer strength, the indomitable presentness of the closing "... the woods remain," despite our actions, it seems. Her voice here thrills, it shrills, it chills. In the ballad, Armstrong seems to present the main characters (Margaret, Tam Lin, the second serving maid, and the queen) from the inside. How she makes this ballad so electric is hard to put into words, but one way is to note how she attacks some vowels. Thus, just before Tam Lin is changed successively into a host of creatures in Margaret's arms, i.e., as we approach the climax whereby Margaret's trust in the face of fear wins him, the Queen of Elfland gave a thrilling cry: "Oh, young Tam Lin's away, away." But from Armstrong's tongue: "[H]oh, [h]young Tam Li-[hi]n's awa-[h]ay, [h]away." It looks awkward, but those interposed *h*s each mark an extra moment of strength expelled from the diaphragm—almost as if Armstrong is blowing us over by the sheer power, energy, and belief of her delivery. Even today, I hesitate to assert such brazen power as acceptable or comfortable in contemporary society. Earlier in the verse, and two verses earlier, she has taken an inordinate amount of time over "she heard the harness ring" and "the stars they blazed like day." There is something special about the melody of this line, in its resolute emphasis on refusing the natural cadence (almost in spite), and at both these points, again, the pure force of Armstrong's delivery is palpable. It is moments like these—not necessarily the most obvious moments to emphasize, for the latter two are incidental to the course of the narrative—which make her conception so chilling, so glorious. But don't read about it, listen to it. As Armstrong herself noted:

> Given that I've sung this more than any other ballad ... it's strange that I find it difficult to know what to say about it ... At its heart there is a mystery and I have no

desire to analyse this away—even were it possible—I simply know that its power lies somewhere in the glorious weaving of words, images, story and tune and in something magical about tales of transformation … Singing it still thrills me.[3]

That's one set. The second proceeds from Blowzabella's Balkan-inspired instrumentarium, which has influenced so many strange reaches of music in the folk tradition these past forty years, and not only in the United Kingdom: Flemish and Macedonian bagpipes; various Renaissance recorders; soprano saxophones; hurdy gurdy and plain fiddle with no vibrato; and shawm, bombarde, musette and bassoons, and the odd drum. So impolite, so lacking in decorum, in convention, but (therefore) so *real*. The subtlety of the playing continually matches the weight of the lyrics. There's the way the melody in the bagpipe (always a monophonic instrument) splits into two at the end of "In the Garden," as if opening the door to a new mode of perception. There's the way the recorders twine about the melody in "The Queen of Air and Darkness," a beautiful sonic metaphor for the way the queen beguiles Tam Lin; after she has lost him, a lone recorder wanders aimlessly to the close. There's the way the bagpipe teeters on the edge of acceptable tuning just as Frankie Armstrong's voice does the same in "Holding Song." There's the sound of danger in the way they both skip along the beam, just about keeping balance. The ballad's shapeshifting sequence becomes in this song a chase of emotions of commitment and anger as *she* nevertheless holds fast to *him*, reaching a positive close in "… maybe we can trust." "Despite everything" one feels like adding. There's the elemental sound of "Earth, Air, Fire, Water," particularly the last two verses—the harshness of the tone of the instruments betokens uncomfortable reality. You don't need a rhythm section to portray emotional force, but denying it too has no place in contemporary society.

So, in those ghastly years from which there's as yet been no U-turning, *Tam Lin* shines as a beacon for a different way of perceiving things, and as I listen back again to the "godmother of the natural voice singing movement" and her assorted train, I glimpse again that seemingly uncultured, anti-"cultured" ("un"?-)reality we all ought to encounter once in a while.

Allan F. Moore is the author of *Aqualung* (#14).

CHAPTER 27
SCRITTI POLITTI'S *CUPID & PSYCHE 85* (1985)
Dan LeRoy

A number of mythological characters with familiar names have stories unfamiliar to many of us. Two such figures are Cupid and Psyche, star-crossed lovers from Greek antiquity. Cupid, sent by a jealous Aphrodite to wound Psyche with an arrow, stabs himself instead and falls for his intended prey. He plots a way to consummate his passion with Psyche each night, darkening the room to mask his identity. But when she discovers him, Cupid flees, sending Psyche on a quest around the globe and even into the underworld to find him again.

Conflating fable and fact is a dangerous game, doubly so when one mixes myth with pop music. Yet it's tempting to consider Green Gartside as Cupid's modern incarnation. The reluctant leader of Scritti Politti achieved the perfect sound and stardom he desired—and then ran from it all, eluding and frustrating those who loved him. It's a tortured analogy, to be sure: Gartside as Cupid, and the heavenly music he helped to create on *Cupid & Psyche 85*—plus the adulation that followed—as the collective Psyche he's tried to outrun. Gartside, one of the most erudite figures in the annals of pop, would likely despise it. But Gartside's Cupid-like ambivalence has long been a subject of fascination, especially to those who know him well. Bob Last, the Scottish punk impresario who managed Scritti during the *Cupid* era, thought the demise of the band came down to "Green's inability to inhabit the archetype of the pop star." "On one level, he wanted to write a pure love song. And on one level, he wanted to be a pop star," reflects Last. "And on another level, he was deeply uneasy and critical about what that meant."[1] That uneasiness kept Scritti's time in the spotlight brief. But the band stood squarely within its glow on *Cupid & Psyche 85*, when Gartside, keyboardist David Gamson, and drummer Fred Maher sculpted pristine pop-soul with a studio fastidiousness equaled only by Steely Dan.

Might there be some truth—even some reproach—in a line Gartside once sang, on the 1988 single "Oh Patti," when the temple of Scritti's Olympian sound was under siege from within, and even Miles Davis's muted trumpet could only bear wistful witness? When he advised: "Don't feel sorry for loverboy / You know he wants the world to love him / And then he goes and spoils it all for love," was Gartside talking about any old loverboy? Or about Cupid? Or about himself?

***

It's a scorching July afternoon in 2006, and heads swivel when Green Gartside strides into the lobby of the Soho Grande. At six feet, six inches, he towers over nearly everyone else at the hotel, but he also possesses that air of not quite belonging that naturally draws the eye. To say Gartside has returned from the wilderness is only slight hyperbole. He's spent the last few years exiled in East London and his native Wales, and has come back bearing a new album. It's a home-brewed affair called *White Bread, Black Beer* in tribute to his "normally appalling" diet. (Gartside's last outing, 1999's *Anomie and Bonhomie*, was preceded by a similar Welsh retreat of nearly a decade.)

Although he recorded it himself in a bedroom, the new songs arrive in that same effortless way Gartside's singles used to drift above the radio waves, too clever to be pure pop and too cool to be R&B. The changes, perhaps, are more cosmetic. Gartside's hair is red now, instead of the frosted blonde once seen on MTV, and he has a beard to match. But he's courtly as ever; at one point he offers to give up his chair to a woman seeking an outlet for her cell phone. "Your need is greater than ours," he remarks.[2]

Yet while he might draw on his considerable social graces to get through this interview, he isn't necessarily enjoying it. In fact, he begins to loosen up only when describing the vow of silence he imposed upon his new band, largely amateurs he met at an East London pub. Like Cupid, the revelation of his identity would spoil it all. "Everybody knew, 'Don't speak to him about Scritti.' Word goes around that you do *not* talk to this man about his past, ever," Gartside insists. He's smiling, but he doesn't seem to be joking. "To this day, we haven't spoken about it."[3]

***

There may be no better explanation of that unspoken past than what David Gamson— the classically-trained American keyboardist who helped Gartside craft Scritti's signature sound, bit by painstaking bit—once revealed, not long after *Cupid & Psyche* debuted. The album had already generated hits: "Wood Beez (Pray Like Aretha Franklin)" and "Absolute" were overseen by R&B icon Arif Mardin, who showed Scritti how crushingly huge beats could coexist with Gartside's delicate vocals and the band's melodies to die for. Meanwhile, "The Word Girl" was a slicker update of the 1982 single "The Sweetest Girl," sublime reggae filled with the same longing and emptiness. Produced by the group, who had learned well at Mardin's elbow, it would be Scritti's biggest UK success. Yet Gamson confessed to *Electronic Soundmaker*'s Pete Phillips that the greatest pleasure of the experience was purely aural. "When you MIDI four DX7s with a DX1, some of the sounds you get are beyond words," Gamson enthused. "Sometimes we'd just stand there and listen to these incredible sounds we were making. We didn't even intend putting them on the tracks, but just to listen to them was a joy."[4]

Gamson has since logged three decades as a producer and songwriter for megastars like Kesha and Kelly Clarkson. If he didn't know how the industry worked then, as a college student who got class credit for producing *Cupid & Psyche 85*, he does now. And he can only look back in wonder at the freedom Scritti received to pursue these castles of perfect sound. "At some point someone at the record company said 'We're not giving you any more money,'" Gamson remembers, "and we were done. Otherwise, we'd probably still be at it."[5]

***

Knowing how the sound of *Cupid & Psyche 85* was achieved makes it more marvelous still. Listen, for example, to Fred Maher describe the way in which each of his drum hits was recorded separately, then run through its own AMS digital delay. "It was nightmarishly difficult," concedes Maher, who now creates content for Digital Theater Systems, a professional audio company. "But that was a point of pride for us."[6]

Musicians noticed. The bright, syncopated funk of *Cupid & Psyche* was rapidly assimilated into the 1980s mainstream, although not even the harder-edged hits of Jam and Lewis, such as Janet Jackson's *Control*, could duplicate it. But when he heard songs like El DeBarge's Top Three smash "Who's Johnny?," Maher thought he discerned the sound of trouble ahead. "Suddenly everything that we had done, all the trouble that we went through on *Cupid & Psyche*, all the painstaking and agonizing tweaking and futzing and solving all kinds of technological problems in the studio—all of a sudden, there's like this quantum leap in technology, and it's like, 'Oh, crap! Everybody can do this now.'"[7]

Yet, while only Scritti could truly do Scritti, the follow-up, 1988's *Provision*, still left the band feeling empty. Maher essentially departed the group early in a two-and-a-half-year studio slog that made Gamson physically ill and Gartside homesick for the wilds of Wales. No one remained to appreciate an album where the funkiest moments made the group's informal philosophy, "Machines groove better than humans," prophetic.

The unexpected happy ending is that Rough Trade, Scritti's original label, has bought back the masters of three Scritti albums, including *Cupid & Psyche 85*, and plans to reissue them. "I can't think of anything Green has ever released that hasn't been of a certain standard," observes Rough Trade founder Geoff Travis, who first signed a fledgling Scritti to his label in the late 1970s. "And that standard is very, very high … I mean, you look at Neil Young, and the last twenty-three records are awful, Neil. What's wrong with you?" asks Travis, chuckling at the question. "What Green has done is very rare."[8]

***

Might the reappearance of *Cupid & Psyche 85* lessen Gartside's ambivalence about his own past? The best advice is not to hold your breath. In the summer of 2018, Green agreed to speak about *Cupid & Psyche* for this chapter. Shortly before the telephone interview, he requested that questions be emailed instead. Remembering that Green once brought prepared notes to a meeting with a reporter, this was hardly surprising. And as summer turned to autumn, and autumn gave way to winter, the answers remained elusive. "Green can be slow to reply," his publicist at Rough Trade apologetically explained. This was hardly surprising, either. It was Green, after all, who once proclaimed "*All* memories are bad."[9]

***

A dozen years ago, in the Soho Grande lobby, Gartside patiently discussed his most successful album. But asking about his Psyches—those who got hooked on Cupid with *Cupid*, and had since haunted online message boards, and even built Scritti-themed websites, to pass the long years between records, trading hopeful rumors about their eventual release—elicited a more pained reply. "I must admit, I never, ever looked at any of that stuff. That would make me incredibly uncomfortable," Gartside confessed. "I don't listen to my own records. The BBC made a documentary about me … an hour-long film. I've never seen it. I don't want to know. I know that it would make me uncomfortable."[10]

To be a music fan can involve heartbreak on any number of levels, from the disappointment of a substandard album to a star who fails to live up to our standards, however unreasonable. It can also occur when someone would rather not acknowledge the genius we think we hear on a favorite record. When someone would rather we simply stopped talking about it, life-changing as we think it may still be. But there can't be a Cupid without a Psyche, nor can there be a Cupid and Psyche without heartbreak. Desire and the struggle to fulfill it—the subjects from the first moments of "The Word Girl," Side One, Track One of *Cupid & Psyche 85*—have always been integral to Scritti Politti's language, and the broader language of pop. Without a pursuer, pop's whole bargain goes wrong, as the increasingly solipsistic state of modern music proves. How many of its figures will demand our attention for thirty days, let alone thirty years? And if there are any, how many of us will *give* them that attention, instead of diffusing it across an increasingly wide and shallow palette of momentary choices?

There aren't enough Cupids like Gartside. Perhaps there aren't enough Psyches like us, either. So don't feel sorry for loverboy. Or for yourself.

Dan LeRoy is the author of *Paul's Boutique* (#30). Follow him on Twitter @danleroy.

CHAPTER 28
NEGATIVLAND'S *ESCAPE FROM NOISE* (1987)
Kembrew McLeod

As a teenage hipster-doofus record-store clerk, I was drawn to the way Negativland held up funhouse mirrors to our media-saturated culture. The San Francisco Bay Area group's collage aesthetic felt like a natural response to that environment, especially because I had grown up in the 1980s listening to hip-hop. Through digital sampling, I had already absorbed the notion that sounds could be liberated from their original sources, but Negativland opened up a new world when it released *Escape from Noise*—eventually leading me to become a media maker and scholar of copyright and collage. While hip-hop's boisterous assault on intellectual property law went multiplatinum, crashing the culture industry's party, Negativland's oeuvre provided an arty aural B-side that also set the stage for remix culture's eventual takeover.

In titling their 1987 album *Escape from Noise*, which was released on the influential indie-punk label SST Records, they were referring to the ubiquitous pop-culture cacophony that blankets us all. But instead of *literally* escaping, living off the technological grid, the group engaged with this brave new world by injecting subversion into the mix. "One of Negativland's artistic obsessions," the group stated in its 1995 book *Fair Use*, "involves the media, itself, as a source and subject for much of our work. We respond (as artists always have) to our environment, an environment increasingly filled with artificial ideas, images, and sounds."[1]

Negativland liberated sonic sources from their original context, just as the Dadaists collaged words and images at the beginning of the twentieth century. But when Negativland released its debut record in 1981, its members were just teens making noise who had little knowledge of the history of appropriation art. "When we were doing early Negativland recordings," said founding member Mark Hosler:

> the television set was mixed in, we played tapes from game shows and interview talk shows, and I'd have a mic outside recording what was going on in our neighborhood. You see, I'm a kid. I've grown up in a media-saturated environment, and I'm just tuned in to it. I was born in 1962; I grew up watching *Captain Kangaroo*, moon landings, zillions of TV ads, the Banana Splits, *M*A*S*H*, and *The Mary Tyler Moore Show*. When I started messing around with sounds, there was no conceptual pretense at all.[2]

This reflects the attitude of a great many artists who have used collage as a tool to create their art. Not many people consciously say to themselves, *I'm going to deconstruct texts from the media barrage in order to undermine the dominant culture's ideology.* They just do it because it feels natural. Future Negativland member Don Joyce—whose initials were, appropriately enough, DJ—began creating sound collages while doing his long-running radio show, *Over the Edge*, which debuted in 1981 at the Berkeley-area station KPFA. Older than the rest of the group and well versed in the history of collage, he played the role of Sonic Elder. "They were a bunch of kids who were making records in their bedroom," Joyce said, "and they were doing a lot of collage musical stuff, collecting sounds. I invited them up to the show, and they brought keyboards and instruments and noise makers and sound generating devices and electronics, and they set it all up and started playing live."[3]

"KPFA had all kinds of reel-to-reels," Hosler recounted, "tape decks and turntables, and auxiliary inputs and mixers, and extra studios with microphones and you could put callers on the air. Immediately, we just started playing four records at once and turning everything backwards, and stopping and starting stuff, and bringing in tape loops."[4] The younger members of Negativland took full advantage of KPFA's equipment, and they soon absorbed Joyce into the group—which led to the creation of their landmark album. "I think that, by 1983, Don was playing live with Negativland onstage," Hosler recalled. "We decided, 'let's all move in together and build a studio in the living room,' and we worked on *Escape from Noise*."[5]

"Negativland had found its 'lead vocalist' without even realizing they were looking for one," the group wrote in a statement on its website soon after Don Joyce's death in 2015, at the age of 71. "It was Don who took the idea of reshaping previously recorded words—in a pre-sampling age—and ran with it to an extent and depth never before heard, and never equaled."[6] For instance, *Escape from Noise* contained the college-radio hit "Christianity Is Stupid," which sampled Rev. Estrus W. Pirkle's sermon about state-sponsored mind-control programs. Pirkle spoke of a dystopian future in which communist prisoner-of-war camps used loudspeakers that repeated "Christianity is stupid, Communism is good," a soundbite that worked perfectly as the hook to an industrial dirge that Negativland augmented with ominous, minimalist guitar riffs.

Spoken-word recordings made by another Christian zealot also provided aural grist for "Michael Jackson," a surreal sonic portrait of 1980s pop culture that reflected the nausea of living in Ronald Reagan's America. Likewise, the remixed soundbites in "Time Zones" capture the Cold War's premillennial anxiety and the possibility of nuclear annihilation—"Do you know how many time zones there are in the Soviet Union? *Eleven*"—all without sounding heavy-handed. However, *Escape from Noise* wasn't entirely composed from found sounds, for it incorporated tracks with traditional musical instruments ("Nesbitt's Lime Soda Song") and electronic compositions ("Car Bomb"). It also included audio contributions from the Church of the Subgenius's Ivan Stang, as well as several notable Bay Area artists who participated in urban field recordings collected by Negativland. For example, the album liner notes state that the Grateful Dead's Mickey Hart and Jerry Garcia played chimes, percussion, mouth sounds, and "processed animals"

(Hart provided Negativland with recordings of insects and animals, treated with various electronic effects, that he specifically made for *Escape from Noise*). Additionally, pop deconstructionists The Residents added hoots and clanging, and toilet-flushing sounds were provided by Dead Kennedy's Jello Biafra. It took a countercultural village to create *Escape from Noise*.

Not long before Negativland's national tour to support the album was to begin, the group's members realized that none of them could afford to take time off from their day jobs. They needed a reason to cancel but not just *any* reason. "One of the band members, Richard Lyons," Joyce recalled, "found this news article in the *New York Times* about a kid, David Brom, who had killed his family in Minnesota with an ax. The story mentioned his parents were very religious."[7] Negativland drafted a press release that suggested the FBI had asked the band to stay home while it investigated what role "Christianity Is Stupid" might have had in the killings.

"What really made the story work," said Hosler, "and what gave it legs was that it was tied into the fears about back-masking and hidden messages in rock music."[8] Every media virus needs a host body to feed on, and the 1980s Satanic Panics carried Negativland's prank far and wide. The California music and culture magazine *BAM* reprinted the press release almost verbatim, and Channel 5, the local CBS affiliate, ran with the story. "Good evening," the news report began. "Topping Nightcast—a possible link between murder and music … Four members of a midwestern family were murdered. The sixteen-year-old son is the prime suspect. Members of the experimental rock group Negativland have been drawn into the case."[9]

Even though the band spent much of the interview with Channel 5 discussing the news media's appetite for the sensational, predictably, none of that made it on air. Viewers were instead treated to the following conjecture: "A Negativland album may have sparked the last family dispute, and in particular, the song 'Christianity Is Stupid' may have been involved."[10] Soon after, the *San Francisco Chronicle* gave Negativland a ring. Because the group's members were growing uneasy about the nature of this attention, they told reporters that the FBI had asked them not to discuss the case. After the *Chronicle* went forward with an article that recycled Negativland's unsubstantiated claims, the group observed: "It's now abundantly clear that a major source for news stories is often other news."[11]

Validation from just one respectable outlet can help grease the wheels for the rapid dissemination of a prank or hoax. "We noticed right away when each new article appeared," Joyce recalled, "that the same errors would pop up."[12] The only exception was the *Village Voice*, which reported on the band's press release with some skepticism. Music critic R. J. Smith and media critic Geoffrey Stokes even went so far as to track down a Negativland member at his job to confirm the story. "I do remember sitting there at the *Voice* processing this story," Smith said two decades later. "I was talking about it with Geoffrey, watching his response, and just thinking it didn't smell right, that it seemed outlandish on the face."[13] Of all the reporters who covered this story, they were the only ones who didn't credulously rehash the original press release and subsequent news reports.

Given that Negativland was already in the habit of taping television and radio broadcasts for its sound collages, the band documented the snowballing story surrounding "Christianity Is Stupid." They remixed and reworked that news coverage to make a concept album, 1989's *Helter Stupid*, which scrutinized the same media outlets that carelessly examined them. It was similar to the tactics employed by the hip-hop group Public Enemy—which happened to release the song "Bring the Noise" in the same year *Escape from Noise* came out—by remixing media coverage about themselves on their own records. In both cases, these groups produced mediated meta-commentaries on the echo chamber we call mass media, calling into question the distinction between truth and fiction, information and spectacle.

Their irreverent mining of popular culture put the group on a collision course with some high-profile music-industry gatekeepers—particularly U2's record label and song publishing company. Negativland's 1991 *U2* single made the mistake of sampling that group's music, the crown jewel in Island Records' multiplatinum crown. More troubling (to Island, at least) was that fragments of U2's music commingled with hilarious, gut-busting moments of tongue-tied obscenity by veteran DJ Casey Kasem, sampled from tapes that were likely smuggled out of Kasem's studio by a disgruntled, abused staff member. "This is *American Top 40*," said the congenial-sounding Kasem, "right here on the radio station you grew up with. Pubic Radio 138—*OH, FUCK!*" Kasem also flubbed his lines in a segment about the aforementioned Irish rock band. "That's the letter U and the numeral 2," the host announced, starting off innocently enough. "The four-man band features Adam Clayton on bass, Larry Mullin on drums, Dave Evans, nicknamed 'The Edge,'" and then Kasem grew agitated. "Wait, this is bullshit. *Nobody cares!* These guys are from England and WHO GIVES A SHIT? Just a lot of wasted names that don't mean DIDDLEY SHIT!"[14]

Negativland's *U2* single was released with little fanfare on SST, but within ten days of its release Island Records and U2's song publisher, Warner-Chappel, served Negativland with a lawsuit—setting off another wave of publicity for the group. "We may not have had a hit single," Hosler has said, "but we had a hit lawsuit!"[15] Although their *U2* release made them infamous, *Escape from Noise* planted the seeds that ensured Negativland would have a disproportionate influence on popular culture, especially for such an under-the-radar band of misfits.

Kembrew McLeod is the author of *Parallel Lines* (#111).

CHAPTER 29
FRANK BLACK'S *FRANK BLACK* (1993)
Zeth Lundy

This is how I see it. In 1992, Charles Thompson had been playing the role of Black Francis professionally for five years. Black Francis was fronting the Pixies—a seminal Boston band that wouldn't be truly appreciated until it was defunct—with some of the most unorthodox songs of sex, religion, outer space, and pop-culture esoterica. There are songs about tattooed tits and sliced-up eyeballs, songs about monkeys that have gone to heaven and redneckers that get us pissed—all served up with anxious, splinter-ridden-pop aplomb. They score some modern rock hits with "Here Comes Your Man" and "Velouria" (both of which buck the band's more abrasive hallmarks), but in general find more success in the United Kingdom than their native United States. For one EP and four LPs, Thompson does the Black Francis thing, oscillating between unhinged shrieks and cutesy croons, while the band weathers underground huzzahs and escalating personnel tensions. The Pixies grasp for the big time with an opening spot on U2's *Zoo TV* tour in 1992, but ultimately the pressure gets to them and they go on hiatus.

Thompson infamously announced the break-up of the Pixies to the press first, and then to the rest of the band—via fax, so the story goes—and tabled the Black Francis persona for the next twelve years. Because this wasn't just about the rigor of the road, or the dynamics of band member relationships, or the pressure to survive as a small fish in a pond of big honkin' rock 'n' rollers. There were other things at stake here. There were other people that Charles Thompson needed to be.

In March 1993, Thompson quickly rebounded with *Frank Black*, the eponymous debut by his new, inverted *nom de rock*, and it's everything that the Pixies were not. Some would call this album an inevitability—that moment when an idiosyncratic indie artist matures, arguably compromises, and makes a big-time legit rock rekkid, aka *sells out*—and sure, there is definitely some truth in those assumptions, but it's not so black and white. It's an opportunity, not just for a creative rebirth as a completely different artist, but to subversively plant those underlying idiosyncrasies into something more welcoming and ready for the big time. For the first time in his career, Black wasn't taking himself so seriously: his intensity, his eccentricity, and his fondness for oddity are all intact on *Frank Black*, but they are dosed with dollops of levity and irreverence: the perfect recipe for a B-side. Here, Black is more playful than even the Pixies' lightest material had hoped to be. It's not an album that anyone asked for or was expecting, and, in the wake of the Pixies' indefinite reunion, is an album disregarded by the masses.

Nevertheless, it remains a definitive statement on turning idiosyncrasy into something universal.

***

Frank Black opens with a ginormous red herring that illustrates the yin/yang of Black's changeling persona. "Los Angeles" kicks the Beach Boys' well-worn *clichés* of California into the far-flung reaches of the outskirts of utopia: to Patagonia, to Moleville, even to the year 2525. "I wanna live in Los Angeles," Black sings cheekily as the song accelerates into hard rock overdrive, "Not the one in Los Angeles." It's an anthem about Los Angeles, but it's not about Los Angeles. Discuss.

"Los Angeles" is the most dramatic example on the record of *Frank Black's* spliced halves: the song moves from super-hard rock juggernaut to blissed-out acoustic dream pop, a sudden move that sums up the Black Francis > Frank Black paradigm shift nicely. In the music video directed by They Might Be Giants' John Flansburgh, Black tools around on a hoverboard with his guitar strapped to his back while a long-haired metal band lampoons the whole concept of "hard rock." (Not exactly dissimilar, perhaps, to Black Francis lampooning rock music with the Pixies', err, "Rock Music," a prophetic nugget consisting entirely of wordless howls.) The wide-open cinematic space conjured up by the song's extended second half/coda is the flipside of the Pixies' claustrophobic modus operandi: here, Frank Black's got nothing but time.

Likewise, the mid-album instrumental "Tossed," featuring a generous helping of saxophone from They Might Be Giants' John Linnell, is like an inverted California surf tune. Evoking winding coastal highways and never-ending Pacific Ocean vistas, "Tossed" celebrates the freedom to jam blissfully for four minutes without having to utter a word.

The big, widescreen sound of the album in general is no doubt due in part to Black's collaboration with Eric Drew Feldman, a multi-instrumentalist with a dream weirdo-rock *résumé*. A member of Captain Beefheart's Magic Band, Fear, and Pere Ubu, Feldman first met Black when Pere Ubu opened for the Pixies; he would join the band in the studio on keyboards for *Trompe le Monde*. *Frank Black* is synth heavy, not in a Toto kind of way, but in the way that lends a lush foundation to each track, not to mention the occasional plastic sci-fi squeal.

Rounding out the record's core trio is Nick Vincent, a drummer who played alongside old-guard royalty like Art Garfunkel, John Fogerty, and Carole King. His boxy, thunderous drums are the album's unsung muscle—not to mention very similar to those of Malcolm Travis, whose power trio, Sugar, debuted six months earlier with a frontman who was also executing a 180-degree turnaround from his critically acclaimed 1980s college-rock group. Bob Mould's artistic rebirth following the disbanding of Hüsker Dü is coincidentally similar to Black's, and both records unknowingly set a tone for the legions of super-power poppers that followed in the 1990s.

To say that Feldman and Vincent play with the confidence of seasoned pros isn't a slight to the Pixies—and anyway, their bag never was the "seasoned pro" kind. Still, the Pixies' Joey Santiago is here, a holdover from that past musical life, throwing around his lead guitar shards and keeping one of *Frank Black's* feet firmly planted in the Pixies' world. But if the Pixies were a cabin, then the Black/Feldman/Vincent team weatherize that cabin with some insulation and new windows. We can wax nostalgic about the drafty, rough-edged cabin, but you know … this cabin upgrade feels pretty nice, y'all.

***

Frank Black hit stores a year and a half after the Pixies' 1991 swan song. Despite being one of the band's best albums, *Trompe le Monde* was also the record to feature the smallest number of identifiable contributions from the band's other creative powerhouse, Kim Deal; some fans deride it as a Frank Black solo album in everything but name, not to mention Exhibit A for how undemocratic the band had become. (Cue Guided by Voices' Robert Pollard, who once opined, "Sometimes I think a band can get over-democratic and when that happens, you can't get anything done."[1]

I had arrived at the Pixies a few years earlier, along with many other soon-to-be fans. In the summer of 1989, I was visiting my grandparents in Portland, Maine. My grandmother and I went to the Maine Mall where I hit up the local cassette emporium (Tape World? Record Town? Strawberries?) and bought two live tapes (the Rolling Stones' *Still Life* and Depeche Mode's *101*) and the Pixies' latest, *Doolittle*. (Even at 11 years old, the Stones tape sounded lame and D.O.A., but Depeche Mode was shockingly new to a kid from the sticks, so it balanced out.) I bought *Doolittle* because I had seen the music video for "Here Comes Your Man" at my grandparents' house that week, and it was a quirky pop confection made explicitly for my ears.

Of course, *Doolittle* as a whole sounds nothing like that one song, and as a result I had a harder time combing through some of the album's darker, thornier moments. (What can I say—I lived a sheltered life!) I kept trying, both with future and past Pixies albums, and I continued to pluck out pop-hued favorites: "Brick Is Red," "Allison," "Motorway to Roswell," "Caribou." When *Frank Black* happened, it took everything I liked about the Pixies and ran with it—even delivering it all with some bright cover art that promised a sunshiney new day. Black hasn't written many lovelier songs than "Places Named After Numbers," which sounds like a tune Burt Bacharach would have written had he spent his formative musical years in clubs like the Rathskeller and the Bat Cave. Likewise, "Two Spaces" is his giddiest offering to date, its infectious melody and insatiable structure matching the weightlessness of its words: "I want to want to be / So high above the weather."

I've always seen the closing trio of "Adda Lee," "Every Time I Go Around Here," and "Don't Ya Rile 'Em" like a string of tunes from *A Hard Day's Night* or the B-side of *Nevermind*. They don't share the idiosyncrasies of some of the other songs on the album, and their straight-ahead composition and all-killer-no-filler delivery creates a feeling of sublime sameness. If the preceding twelve songs have set up an intricate sequence of dominoes, these last three are the rapid, cathartic collapse of the domino chain.

***

So wait, do we classify *Frank Black* as edgy Dad rock? Are we talking about an artist who has ditched confrontational-yet-catchy art rock for something with a warmed-over popist heart? Nah. *Frank Black* isn't the sound of compromise so much as it's the sound of shifting up to the next gear, of shedding a veil of self-seriousness. It's the distance the Clash traveled between "White Riot" and "Train in Vain." It's the contrast between the Rolling Stones, skulking around as rough-and-tumble *artistes dangereux*, while the Beatles were raving up the Shirelles' "Boys" with Ringo on lead vocals. Self-deprecation can be maturity, and maturity needn't be a dirty word.

To the Pixies diehard, however, both Frank Black the singer and *Frank Black* the album exploited Black Francis's freak/weirdo/fringe persona to goofball stature. After all, there he is in the CD booklet's liner notes with a Fu Manchu and kimono, with a (fake?) lizard and trick glasses, with a dang suit and tie—like a real square! On *Frank Black*, there's no "Planet of Sound," no "Tame," no "Rock Music." No barbaric yawp missive hurled over a nervy rhythm section, no assaulting screams, no uncomfortable imagery. Whereas Black Francis once hollered "TAAAAAAAME!" and made it sound ominous and forbidding, now Frank Black blurts "JERK! JERK! JERK!" with a knowing eyewink and tongue planted in cheek.

The "JERK!" song is "Ten Percenter," one of the album's burly riff machines, where Black offers a slightly coded homage to Iggy Pop, an idol who knew a thing or two about straddling the worlds of self-deprecation and dead-seriousness: "I'm trying to be a guy who's hailing from Ann Arbor." Never before had we heard Black Francis sing about something as wonderfully banal as his influences. Here, "I Heard Ramona Sing" preaches about the staying power of formative musical discovery, namely the Ramones. "I heard Ramona sing," Black sings over a stuttering rhythm and major/minor chord fluctuations. "And I heard everything / The speed they're traveling."

For as strange as Black's song structures could be, this album achieves a Zen-like clarity of voice that the Pixies would only obscure. "Adda Lee," a power-pop eulogy for a deceased friend, was described by Black as "a little ditty about a very big thing." Perhaps the most personal moment on the record, it's also tellingly the most simple and direct: "And the lake sings / And the dogs don't." In this way, *Frank Black* doesn't try so hard: streamlined and emotional, laid bare and vulnerable, a transmission from a fellow oddball who's just like the rest of us.

Zeth Lundy is the author of *Songs in the Key of Life* (#42). He tweets @zethlundy.

CHAPTER 30
RODAN'S *RUSTY* (1994)
Michael T. Fournier

There's currency in heaviness. A T-shirt check at any rock show yields culprits: Converge, Neurosis, Sunn O))), Jesu, umpteen others. Bands like this get capital letters: they are "Uncompromising in Their Vision," they are "Terrifying and Pummeling." And nothing against them. Some of their records (and shirts) grace my collections. Based on the popularity of heaviness, I'm surprised there aren't more Rodan fans. The band's lone album *Rusty* is an overlooked, heavy gem.

Granted, the band was short-lived: its first recording was on September 25, 1992, and its final show was on the same date in 1994. During that time it recorded a seven-inch, an LP, some comp tracks, and a session with John Peel. Maybe it's the band's relative lack of output that accounts for its obscurity. Certainly Rodan is heavy, but not in the sense of any of the bands mentioned above. The occasional metallic chug is present, sure, but the LP *Rusty* relies on an emotional heft, bringing listeners to the precipice of comfort and honesty again and again with nary a break. Rodan builds tremendous crests that sometimes peter into nothing, and other times deliver altogether unexpected crescendos saturated with barely discernable vocals, sometimes single, other times from multiple singers. Patterns are briefly established and broken. Ambient noise crashes in the background, adding more disquiet to the proceedings. *Rusty* is not an easy record to listen to.

Rodan hailed from Louisville, Kentucky, a town with an amazing, insular history. Punk, new wave, and hardcore bands like Malignant Growth, Babylon Dance Band, Your Food, Endpoint, and Sunspring lay the groundwork for the town's ever-evolving scene.

The most common point of delineation for Rodan comes in Slint, the mathy quartet whose album *Spiderland* remains one of the most cryptic and haunting albums of the 90s. It's easy to see where these comparisons come from: like Slint, Rodan was steeped in obscurity and apocrypha,[1] folding at what appeared to be its apex, never attracting the attention it deserved during its short lifespan. Rodan's song constructions are complex and challenging, as are Slint's. And heavy.[2] And, like Slint, Rodan is its own thing, despite commonly affixed math-rock/post-rock tags.

***

Rusty was recorded by Bob Weston in Steve Albini's home studio in Chicago. The members of Rodan were starstruck. Weston, after all, was a guy who had played in the

Volcano Suns, and continues to play in Shellac, recording them in the studio owned by the guy from Big Black who recorded Nirvana and Jesus Lizard and umpteen others.

The initial wallop of *Rusty* is in the sequencing of its first side, which reveals the duality of the record as a whole. Intro "Bible Silver Corner" is a beautiful song, full of wistful, sometimes plaintive guitar picking. It evolves in movements like a classical composition,[3] with themes and repetitions and callbacks in its gentle orchestration. Then it's on to "Shiner," the shortest song on the record.

In *The New Analog*, author Damon Krukowski discusses the digital vs. analog paradigm, placing the argument in the context of the new millennium. Digital favors signal, whereas analog favors noise: in a digital context, everything that's not signal tends to be removed, whether the idea is literal (as in using recording tools to remove extraneous sounds) or metaphorical (songs on streaming services being removed both from the context of the albums on which they originally appeared, and from the context of the artist's oeuvre).[4] Krukowski mentions the Beach Boys as an example, providing a list of spots on *Pet Sounds* where the group's flubs can be heard on the final product: the band giving the studio engineer directions, people blowing cues. Similar gaffes can be heard on early Beatles stuff, where the band members don't quite nail their harmonies in otherwise spotless analog performances.[5] As I read Krukowski's book, the Beach Boys made me think back to *Rusty*: Rodan *loved* noise. British group Talk Talk's 1991 album *Laughing Stock* was a touchstone and inspiration. Prior to digging into Rodan, the extent of my knowledge about Talk Talk was their eponymous 1980s' single—I heard the song playing on a satellite radio 1980s' station in a bar just last week. With a bit of knowledge, though, the connection makes sense.

I interviewed Rodan guitarist/singer Jason Noble before his untimely passing in 2013. He said Rodan wanted to "establish a mood," claiming *Laughing Stock* as inspiration. For that record, Talk Talk singer Mark Hollis and drummer Lee Harris gathered musicians together in a room and improvised for hours, whittling the sessions down to an album-length composition. Throughout *Rusty*, members of Rodan are busy creating a mood by creating chaos. Listen in the background: unexpected crashes and clamor. "There are just moments," Noble said, "where there's stuff happening, where it might be one of the bandmates in the room making stuff happen."[6] Heavy noise, in other words—not signal—to create atmosphere. The specific atmosphere in *Rusty* is claustrophobic and harrowing. Throughout the album, the band calls back to its opening, causing listeners to remember the relative calm of the beginning. Over time, the effect is nightmarish: listeners realize they're mired in the proceedings, but can't wake up. The only way out is through.

According to Noble, the sequencing was very much an attempt to emphasize the dynamic sides of the band. "I think it was very conscious that we would have the extremes on the front side of the record," he said.[7] Indeed, "Shiner" is the fastest song on the album—and its speed was an uncharacteristic side effect of environment. Because the band was in Albini's studio, recording with Weston, they were full of edginess, and, according to Noble, played the song way faster than usual as a result. A quick look around YouTube confirms this—other performances of the song[8] don't contain the same nervy energy as captured on the album.

"Shiner" hints at the precision and mathy changes to be found in later songs. Rodan stops on a dime for the "pop pop!" part—the bridge?—which comes about two-thirds of the way through the song. These tendencies come to the fore in the short album's centerpiece, "The Everyday World of Bodies," a distillation of everything in the first two songs on the album—if, that is, an 11.5-minute opus can be called a distillation. Fans of heavy stuff will find familiar signifiers to start the song: guitar chug and palm mutes form the first movement, before screamed male vocals kick in. Then, amidst harmonics and single picked notes, bass player Tara Jane O'Neill doubles the spoken vocals which outline—what?

"Everyday" has always been a difficult listen, and the band does what it can to create obfuscating layers. From the start, the word "bodies" could refer to corpses as much as corporeal concerns, alluding to ominous violence. The song's fractured narrative gestures towards the literal with mentions of trains—the classic metaphor for sex—and certainly the song's lyrics detail a sexual situation. The most memorable part of the song—and the easiest to sing along to in the car—is the repeating "come on come!" bit, punctuated by a flurry of fills by drummer Kevin Coultas. But singing along equates to cheering on some kind of dysfunction—or becoming implicit in it. Is this song just about sex? Why is the lyrical "you" kneeling, sick, in the bathroom?

Amidst Drive Like Jehu-esque guitar slides, O'Neill's vocals disappear, adding to the song's disease—but she reappears, as does the "come on come!" bit and the song's opening theme of rain. And there are mistakes in the song, performed live in the studio, which add to its overall creepiness (and noise). These flubs are no surprise in a song so brazenly technical. According to Noble, the band's songwriting process centered on "what's gonna be fun to play, which is not what people probably first think about when they think about the stuff … it was doing something that would push us."[9] By pushing as hard as they did, incorporating difficult musicianship, and leaving room for interpretation, "Bodies" continues to be a masterpiece of mood, tone, and math.

Side B showcases Tara Jane O'Neill's vocals and continues the harrowing tone of Side A, focusing on childhood trauma and nightmares. "Jungle Jim" quickly descends into nightmare territory, with off-kilter lullaby veering into a pummeling riff. A favorite toy becomes something more sinister, evoking Stephen King-like imagery that is also found in O'Neill's "Toothfairy Retribution Manifesto." In that song, the album's closer, a child (perhaps the same one from "Jungle Jim") leaves the playground holding "a handful of teeth." The titular tooth fairy, though, is not benevolent. It's a grotesque thing, all black feathers and joints that make eerie sounds as it crawls across the floor. The narrator thinks about all those who have wronged her, and how great it would be to be paid by the piece for her misery.

Sandwiched in the middle of O'Neill's duo is "Gauge," a song about drug abuse, which shares the same nightmarish quality as its bookends (and the rest of the album). Once established by Side A, the second side reinforces the blurred line between reality and nightmare, both with its lyrics and arrangements. In "Gauge," dual male/female vox trade lilting lullaby lines. But sleep is full of terror, emphasized by alternately precise and sloppy lurching arrangements and background noise. After repeated listens, it's easy to loop "Gauge" back to "The Everyday World of Bodies," where someone lies sick on the bathroom floor.

The nightmarish quality of Side B offers something resembling hope: maybe the first side of the album was all a dream, a nightmarish distortion. It's pretty to think so. But in such an unrelentingly bleak record, little hope of escape seems possible. The sleeping pills of "Gauge" are the only way to escape an endless cycle of trauma, and, as evidenced in "Bodies," they are no escape at all. Rodan doesn't let us off the hook so easily.

***

Rodan's lone album stands up to scrutiny, and remains a rewarding—though harrowing—listen. With such an intensity, it's no surprise the band's lifespan was so short. According to Jason Noble, there was no catastrophe or calamity that caused the band to break up—after a point, he says, it "didn't feel right" to continue.

Jason Noble died of synovial sarcoma in August 2012. Original drummer Jon Cook, later of Crain, passed away in February 2013. Touch and Go Records released *Fifteen Quiet Years* following these two untimely passings. It collects demos, alternate takes, and songs from the band's Peel sessions.[10] These recordings are fascinating and vital throughout. But whether intended or not, the odds 'n' sods serve as a reminder of the greatness of *Rusty*. Rodan's creepy cohesion and commitment were never stronger than when the band recorded in Chicago.

Michael T. Fournier is the author of *Double Nickels on the Dime* (#45). Find him at michaeltfournier.org.

CHAPTER 31
KENICKIE'S *AT THE CLUB* (1997)
Emily Mackay

Well, do you want to sell records or not? It's a question that's dogged popular music ever since there were records to sell. The idea of "selling out" as a sin or a subversion was codified in the punk era, but reached its crisis in the 1990s as grunge crossed over to the radio-friendly, unit-shifting mainstream. The ascent was documented in the film *1991: The Year Punk Broke*, the crash three years later in Kurt Cobain's suicide note: "all the warnings from the punk rock 101 courses over the years [have] proven to be very true."[1]

But Britpop, wayward descendant of punk rock and 1980s indie, was not deterred. Over the next couple of years, it would hit its commercial peak, with Oasis' *Definitely Maybe* becoming the fastest-selling debut album in UK history in August 1994, overtaken by Elastica's eponymous debut in March 1995.

Meanwhile, in Sunderland, north-east England, Pete Dale, inspired by the indie underground and the DIY culture of riot grrrl, had set up an arts organization called Slampt in 1992 with then-girlfriend Rachel Holborow. At a Slampt gig in summer 1994, they came across two smart, witty, young women. One of them, Lauren Gofton, was the sister of Pete Gofton of local band Bone. She'd been friends with Marie Nixon, Bone's new guitarist and her fellow St. Anthony's Girls Catholic School pupil, since they were 6. Three weeks later, she posted Slampt a cassette tape entitled *Uglification* that she, Pete, Nixon, and their schoolfriend Emma Jackson had recorded under the name Kenickie.

The nine songs were rackety, idiosyncratic, hilarious. Three more tapes followed: *The Janet Ellis Conspiracy*, *Glamour for the Criminally Insane*, and *Return to Shrimp Valley*. Kenickie, which Lauren described in Slampt fanzine *Fast Connection* as "the phenomenological reconstruction of debutante life in post-industrial Sunderland,"[2] became Slampt's darlings.

In June 1995, Kenickie released *Catsuit City*, an eight-song EP with sleeve artwork by Lauren Gofton that depicted the band as cat-headed, shade-wearing secret agents: Marie Du Santiago, Emmy-Kate Montrose, Johnny X, and Lauren Laverne (Gofton). The seven-inch picked up excitable reviews in *Melody Maker*[3] ("the very essence of pop") and *NME* ("unnervingly bold 'n' bitchy blasts of post-riot grrrl petulance"[4]), got them a Peel session, and pricked up A&R ears—attention that soon resulted in tension with Slampt.

In the contemporary film *Slamptumentary: 1995, The Year Punk Got Fixed*,[5] Holborow, folding fanzines at the kitchen table, says: "One of the problems with being involved in putting out records is that people suddenly start thinking 'Ooh, we could be famous!', and I really hate people that want to be famous." "We did sort of sacrifice their principles," Laverne counters, "but that was their principles and not ours …"

Things soured even more after Kenickie recorded the "Skillex" single for Fierce Panda, a London label set up by *NME* journalists John Harris, Paul Moody, and Simon Williams. The Laverne-penned lead track, "Come Out 2Nite," established their core sound: girl-group harmonies and handclaps roughed up with glammy, lo-fi punk. To Slampt, it was betrayal.

A split tape that Pete Gofton and Laverne's side-project Muchos Gratsias had recorded with Dale and Holborow's Science Fiction subsequently found itself titled, on the Science Fiction side, *Fuck Sellouts up the Arse*. Holborow wrote a fiery column in *Fast Connection*: "If you are planning on using an indie to give you 'hip credibility' and then scarpering as soon as a major offers a deal then you can fuck off."[6] In it, she also describes her new tattoo, which reads: VIVA LA PUNKA; Dale had an identical one. "I can now see at the age of 24, I was naive," Dale says. "We had this vision, after Nirvana and riot grrrl, that there should be a return to an indie-alternative-DIY underground … and we thought Kenickie could be standard-bearers for that."[7]

In a *Melody Maker* feature, the band hit back, calling Dale and Holborow patronizing, comparing them to missionaries and implying that Slampt was bankrolled by Jonathan Holborow, editor of the *Mail on Sunday* and Rachel's father. This was not true, and the *Maker* had to print a correction after an irate call from Holborow Sr.

Catsuit City had meanwhile found its way to Saint Etienne's Bob Stanley. He and his bandmate Pete Wiggs had been approached that year by EMI to run a subsidiary. At the time, faux-indie imprints on majors were the object of some scorn in the music press, so the pair named their venture Emidisc—not just after EMI's historical test-pressing label, but to make its nature totally transparent. There was another strand of 1990s thought that recast selling out as a positive, even a moral imperative, against the exclusive elitism of the indie underground. If you want to get your message out, reasoned Britpop's big beasts (and the stranger creatures the majors netted along with them), don't you want as many people to hear it as possible? "Who says there's anything wrong with selling out?" Laverne asks in *Slamptumentary*. "We're just out for a laugh." "And we're prepared to take you with us," adds Nixon.

Kenickie's first Emidisc release, "Punka"—a clear reference to Dale and Holborow— took the shout-and-response riot grrrl template used by many Slampt bands and turned it back at them. "P-U-N-K-A, underground cliché," sang Laverne, deadpan. "My one wish is to be as punk as you when I grow up / If punkas ever do grow up."

"Mistakes were made on both sides," says Pete Gofton now, wryly, of the Slampt spat. "But in terms of the band, I wouldn't do anything different." To Kenickie, he argues, the selling out/staying pure binary just didn't seem relevant. "A lot of the records I listened to were anti-mainstream. But at the same time, Nirvana and Sonic Youth were on Geffen, and so was Beck, and most of the music you knew about, you read about in the *Melody*

Maker."[8] "If we hadn't signed to a major label, we would have all gone to a university," says Emma Jackson. "It was like, 'let's just take this as far as we can.'"[9]

That decision benefited many young ears and minds, many more so than if they'd stayed on Slampt. Britpop was predominantly white and male, and Kenickie experienced its share of industry sexism: reviews were sexualized, sound men were difficult, roadies assumed they were groupies when they supported the Ramones at Brixton. They were offered an *NME* cover, but on the condition that they would strip and be painted gold in a replica of a 1993 Manic Street Preachers shoot. Nonetheless, they complicated the dominant narrative: a young, predominantly female band whose members were fearless, funny, fabulous, and bracingly matter-of-fact about it. "We're just telling the truth. We're clever. Deal with it," Laverne said.[10]

Embracing the chances that came their way, the members of Kenickie moved to London and, in 1996, headed to Sawmills in Cornwall, most famous as the birthplace of *Definitely Maybe*, to make their major-label debut. Here, with resident engineer John Cornfield overseeing production, they laid down the slashing chords, punk sneer, and sha-la-la-WOOS of "Spies" and the thrashing chords of the out-on-the-town anthem "Nightlife," with its manifesto middle-eight ("We are NOW for your inspiration / Soundtrack to the times / We are YOUNG for your desecration / Destroy what you find!"). The strident Shangri-Las snark-and-response of "In Your Car" distilled the spirit of the session into a brilliantly basic chorus: "YEAH YEAH, YEAH YEAH, YEAH YEAH YEAH!"

Interviewed in *NME* shortly before the release of *At the Club*, as New Labour was about to sweep into power in a landslide election victory, Nixon compared Tony Blair to the "In Your Car" hook. "He's like the thin end of the wedge lodged into the man in the street's ear, and maybe we can use him to prise open his cranium and get some real socialism in there after 18 years of shit!"[11] As for underground purity, she was dismissive: "They call it credibility. It's not, it's rank stupidity." As in pop, so in politics: spoonfuls of entryist sugar to help the medicine go down.

And it was all their own plan: the only "major-label interference" was on "Millionaire Sweeper," which Stanley asked Laverne to re-record and soften the vocal. The song, with its "Be My Baby" drum intro and tale of young pregnancy, is a pure and wistful heartbreaker in contrast to the more bitter yearning of "People We Want," where Laverne snarls sourly, "Well, it's *nice*, to be loved by someone / This love life is taking too long." That latter track was laid down at Moles Studio in Bath, where Kenickie crafted songs with a strange, sweet sadness that shadowed the bright ebullience.

"Come Out 2Nite" and "Classy," recorded at Sawmills, try to dance themselves out of their skins, celebrating the nightlife the band had embraced after moving to London, where they frequented Britpop's biggest scene nightclub, Smashing. The album's title, and the sleeve shot at none-more-1990s hotspot the Atlantic Grill, reflect their commitment to the life-changing power of self-willed glamor. "Where I Was Made," recorded at Moles, is waking up in your clammy flesh the next morning, and learning, reluctantly, to live in it: "The good lord rubbed my face to give it shape / And he formed a callus."

"Robot Song," sung by Nixon, examines emotion with cool distance, shuddering at vulnerable humanity: "I hate the taste of skin / It's terrifying." It's a sullen, looming track, Numan-esque. "Originally, I wanted to write a song about robots because robots are cool," said Nixon. "Then I thought it through, and realised robots don't have such a great time ... In the song, it wants feelings, it gets them, but they drive it mad."[12] "Acetone" closes the record with a rare moment of unbarbed, punchline-free yearning, a deeply alienated love song of bus station seats, sick stains on streets, and elegiac strings.

Balanced between fearless forward momentum, dizzying disorientation, and pure fun, *At the Club*'s poise is perfect, all the more so for being unsustainable, caught at the crest. The album made it to number nine on the charts, but the post-Britpop feeding frenzy that had led major labels to sign bands like Kenickie was already satiated.

Nixon would later say that the one thing EMI did that they hated was re-releasing "Punka" in 1997. Its second run only just scraped into the Top 40—a poor performance for a guitar band by the era's inflated standards. A year later, their second album, *Get In*, with its glitzy but skewed pop and its complicated emotions, failed even more dramatically to deliver the sales EMI expected. At the end of a disillusioned autumn tour, Kenickie split on stage at the London Astoria. "We were Kenickie, a bunch of fuckwits," said Laverne.

Were they? Is theirs a cautionary tale? They didn't stay pure, and they didn't really "make it," either. But Kenickie were everything to those that heard their call. And in many ways, their story is a better illustration of the richness and the pitfalls of that period than the old yarns about Blur and Oasis. "We're on our backs, looking up at the stars," sneers Nixon in "Classy." *At the Club* is the sound of seeing where the rush can take you, a foot in the underground, its head in the clouds, its heart pounding fit to burst.

Emily Mackay is the author of *Homogenic* (#127). Find her at emilymackay.contently. com.

CHAPTER 32
GUY'S *GUY* (1988)
Patrick Rivers

Guy (Music Corporation of America [MCA] 1988) is one of the great hip-hop albums of 1988. It is also one of the great R&B albums from that year. Further, it was the first album-length manifestation from the progenitor of New Jack Swing, an inevitable stylistic merging that remains a foundation of the production and sound of high-profile black music and the amorphous genre of pop music. Dispensing a mouthful of arguable accolades is perhaps excessive, but these positions are stated because considerations of *Guy* are not as prevalent as other seminal 1988 hip-hop recordings. The album is overshadowed by Teddy Riley's work with Michael Jackson and "No Diggity" (Interscope 1996) and by his group BLACKstreet. As such, *Guy* is a B-side that, as the appreciation of Riley's work increases, will get more play.

Enthusiasts of hip-hop history are generally familiar with the concept of a hip-hop golden age that saw maturity in the lyrical, performance, and production aesthetics of hip-hop music. 1988 is commonly marked as the inaugural year of the era.[1] But, for cultural critics, journalists, and scholars that document hip-hop music, there remains a reflex to promote the genre through recordings dominated by a rapper. With the exception of sampled records, hip-hop had spiritual clashes with R&B—many R&B performers and radio programers disparaged hip-hop music until the 1990s, for many years the popular discourse of hip-hop ignored the influence and importance of disco, and the promotion of hyper-aggressive blackness complicated connections to the perceived docile demeanor of 1980s' R&B. Consequently, the twenty- and now thirty-year anniversaries of the heralded year neglect to mention hip-hop-infused R&B such as heard on *Guy*.[2] In a twist to the 2018 run of content about 1988, Stereo Williams published an article specifically about the watershed summer of 1988 when Teddy Riley's New Jack Swing planted its flag.[3] Three months prior, though, the entertainment journalist and documentarian wrote an article that solely profiled rappers from the critical year.[4]

Guy is not a rap album, but it is a hip-hop album. Before Harlem-born musician and producer Teddy Riley crafted the beats for the album, he absorbed local hip-hop aesthetics. By 1987, the sound aesthetics of hip-hop beat-making in New York City were forming into a common practice facilitated by the manipulation of digital samples and resulting in dense rhythmic arrangements of sounds. Riley began his production career after his local R&B teeny bop trio, Kids At Work, failed to gain an audience in the wake of New Edition's popularity. Enticed by the allure of hip-hop, he started hanging around Harlem and the Bronx to learn from and collaborate with rappers. Riley helped to arrange the beat for "The Show" (Reality 1985) by Doug E. Fresh and the Get Fresh Crew, and produced notable 1987 singles by Heavy D & The Boyz, Kool Moe Dee, and The Classical Two with contemporaneous drum machines. Besides sequencing funky bass lines, he exploited the swing parameters of the Oberheim DMX and Korg DDD-1 to distinguish his beats.

Interestingly, Riley's success at producing rap and the unnecessary walls erected between genres almost kept the young producer from R&B music. "I didn't want to do R&B because the first record I made R&B, it flopped. It was with a group called Kids At Work," explains Riley in a 2018 interview.[5] In the same interview, he credited singer Keith Sweat for persuading him to employ his production style in the service of expanding the sound of R&B. Riley paraphrased Sweat's proposition: "If you just play the church chords and put that with the hip-hop beats we'll come out with something dope." The 18-year-old Riley agreed, and when Sweat called two days later, the beat for "I Want Her" (Elektra 1987) was waiting for him. The song was the debut hit for Sweat and reinvigorated Riley to take another chance at R&B.

Around the same time—mid-to-late 1987—he creatively reunited with Timmy Gatling, a member of Kids At Work, and they began crafting the music that became *Guy*. Clurel Henderson, the third member of Kids At Work, declined to rejoin the group and released one solo album in 1988. The open spot was offered to Aaron Hall, a Brooklyn-based singer and pianist who worked with Gatling at a department store. As a songwriter and bassist, Gatling was a complement to Riley, and they were young Harlem musicians seeking more from contemporary R&B: "We loved R&B music … but we just wanted it to have a little more edge. We wanted it to define where we were coming from."[6] Acts like Rick James and the Mary Jane Girls were edgy, but Gatling and perhaps other young musicians understood R&B through the adult contemporary, quiet storm-stylings of Anita Baker and/or the post-disco sound of boogie heard in records by Midnight Star.

Performers, songwriters, and producers are acknowledged and appreciated for the creative development of a style of music. But, in several cases, those roles succeeded and gained their acknowledgment because a record company understood their artistic goals and worked to establish a platform for their music to reach an audience. Uptown Records was an ideal home for Guy and Riley's production style. As the profile of hip-hop grew, Uptown became an institution that positioned a collective of producers, singers, rappers, and executives in the vanguard of black R&B expression. In 1987, former rapper and Def Jam Recordings executive Andre Harrell founded Uptown. MCA gave him the imprint following the sales success of his compilation project *Uptown's Kickin' It* (MCA 1986). Ostensibly, Riley's profile grew as his productions populated R&B radio programming and Harrell aspired to have the young producer develop Uptown's sound. "I remember when Andre introduced me to Teddy Riley and was telling me this guy is going to change the game," explains entertainment lawyer Bob Celestin, who served as the first vice president and general manager of Uptown Records; however, continues Celestin, "[Teddy] wanted to be an artist, it wasn't Uptown's decision."[7]

Riley—with Gatling and Hall as Guy—embraced the opportunity to take another shot at being a recording artist and his manager/mentor, Gene Griffin, ensured that it happened. Griffin shepherded the young Riley into the music industry but their relationship dynamic did not always benefit Riley and became a point of contention for Gatling who was displeased with Griffin's role in the decision making for the group. Gatling's discontent resulted in him being replaced by Damian Hall, a drummer and the younger brother of Aaron, but not before the Gatling-included cover photo for *Guy* was selected for the album. Uptown Records did not meddle with Guy's debut album—which was mostly recorded before the band signed to the imprint—and supported what was not yet called New Jack Swing because the combination of R&B and hip-hop sonically communicated Harrell's ethos for the company. According to Celestin, "Uptown for [Harrell] was a certain amount of sexiness and class the company and the artists would exude."[8] Industry executive and manager Jojo Brim, a producer at Uptown in the early 1990s, further describes the meaning of New Jack Swing:

> It was upwardly mobile. It was aspirational and inspirational. And that's what a lot of us were. We were humble in our means—none of us had silver spoons—but we weren't the desperate, like ghetto, like "everybody gotta die," from the 'hood [people]. We weren't that. We wanted something more. New Jack Swing sonically represented that more, and the artists that went along with it spoke to that.[9]

In 1984, Grandmaster Flash and the Furious Five member Melle Mel famously rapped the introduction to Chaka Khan's hit record "I Feel for You" (Warner Bros.), and in 1988 Midnight Star released the single "Don't Rock the Boat" (Solar) featuring rapper Ecstasy from the group Whodini. These records fused rapped verses onto electro-based R&B tracks, but spiritually lacked the edge Gatling spoke of to represent the young people growing up with hip-hop. In nine months starting in September 1987, Riley-produced records demonstrated how hip-hop aesthetics could be assimilated into R&B and established a formula for a wide-reaching urban black music. Keith Sweat's "I Want Her" and Johnny Kemp's "Just Got Paid" (Columbia 1988) were hit records that forecasted the new wave of R&B.[10]

The 1988 rollout for *Guy* began on April 12 with the single release of "'Round and 'Round (Merry Go 'Round of Love)" and continued on May 31 with "Groove Me." The first single begins with some sung studio chatter from Riley ("yeeeaaaaay"). After he utters "kick it," the kick and snare drum attacks puncture through the speakers (or headphones), introducing a percussive decibel level comparable to the power of Run-D.M.C. and Public Enemy recordings.[11] The bassline for "'Round and 'Round" is reminiscent of Michael Jackson's "Thriller" (Epic 1983) but is performed with the thick and gritty synthesizer bass heard on Bobby Brown's "My Prerogative" (MCA 1988). While bass and drums are essential to R&B aesthetics, they are usually attenuated to promote the main vocal. The sonics of the first single transmitted an aesthetic that distinguished hip-hop recordings at the time. For the second single, Riley further fused hip-hop and R&B with the assistance of the newly released AKAI MPC60, the first in a series of all-in-one drum machine, sampler, and sequencer that continues to define the beat-making practice of hip-hop. Excluding the synthesized bass, "Groove Me" is a sample-based track—once sampled into his MPC60, all the elements of the beat were at Riley's fingertips. Demonstrating Riley's embrace of hip-hop aesthetics, he re-flipped samples from Eric B. & Rakim's seminal single "Eric B. Is President" (4th & Broadway 1986) into the beat for "Groove Me"—particularly popular breaks from "The Champ" (Pama 1968) by the Mohawks and James Brown's "Funky President (People It's Bad)" (Polydor 1974). Lastly, Riley deftly merged the aesthetics of the two genres by sampling the background vocals of the group and triggering them into a twelve-bar blues that ingeniously ends with a turnaround featuring a reversed vocal sample!

Guy was released on June 13, 1988. Besides the first two singles, most of the remaining tracks on the album have persisted on R&B radio stations, been sampled and interpolated by producers, and are staples at family cookouts. Interestingly, despite having some of the funkiest and hardest beats of 1988, the album lacks a rap verse. Uptown Records was affiliated with several rappers, including Heavy D, and Riley was actively producing Kool Moe Dee and Spoonie Gee. While not confirmed, it is reasonable to conclude that Riley intended to release an R&B-vocal-driven album to display the expanse and utility of his hip-hop-based production style. *Guy* is a sonic force comparable to Public Enemy's *It Takes a Nation of Millions*, and, arguably, the former had more influence on commercial popular music. The rhythms, samples, and vocals reflected R&B's past and perhaps provided an indication of hip-hop's future ubiquity—by the 1990s, many hip-hop beats were suited to the lyricism of a rapper or emotive squalling of an R&B singer. *Guy* was part of an aesthetic shift in black music, a full signal to the coming generation of performers and producers that the rules had changed: R&B could be made with samples of R&B.

Patrick Rivers is the co-author of *Uptown Saturday Night* (#125).

CHAPTER 33
SLEEP'S *DOPESMOKER* (2003)
Erik Davis

I'm, like, totally baked right now, at least in spirit, which is where you want your head to be when said head gets slapped upside with *Dopesmoker*, a master arcanum of frankincense-fried stoner rock released by the San Jose metal trio Sleep in 2003. The album is mostly taken up with a single eponymous song, an hour-long, seemingly endless track that rears up like the monolith in *2001: A Space Odyssey*: cosmic, hieratic, a monster of obsidian minimalism. The song's central riff is a thick slither of sublimity that rears up from the tonic to the fourth like a petroleum cobra, hovering there for seeming eons over a time signature you can never quite grok, scrawled as it is in a nameless hand. Then, at a point you can never quite call ahead of time—despite all the opportunities this righteously repetitive song affords—the serpent swallows its tail, the riff falls to the tonic again, and the eternal recurs one more damn(ed) time. When bassist Al Cisneros finally gets around to singing, or growling, sometime after the eight-minute mark, he underscores the ambience of the implacable by sticking to a single pitch, like a grizzled Orthodox cantor too emphatic to bother with melody.

With "Dopesmoker," Sleep sealed the tomb of the very genre—doom metal—that the band was also instrumental in defining. It did this by minting an absolute statement that stands ever-more supreme for having been released in multiple versions under multiple titles—including its earlier 1998 release as "Jerusalem"—and with multiple icons of pothead imagery serving as cover art. These manifold expressions remind us that there is always a metaphysical gap between the absolute and its various incarnations, whether in vinyl, lossy code, or discs of data—in some ways the preferred, push-button format. This distance from the absolute is what makes this otherwise monumental work a B-side. By forcing listeners to imagine the track that mystically connects all these different variations, each concrete instance points beyond itself. So, while there is no definitive version of the song, the slab abides.

And the slab abides because it rests on the two great mysteries we know amidst our certain earthly doom. One of these mysteries is time, and how we are both made of it and unmade by it. But art and spirit also remind us that time is malleable. Even the machinery of mere repetition—turntable, disc drive, or otherwise—engenders all manner of turbulence and stasis, loops and echoes, backwash and sludge. Time is particularly malleable to minds altering their consciousness, or to music altering such minds. Heightened, stretched, robotic, or stilled, time is the unsilly putty of all our sounds and soundings. Volume helps. "Dopesmoker," which can scrape you down to quivering soulstuff if you devote your ears to its hallowed tedium, gives us time to spare, or time to lose. But be warned: its time does not fly.

The other mystery we know on this restless orb is that the alkaloids of certain plants release intoxicating vapors in the human nervous system. Many of these magic plants have, in turn, helped form the experiential crux of mystical religion. The ancient yogis had their soma, Greek philosophers guzzled their *kykeon*, and Amazonian doctors brewed up their nightshades, tryptamines, beta-carbolines.

And then there is cannabis. In its sticky fuzz, its hypnogogic conjurations, its contemplative lethargy, "Dopesmoker" is at once an apotheosis and hypostasis of bud. The first couple of lines of grease-monkey recitative that Cisneros provides are also a ritual protocol, aimed directly at the listener, who is assumed to also be a seeker of sorts:

Drop out of life with bong in hand
Follow the smoke toward the riff filled land.

Perform these gestures of ascetic hedonism, and you will drift into a timeless, hazy holy land. *Jerusalem*. This is not something to believe, let alone something to be entertained by. This is something to practice. All praise cannabis, and all that it has inspired.

Is this blasphemy? Here and elsewhere, including his work with the mighty Om, Cisneros regularly invokes Levantine religiosity. "Dopesmoker" references the Jordan, Zion, the Nazarene, and the Son of the God of Israel. You should not be shocked here, or give in to the faithless temptation to read this as "transgression." Even Sleep's riff progenitors Black Sabbath sang sweetly of Christ at times (perhaps because Christ was the *Christos*, the one anointed with *sweet leaves* and *secret oils*). On the surface, it might seem that Cisneros is simply ignoring the limitations of doctrinal creed in favor of the vibe: the strange scents, glinting images, and stoner beards of Orthodox style. But Cisneros also knows the deeper secret: that the ritual arts of the old faiths—the icons, the precious metals, the ancient modes—*point beyond aesthetics*. Art and music, like cannabis, are not just exotic packaging, at least in these sacred environs. These are *portals*.

Which is not to say that "Dopesmoker" has no need of catechism. The "creed of Hasheeshian" that Cisneros presents in "Dopesmoker" may be a *Dune*-like phantasia of weed-priests and hemp-seed caravans, but it's still a creed, a guide for living. This guide is also more than the product of the stoned imagination, or whatever section of the bookstore stocks "the Chronicle of the Sinsemillian" (probably near *The Silmarillion*). No: the song's "chalices" and "groundations" also allude directly to the heavy-lidded Zion pilots of Rastafari, the most influential cannabis religion in the real world, and certainly in the Babylon of popular music. These are crucial echoes, especially in a metal record made by the usual white boys. For Sleep offers a sacred mode of weed jamming that far transcends the dormboy fetish for the Jamaican herbsmen of yore. "Dopesmoker" is communion.

To truly listen to *Dopesmoker*, to allow its eternity in an hour to change you, you must allow the fumes of its musical chalice to transmute the metal of your own bones. Like a flame, you yourself must blaze. The aim is not just to smoke dope, in other words, but to become another kind of being entirely: a "weedian," a "lungsman," a "marijuanaut." A *dopesmoker*. This is the cannabinoid covenant offered herein, oh wanderer of the wasted.

Erik Davis is the author of *Led Zeppelin IV* (#17). Find him at techgnosis.com.

CHAPTER 34
THE BLOOD BROTHERS' *CRIMES* (2004)
Ethan Hayden

A jittery electronic texture softly materializes, simmering and breaking like an aged smoker trying to speak clearly. Soon, two hard-panned guitars enter, alternating regular but seemingly unintentional noises, together a lurching machine pumping out clouds of black sound. This sick engine then doubles in size, augmenting its bilious rhythm with a pummeling percussive pulse as it speaks in two voices at once, describing a burning world worn ragged by toxic air, a landscape of "cement lawns" and "amputated horizons." It tells of industrial chimneys pointing skyward like middle fingers to a younger generation whose planet has been maliciously desecrated. Resentment over this transgression reaches fever pitch a minute later when the voices scream violently with accusatory abandon: "Thanks for the fucked-up future / We can learn to love misery!"

So begins "Feed Me to the Forest," the opening track on The Blood Brothers' 2004 album *Crimes*, a record which spends much of its thirty-nine-minute duration savagely decrying ethical abominations of all kinds. Fifteen years after its release, the song's apocalyptic desperation seems less exaggerated than prophetic: the intervening time has seen nine of the ten hottest years on record, unprecedented wildfires feeding California to the furnace, and lawsuits against the federal government on behalf of future generations, in an effort to establish a legal right to a non-fucked-up future. But at the heart of *Crimes* is more than just prescient denunciations: the album's abject rage articulated an acute sense of societal dejection, while exposing the obscene double standards of the social unconscious.

Caramel apple corpses singing ...

Crimes was The Blood Brothers' fourth LP, recorded in the wake of the maelstrom that was the Seattle band's prior album: ... *Burn, Piano Island, Burn* (2003). *Burn* was composed in-studio, allowing the band to leisurely sew together an elaborate tapestry of high-tempo screeching frenzies, complex math-rock time changes, and—in a first for the band—songs over four minutes in duration, some of which even ventured into proto-prog extended forms. The result, while a transcendentally relentless listen, turned out to be utterly draining to perform live.

Crimes was approached as a kind of corrective. Many of the album's songs were written and refined on the road, the band embracing practicality and space over dense musical mayhem. But, rather than a "back to basics" approach, *Crimes* was far broader in its stylistic and instrumental palettes than its predecessors. Bassist Morgan Henderson maintained a menagerie of synthesizers, contrabasses, laptops, and accordions, granting some pieces lush textures and others tightly-wound rhythmic configurations. Few songs were orchestrated with hardcore's traditional crusty power chords and D-beat drumming—although "Beautiful Horses," the album's shortest song, came the closest. Instead, there was the top-heavy reggae of "Wolf Party," the darkly casual lounge of "Live at the Apocalypse Cabaret," and the barking carnivalesque of "My First Kiss at the Public Execution." "Peacock Skeleton with Crooked Feathers" is a quasi-samba led by a syncopated Wurlitzer, whose elaborate rhythmic texture is laden with shakers, bongos, and flickering hi-hats courtesy of percussionist Mark Gajadhar.

While such postmodern genre-hopping may seem decadent, *Crimes* was counterintuitively the record in which The Blood Brothers' aesthetic became the most focused. The band's two co-vocalists, Jordan Blilie and Johnny Whitney, had always been an alternating current of full-throated tumult, but here each singer found their way into more circumscribed vocal ranges: Blilie embracing a restrained, menacing lower tessitura; Whitney leaping to stratospheric shrieks. Guitarist Cody Votolato used his instrument not as a vague source of abstract noise, but as a clear articulator of rhythm and harmony, often preferring lean monophonic lines to dense chords, and always foregrounding the physicality of his gestures. Together, the band cohered into a defined diversity, like the sinewy spaciousness of the album's single, "Love Rhymes with Hideous Car Wreck."

The sins are in sound …

Musical arrangements were not the only thing more focused on *Crimes*. In the past, the band's lyrics were a profligately florid field of horrifying but abstract metaphors, dripping with violent adjectives and purple prose. The Blood Brothers' ability to surpass the grotesqueries of occult metal lyrics with extra degrees of flamboyant non-sequitur was always part of the band's campy sass aesthetic; however, on *Crimes* these tools were refined and pointed towards the contemporary political climate. The sinister parade of characters that populated the lyrical landscape—the Peacock, the Scarecrow, the Fifth Horseman—were more easily recognized as avatars of politicians, media personalities, and religious leaders. Written in the wake of the September 11 attacks, the War on Terror, and the corporate media's eager manufacturing of consent for the Iraq War, the album sculpts a nightmarish terrain from the era's anxieties and paranoia.

In the aftermath of the 2016 election, it is easy to forget how unsettling the environment of the Bush years was, but *Crimes* is a stark reminder, painting the cultural id as a dark topography of transgressions, an American redux of *The Garden of Earthly Delights*. We see images of bloodthirsty crowds, hungrily licking their lips as hawkish politicians seduce them with stripteases ("Devastator"). "Teen Heat" condemns the corporate exploitation of sexuality in popular music through the Fifth Horseman, a record executive who "stuffs the radio with singles until it's sick to its stomach," while drooling crowds respond with unconstrained desire: "We want it! We need it!" "Live at the Apocalypse Cabaret" turns its gaze towards religious figures, decrying a litany of horrendous acts including a homophobic murder, a man imprisoning his own daughter, and priests masturbating within the walls of their churches. Throughout the album, the titular crimes are predominantly crimes of corruption, committed by those in positions of power, and gleefully celebrated by society at large. While "My First Kiss at the Public Execution" takes place at the gallows, there is no mention of the offenses of the condemned. Instead, the narration is much more focused on the audience's alarming bloodlust, and one cannot escape the implication that the only crime taking place is the execution itself—the conscience being "choked clean" is that of its spectators—a crime that, like so many on the album, exists with impunity.

The notable exception is "Love Rhymes with Hideous Car Wreck," a morality play in which a man discards his partner for the allure of a younger woman's body, only to meet his karmic retribution in a debilitating car crash. The band's cryptic taunts revel in the Old Testament vengeance, the *schadenfreude* of a punished betrayal. While the song's pseudo-feminist sexual ethics are not without their problems, they do name and condemn some of the darker manifestations of misogyny.

The issues addressed in "Love Rhymes" and the aforementioned "Teen Heat" are representative of The Blood Brothers' move past the more testosterone-fueled traditions of hardcore. This sensibility was no doubt informed by their home state's rich legacy of feminist punk—via riot grrrl and K Records—indeed, *Crimes* producer John Goodmanson had recorded albums for Bikini Kill and Sleater-Kinney. This influence was manifest not just in their lyrics, but musically as well. Blilie's and Whitney's shrill cries were never screams of aggression or dominance, sounding far more like Fay Wray's frightened screeches than the brutish howls of death metal. *Crimes* also saw a continued emphasis—established early in the band's career—on quirky post-punk dance rhythms over macho breakdowns, the band's frenetic spazzcore always more at home on the dance floor than in the pit, as can be clearly heard in the offbeat gyrations of "Trash-Flavored Trash" or the buccaneer boogie of "Celebrator." The band's Bowie-esque glam (marked by tight jeans, colorful bandanas, and the occasional white belt) further undermined masculine hardcore tropes, and, when coupled with Whitney's gender-defying soprano, became the object of tiresome homophobic heckling at shows—the same barbarous groupthink *Crimes* denounced frequently arising at the band's own performances.

I peel the wrapping paper back …

While *Crimes* is an album of judgment, its condemnation is rarely one of self-righteous blamelessness. Throughout the album, there is the distinct sense that *all* are stained by the transgressions being chronicled. Even further, there is a pervasive sense of persecution, as if those ominous caricatures from whose sins the album recoils in horror are *themselves* acting as the arbiters of criminality. This is most evident in the title track, in which, over a tumbling tom-laden beat, the narrators sing of Junk Island, a floating inferno where all of society's rubbish is sent to be incinerated. They speak of being refuse themselves, of being discarded like condom wrappers, and, in the dramatic funeral dirge refrain, they lament: "We're scrapped valentines / We're tangerine rinds / We're crimes, crimes, crimes, crimes, crimes."

This notion of being a crime is significant. The band does not sing of being *criminals*— criminals are sexy and mysterious, like Bonnie and Clyde or the mobsters of early Hollywood. Criminals have personality, ambitions, agency, and even, in many cases, power. Where criminals act in violation of the law, *crimes* are violations themselves. To be a crime is to be one whose very existence is a transgression, to be abject and exiled. Such a sense of exile can be found throughout the album: in "Peacock's" paranoid persecution complex ("Who do you trust when your friends take a match to your front lawn?"), "Celebrator's" terrorized outsider perspective ("I just want to join the party / but the confetti falling is razor sharpened"), or "Beautiful Horses'" taunts of failure ("You're so fucked up, you're a fucking mess!").

In light of this oppressive atmosphere, perhaps the depraved landscape of *Crimes* is not an exaggerated allegory, but rather a direct glimpse into the American unconscious *c.* 2004. At the time the album was recorded, the dominating conservative ideology was predicated on a gatekeeping of morality, family values, and being "tough on crime." *Crimes* rips past this rhetoric, exposing it as a paper-thin veil over the monstrosities of homophobia, racism, and imperialistic xenophobia. Being "tough on crime" was merely a polite euphemism for being tough on those not predisposed with certain racial, sexual, or class privileges. If such euphemisms were the culture's presentable A-side, *Crimes* was the growling B-side, a rhythmic version that skinned off the mellifluous surface to reveal the bleeding, snarling underbelly. With mass incarceration booming under pretenses like the War on Drugs, it became clear only a particularly narrow band of infractions was being punished. As the new decade began, over 100,000 people of color were incarcerated for drug charges while only a single banker was held accountable after the financial crisis. In "Crimes," the band reveals the ghastly realities of this ideology: it is not criminals that are being cast off to Junk Island, but people whose very existence is a crime.

Post-2016, this dark unconscious now seems far less repressed. While The Blood Brothers had to "peel the wrapping paper back" to unmask the latent American id, it is now barely concealed. With the election of the forty-fifth president, American conservatism surrendered its euphemistic claims to moral superiority in favor of explicit demagoguery, making it devastatingly evident that to be of certain race, class, or gender identities is to be a crime, while being a criminal is still safely lucrative.

Ready to explode …

If *Crimes* begins with hot machines pumping away the future, it ends where the exiled labor their futures away: on the chain gang. The album's final track, "Devastator," opens with an amorphous call-and-response led by Whitney's crackling yelps. Soon, the chant blossoms into a work song, accompanied by a tambourine hitting the backbeat like a rain of pick-axes at Parchman Farm. The Devastator is the last in the cavalcade of *Crimes*' burlesque characters, a war profiteer who sees "Neon black corpses, stacked, eclipse the horizon," like Walter Benjamin's angel of history. The song's "war gang hiss" is suddenly interrupted by a fearsome blitzkrieg as Blilie depicts the violent clamor of bayonets over Votolato's jagged asymmetrical rhythm—the retching screams and incessant sonic battery manifesting not only horror at Devastator's atrocities, but a kind of bodily purging of such abject criminality. Fifteen years on, *Crimes*' analysis of the American unconscious seems startlingly prophetic, making its final, cryptic couplet all the more ominous: "Neon black future charging like a bull / with a funeral bouquet ready to explode."

Ethan Hayden is the author of *Sigur Rós's ()* (#99). Find him at ethanhayden.com.

CHAPTER 35
BORIS' *PINK* (2006)
Paula Mejía

One morning in May, right around when the seasons turned, a former flame and I lay in bed on a too-early Saturday, groaning into our respective pillows. A screwdriver sung into the walls, and a bag of leaden weights, slowly dragged across the floor upstairs, had stirred us from sleep (at least, that's what it sounded like). Now we were up. But the thrum made it too loud to have a conversation, and the power tool's uneven sputtering sounds made us burst into laughter every time we looked at each other or started kissing. Eventually I put Boris's 2006 album, *Pink*, on the turntable—as I had many times to counter the noise sputtering around in my own head. Only this time the noise happened to be outside of it.

For their twenty-five-plus years as a band, Boris, a trio hailing from Tokyo, Japan, has played amorphous experimental music, often leaning towards metal and noise, that consistently bares its soul. "This sort of consistent noise is definitely a vital part of the Japanese psyche, and it's been a big influence on us," the band has said. "Noise is a vital part of the Japanese mentality, particularly when making music. Noise is Japanese blues."[1] A collective effort between three musicians named Atsuo, Wata, and Takeshi, Boris is an ever-evolving project that deftly resists any kind of categorization or comparison. Boris frequently releases disparate-sounding albums that at once sound uniquely like Boris while being incomparable to anything on Earth—even themselves. This ranges from a truly grave-sounding doom mainstay called *Amplifier Worship* to an idiosyncratic experiment they forged with the incomparable Merzbow where the two albums were meant to be listened to at once.

Pink exists somewhere in-between. While Boris's *Pink* is a beloved release for many pre-existing fans of the band, it remains critically underrated, especially within the canon of heavy music that's been historically dominated by straight white men. This album became more of a breakout for the band worldwide, despite the fact that it had been heavily ingrained in Japanese heavy rock circles since the mid-1990s and *Akuma No Uta* became a beloved cult work upon its 2003 release. But *Pink* is a testament to the fact that musicians are hardly bound to the trope of near-flawless first albums. As one of Boris's mid-career swings, *Pink* immediately hit its mark—combining Wata's propensity for unleashing unrelenting guitar swells, Atsuo's constant spitfire drumming and singing, and Takeshi's rhythmic prowess—and thrust the band into unknown psychedelic territories. What makes it endlessly listenable is the fact that *Pink*'s emotive weight, no matter how many times you've listened to it, is also impossible to predict.

It's been noted, sometimes critically, that *Pink* is one of Boris's most "listenable" albums. But its ample entry points, sonic diversity, and accessibility only render *Pink* more resonant, both within Boris's discography and in experimental canons alike. For how non-linear and expansive the styles of music are therein, *Pink* resonates with a whole lot of people who each look for varying sounds and ideas whenever they put on a record. Songs such as "Farewell," the opener, are dusted with swathes of delay pedals; a fever dream for ardent shoegazers. The wild, expansive thrums of "Just Abandoned Myself," a sumptuous, eighteen-minute-long reckoning, is a case study for the spatially minded. And the doomsday crawl of "Blackout" is a beckoning to those who don't feel lost by sludge's depth, but instead freed by it. Perhaps there's a metaphor in the liner notes, as Zach Baron noted in *Pitchfork*: "[it] peel[s] apart into small individual squares resembling either Pantone chips or acid tabs ... the implication was surely meant to be ambiguous: Whatever you were looking for, you would find."[2]

Perhaps Boris was looking for something bigger than the sum of its parts when it was recording *Pink*; the band even shed trusted gear in the service of finding sounds in other ways. (One example: after many years, Wata took the Big Muff, one of the biggest-sounding and most pre-eminent distortion pedals made in history, off her pedalboard—which had been in constant rotation before then.) Reflecting on the album a few years later, Atsuo said: "Well, in that madness that was *Pink*, we just got so tired of chasing some kind of cool, rock image. I felt like we were chasing something, it was like we wanted to be something greater. But after all that, we got and have been reflective."[3]

As Nina Corcoran notes in Consequence of Sound, 2006 was also the year that technology and identity began to merge in unprecedented, hyper-personalized ways.[4] Look no further than the language surrounding the self used to market the musical technology commodities of ten-ish years ago: personal and uber-portable iPods, and YouTube (which was emerging both as a platform for viral video and a place of discovery, eventually evolving into a fascinating trove for rare music). This particular cultural moment also coincided with a peculiar shift in how we talked about music with each other. Around then, I felt that it was no longer beyond the pale to admit—and even celebrate—the fact that you liked a lot of different opposing sounds. And sometimes all those songs appeared on the same burned CD. And maybe, much like on *Pink*, these varied styles appeared all on the same album.

But even when setting out to make a massive, throttling album, Boris never seemed to be concerned about forging songs meant to be listened to from nosebleeds. Some of the songs on *Pink* that loom the largest, to me, aren't necessarily the shredders. The guitar rippling through "My Machine," easily the slowest song on the album, also makes it feel like the heaviest one. Listening to it feels not unlike slowly, painfully, releasing an exhale that's been burning a hole in your chest for some time. This is intertwined with an idea that Atsuo brought up in a recent interview with Bandcamp, in which he said that he hopes Boris's music gets "across the diversity of 'heavy'".[5]

Within that radicalization, of carving out new forms of heaviness, lies the idea that some things are just not always pleasurable to listen to, either. "Just Abandoned Myself" is the whirring, noise-driven ride that closes out the album, and it has devastated me as many times as it's delighted me. Still, I turn to it when I'm seeking something that barrels on—a counterbalance—when I need to work through something or see it in another way, or even drown out environmental noise. *Pink* absorbs the full weight of my sadness and my exhilaration, always roaring back, and, in turn, reflecting my own self back to me.

Paula Mejía is the author of *Psychocandy* (#118). Find her at paulamejia.com.

CHAPTER 36
STARS OF THE LID'S *AND THEIR REFINEMENT OF THE DECLINE* (2007)
Walter Holland

The machine says I've played Stars of the Lid's album *And Their Refinement of the Decline* hundreds of times. This would seem to imply that I've listened to the album a healthy amount, but I confess that, while I've *heard* it more times than I can easily count, I've never listened to it. Not once. I'm not sure I could.

For a decade, *And Their Refinement* has been my cherished "writing music," that is to say it's a piece of periodically executed aural code that temporarily generates a kind of alternate consciousness, which might only be to say it's art. Begin: doubled horns an octave apart sustain just five tones in thirty seconds, then a synthesizer creeps in at the edge of sense like a fluorescent light shifting almost imperceptibly from red to blue, completing the implied A-major chord. Isolated percussion, almost accidental. Nearly six minutes of this. Mourning horns, dawn swell, and dusken hush from a laptop computer, near to no movement. Six minutes of this one idea and no other, or, more to the point, this *feeling*, and after those six, 114 more such minutes to go.

The opening track really is called "Dungtitled," and the closing track "December Hunting for Vegetarian Fuckface." There really are strings and a Frenchman. There really is a sort of backhanded tribute to Fulham FC. You really can count every tempo on your fingers.

And Their Refinement approaches the theoretical minimum information density for a work of art that runs twenty minutes longer than *The Princess Bride*, and it might be one of my favorite places in the whole world. Two hours of indispensable yang with no yin; what could be more B-side than that?

The thing about art, "psychedelic" not least, is you have to make time for it (to change)—that is to say, make *headspace*. You can't get a "quick hit" of psychedelia the way you can from, say, a three-minute punk tune or "We Will Rock You" or "The Imperial March" or, for that matter, a national anthem, because psychedelic art is a technology of psychotropism, and change takes time. Think of how pointless *Eraserhead* seems until you give up on the idea of it having a point, or the way the dumbass dude-comedy set pieces in the codlynchian *Southland Tales* cross-reference and interleave until its dreaming starts making the kind of sense that's ... not. Think of how simpleminded a single Bernard Xolotl or Terry Riley track seems, just-pretty-enough elevated to a whole stupid principle of being in the world. But think too of the way you feel after floating down the full length of *In C* or *The Golden Mean*, or the Veneta "Dark Star," the sixty-ninth love song, the Scouring of the Shire, "December Hunting for Vegetarian Fuckface," and yes please know that we're implying or assuming or just gesturing at the following:

1. consciousness is multiple and malleable and crucially *decentered*

2. art criticism's fundamentally a declaration of/by/from/within a consciousness rather than any kind of useful statement about the art in question, really almost always ever

3. accounts of weird experience emerge from a kind of radically shifted private reference frame, a whole other "world" in Nelson Goodman's sense of a world-*version*, so that their irreconcilability to the norms of the dreadful ordinary paycheck-world should be understood not as evidence for their unreality but rather a beige-dull fact about parallel, um, *cosmos*

4. we're striving here to come at art not "for its own sake"—we're all dying by degree and nothing a brain as complex as yours can cook up is ever purely or primarily "for its own sake"—but rather *on its own terms*

5. and I'd like to not *so* much argue as hand wave at you that point #4 is an ethical imperative from which the rest of this chapter flows, hopefully smoothly; but if that doesn't fly, then

6. fuck it, plus cf. points #1–5, *supra*, and #6 most of all.

Now, the duration (or convertibly the spatial extension) of psychedelic art is essential to its working because it needs to be processed in flux, from within a private universe in chaotic motion. It remaps the sensory/cognitive apparatus with which it's meant to be processed; yes, you can lie around for two hours just floating on it, but your changing inner context is in a sense—academics use "in a sense" to mean "none of my claims are verifiable," ha ha ha—the true object of the art's work. "The journey" the hippies go on about, which is why *And Their Refinement*, a pretty void, a work of art perversely empty of apparent musical information and in which every instant feels instantly, almost willfully, forgettable, seems to me a perfect success on its own terms. It creates a world sensible *only* from an internal vantage, and manifests the conditions of possibility of that transformed seeing. Put *slightly* less pretentiously, it teaches you how to hear it, but the lesson only makes sense in the hearing—"hearing" rather than "listening" because (speaking just for myself here) if active musical listening is part patient attention to the moment and part predictive attention to the possible futures that that moment suggests, then *And Their Refinement* perversely resists active listening. There's nothing to listen *to* or even really *for*, unless you're the kind of synth-dweeb who delights in figuring out what gates and envelopes and transforms were applied to a poor defenseless A-major to make *that* sound. It's nearly as boring as academic minimalism, except that the two synth-dweebs in Stars of the Lid have a functioning sense of humor …

But what if that boredom weren't a failure state of such art but rather a provision, a transient phase of its reception? Have you never been joyfully or even ecstatically bored—Sunday noon with a lover over, 200 pages from book's end as concerns multiply but means have not yet begun to gather, visiting for the dozenth time the cursed Impressionist gallery, talking about work during the seventh-inning stretch, watching the commercials for Christ's sake? Forests are boring, plane rides, backrubs, comforting words, weddings, work ... until all of a sudden they aren't, some inner bit flips so hard you can feel it and suddenly your sensorium comes alive and your anxieties (maybe boredom is anxiety, reality-envy: ugh why isn't my world *otherwise*) recede like empty threats. And you're right there with(in) the thing itself.

I do wonder all of a sudden if instead of this album being my "writing music," both the music and the writing might not be components of a ritual whose point is less the work than the headspace that the work creates. And words, even these ones, an epiphenomenon: social manifestation of the working. A magical effect.

And Their Refinement doesn't particularly reward close attention but one of the all-time stupid small but hugely consequential critical fallacies is that Grrrrreat Art is owed a *specific kind of attention*, that "greatness" is depth which inheres in the text rather than the experience. It's just as wrong to approach an album like this looking for "reward" of some sort as it would be to expect a pen pal to reward you for your letter. Work is change, art is a means of effecting change at a distance: the technique of ecstasy as the man said, or of joy, weird melancholy, a laugh, whatever. But those feelings aren't pellets that pop out of your record player when you solve the maze and push play; I suppose the long slow wavy groovy floaty feeling this album tends to create (to afford?) is one facet of an act of cocreation, of *giving* and *presentness*—present mostly in the writing while hearing, for me, though YMM-obviously-V. The work and the music deepen together, in my writing/hearing experience; that deepening takes time, so this music needs to be long and wavy and to fall and rise like breath, so that your own breaths make sense in the hearing and the sense, more so than the breaths themselves, becoming an element of the alternation of your consciousness. This is all to say that if *And Their Refinement* isn't obviously impressive or interesting, neither is a lake, frankly; and then you're in it eyes closed and weightless and all strange creatures beneath and the earth turning, turning, and there you are turning with it. Into something.

Walter Holland is the author of *A Live One* (#109). He tweets @waxbanks.

CHAPTER 37
THE RANGE RATS' *THE RANGE RATS* (2010)
Michael Blair

At the start of the summer of 1985, Fred and Toody Cole piled clothes, guitars, camping gear, and just enough cash for gas and a trip to the casino into their Volkswagen van, pulled out of their home in Clackamas, Oregon, and lit out south toward Nevada. For three months, they would leave everything they'd spent the last several years working on behind—the music shop and general store they'd built from reclaimed wood, their petering-out and now 8-year-old punk band, The Rats, and their three adolescent children. "It was our *first* midlife crisis," Fred remembered years later, and the form it took resembled both a standard married couple's second honeymoon and, like most things with the Coles, the stuff of American myth.[1]

By day, they'd cruise the highway or settle in for gambling sessions, favoring the lottery-style game Keno. By night, they'd play country and western music at taverns and union halls in almost-abandoned mining towns along the Nevada-California border, accompanied only by a primitive Roland drum machine nicknamed "rollie" on account of its brand but also its penchant to maddeningly quicken or inexplicably slow down its beat as it chugged along toward the end of a tune.[2] The crowds, though, didn't care. "It was a big major event for them to hear a live band," Toody recalled.[3] They would play for hours on end for dancing crowds much different from those at Satyricon in Portland. Sometimes people would tip them to play the same song—like Willie Nelson's "Crazy"—over and over again, until the audiences finally got their fill.

They called this new band The Range Rats—a punk band gone to pasture—and while their set up was spartan, the tip jar would become stocked enough by the end of the summer to allow the Coles to ditch the backseat of their van or their tent and rent a room for $60 a week at the Pony Express Motel. In fact, they would eventually record an entire album of original Range Rats songs—a few with a couple of other musicians, a few simply Fred, Toody, and rollie—but the tapes were shelved until 2010, when they were finally released by the Portland-based label Mississippi Records.

The intervening decades were defined by another band fronted by the Coles—the enduring Dead Moon. That band—with Fred and Toody covering guitar, bass, and vocals, and Andrew Loomis on the drums—would release over twenty LPs and singles in just about as many years, tour Europe and the continental United States many times over, and become one of the most fiercely loved rock 'n' roll bands of the last thirty years. In the process, the band members also redefined the meaning of "DIY"—self-recording their albums at home, cutting vinyl using their own mono lathe, and releasing and distributing the records on their own label, Tombstone.

Much has been written about and much more is still to be made of the Dead Moon legacy. It's one filled with all kinds of lore: the mono lathe Fred Cole used to cut their records that had also been used to cut the Kingsmen's classic, "Louie, Louie," and Fred Cole's own musical history that stretched just as far back, as the teenage rocker behind 1960s acts like Deep Soul Cole, the Weeds, and the Lollipop Shoppe. Beyond historical footnotes like these lay the mysterious landscape that arose from their songs, their lyrics, their album covers and logos, and even from their name itself, two syllables plunked down with a kind of prophetic dread. Dead. Moon. This world is riddled with icons pulled from the graveyard of the American West, the product of the imagination of people who are, as the title of the 1991 album puts it, *Stranded in the Mystery Zone*. As other songs and covers remind, such a place can only be called *Destination X*. A place where the crescent moon turns into a skull. Where an unknown passage cuts like a knife through the eyes. Are those normal eyes or Evil Eyes? The D is for Disaster. The N is for the Night. M is for Mona. *Who is Mona*? Tombstones appear in the mist. Thunderbolts and nightsticks fall out of the sky. There's a Fire in the Western World. Johnny's Got a Gun. Strange Pray Tell. Out in the Blue. A Miss of You.

On "Dead Moon Night," the crack of Fred's howling voice, his ominous guitar refrain, Toody's deadening drone on bass, Andrew's endless thundering on the snare drum—these things don't make metaphors out of the long night and the journey to the other side; they deliver the feeling of death straight to the stomach. But much like the story of the Range Rats, there is often an unadorned everyday uncertainty that lies beyond the myth and the iconography. Take Fred's description of "Dagger Moon," a plaintive and stark song filled with images of jagged wire and chambers coated in shadows and rusted tarnish.

> Dagger Moon is worrying about your job, worrying about money, worrying about does somebody love you, worrying about are you sexy enough, worrying about is your nose too big, worrying about your hair, how old you are, can you hear, can you see, whatever your hang-ups are, your weight. God, you look at yourself in the mirror and you think, Oh fuck this can't be me. It's release me from that. Please just let me go, I don't want to have these addictions to these worries.[4]

On the one hand, there is a potent metaphor: a dagger moon, something that both cuts below and looms above at the same time. Yet it's not the dagger moon that Fred hangs the song's meaning on, but rather the pleading to be released from it.

Nowhere is this kind of plea more present than in the Coles' country songs as The Range Rats. What first appear to be stylized compendiums of Western genres—the album cover imagines each song title as its own fictional dime novel—actually reveal themselves to address the joys and confines of married love, the turn from youth to middle age, or simply loneliness and emotional desperation. Good country songs do the same thing, transforming a collection of highly familiar, perhaps even *clichéd* images—the smoke-filled honky-tonk or cantina, the cold jail cell, the singing waterfall, a pair of silver wings, a train rolling down the tracks, the whiskey bottle broken on the ground, the golden wedding ring slipped off the finger, the bandit standing over the smoking gun—into something more personal, idiosyncratic, or strange than their well-worn source material suggests. And if hum-along standards like the ones the Coles played live are like hit singles, then the endless ways in which those standards get messed with and turned into something else become their messy and unresolved mirror-image B-sides.

Fred and Toody's B-sides depict a world of stagecoaches and bootleg whiskey on "Thunder Road," fires and disasters along the border on "Vaya Con Dios," a woman fleeing her lover and taking a job on "A Fast Freight Train." As they chart their way through the old Wild West, the songs also record the journeys of a middle-aged married couple on the road for the summer in the America of the mid-1980s: sleeping some nights in a van, some nights under the stars, and some nights in a roach-infested motel not far from the casino. And some nights they're not sleeping at all—instead playing Patsy Cline over and over again for dancing couples far older than they are. The Coles sing on stage next to their drum machine; they are together, but they are alone, the songs seem to be saying. They don't know where they're going, but they know they need to go together. "Two of us are better than just one," they sing on the opening track.

The final song is a reinterpretation of an old standard, "Vaya Con Dios," or "Go with God" in English, most famously recorded as a duet between another married couple, Les Paul and Mary Ford, in 1953. It's a ballad of lovers parting ways, who will never meet again but will carry the memory of each other for the rest of their days. "Wherever you may be, I'll be beside you," Mary Ford croons, "although you're many, many dreams away."[5] The Coles' version, by comparison, is more desolate and unconsoling. The warm warbly waltz of Les Paul's guitar has changed into something muffled and jagged; the song is filled with gaps and silences punctuated only by the defeated sputtering of rollie and the clipped refrains of Toody's bass and Fred's guitar.[6] "I've taken everything I could," Fred begins singing. "And maybe gave more than I should." Toody sings next: "As the leaves begin to fall, I am the one who's lost it all." And then the two of them together: "Fought for love and lost the war. I will touch my land no more. Vaya Con Dios." What's left for the lovers by the end of the song are burning fields, smoke rising up onto the banks of an endless river, summer leaves falling, dying. "When I go, don't ask me why," Fred pleads.

And yet there's still some kind of release, at least for me. A nostalgic song about carrying memories with you turns into one about the very impossibility of remembering things as they were. Something in the translation of an old familiar standard into a new haunting one is enough to pull my own memories out, but they're foggy. Staring in the mirror as a 12-year-old wondering what I'd end up looking like. Walking home from dinner through a park with someone and thinking this is the closest you can ever come to knowing someone else. Sitting on a couch in the basement listening to my aunt and mom talk about summer nights as kids on a public lake in northern Wisconsin in the early 1970s. When the parents fell asleep in their cabins, the kids would sneak into a row boat stocked with beers and cigarettes and paddle out into the dark.

Michael Blair is the co-author, along with Joe Bucciero, of *Colossal Youth* (#121).

CHAPTER 38
DANIEL LOPATIN'S *CHUCK PERSON'S ECCOJAMS VOL. 1* (2010)
Marvin Lin

One of my favorite episodes of *The Simpsons* is Season 5's "Cape Feare" (October 7, 1993). In it, Sideshow Bob once again seeks revenge on Bart, who had years earlier exposed his attempt to frame Krusty the Clown for armed robbery. Now several years into his prison sentence, Sideshow Bob tricks the parole board to release him and quickly pursues his 10-year-old nemesis, prompting the Simpsons to change their surname and relocate to a houseboat. As they prepare for their trip, it's revealed that strapped secretly to the underside of their car is none other than Sideshow Bob, who is subsequently tortured by speed bumps, scalding coffee, and a cactus farm before the Simpsons finally arrive at their new home. Exhausted and in pain, yet free now from the horror of the covert tagalong, Sideshow Bob unstraps himself and crawls out from under the car—only to immediately step on a rake. The rake, of course, slams violently into Sideshow Bob's face, as he emits a deep, quivering groan. But before he (or the audience) can process the irony of the situation, Sideshow Bob suddenly steps on *another* rake, which is followed by another groan. Then *another* rake, followed by yet another groan. Then another. And another. And another. And another. And another. *And another.*

***

Repetition is a form of change. Brian Eno taught me that. But repetition also creates value, compounding with each iteration and building in cumulative ways. We can predict how future repetitions will play out on a technical level, but can we predict how we'll feel? Sideshow Bob's rake predicament is fascinating to me not because it repeats a funny joke, but because the hackneyed gag itself is only funny through the excessive repetition, shifting from being funny to unfunny to mildly irritating, and then suddenly to becoming *even funnier* than when the first rake hit. By the time the sequence ends, after roughly thirty seconds of looped slapstick absurdity pushed to its limits, the scene has undergone a wild transformation, and so too our reactions to it.

Daniel Lopatin is an expert in delivering such transformations, in playing with the ambiguity and disorientation before a reversal sets in. His music finds us where we're vulnerable, between our fragile mythologies and the memories of our material experiences. This is why his music can sometimes feel uncomfortable: working primarily as Oneohtrix Point Never, Lopatin routinely destabilizes our expectations, unsettles our desires, and disrupts our narratives. Out of this rubble, he constructs new experiences through a sensual, provocative combination of sound and image, achieved through his early fantasias of claustrophobic synthscapes and the subsequent hyperdawning of dense simulations (2013's *R Plus Seven*), reimagined tropes (2015's *Garden of Delete*), and studious myth-building (2018's *Age Of*), two eras bifurcated by the haunting rupture that was 2011's masterpiece *Replica*.

And yet, as successful as he's been as Oneohtrix Point Never, I think his most transformative work—and the one that led directly to the sample-based vignettes of *Replica*—is a scrappy, relatively unacknowledged, "B-side" cassette tape entitled *Chuck Person's Eccojams Vol. 1*. Released in 2010 by The Curatorial Club in a modest edition of 100, the fifteen-track tape takes cues from appropriation artists like Steve Reich, Christian Marclay, and John Oswald, with its primary methodology derived from DJ Screw's "chopped and screwed" technique. Like the late Houston hero's narcotic treatment of 1990s rap songs (as well as Lopatin's own Screw-influenced DJ sets and *Heaven Can Wait* mixtapes with co-conspirator Joel Ford), Lopatin's approach on *Eccojams* is simple: isolate short snippets from commercial pop songs of the 1980s or 1990s, layer effects like pitch shifting and echo, and loop them over and over and over.

From its understated fade-in to its gorgeous fade-out, *Eccojams* strings us through its concentrated poetry with an exquisite, mesmerizing procession of down-pitched melodies and cavernous echoing. These sampled flecks of pop—from Fleetwood Mac and Teddy Pendergrass, to Peter Gabriel and Heart—are looped with little regard for their original contexts, each repetition further stripping the source material of its historical and cultural baggage. The sublimated desires are castrated here, the very semantic conditions that gave meaning to the lyrics eroded. Like the Chuck Person moniker or the flattened Ecco the Dolphin cover art, the samples become empty shells, Pop Music turned into "pop music," severed quotations searching for a semiotic refresh.

Rather than interrogating our taste profiles or attempting to expose the music's artifice, Lopatin restages the lyrics to engage his own affective relationship with the songs, recasting these shards of modern life as mantric sources of despair and dislocation. On "B4," for example, the romantic lyricism of Chris De Burgh's massive hit "The Lady in Red" is rendered here as a quiet existential nightmare, with the line "There's nobody here / It's just you and me" reduced simply to "There's nobody here," looped for over two desolate minutes. Elsewhere, Lopatin hones in on phrases, usually short respites from the overall tone and sentiment of the originals, to express emotional defeat ("There was no way to compromise"—Phil Collins), suffocating anxiety ("Hurry boy, she's waiting there for you"—Toto), and unrelenting paranoia ("Where'd you get that information from?"—Alexander O'Neal).

But as eternal as the reframed lyrics may seem, *Eccojams* continually threatens to eschew meaning altogether through its ceaseless, hegemonic repetition. Whatever feelings are evoked through Lopatin's hybrid text eventually dissipate into an impressionistic, disembodied chorus of syllables and phonemes, locating the throbbing void beneath pop culture's glistening surfaces and exposing it for what it is: a space of possibility. Rather than simply destroying or cementing meaning, *Eccojams* shows how malleable, how contingent meaning can be while still fulfilling our appetite for deeper emotional connections to what we might otherwise disregard as cultural trash. It's a corollary to our mediated lives, nestled somewhere between spectacle and subversion, between communication breakdown and memory failure; and it serves as a reminder that, no matter how many times something is repeated—whether it's a sanctified pop lyric or a classic rake joke—nothing is truly fixed and everything is ripe for transformation.

***

But who is this Chuck Person anyway? In an interview with music writer Simon Reynolds, Lopatin interrogates his role as an author of these eccojams, but, interestingly, not in relation to the original composers of the sampled material. "I'm uncomfortable with the idea that I'm an author of this stuff," he explains. "I'm just participating in stuff that's happening all across YouTube, kids doing similar things all over."[1]

It's fitting that Lopatin's concerns are with new forms of creative expression rather than the old dinosaur that is "originality." More than a year before *Eccojams* was even released, Lopatin, bored at his job, started uploading videos to YouTube with little fanfare, composed of audio and visual material sourced from YouTube itself and released under the username "sunsetcorp." Like its musical counterpart, the found visuals—MS-DOS video games, Japanese TV advertisements for dated consumer electronics, rudimentary vector graphics, Soviet-era programming—are slowed down and looped in dizzying yet seductive ways. Featuring a couple of tracks from *Eccojams* (including a Michael Jackson tribute as KGB Man), two unreleased songs, and more, the sunsetcorp videos offer a spellbinding visual response to the degradation of our collective memories and the failed promises heralded by nascent, obsolescent technologies, uploaded out of seemingly nowhere and from seemingly no one in particular.

Young musicians these days play a similarly amorphous role. Subject to the technological possibilities and limitations built into a given medium, some of the most daring artists act less like musicians proper and more like information manipulators, shaping art out of an unprecedented archive of audio and visual material. And in an age of media saturation and intuitive symbol play, in which the rapid and anonymous production of repetitive phenomena like copypasta and Drake memes contribute deliciously absurd ways of reacting to information overload, it's always only a matter of time before self-devouring practices occur, especially through the liquid methodologies of a hyperactive, meta-aware userbase that's able to easily wrest hidden vestiges from its source material and present them anew.

This is why I find eccojamming such a beautiful mode of music-making to complement this era of repetition and appropriation: like the hypnagogic pop artists, like the hauntologists, like the chillwavers, like the witch house dwellers, and like the seapunks, eccojamming arrived in and perfectly reflected a moment when the recent past was becoming even more noticeably flattened by the subsuming topology of streaming internet culture, when our behavioral patterns were becoming more clearly determined by algorithmic pressures, when our mediums were slyly moving us away from the World Wide Web and toward the semi-closed platforms from which we still can't escape. But these platforms—from Reddit, Last.fm, and Twitter, to Bandcamp, 4chan, and Turntable.fm— were also where virtual communities could quickly coalesce, interfaces staked out as repositories, as incubators, for creative energy and collective movement.

One such virtual community is vaporwave. Crediting *Eccojams* as its genesis and taking additional cues from early YouTube eccojammers (jusabanksta, EEGPROGRAMS, Night Goat), enigmatic proto-vaporwave artists (Nonage, 骨架的), and James Ferraro's *Far Side Virtual*, vaporwave expanded the eccojamming reach to transform disposable cultural debris like boardroom muzak, kitschy smooth jazz, and elevator music into sound memes for a new generation. Led by young, mostly anonymous net-based producers like Vektroid, Midnight Television/Computer Dreams, and INTERNET CLUB, vaporwave's viral propagation throughout the internet was aided in large part by anachronous, post-ironic imagery of early digital culture, dead symbols of capitalist globalization, and tokenized artifacts from different eras and cultures.

But if eccojamming helped open up the so-called avant-garde to echoing loops of pop music and bland, minimally reworked lounge music, what does that say about originality in the twenty-first century? About taste? What might these works imply about authorship and the proliferation of like-minded artists? Lopatin expressed his thoughts about the unprecedented influx of vaporwave producers in a Reddit Ask Me Anything (AMA):

> the entire point of eccojams was that it was a DIY practice that didn't involve any specialized music tech knowledge and for me it was a direct way of dealing with audio in a mutable, philosophical way that had very little to do with music and everything to do with FEELINGS and I'm happy to see that it actually turned out to be true, that people make the stuff and find connection and meaning through that PRACTICE is all I could ever hope for. Its folk music now.[2]

***

We like telling stories. This is how we cope. But our futures are our fictions, pitched against the darkness of the unknown. *Eccojams* asks us not to imagine new futures by pillaging the past, but to linger in the instantaneity of the exclusive, ecstatic now by reconstituting the past *as* the present. Rather than simply promising new aesthetic worlds or wielding critiques of our failed economic systems and political sideshows, the tape reinvigorates our need to feel in a moment when our desires are increasingly mediated and exploited by the platforms through which we express them. *Eccojams* catalyzed this emotional urgency by offering a simple practice with minimal barriers to both entry and distribution, setting into motion a meme-optimized, entropically defined eruption of feelings for nearly anyone to pick up, elongate, and articulate as they wished. *Eccojams*, it turns out, was a gift, and I've been feeling better and emptier ever since.

Marvin Lin is the author of *Kid A* (#76). Find him at marvinlin.com.

PART THREE
MEMORABILIA

CHAPTER 39
THE BAND'S *ROCK OF AGES* (1972)
Steve Matteo

There was a time when the long-playing record album really meant something to the culture at large. Even before *Sgt. Pepper's Lonely Hearts Club Band* by The Beatles solidified the pop album's place as an art form in 1967, the rock album was a totemic and iconic talisman of the baby boomers. Those of us who were around in the mid-1960s through the late 1970s, and who held the rock album in high esteem, sometimes still cling to particular examples of it in our lives. The baby boomer rock album fan is part of a more varied group than some might think. Those that were born in 1946 had a very different perspective on the music than those born in 1964. I was born around the middle in 1958, and the rock album became a distinctly tangible and significant part of my life when my family got a complete stereo system at the end of 1971.

It was the sudden easy and broad access to FM radio that accelerated my rock album education. While only a handful of underground or progressive FM rock radio stations had been around since late 1966, such stations were ubiquitous by 1971. It's hard to convey at this point in history how that relatively new music medium (progressive FM radio) shaped the evolution of the pop and rock audience of that time.

Cruising a handful of stations in the tri-state New York area exposed me to albums I had never heard before and the debut of new releases. 1971 heralded the release of the live, triple album *Concert for Bangladesh*, which captured arguably the peak period for live albums. In 1970 The Who had released *Live at Leeds* and the Rolling Stones had released *Get Yer Ya Ya's Out*, easily the best live albums from these two groups as well as two of the best live albums in rock history. Also in 1971, The Allman Brothers Band released *Live at Fillmore East*, a venue that gave us that same year the grossly underrated *Performance: Rockin' the Fillmore* from Humble Pie, the band Steve Marriott of the Small Faces formed with Peter Frampton (who would go on to release his own monster live album *Frampton Comes Alive* in 1976). While not critically acclaimed, other significant live albums of the period were the soundtrack of the Woodstock movie and *Four Way Street* from Crosby, Stills, Nash, and Young.

A watershed album recorded in 1971 but not released until 1972 was the live album *Rock of Ages* from The Band. While my love of all the albums mentioned here so far is acute, *Rock of Ages* still consumes me. Recorded at the concert hall of the Academy of Music in New York around New Year's Eve 1971, the double record was the first live album from the group after four studio albums. The group was formerly known as The Hawks and backed up Canadian rockabilly singer Ronnie Hawkins beginning in 1960, which would last until 1964. From 1965 until 1967, the group served as Bob Dylan's backing band when he became an electric artist, although drummer Levon Helm, the only American in the group, would often be replaced by Mickey Jones and briefly Sandy Konikoff. The other members, all Canadians, were Robbie Robertson, Rick Danko, Richard Manuel, and Garth Hudson.

The group became The Band and released the seminal country-rock album *Music from Big Pink* in 1968. The legendary group simultaneously put Woodstock on the map as a key locale of an emerging new sound, which also included the band's former employer and Woodstock neighbor Bob Dylan. Both Dylan and The Band were managed by Albert Grossman, who was located there long before the others. Dylan's presence in Woodstock was one of the main reasons the promoters of the festival chose the area for their concert, which initially was intended to raise money to build a recording studio there.

It's hard to say why a particular artist, group, or piece of music grabs one, but hearing The Band performing live on record knocked me out, and it wasn't long before the album became a part of my small but growing album collection. The sheer power of this dazzling five-piece group playing on stage at a concert hall with eleven years of being on the road behind them, backed by a five-piece horn section, was a revelation. The blend of rock, R&B, country, and jazz made for a truly unique sound and the vocal interplay and harmonies of Levon Helm, Richard Manuel, and Rick Danko made them distinctive.

Reading the liner notes revealed that Allen Toussaint did the horn arrangements. It would be years before I would fully comprehend the significance of his contribution to the album and to American music in general. It would be many, many more years before I would interview Toussaint.

I listened to the album over and over again and every little nuance of the performances and sequencing became ingrained in my musical DNA. I would finally see The Band roughly four years later in the middle of September 1976 at the very same venue where *Rock of Ages* was recorded (by then renamed the Palladium). The concert occurred roughly ten weeks before what would become *The Last Waltz*, the group's farewell concert in San Francisco on Thanksgiving Day.

The concert was electrifying and very closely followed the set list from the *Rock of Ages* album. A friend who was not going to the show recorded the concert for me off the radio as the premier New York rock station WNEW-FM was broadcasting it live. I still have the cassette, and despite the Maxell tape logo being a bit frayed, the audio is intact. Hearing the seamless transition of "The Night They Drove Old Dixie Down" into "Across the Great Divide," just like on the album, was spine-tingling. While the group's farewell show would happen about two months later, my musical relationship with the album and, more importantly, with the group, was only just beginning. While The Band did release more music after *The Last Waltz*, the original five-piece group would never play together live again; however, the various members would play together as part of different projects and would reunite, without Robertson, in 1983. It was on one of those tours that I met Rick Danko and Levon Helm, and interviewed Helm extensively. We met backstage after a show in Roslyn, New York, at My Father's Place, a legendary suburban club that has recently been revived in a different location.

The music of *Rock of Ages* swirled through my head as I interviewed Helm. While various studio works of the group rank as some of the greatest albums of the period and songs written by members of the group, particularly Robbie Robertson, only become more vital as the years go by, it's those performances of the group's primary repertoire that stay with me. The album has been reissued over the years many times, with additional performances of various songs added, including some with Bob Dylan, but that original double-album version for me remains essential listening. The unfussy, brash, swinging blend of American musical styles never sounds dated, because the group followed no trends and created its sound from the music the members grew up with, learned to play, and chose to honor. That music ranged from the earliest country sounds to electric and acoustic blues, many of the influential jazz sounds of New Orleans, R&B, soul, and, of course, early rock 'n' roll.

I would come to understand that Robbie Robertson's keen songwriting had much to do with why the group was so successful. This is true, though Rick Danko co-wrote many of its key songs and Levon Helm's growing up in the South and transmogrifying that history made the music more authentic. Helm was a charming, affable, Southern gentleman when I interviewed him, with an occasional prickly side that I did not detect that first time we met. He was very welcoming and acted more like one's next-door neighbor than one of the greatest singers rock has ever produced. He even invited me up to his place in Woodstock, enticing me with tales of his wife's noodle cake.

I would interview Helm two more times and meet up with him again, but that night backstage after the show afforded me the most intimacy. I would also interview Robbie Robertson twice. The first time, in 1991, it was in person and Robertson was a bit guarded, but not uncooperative, and was filled with many excellent stories, befitting the title of the album he was promoting at the time, *Storyville*. I would interview him again in 2011 upon the release of *How to Become Clairvoyant*. Robertson was a completely different person, claiming he remembered me from our first encounter, and he was extremely open and talked freely during our interview.

Nowadays, the live album seems to be no more than a curio for hardcore fans or a tour souvenir no more important than the obligatory concert T-shirt. The sheer force of live rock music from that period is incalculable in raising the art form to new heights. Today's pop music scene, dominated by cute girl singers, electronic music, auto-tune, solo artists, and a focus on image and Twitter followers, does not create an environment for musical artists to release great live albums. The visceral thrill of groups creating timeless musical magic on stage that begs to be preserved seems like a quaint notion. I chose *Rock of Ages* because live albums rarely appear on lists of best albums of a genre or year. They are, sadly, but also maybe wonderfully, relegated to becoming B-sides. The significance of live rock albums from the 1960s and 1970s is a key to understanding the musical culture of that watershed period. The fact that many of the aforementioned albums still resonate today and are only enhanced by their longevity speaks to the quality of the music of that period. Sure, there are plenty of excellent live groups and even solo artists making music today, but how many have put out live albums and, of those albums, how many will still sound great even ten years from now?

Steve Matteo is the author of *Let It Be* (#12). Find him on Twitter @MatteoMedia.

CHAPTER 40
BRUCE SPRINGSTEEN'S *BRUCE SPRINGSTEEN AND THE E STREET BAND LIVE AT THE GENEVA THEATER* (1974)
Bruce Eaton

In today's world of massive every-note-ever-recorded box sets and affordable high-quality recording equipment, it's hard to imagine that a significant chapter in the development of a major artist would go virtually undocumented. But such is the case with Bruce Springsteen—and no matter how many of his official releases you listen to, his sonic story can't be fully told without a "recording of independent origin" to fill in a vital gap.

It might be hard today to imagine Springsteen as being anyone other than The Boss: a cultural icon loved by millions. But in October 1973, Bruce was just another struggling musician trying to pay his bills and sell enough records to avoid getting dropped by his label. As head of my college's student concert committee in upstate New York, I booked Springsteen to play at the Geneva Theater—a musty small-town Victorian opera house near campus. The fee?—$2,000—a fair price for someone with one album to his virtually unknown name. Watching from the wings as Springsteen and his band systematically whipped the initially skeptical (and less-than-full) house into a frenzy, I kept asking myself "why isn't this guy one of the biggest acts in the world?"

I soon graduated, but with Bruce Fever now running high on campus, the college determinedly booked a return engagement. This time, on a frigid Saturday night in December 1974, the theater was packed. One of the most magical attributes of rock and roll is that, on any given night, any given band—even one playing at the local bar down your street—has a shot at being the best in the world. The word was spreading. Springsteen and the now officially-monikered E Street Band could make you feel like they were the best band in the world every single night out. And that night I walked out of the theater believing they most certainly were. Or were they?

Perceptions and memories of a live show are tricky to say the least. But over the decades—with many notable Springsteen concerts—I could never shake the feeling that there was something special about that December night that had never been captured on record. Improbably, a high-quality audience tape of the Geneva concert surfaced in 2015. Even on first listen it was readily evident that the show was not only as good as I had remembered, it was better. And as high as the peaks have been in Springsteen's career to date, this peak—reached ten years before he conquered the sports stadiums of the world—stands as their equal. The tape didn't just reveal a particularly hot performance. There was something quite concrete about what set the Geneva concert apart from those

I witnessed over the ensuing years. Ultimately, the Geneva recording proves to be an essential document of a unique six-month phase in Springsteen's career before *Born to Run* landed him front and center on the national stage—one that's largely forgotten except by those who actually experienced it live.

Early on, Springsteen was often touted as yet another artist in a long procession of Next Dylans. On the surface it made some sense. Springsteen had the scruffy looks and the dazzling hyperactive wordplay of early Dylan. Musically speaking though, Springsteen's first two albums more often elicited comparisons to Van Morrison than to Dylan. The first time I played *Greetings from Asbury Park* while pondering the possibility of booking "this Bruce guy," I reflexively expected Morrison to break in with the vocal on "Spirits in the Night." That reaction nudged me to take a chance on Springsteen. A few months later, after hearing the sweeping *The Wild, The Innocent, and The E Street Shuffle*, it was not a stretch to conclude that, if Morrison was out in California with his Caledonia Soul Orchestra, Springsteen was fronting the Jersey Shore counterpoint.

While a number of the tracks on Springsteen's first two albums shared Morrison's penchant for nimble, soul-drenched swing, others offered evidence that Springsteen had spent considerable time immersed in Morrison's grand epic *Astral Weeks*. Like Morrison, Springsteen painted stream-of-consciousness pictures of people living on a spiritual edge in a world that seemed both immediately real and at the far reaches of imagination—a world you wanted to dive into heart first. The *Astral Weeks* connection wasn't conjecture—it was reality. Springsteen himself has declared *Astral Weeks* as "extremely important for me … it gave me a sense of the divine," adding that "there would be no 'New York Serenade' without *Astral Weeks*."[1] If *The Wild, The Innocent, and The E Street Shuffle* can be considered Springsteen's *Astral Weeks*, then it's not a stretch to say that the Geneva concert recording is Springsteen's counterpart to *It's Too Late to Stop Now*—Morrison's dynamite 1974 live album.

A photo taken during the 1974 concert shows Springsteen, dramatically backlit (lighting engineer Marc Brickman would go on to become one of the world's pre-eminent lighting designers), with another figure: a beautiful woman in a flowing dress playing a violin. Today, nightly set lists and band personnel changes fly around the internet in seconds. Suki Lahav's presence—she had been performing with the band for several months—that night was as mysterious as it was unexpected. Whether you were in the audience that night or were listening to the recording decades later, her compelling contribution becomes obvious mere seconds into the concert.

The crowd whoops loudly in recognition as pianist Roy Bittan chimes in with the opening notes of "Incident on 57th Street" and then Lahav enters with a heartbreakingly note-perfect accompaniment. Springsteen steps to the mic and begins to intertwine the tale of Spanish Johnny and Puerto Rican Jane with Lahav's aching violin. There's a subtly and expressive range in Springsteen's vocals—no trace of the bark or twang that later crept in—drawn out by the violin that would not (and probably could not) make the jump to larger venues. The crowd explodes into wild cheers well before the final notes ring as the remaining band members take the stage, the roar rolling on for a full sixty seconds past the start of "Spirits in the Night." It's as if Springsteen is already the Biggest Show on Earth.

The set list for the evening leans heavily on Springsteen's first two albums. But early in the show he steps outside his lane and kicks the Next Dylan notion to the curb with a riveting cover of Dylan's own "I Want You." It's a bold move but Springsteen—with Lahav by his side—is up for the challenge. It's been oft-speculated that Springsteen was quite smitten with Lahav, then married to his sound engineer. Whatever the reality, the electricity is palpable as Springsteen's expression of romantic want borders on pure desperation.

When Springsteen breaks a guitar string mid-set, Clarence Clemons takes the mic and leads the band through a swingin' cover of the Lambert, Hendricks & Ross vocalese nugget "Gimme That Wine." It's a light note before the performance takes off into the stratosphere for the next sixty-six minutes. Over a mere four songs Springsteen grabs the wheel and takes the audience on a tour of a mystical nocturnal underworld running from Harlem to the Jersey Shore. Call it what you want—a backstreets urban opera or a rock and roll answer to *West Side Story*—it's like listening to a movie.

Hearing the then-unreleased "Jungleland" was all the proof you needed that Springsteen was indeed a major artist. The groove on "Kitty's Back" is pure "Moondance," stretched out over eighteen minutes, swinging as hard as Springsteen's nearby Jersey neighbor, Count Basie. The main set could easily have ended here and with a few encores everyone would have gone home satisfied. But instead, Springsteen tells the amped-up crowd, "Sit back … we're still going," and launches into an epic twenty-five-minute "New York City Serenade."

As the performance unfolds, Springsteen-as-narrator is buried in a cloud of existential dread near the seedy Port Authority Terminal, desperate for companionship beyond what's being sold on 42nd Street. Over and over he promises a girl—"little stranger"—who looks as lost as he is, that "I'll be proud of you" as they walk together down Broadway to a quiet nearby place with "this, uh, uh, color TV" (Bruce clearly has no set script at this point). Springsteen for sure has no money and love is never mentioned, but it's clear by the song's end that, to him, expressing pride in someone else may be even more important than offering money, or even love. With hindsight, Springsteen's well-known real-life struggle to win his father's approval almost certainly wells just beneath the surface. Over and over, he repeats "and down and down and down and down" as his room spins "round and round and round and round." Little Johnny is calling from the alley—perhaps to join him in a sketchy caper—but Springsteen cries "I don't want to hear it!" as church bells ring. Morning approaches and Springsteen unsteadily suggests that he and the girl can maybe steal away and leave the city. "We can make it … we can take it," he promises, and then, as the band kicks into double-time, Springsteen takes a big swing at all his self-doubt, repeatedly shouting "I'll be proud … I can take it!" It's a draining performance that virtually defines "tour de force" (as well as being Exhibit A for bassist Garry Tallent being the stealth MVP of the E Street Band).

After a raucous "Rosalita" closes out the set, there are multiple encores before Bruce announces "this song may be the best dance song ever recorded" and the band tears into a blow-out version of Gary U.S. Bonds's "Quarter to Three." At this moment, they're the local bar band that is indeed the best combo on the planet.

Springsteen would return to the Geneva Theater the following July for the second date of the *Born to Run* tour. The ethereal Lehav had gone back to her native Israel. In her place was guitarist Steve Van Zandt, resplendent in a flashy Joisey pimp suit. The E Street Band juggernaut was now fully assembled, tuned up, and driving off the lot to conquer the world. A hit album and magazine covers were just down the road, and Springsteen's music was already becoming streamlined. Over time, the song structures became more conventional, the swinging rhythms gave way to straight-ahead rock beats, and the impressionistic tales of wild characters were replaced by a more personal and direct voice: Bruce's. The early songs really weren't cut out to get much radio airplay, but "Dancing in the Dark" certainly was.

Beyond being a window on this phase of Springsteen's career, the Geneva recording raises an intriguing scenario. It's entirely possible that, if the internet and today's affordable recording technology had existed in the early 1970s, Springsteen's first manager, the underrated Mike Appel, would have been able to produce a quality live recording on the cheap and make it readily available online to fans rabid to spread the word. If this early version of Springsteen had found a large-enough audience in time to lift the financial and record label pressures off his shoulders, might he have pursued his muse in a different direction, delving deeper into the mystic before pulling into the Cadillac Ranch?

One hazard of going to hear a lot of live music is that you run the risk of becoming *that* guy—the bore who reminds you that he saw an artist *waaaay* back when they were virtually nobody, and, of course, they were *waaaay* better way back then than they are now, but of course you don't know that because you weren't there. I'm not going to be that guy. You can form your own opinion. But if you want to better understand why people who encountered Springsteen before *Born to Run* walked away in a spell, a good place to start is Geneva, New York.

Bruce Eaton is the author of *Radio City* (#65). Find him at http://bigstarbook.blogspot.com.

CHAPTER 41

TALISKER'S *DREAMING OF GLENISLA* (1975)

John Cavanagh

The dog on the front cover was the first attraction. Until I was 9, my family had a cairn terrier and, although Dougal, Talisker's mascot, was a white West Highland terrier, the resemblance to our dear-departed Brownie was enough of a tug. The title *Dreaming of Glenisla*, the cheerful dog on the front, and the pieces listed on the back, such as "Ca' the Yowes"—a folksong collected by Scotland's most famous bard Robert Burns—and "Mingulay Boat Song," added up to something that, in the Scots vernacular, looked "couthy": this might well have been an album of accordion quaintness, played by red-nosed blokes in big wooly jumpers.

This impression was thrown into sharp relief by the rear of the sleeve and rather severe-looking photos of the band, who appeared anything but "couthy." The direct-to-camera stare of band leader and drummer Ken Hyder topped an arch of pictures supported by profile shots of reed players Davie Webster and John Rangecroft and double bassists Marc Meggido and Lindsay Cooper.

I'd spotted the LP in Glasgow's 23rd Precinct shop, where the assistant let me hear a sample of the music. Had he played the flowing, melodic title track and opener to Side One, I may have bought it straightaway. Instead, Side Two's opener blasted out, leading off with a traditional tune played on a tin whistle to a heavy drumbeat and twanging basses for a couple of measures before the tenor sax came in and it spiraled off into free blowing of a sort very new to me. I'd heard Chick Corea's *outré Sundance* album by then and understood that jazz didn't necessarily mean choruses and breaks, but the treatment of the folk tune "Mrs. MacLeod" was both confusingly strange and oddly unforgettable. I didn't buy it, but I kept thinking about what I'd heard.

The wide scope of my childhood listening was much encouraged, especially by my dad. Our shared interest in radio included the BBC's *Jazz in Britain* show, and a couple of weeks after I'd chanced on the Talisker album, we noted they were featured in a half-hour session. This session was duly recorded, and it highlighted the contrasts of Talisker: from melodic and spiritual to wild whooping and frantic free improv. Whatever it was that drew me to this odd concoction, the appeal was not waning.

My sister Jean deserves credit for buying the LP for my eleventh birthday, especially as her taste in harmony pop (Graham Nash, the Hollies, etc.) meant that Talisker's music would drive her up the wall! Perhaps the fact she'd been married a few weeks before helped matters: she could give the thing to me and retreat to a safe distance. For me the album was more than influential: it was life-changing and a runaway first choice to spotlight in this collection of B-sides.

A central figure in Dundee-born Hyder's early life, who still receives regular credit in his discourse today, was his granny. Her impact is clear on the second piece from *Dreaming of Glenisla*, which contrasts "Diddlin' for the Bairns" with "Lament for Dairmid." Hyder sees the wordless vocal rhythms uttered by his grandmother whilst bouncing his infant self on her knee as his first access to freeform music: this "diddling" was made up on the spot, never the same twice.

Talisker existed for around three years before the *Dreaming of Glenisla* album was made in June 1975, starting out in a more conventional jazz mode before evolving the process of employing Scottish themes. This evolution was sparked by two sources. Hyder's attention was caught by something Charles Mingus said about the tendency for European jazz to model itself on the American form. Mingus postulated that, as American jazz grew out of folk-forms and Europe was rich in those, why not try making jazz expression from something that could be found closer to your own roots? The main catalyst was Hyder's drum teacher John Stevens. His influence over the creative music coming out of London in the late 1960s/early 1970s with his own playing and via his Little Theatre Club is vast. Hyder recalls the breadth of Stevens's interests and knowledge: "He blind-dated me by playing this LP. He said 'Where's that from?' I'm listening to these women singing, the rhythms, and I said 'Sounds North African, John.' It was a School of Scottish Studies record, women in the Hebrides singing waulking songs for teasing out the tweed and I'm thinking: how come I didn't know about this?"[1]

The coupling of "Diddlin' for the Bairns" and "Lament for Dairmid" reflected Hyder's growing interest in "pibroch," an extended form of Scottish bagpipe music. In present times, pibroch has been formalized into a strict style, but Hyder maintains its evolution, dating back hundreds of years, was one of themes and variations and, therefore, an early form of jazz. Albert Ayler and John Coltrane were both interested in the modes and drones of Scottish music, and the "Lament for Dairmid" is a powerful and emotional piece I'd like to think they would've enjoyed.

Another aspect of Scottish music opens the lengthy track that rounds off Side One of the original LP: the drum salute, a type of drumming associated with pipe bands. Many years later Hyder would discover its connection to bebop. In the 1980s, Max Roach came to London to accept the dedication of a park in Tooting to his name in honor of his activities in the US Civil Rights movement. As Ken Hyder was a drummer, involved in left-wing politics and lived in nearby Balham, he was the ideal choice to meet up with Roach for the occasion. Max Roach, that doyen of bebop drummers, was very interested in Hyder's music. It transpired that his own first drum teacher was a Scottish pipe band drummer. As Hyder says: "that explains why there's so much 'rrrrrrrr' in the snare-playing in bebop!"[2]

Following the drum salute, the "Lament for Mal Dean" is a beautiful piece, again modelled on the pibroch form, in homage to a friend who died in 1974. Mal Dean is probably best remembered now for his visual art, including cartoons. Hyder also knew him as a trumpeter in the Amazing Band, a free jazz outfit formed by Dean, where

Hyder took over as drummer from Robert Wyatt and was, in turn, replaced by Charles Hayward.

The more I listened to the album and the taped BBC session, the more involved I felt by the free playing. That Side Two opener, which caused confusion on first listen, now seemed joyous, as the medley, beginning with "Mrs. MacLeod," flowed through two more folk tunes: "Raasay" (named after the Hebridean island) and "Soldier's Song."

The dynamic of the album eases for a heartfelt and un-jazzy version of "Ca' the Yowes" led by John Rangecroft's clarinet. The playing of both "Rangie" and "Wee Davie" Webster inspired me to take up an instrument. But fiscal necessity dictated the choice between clarinet, tenor, or alto sax: a clarinet was about one-third of the price of the brass reed instruments. I still have and play the clarinet I started out with in 1976.

Something of a Mingus-band swing combines with the snap of a Scottish strathspey in the next piece on Side Two of the LP: Talisker's take on "Mingulay Boat Song," written by Hugh Roberton, founder of the Glasgow Orpheus Choir, in the 1930s. This would be one of the first songs I ever heard, thanks to the version by Robin Hall and Jimmie MacGregor.

Full-scale wildness erupts next with "Heel an' Toe, Foot an' Moo," which Hyder describes as an attempt to capture "the jaunty and jocular side of Scottish music."[3] Once the free-blowing subsides, Davie Webster lapses into riffing on the traditional tune "Cock o' the North," as Hyder punctuates with snare rolls and the basses ascend/descend around the theme.

The final piece on *Dreaming of Glenisla*, "Homeward," shows the beginnings of another leitmotif in Ken Hyder's interests: "spirit music" and here, specifically, Gaelic psalm singing, a form found mainly in Scotland's Western Isles. John Rangecroft's tenor takes the role of precentor, giving out the call to which the band, as a vocal group, responds.

Glasgow's Third Eye center was a place of huge importance to my childhood. As an 11-year-old, there was no way I could've seen Talisker had they played in the usual sort of licensed venue. The Third Eye possessed a more open-minded outlook and the night of May 11, 1976 was pivotal to so much that followed for me. I'd heard more Talisker the previous week when another BBC session aired on John Peel's show, which heightened my excitement. I counted the days to the concert.

In the pre-punk era, one did not generally see males in public who dressed in tartan pajama trousers, padding about in socks, but my mum and I were joined by such a figure before Talisker played. From across the room Davie Webster had spotted my Talisker hat—a red woolen creation with white lettering woven in, made by my mum—and he arrived, proffering share from his box of dates.

Webster soon gathered my level of interest in Talisker and that I wanted to meet the leader of the band. Much later I heard the story from Hyder's point of view. Webster told him, "There's a boy over there who wants to meet you," adding "I mean a wee boy: he's with his mum!" And thus I met Ken Hyder.

I'd been made to feel very welcome by this band whose whole set was an exhilarating introduction to watching the interaction of improvisers as well as hearing music which depended on spontaneity and understanding of form. "Dreaming of Glenisla" itself was dedicated to me during the show. By now the main theme was stated by the whole band, in contrast to the LP, which begins quietly on clarinet and bowed basses.

Thereafter I felt adopted as Talisker's mascot (not in a competitive way with Dougal, you understand), being sent tapes of new pieces and introduced to sounds Hyder thought I ought to hear, be they Dollar Brand or a new African talking drum he'd just acquired. Within the band, however, I became known as "The," short for "The Fan"!

Dreaming of Glenisla established a questing spirit that Hyder still pursues. Talisker would release three more albums with floating personnel, playing into the mid-1980s. Meanwhile, Hyder's longest-lasting playing partnership is with Tim Hodgkinson, spanning over four decades and including the trio K-Space. Here Hyder and Hodgkinson were joined by Tuvan shaman Gendos Chamzyryn, reflecting Hyder's interest in Tuvan music and culture. Studying there for over twenty years, he is a fully qualified shaman.

Although preferring to create anew, Hyder sanctioned the reissue of *Dreaming of Glenisla* by Canada's Reel Recordings label in 2007. This reissue allowed me to pay back something to a record that had such a personal impact: the extra material on the CD exists because I'd captured it on tape when I was 11.

Perhaps the ultimate rounding of a circle came in 2010 at the Glasgow Improvisers Orchestra *GIO-Fest*, held in what was the Third Eye center, now the Centre for Contemporary Arts (CCA). Ken Hyder was a special guest; I was MC for the event. Before Hyder played his opening solo set, I introduced him, telling the story of how we'd met in the same building thirty-four years ago. When I got to the part about the Talisker hat, I produced that very garment and wore it again as I completed my introduction. I then reflected on how all of life is a sequence of improvisation, each chance move having an effect on what follows, and I wondered how different my life might have been if Ken Hyder's dog Dougal hadn't graced the cover of Talisker's debut album.

John Cavanagh is the author of *The Piper at the Gates of Dawn* (#6). Find him at johncavanagh.co.uk.

CHAPTER 42
THE VILLAGE PEOPLE'S *CAN'T STOP THE MUSIC: THE ORIGINAL MOTION PICTURE SOUNDTRACK* (1980)
Rebecca Wallwork

Like all good things, it starts with Steve Guttenberg. Before *Police Academy* and *3 Men and a Baby*, we see The Gutt dressed in white jeans, a green polo, and roller skates. He is begging his record-store boss for the night off. No dice. So, he quits on the spot over the store's loudspeaker, proclaiming: "My time is now!" before butt-sliding over the counter and hitting the streets of midtown Manhattan on his skates. Cue the music! Cue the cheese!

Can't Stop the Music, the 1980 fantasy biopic of the Village People, starts thus, with the indelible image of Steve Guttenberg skating down Broadway, pumping his fists in the air. Indelible, at least, to me. (Some things can't be unseen; The Gutt on roller skates is one of them.) The movie that follows is a shameless promo reel for the Village People, held together by lashings of quippy dialogue and a gossamer excuse for a plot. *Can't Stop the Music* holds the distinction of receiving the first-ever Razzie Award for Worst Picture. The accompanying soundtrack yielded but one hit, "Y.M.C.A." And yet, despite these flaws, the movie and its soundtrack are lodged in my internal jukebox. Why? How can something so shit be so good? And how would an objectively bad movie and album, now almost 40 years old, hold up to re-examination?

I dialed up the movie and downloaded the soundtrack. One thing was immediately clear: it isn't the nostalgic passing of time since the album's 1980 heyday that affects how I feel about *Can't Stop the Music* today. It's the time and place I'm in and you're in. If I had written this fifteen years ago—or ten or three—it would have been too easy to devolve into snark, or to dismiss my interest in the album as an exercise in self-deprecating irony. But here, in 2019, there is no room for irony. Snide sarcasm, be gone. The world is in the hands of a sexist, racist man-child, and every day brings new horrors and indignities. The good thing is that urgent times have a way of stripping away the bullshit. It's never felt so important to claim our passions and stand up for the things we love without reservation—because if not now, when?

And, so, I'm here to report that *Can't Stop the Music* is much more than a tongue-in-cheek guilty pleasure. It's a manifesto. The title track nails it. Think about the lyrics for a second, and don't pretend you don't know them: "You can't stop the music / Nobody can stop the music." That is the simplest, most eloquent expression of what everyone reading this book feels about music. You don't have to like the Village People to admit this, just take the song at its word.

I loved this album without irony—or life experience—as a child. I had no inkling of the Village People's role as crown princes of the gay club scene and was oblivious to the "disco sucks!" backlash. *Can't Stop the Music* (surely purchased by my mother) was a favorite in my house—and in my homeland, where it hit the top of the Aussie charts. (In the United States it only made it to #47.) If I wasn't watching the movie on VHS, I was poring over the record's gatefold sleeve, reverently cataloging the collage of stills from the film as I listened to the album. Everything I loved about it then I love still, because it's pure and true in a world that is currently anything but.

OK, so back to Guttenberg. His big entrance, "The Sound of the City," (performed by David London, not a member of The Village People) is a corny, jingly love letter to New York. His character Jack Morell, a fictionalization of real-life Village People creator Jacques Morali, is listening to music and he is ecstatic! He is pure joy as he skates between cabs and buses, around garbage trucks and Midtown traffic, sailing onto the sidewalk, waving to mannequins in department-store windows, breaking into parades, and gliding into Washington Square Park, where people are juggling and dancing in fountains and skating just like him. His New York is bright and sunny and friendly, all color and movement and moxie—"A city with gusto!" It's a big show. "It's what's happen-*ing!*"

Who wouldn't want to live in New York after such an endorsement? I moved halfway around the world to the city—*and* worked in a record store, just like Jack Morell did. (I do not roller skate.) "Sound of the City" is upbeat and unashamedly celebratory. There is no need for subtlety or nuance when a song can get you off your ass and onto the dancefloor. Irresistible, infectious pop with an inescapable hook and a straightforward story? I'm all in.

That's the thing. The soundtrack to *Can't Stop the Music* is nothing if not straightforward. It is what it is and *it's a lot*. Take "Milkshake"—a frothy song about the virtues of dairy. In the movie, it's staged as a TV commercial, a bubbly set piece that Busby Berkeley might have dreamed up—if only he had thought to cast six grown men in sparkling white versions of their signature costumes alongside a troop of showgirls. It's fabulous, it's ridiculous, it's a riot. The song alone is a paint-by-numbers earworm, but the movie elevates it to inexplicably delightful.

The "Y.M.C.A." sequence in the movie also takes some cues from Hollywood musicals, whisking the Village People and their co-stars into a "Y" to "hang out with all the boys" using split-screens and kaleidoscopic collages of jocks cartwheeling across the screen. The group members sing poolside in jogging suits and stare wide-eyed at the communal shower crammed with hunks. There's table tennis and squash and dancing on stationary bikes. There's diving and skipping and gymnastics with chiseled male bodies flying through the air. Judo and wrestling and slow-mo boxing; volleyball and basketball and one-armed push-ups. Finally, exhausted, everyone falls to the floor like dominoes. Of course, this is one song that transcended the soundtrack, in large part thanks to jazz composer Horace Ott, who arranged the horns and strings that made it such an indefatigable wedding, bar mitzvah, and ball-park hit.

In the middle of all this testosterone is Valerie Perrine as Samantha Simpson, the movie's female star. She is Jack Morell's roommate and helps corral her friends from

Greenwich Village to populate his new singing group. Samantha leads a glamorous downtown life with a plant-filled apartment, a wise-cracking best friend and an enviable backyard strung with party lights. (This was what life as a grown-up must be like, I assumed as a 4-year-old.) It is in Samantha's backyard where the Village People first come together to jam, singing along to "Magic Night"—a song that isn't embarrassed to claim: "When I'm with my friends, there's magic in the air" and that "Magic's in the music." Yes, it's trite but it's not wrong. Nights filled with friends and good music *are* magic. Earlier in the movie, Jack points out to Samantha while he's DJing that everyone in the club is so happy: "They've forgotten everything that gets them down. That's what it's all about, isn't it? Music is magic. I want to make that magic!"[1] I refuse to scoff at that sentiment. I'll take any chance I can right now to *not* be cynical, to *not* feel jaded and beaten down by the news cycle. Yes, *Can't Stop the Music* is goofy but it's *happy*, goddamn it, and it believes in the power of music and friendship. I'm not embarrassed to stand, and dance, for that.

This is a kid-friendly Hollywood flick from the 1980s, so setbacks in the storyline are few—until the "Milkshake" commercial is deemed a little controversial by Madison Avenue. Does that get the Village People down? It does not. It propels them to a triumphant debut in San Francisco, where they perform at a gala organized by the society-lady mom of their new lawyer. (Their lawyer is played by none other than Caitlyn, then-Bruce, Jenner.) Each heavily-sequined Village Person arrives on stage in full method-actor mode—the cowboy bursts through a saloon door with guns blazing, the construction worker straddles a tractor, the cop and Leatherman ride in on their bikes. It's time to bring the house down with the title track, the manifesto that says music makes the world go around.

"Can't Stop the Music" knows, like you do, that music is fucking awesome. So awesome that it would be easier to catch a falling star than stop the music. Easier to perform meteorological miracles like sending rain back than stop the music! You can't stop the music. Don't even try. Are the lyrics cheesy? Yes. (Remember, we are talking about the worst film of 1980.) But when we're one Tweet away from one more affront, one more humiliation—or worse—I'm willing to pardon sentimentality if the sentiment is true. I know that I can't stop the music and I do not want to.

"Amid feelings of despair and uncertainty, disco life offered a thrilling escape from the darkness of everyday living in an age of diminishing expectations," wrote the authors of *Dancing in the Dark: Youth, Popular Culture, and the Electronic Media* in 1990.[2] It's hard not to read that line and feel the downward pull of diminishing expectations today.

By every critical metric, *Can't Stop the Music* is a terrible movie and an average disco album containing one legitimate hit. But, combined, they have the power to transport me—and maybe you, too. Revisiting this record gave me a reason to get off my phone, get out of my head, jack up the volume, and *dance*. I even forgot for a second that another relic of make-believe 1980s New York is now in residence at 1600 Pennsylvania Avenue. What's that if not magic?

Rebecca Wallwork is the author of *Hangin' Tough* (#113). Find her at rebeccawallwork.com

CHAPTER 43
HARUOMI HOSONO'S *PHILHARMONY* (1982)
Bryan Waterman

What happens when you discover music later in life that you wish you'd known as a teenager? Can particular sounds and rhythms create a musical False Memory Syndrome? Or do they bring you back to who you were before, but with a better sense of context, like a B-side you forgot to play the first time around?

Sofia Coppola's *Lost in Translation* (2003)—with Bill Murray memorably crooning Roxy Music in a Tokyo hipster karaoke—came at a moment in my early 30s when all my mixes included something by Bryan Ferry. Exquisite vindication! Originally released in 1982, on the cusp of my teenage years, "More Than This" wasn't on my radar then. We played *Avalon*'s title track in middle school orchestra but I didn't know the band, and in 2003 I still undervalued the album. Murray's version was a meditation on aging: "More than this, you know there's nothing / More than this." Had I already peaked? Was that okay? *Lost in Translation*'s only Japanese song hit me even harder. Happy End's "Kaze Wo Atsumete" sounded like 1970s AM country rock—in Japanese. It was like an alternative childhood. In that magic moment, file sharing still fresh, I nabbed Happy End's *Kazemachi Roman* (1971) with a few keystrokes. The internet informed me that Happy End's bassist, Haruomi Hosono, who composed this song, had a few years later founded Japan's most influential electropop band, Yellow Magic Orchestra (YMO). That revelation threw me headfirst down a Harry Hosono rabbit hole. Fifteen years later I still haven't emerged.

My introduction to YMO and friends came just as the Web changed everything. Hyperlinked reviews and recommendation algorithms helped historicize my tastes. File sharing sites filled in my collection's corners: Ferry's solo albums, Eno's pop records, then everything else Eno had touched as I realized his prints were all over my music all along. My earliest downloading spree culminated in Daryl Hall's *Sacred Songs* (1980), featuring Robert Fripp's spaced-out trips. Hall and Oates's *Rock and Soul, Pt. 1* (1983) had been an early teenage cassette-club selection, but Fripp's sonic detours here unexpectedly overlapped with my new Eno-mania. What would I have thought of *Sacred Songs* if I'd heard it in 1980, or even in 1985? What if I'd heard *Music for Airports* (1978) before *The Unforgettable Fire* (1984)? Or what if Michael Jackson had managed to include his cover of YMO's "Behind the Mask" on *Thriller* (1982), as originally planned? Would I have found YMO's *Solid State Survivor* (1979), a heavy rotation in my early 30s, twenty years sooner? Would I even have noticed the Japanese influence in the middle of a decade when *everything* was turning Japanese?

When I first heard Hosono's *Philharmony* (1982), sometime around 2010, I still didn't know enough of his solo work to contextualize it adequately. The first Hosono solo LP I'd owned, *Hosono House* (1973), was country-psych along the lines of Happy End. I knew about his Western pop fetish via Tin Pan Alley in Chinatown, his 1970s homage to American songbook orientalism, and I'd heard *Paraiso* (1978), his loving foray into Quiet Village kitsch. I'd had YMO's first two records—Bally/Midway arcade dancefests—for almost a decade. I hadn't yet heard the last few YMO records, so I couldn't have known how much *Philharmony* shares with Hosono's credits there. And I didn't know yet about his subsequent release, *Video Game Music* (1984), which featured covers of classic game themes (Pac-Man, Dig Dug, Galaga), one-upping the way YMO had sampled Space Invaders on their 1978 debut. But even if I'd heard these records, I may not have been prepared for the transition between *Philharmony*'s first two songs.

The album opens with a New Wave nod to Japanese intonation, pentatonic arpeggios ushering us into video-game landscapes, the word "Picnic" busted into parts until it hardly has a real-world referent. And then: a remake of Luigi Denza's century-old Neapolitan pop song, "Funiculì, Funiculà"! Somehow Hosono had reverse-engineered the entire age of mechanical reproduction in just two tracks. A sheet-music bestseller in the 1880s, commemorating the opening of a Mount Vesuvias cable car, "Funiculì, Funiculà" worked its way into European music as a faux folksong: Strauss, Rimsky-Korsakov, and even Shoenberg assumed it was traditional, lifting the tune for their own work. (I'll admit I learned this from Wikipedia; *I* knew the tune from Goofy and Donald's rendition in Disney's *Mickey and the Beanstalk*.) Stretching the chorus's refrain to the verge of endless loop, Hosono's version does two things totally new: it blurs the East-West borderline (who owns music so endlessly sampled?) and it sounds a note Hosono returns to frequently, that computers aren't futuristic so much as a way to "re-experience music in the past."[1] If *Philharmony* forms a bridge to Hosono's later ambient work, it also retains his pop connoisseur's sensibility and sense of humor.

This odd-couple opening previews the album's toggling between poles: digital mallets, gongs, zithers, and bamboo flutes on one hand, all evoking computer countrysides, and straightforward pop songwriting on the other, as urban and urgent as Lou Reed's. At either pole there's a digitally sampled stutter. "Luminescent/Hotaru" sends fireflies dipping to drink, but Side B's "Living-Dining-Kitchen" domesticates pop consumption, its speaker stuck between noodles and a Big Mac, the insistent drum track pitching the dancefloor as a third option. By album's end, the breathless Speak-and-Spell of the title song's carnival chorale fades into "Air-Condition," layering Frippertronic hums with gong loops, so processed they sound like wind chimes on a high-rise balcony: white noise of the urban sublime.

All of this serves as set up and release for the album's showcase song. When "Sports Men" finally hits in the middle of Side B, its loping, off-kilter beat is almost familiar, echoing "L-D-K" and "Funiculi, Funicura" as well as Hosono's work on YMO's two 1981 albums, *BGM* and *Technodelic*. "Sports Men" starts like a tightly wound cousin to "Cue," the gorgeous Hosono co-write from *BGM*'s Side B comedown. Cantering whistles and flutes extend the possibility of pleasure in a hypermodern world. But then Hosono enters, singing in English about everyday anxieties: anorexia, insomnia, apoplexy. You know. Bombarded by media messages about masculinity ("get into shape," "be strong," "hold her tight") he can't even roller skate or play ping-pong. But still he vows, cheerfully, to "be a good sport." He'll be a sportsman. For years, and after hearing a half-dozen versions of this song, including Hosono's own bluegrass arrangement on *Flying Saucer 1947* (2007), I was certain he also sang a line about not being able to "find the right church"— surely another failure of modern manhood. Instead, he's saying he can't "find the right *charge*." His electricity's off. And then you notice what the backup singers are chirping, in stereo, as they strap you to the table: "Twitching, probing, twitching, probing." Your programing's fucked! Lay back and reboot. As an anthem of beset manhood, "Sports Men" concedes nothing to its near-contemporary, Talking Heads' "Once in a Lifetime."

For years I couldn't find much in English to guide me through Hosono's music. But Paul Roquet's recent work on Japanese ambient media makes me realize YMO's *BGM*, which stands for "background music," offered an important clue. Hosono helped bring ambient music to Japan just as "personal media" (e.g., the Walkman) arrived with their "technologies of self-care" and "mood regulation." Like Eno, whose ambient works inspired him, Hosono would develop an ambient aesthetic that provided both "embodied security" and "impersonal topograph[ies] for listeners' anonymous drift." The effect is an "ambivalent calm" that still accounts for "the precarity of contemporary lifestyles."[2] *Philharmony*, documenting the transition to Hosono's ambient phase, registers all of the precarity before that calm. "Speaking of YMO, I am wondering why you were so uptight in those days," former bandmate Ryuichi Sakamoto asked Hosono in a 2000 conversation. "I don't know. We were young," Hosono replied. Maybe being uptight is just what "youth" meant. "You were in your thirties then, Hosono," Sakamoto laughed. "You were pretty high strung."[3] The time warp opened here makes me wonder again: what would I have thought of *Philharmony* if I'd encountered it new, during my own teenage years?

When I did discover it, the record settled well with other music I'd gravitated to in my 30s: Kraftwerk's *Computer World* (1981), Neil Young's vocoder-assisted *Trans* (1982), The Buggles' *The Age of Plastic* (1980). None of these albums meant anything to me when I was 15, but fifteen years later they evoked just the right mood. Had I returned to the motifs of early 1980s computer music to help me grapple, again, with aging? Or, as Hosono has suggested, is "[e]lectronic music by its nature … a universal language," the same way computers make the recorded past—everyone's past—universally available?[4] In an interview that accompanies *Philharmony*'s 2018 vinyl reissue on Light in the Attic Records (its first release outside Japan), Hosono says his whole approach to songwriting changed with his first E-mu Emulator, which let him sample and filter sounds through electronic keyboards.[5] *Philharmony*'s songs, among the early results, reveal how such tools pushed Hosono both toward and away from cultural specificity. When asked whether video-game scores might be "a new kind of electronic folk music," Hosono answers that computer music's origins might illuminate the origins of music itself. Reduced to basic inputs—"PITCH, STEP, and GATE"—electronic music retreats from "'cultural disposition' and reach[es] into the internal world of individuality. On the other hand, this also means that one comes into contact with the DNA within ethnicity at the same time." This tension between folk's ethnic specificity and the "universal language" of electronic music constitutes what Hosono calls "simply the phenomenon of music."[6] This outlook, which authorizes his ambient phase, isn't quite the same one Sakamoto endorsed in the late 1980s, referring to himself as a "stranger" rather than as "Japanese" because he didn't like "nationalities and borders."[7] Instead, Hosono hovers over boundaries, borders, and shorelines, "where different things collide," seeing himself as a type one might find in any culture: someone who appreciates cultural contact zones: "[J]ust as some animal life begins on the shore," he says, "jazz and rock music also came to be."[8]

Tapping the emotional substrata of my own individuality, *Philharmony* pushes me, as I push 50, to recognize how the sounds that structured my emergent identity—New Wave's robots, spaceships, video games, synths—washed up against Japanese shores. Atari's eight-bit soundtracks were there for sure, but so was the Sony Walkman my mother worried would make me antisocial: the personal media that remade the world as my own private cinema. I can't help but think Hosono intended *Philharmony* specifically for cassette, so it could accompany urban wanderings, real and imagined. (It's a different kind of BGM than he'd create on *Watering a Flower*, his 1984 cassette-only release for Muji that ironically let you listen, on headphones, to the same minimalist mood-softener the store piped through the PA.) Was Hosono, recording *Philharmony*, still sorting through the sounds of his youth? Or was he wishing he'd grown up listening to something else? What he's given the world—sometimes sinister, sometimes humorous, sometimes ambient, sometimes past, sometimes future—captures the space between nostalgia and the unsettlingly uncanny. What happens when you wake up in someone else's music? You be a good sport. Stand up, please. Like a sportsman.

Bryan Waterman is the author of *Marquee Moon* (#83). Find him at bryanwaterman.org.

CHAPTER 44
HIROKAZU TANAKA'S *METROID* (1986)
Andrew Schartmann

Canadian composer Alan Belkin once told me that to achieve greatness in music is to expand its emotional range—to reveal avenues of expression previously unknown. Our histories abound with stories of those who have possessed this gift, and it would be uncontroversial to cite the likes of Nina Simone or Mozart as people who have changed the course of music. But what about a little-known figure who wrote music for a toy— one that was expected to die out within a few years of its creation? This brief chapter argues that Japanese video-game composer Hirokazu "Hip" Tanaka and his score to *Metroid* (1986) deserve a place alongside the creators of "A-side" hits like Koji Kondo's *Super Mario Bros.* (1985), which, as part of a game that sold some forty million copies (in contrast to *Metroid*'s 2.7 million), became the earworm of a generation. In particular, the following paragraphs focus on Tanaka's use of silence, as well as his muddying of the boundary between sound effects and music, as unprecedented conceptual leaps in video-game audio.

Released to North American audiences in August 1987,[1] Nintendo's alien-themed *Metroid* hit the shelves amidst an ongoing American obsession with outer space. Sparked by the launch of Sputnik I in 1957, and fueled by the subsequent Space Race between the USSR and the United States, this space craze pervaded all aspects of American popular culture, from movies (*2001: A Space Odyssey*, *Star Wars*) to television (*The Jetsons*, *Star Trek*) to video games (*Space Invaders*, *Asteroids*). Yet, in addition to being perfectly attuned to the nation's pulse, *Metroid* also broke with tradition in a number of ways.

For one, the game expanded upon the side-scroller model to create an open-ended environment. Instead of restricting players to left–right navigation, *Metroid* offered a complex labyrinth of levels that scroll in four directions. To make this design even more challenging, players had to return to previously explored areas with new items in order to probe more deeply into the planet Zebes. These complicating factors resulted in a game oriented more toward adult consumers, who, at the time, were considered by many to be an unviable target market. *Metroid* was also one of the first mainstream games to feature a female protagonist—bounty hunter Samus Aran—although this remained hidden to those who took longer than five hours to complete the game.

These features notwithstanding, it was Tanaka's music that struck me most when I first encountered the game in the early 1990s. As an avid gamer myself, I had played countless titles on the NES and SNES by the time I gave *Metroid* a try. I still remember blowing on the cartridge before inserting it into the machine, hesitant to play this mysterious game that I'd been told was too difficult for someone my age. It *was* difficult. But that didn't matter. From the moment I turned on my NES and encountered Tanaka's cybernetic title-screen track, the budding musician in me knew that I'd just heard something revolutionary. And yet it wasn't the notes themselves that captivated me, it was the space between them. Tanaka was a master of silence.

It was only years later that I discovered just how groundbreaking Tanaka's score— his *Metroid* "album"—truly was. As the composer himself recalls: "[in the early 1980s] sound designers in many studios started to compete with each other by creating upbeat melodies for game music. The pop-like, lilting tunes were everywhere. The industry was delighted, but on the contrary, I wasn't happy with the trend, because those melodies weren't necessarily matched with the tastes and atmospheres that the games originally had."[2] Tanaka expressed his discontent by creating a new kind of video-game music.

His *Metroid* score is, by and large, the antithesis to "pop-like, lilting tunes"; it is built not with "upbeat melodies," but with holes—salient sonic gaps that depict the vast emptiness of space, as well as the hollowness within us as we confront a remote and isolated landscape. Tanaka's music doesn't just "match the atmosphere"; it immerses us in it. It gives room to our thoughts so that we, too, can become lost in game designer Makoto Kano's alien world. As *Gamespot*'s "History of *Metroid*" notes: "[Tanaka's] music superbly evoked the proper feelings of solitude and loneliness one would expect while infiltrating a hostile alien planet alone."[3]

Of course, the use of silence to depict loneliness in a great expanse was not a new concept per se, and had been used widely in science-fiction films. As *Metroid* mastermind Yoshio Sakamoto explains, Ridley Scott's Academy Award-winning film *Alien* (1979) had considerable influence over the game's design: "I think the film *Alien* had a huge influence on the production of the first *Metroid* game. All of the team members were affected by H. R. Giger's design work, and I think they were aware that such designs would be a good match for the *Metroid* world we had already put in place."[4] Given this explicit connection between the game and the film, it isn't far-fetched to assume that Tanaka took note of Jerry Goldsmith's brilliant score. After all, much like *Metroid*, *Alien* owes some of its tensest moments to the absence of sound. Tanaka's conceptual leap, however, lies in how he imported that effect into an entirely different medium—one in which the observer is an active creator of the content itself. Tanaka realized that silence could be leveraged as an immersive tool.

In practice, Tanaka implemented silence in visceral fashion; he made it so that silence was not just heard, but felt. In "Norfair," for instance, he used changing meters to emphasize soundless moments. By establishing a 3/8 meter and then switching to 2/4, he led listeners to expect a new attack on what turns out to be the final beat of measure four. When that expectation for sound is met with silence, the feeling of emptiness hits home quite strongly.

Tanaka created a similar effect in "Secret Area" by alternating between 3/8 and 2/4 meters, but, unlike "Norfair," he did not provide listeners with a hummable tune, offering instead an atonal succession of pitches. In fact, with its lack of tonal center and changing meters, the passage sounds so disorganized that many would refrain from calling it music at all—which is precisely what Tanaka intended:

> I had a concept that the music for *Metroid* should be created not as game music, but as music the players feel as if they were encountering a living creature. I wanted to create the sound without any distinctions between music and sound effects. The image I had was, "Anything that comes out from the game is the sound that game makes."[5]

It's difficult to define how Tanaka differentiated music from sound effects, but his approach is palpable nonetheless, as illustrated by the game's title theme (see Figure 1). In the excerpt shown, Tanaka avoids material that he would describe as melodic (i.e., "something that someone can sing or hum"), composing instead a handful of scintillating tones (Pulse 2) that ricochet off a pulsating drone (Pulse 1, Triangle). The ambiguous quality of the sound leaves us wondering from where it actually emanates: is it a musical introduction to the play about to unfold—a curtain-raiser, of sorts—or is it the sound made by the creatures of Zebes themselves?[6] There's no correct answer to this question, and that is precisely the point. By blurring the music-effect divide and, as a result, the distinction between diegetic and non-diegetic sound, Tanaka dismantled the proverbial fourth wall and furthered the pursuit of immersion through sound in video games.

More than thirty years have passed since Tanaka's *Metroid* reached the ears of consumers around the world, and yet its sonic influence is felt to this very day. Whether

Figure 1

it be *Silent Hill* (1999), in which the sounds of sirens, drips, and rattles straddle the diegetic and non-diegetic divide to horrifying effect;[7] *Shadow of the Colossus* (2005), in which extended periods of silence nudge us to question the moral implications of our journey;[8] or *The Legend of Zelda: Breath of the Wild* (2017), in which silence, sound effect, and music intertwine to create a soundscape that is at once real and fantastic, Tanaka's innovative voice is forever whispering—silently—in the background.

Andrew Schartmann is the author of *Super Mario Bros. Soundtrack* (#106).

CHAPTER 45
VARIOUS ARTISTS' *MUSIC FROM THE MOTION PICTURE PULP FICTION* (1994)
Evie Nagy

Of the thousands of unconscious associations my mind has made with music in my life, the most unshakable is this: I can't hear "Jungle Boogie's" final Tarzan wail and guitar beat, in any context, without immediately hearing the first chord and horn blast of "Let's Stay Together," even when they don't come. For that miniscule moment, the songs don't exist separately in my mind; they cease to be their own top-ten hits recorded two years apart by two different artists, basking in two different kinds of joy. As Kool and the Gang's funk anthem reaches its last few measures, the anticipation of Al Green's romantic soul standard feels as certain and nerve-wracking as any iconic key change (let's go with "I Will Always Love You," for illustration's sake).

Music from the Motion Picture Pulp Fiction is certainly not the only album I've listened to hundreds of times through, but unlike any other, I've internalized its musical curves as deeply as the subtle turns on my daily commute. (That transition from the fourth to the fifth track is especially ingrained only because of the general ubiquity of those two songs in the wild; if the Revels' "Comanche" was a regular on the supermarket PA, I'd be hearing the ghost of the Statler Brothers' "Flowers on the Wall" follow on its heels every time.) And like a lot of commutes, the soundtrack coasts through serene moments while simultaneously being drenched in anxiety. This album was critically acclaimed and commercially successful, but I consider it a B-side because it put its songs in such a fraught new context, so unrelated to the success of the original songs, making them their alternate-universe selves.

Part of the excited queasiness I feel every time I listen to the album, or even hear any song from it, is absolutely by design—*Pulp Fiction* is famously a movie about the mundane aspects of criminal life, the low-stakes car chats and bowel movements between adrenaline highs (either naturally brought on by mortal peril, or the kind literally injected into the heart). The soundtrack is inseparable from the movie's suspended dread, because it includes a full seven excerpts from the film itself. The album starts with Pumpkin and Honey Bunny declaring the sweetest of love nothings before violently threatening a diner full of innocent people, equally vexing the Dick Dale cover of Mediterranean folk song "Miserlou" that immediately follows. There's no getting lost in the slow melancholy of Ricky Nelson's "Lonesome Town" or the breezy rhythms of The Lively Ones' "Surf Rider" when Samuel L. Jackson, as bad motherfucker Jules Winnfield, interjects his recitation of Ezekiel 25:17 and the righteous vengeance against the tyranny of evil men. If you've seen the film even once, it's impossible to hear the easy wistfulness of Dusty Springfield's classic "Son of a Preacher Man" without channeling John Travolta's Vincent Vega in the most stressful moment of his life as an assassin: arriving to take out his boss Marcellus Wallace's irresistible wife Mia, whom he is terrified of even glancing at the wrong way.

Girl, you'll be a woman soon. But Quentin Tarantino's willful musical mind games are only part of it. *Pulp Fiction* came out three days before my 18th birthday, a month into my freshman year in college, where I was winging life 3,000 miles from home for the first time. I saw the film in the theater with a boy I'd been not-so-secretly in love with all through high school; one of my only classmates who also crossed the country for college, he took a train to visit for the weekend, something I considered an incredible coup after three years of losing my nerve at every conceivable opportunity. Watching the scene in Jack Rabbit Slim's where Uma Thurman's Mia talks to Vincent about uncomfortable silences—"That's when you know you've met someone really special—when you can just shut the fuck up for a minute and comfortably share a silence"—put me in a colder sweat than any of the movie's actually dangerous predicaments. Afterwards, we sat silently on a park bench in the dark, where he proceeded to paraphrase that very scene, the echo of Chuck Berry's "You Never Can Tell" reverberating between my hot temples. I proceeded to do what I'd been practicing for my entire adolescence: absolutely nothing. We ended up walking back to my dorm where he slept on the common room couch and took the train back early the next morning. I was Vincent Vega, holding back every physical and emotional impulse I had—the difference being that I didn't have a ruthless crime boss who would murder me if I didn't, just a young idiot's desperate fear of nothing whatsoever. *In the town of broken dreams, the streets are filled with regret.*

I don't know if it was punishment or reclamation or just the fact that *Music from the Motion Picture Pulp Fiction* is a bulletproof collection of retro hits and surf-pop transcendence, but I bought the soundtrack on CD the next day, and listened to it obsessively on and off for the next several months. My college years were defined by an almost superhuman level of procrastination, a constant threat of miserable defeat that I narrowly escaped over and over like the James Bond of half-hearted political science majors. A week before my senior thesis was due, I had about seventy-five pages of 125 left to write; I wasn't a drug person (and wouldn't have known where to get them), so a sustained source of adrenaline was my only hope. I won't give myself credit that it was a conscious tactical decision, but something deep told me to put the *Pulp Fiction* soundtrack on repeat for the next week while I wrote around the clock about the effect of Reagan's judicial appointments on civil rights policy, and I did. I finished the thesis the morning that it was due, fell into a previously unexplored level of unconsciousness, and slept through my alarm until 4:55 p.m., when a friend feared for my safety and banged on my door. *Well I guess you'll just have to go wake him up now, won't you?*

Two years and a few months later, I was having the first dance at my wedding to "Let's Stay Together," a song that my boyfriend and I had agreed without hesitation was "our song," despite the fact that my strongest association with it was disappointment, anxiety, and Marcellus Wallace's ominous speech about pride and loyalty. The high-school boy was there at the reception with his new wife. My first husband and I are now married to other people. *It goes to show you never can tell.*

In all this comfort, I can't take the strain. The album's third track is the "Royale with Cheese" dialogue, in which Vincent blows Jules's mind with tales from his recent three-year stint in Amsterdam. Not only is hash mostly legal, he says, but "you can walk into a movie theater and get a beer. I'm not talking about no paper cup, I mean a glass of beer." It's one of the most quoted movie scenes of the 1990s, second maybe to the courtroom scene from *A Few Good Men*—but, in 2019, when recreational weed is legal in multiple states and cinemas are rated by whether they bring the beer glass to your actual seat, it's downright quaint.

Two decades of perspective and experience later, the apprehension and failure that define my relationship with *Music from the Motion Picture Pulp Fiction* feel inflated and naïve, given the reality of the stakes involved. The associations get messier, though, in the context that *Pulp Fiction* was championed by now-known monster Harvey Weinstein, who, it turns out, attacked Thurman herself among countless others in the wake of the film's success. Not to mention Tarantino's own controversial behavior and creative decisions that have either come to light recently or felt more complicated over time. What feels in retrospect like an outsized attachment to an album also feels insufficient; the distress that inhabits it is both calculated and selfish. But damn are those songs good. *Can I get away again tonight?*

Evie Nagy is the author of *Freedom of Choice* (#104). She tweets @EvieN.

CHAPTER 46
VARIOUS ARTISTS' *CASINO* SOUNDTRACK (1995)
Kevin Courrier

In the summer of 1996, while taking a car trip with a good friend of mine to visit his home in Boston, we spent a majority of the drive listening to a diverse collection of music that he provided as a soundtrack for the hours ahead. One CD in the player featured music I'd come to love growing up—rock, R&B, doo-wop, jazz, traditional pop, and classical—but the disc itself seemed so beautifully programed, so daringly eclectic, and full of surprises. There was a fascinating selection of mixed-genre music you would normally never hear occupying the same CD. (Tony Bennett following Cream? Unheard of!) Within moments, it brought back an era seemingly lost from twenty years back, when FM radio (and the DJs who spun the discs) played to an eager desire in the audience for something new. The DJs were hearing ripe possibilities in music listening, where short pop singles were giving way to conceptual albums, and personal taste began to expand its comfort zone. High and low culture were encouraged to commingle. So when I asked my friend if we were listening to some special mix tape of his own design, inspired by his own enthused taste for genre collisions, it turned out that I wasn't even close to being right.

For the past hour, we'd been grooving to the double-CD soundtrack of Martin Scorsese's gangster melodrama *Casino* from earlier that year, featuring music programed by Robbie Robertson, who was clearly working happily in that spirit of enthusiasm for pop collisions. Robertson was the co-founder of The Band, and Scorsese had hired him as music producer shortly after making *The Last Waltz*, a film about The Band's last concert before retiring from the road. Most of that movie, outside of the actual concert, was about how music came to matter to this community of people who spent their life performing and making a living from it. Curiously, despite the deft selection of tunes that make up the score of *Casino*, neither of us had actually enjoyed the picture, and I barely recalled the individual tracks beyond the fact that music was used as if it were wall-to-wall sound totally irrelevant to the drama on the screen. On its own, however, separate from its movie source, the *Casino* soundtrack had its own dramatic story to tell—and it was far more compelling than the film. On the disc, the sequencing of film composer Georges Delerue (main title theme for Jean Luc Godard's 1963 *Contempt*), jazz vocalist Louis Prima ("Angelina/Zooma, Zooma Medley"), Devo ("[I Can't Get No] Satisfaction"), Mickey and Sylvia ("Love is Strange"), Roxy Music ("Love is the Drug"), Muddy Waters ("Hoochie Coochie Man"), and Bach's "St. Matthaus Passion" created a listening freedom to explore the immensely seductive underpinnings of pop, standards and the classics—a musical merry-go-round that provided you with good reason to experience music you had never tried before. On the other hand, watching the movie *Casino* only got you strung out on the sensations of garish melodrama. The music, largely disconnected from the characters on the screen, functioned like speed as if to get you pumped on the action and to draw attention to the bravura in Scorsese's film-making.

Based on Nicholas Pileggi's nonfiction book, *Casino: Love and Honor in Las Vegas*, Scorsese and Pileggi were basically backfilling the ground of the previous success they had in 1990 with *Goodfellas*, which is also about the rise and fall of an ambitious gangster, and which features a lot of good music used to help him climb the rungs. The criminal protagonist in *Goodfellas* is a young hotshot Irish-Sicilian, Henry Hill (Ray Liotta), who ascends that ladder of the mob until drugs and ratting to the authorities put him on a runaway train to oblivion in witness protection. *Casino* is a more ambitious tale than *Goodfellas*, but it's also far more impersonal. Looking at the rise and fall of organized crime in controlling gambling in the desert oasis of Las Vegas, *Casino* centers on Sam "Ace" Rothstein (Robert De Niro), a Jewish American handicapper who is hired by the Chicago operation in the 1970s to oversee the Tangiers Casino while his enforcer friend, Nicky (Joe Pesci), provides protection for Sam and helps the bosses back in Chicago skim from the club's profits. By the early 1980s, however, the mobsters in their blind zeal to get rich also get too greedy and—after much bloodshed—lose control of Vegas to legitimate corporate interests.

Unlike the great gangster dramas of the past, like *Scarface*, *The Public Enemy*, or *The Godfather*, *Casino* doesn't provide a compelling protagonist, so it takes refuge instead in an overwrought parody of excesses, one that abandons character drama so that the music and outbursts of violence end up filling the holes left by actors with too little to play. The CD soundtrack to *Casino* has a more coherent dramatic structure; the differences between the individual songs provide contrast, conflict, and flow and give us a sense of what was in the air culturally that these violent criminals were breathing in. Although it may still be a common truth that a good soundtrack can't save a bad movie (taste being relative, there are many who feel that *Casino* is actually a *great* gangster picture), this perception changes when the score is no longer an orchestral one with the traditional operatic structure of the classic Hollywood period. When popular music becomes the sole source of the score, we quickly have a personal investment in it since that music wasn't originally written for the picture. This music already had an inner life, maybe in our memories from its time on the radio somewhere in our past, or perhaps today buried somewhere in our record collection. It may also have an inner life, too, in the memories of the characters in the drama we're watching. The task of the director (and screenwriter) is often to locate that inner life and make it the connecting tissue between the audience and the characters on the screen. That's what *Casino* fails to do with its score.

Sometimes incessant bows to sensuality can become like cocaine hyping up dead air, as the use of music proved to be in much of Scorsese's *Goodfellas* and most of *Casino*. While it's hard to argue with the inclusion of indelible tracks in *Casino*, like the transcendent "I'll Take You There" by The Staple Singers (you could argue, however, that Scorsese could have picked a *better* scene than Sam taking his con-artist wife, played by Sharon Stone, to the bank), or Clarence "Frogman" Henry's delectable "Ain't Got No Home" (in the less-than-delectable scene where Pesci's Nicky gratuitously abuses a dealer at the gambling table), or Tony Bennett's "Rags to Riches" (which also underscores Henry Hill's early desires to be a gangster in *Goodfellas*, one of the best uses of music in both pictures), the tunes are overall too busy.

In *Goodfellas*, the music doesn't even go with what we're watching most of the time, as in the scene where Hill is madly dashing about in a state of paranoia being chased by cops in helicopters while we inexplicably hear George Harrison's spiritual ode "What is Life." Scorsese's promiscuous use of pop music here becomes comparable to Hal Ashby's in *Coming Home*, his sentimental Vietnam War drama, where the music pretty much drowns out the picture when it isn't being applied to make points. (The inclusion of The Rolling Stones' "Out of Time" ["You're out of touch my baby"] as Bruce Dern's clearly reactionary military officer marches along kills the appeal of the song.) Only the sadly majestic piano coda to Derek and the Domino's "Layla," used over the discovery of dead gangsters in a trunk, creates a powerful counterpoint to the successful robbery that would ultimately lead to those corpses in *Goodfellas*.

In *Casino*, the pop score is even more scatter shot than in *Goodfellas*. Why not resist including an obvious and sloppy medley of organist Jimmy Smith's take on Elmer Bernstein's "Walk on the Wild Side," The Rolling Stones' "Gimme Shelter," and The Animals' powerful rendition of "The House of the Rising Sun" to illuminate the tragedy of Sharon Stone's heroin overdose? Does Scorsese really need to use the entire seven-minute take of The Stones' "Can You Hear Me Knocking?" as we watch the routine of gathering cash at the gambling establishment? Does he like the song too much to cut it? The soundtrack CDs of *Goodfellas*, *Casino*, and *Bringing Out the Dead* all feature tracks that can get you jumping with pleasure, but in the movies they come across as throwaway punch lines.

Who knows if Martin Scorsese will ever be able to startle an audience again with a song the way he did in *Mean Streets* (especially in that fleeting moment when Charlie lets himself go in a ridiculously spontaneous drunken dance to The Chips' equally ridiculous doo-wop hit, "Rubber Biscuit"). But he still shows a wry cleverness in picking tracks despite the capricious choices in *Casino*. His 2010 psychological thriller *Shutter Island* was less an adaptation of author Dennis Lehane's mystery thriller than it was a cluttered labyrinth and virtual fun-house of the director's favorite film noir tropes. It was hardly fun and barely coherent. On the other hand, once again, the soundtrack put together by Robbie Robertson for the movie is all of that. Featuring Ligeti's modernist "Lontano," Ingram Marshall's "Fog Tropes"—scored for brass sextet and fog horns—Mahler's unfinished *Piano Quartet*, some prepared piano by John Cage ("Music for Marcel Duchamp"), and the dissonant chords of Krzysztof Penderecki ("Symphony No. 3: Passacaglia—Allegro Moderato"), plus Lonnie Johnson's haunting "Tomorrow Night" and Johnny Ray's eerie "Cry," the score is a central nervous system for a movie that just isn't there. The modern music Robertson uses has a way of creating a psychological tapestry that takes into account the modernist perspective on the twentieth century.

There's one track, heard over the concluding credits of *Shutter Island*, however, that conveys a larger tragedy than almost any of the film itself. Robbie Robertson creates an ingenious mash-up of Dinah Washington's mournfully elegant 1960 hit "This Bitter Earth" (heard once before with powerful resonance in Charles Burnett's 1977 *Killer of Sheep*) and British composer Max Richter's gorgeously melancholic "On the Nature of Daylight" (from his 2004 album *The Blue Notebooks*). Robertson offers what critic Bradley Bambarger called "an improbably pure evocation of a shuttering heart."[1] The song is soaked in the harsh experience of being black in America at the turning point of the Civil Rights struggle in the early 1960s. But it's Richter's strings that provide the tears that Washington can't cry. The song made little sense at the end of *Shutter Island*, but it takes you somewhere more substantial and stirring when the film is over. If the music in Scorsese's recent films (with the exception of his purely magical *Hugo*) no longer seems to provide their inner voice, the music itself is never negligible. Which is why the *Casino* soundtrack is always near my stereo despite how forgettable the movie itself is. When Paul Coates defines cinema as a "dream of an after-life from which to comprehend this one," he isn't talking about Martin Scorsese's later movies.[2] It doesn't even begin to describe them. But he could be describing the enduring appeal of a Martin Scorsese jukebox.

Kevin Courrier is the author of *Trout Mask Replica* (#44). He sadly passed away during the editing of this volume.

CHAPTER 47
WESLEY WILLIS' *ROCK 'N' ROLL WILL NEVER DIE.* (1996)
Phillip Crandall

Wesley Willis head-butted me hard enough for the hundreds inside Common Grounds in Gainesville, Florida, to have heard. We repeated "rah" and "raow" to each other in a rock-star communion every bit as life-affirming as I had hoped, and when Wesley stormed the stage and fired up his keyboard—using the same factory-setting pattern he would play, at various speeds and keys, all night long—the jam session was, to crib an adjective Wesley uses nineteen times on *Rock 'N' Roll Will Never Die*, "awesome."

***

"In India, they call them masts, which means a God-intoxicated person," says Bob Fredericks, a friend of Wesley's, in the 2008 documentary, *Wesley Willis's Joy Rides.*[1] "Somebody who acts abnormal, somebody who acts like they're crazy, but they're not crazy at all. They're, in fact, so in love with God, so in love with life, that they act imbalanced…. I think Wesley may be one of these types of people."

Looking back on that concert nearly two decades later, I couldn't tell you which fatty foods or suck-it insults or defeated superheroes or commercial slogans Wesley sang about. I struggle enough trying to convey just how joyous and transcendent that show was.

Wesley was, to use Fredericks's illuminating term, a mast—in love with, intoxicated by, and an inspiring ecstatic force through music.

***

About a century ago, a teenager in India was riding his bike. He would eventually coin the Bobby McFerrin-popularized phrase "Don't worry, be happy," and inspire The Who song mistakenly called "Teenage Wasteland." But before those tributes, the teen crossed paths with Hazrat Babajan, a Muslim saint considered by her followers to be a Perfect Master. "She beckoned Him to her and kissed Him on the forehead," Don Stevens writes, "subsequently revealing to Him His true state as the *Avatar*, the total manifestation of God in human form."[2] (After Wesley head-butted my forehead, he sold me a T-shirt.)

That teen was Meher Baba, and it's through his detailed missions that followers have become familiar with the mast (pronounced *must*). "One of the criteria for recognizing someone who is a mast … is the effect they have on people around them," continues Fredericks.[3] "Usually a mad person, you want to keep away and they have sort of a disturbing effect. Whereas Wesley had the opposite. He could uplift people ... and people liked to be around him."[4]

Fredericks got to know Wesley at Genesis, an art store Wesley frequented when he wasn't out capturing the broad shoulders and busy streets of Chicago in drawings he'd sell to friends and passers-by. In 1989, his mother's boyfriend robbed him at gunpoint of those earnings, and voices in Wesley's head would forevermore insult him, tell him to give up art, and turn any moment into what Wesley called a "hell ride." Diagnosed with schizophrenia (Greek for "split mind"), Wesley would hit right back, publicly cursing out demons that went by names like Nerve Wrecker, Heart Breaker, and Mean Sucker. "I used to hear music in my head between 1978 to 1989 when I was riding Pace buses for joy," Wesley said, "but now since that demon took over me with profanity, I don't ride Pace buses for joy anymore. I'm afraid I might holler on them and get picked up by the police."[5]

Carla Winterbottom, a friend and former roommate, says Wesley was more social than most people with schizophrenia.[6] When he'd check himself into the psych ward during particularly bad times, he'd be "the only bright light up in there," skipping down halls because he'd sold a doctor a drawing. "When he was happy, he was just really, *really* happy," she says. "I remember him putting headphones on and his head moving ... singing along and smiling ear to ear. Part of the appeal was that it would help drown out the voices. I think it was some desperate self-medication."[7]

Fredericks had previously put some of Wesley's spoken-word riffs to a beat, but one day, following quality time spent with Genesis employees who were playing shows by night, Wesley committed himself to letting there be rock. He came home, asked for a notebook, and wrote a handful of songs that night, including "I'm Sorry That I Got Fat."[8] Immediately, the force that provided Wesley with "joy rides" became the very force Wesley gifted back to the world. "Never had a doubt in his mind that he was going to become a rock star," says Winterbottom. "It was funny, sweet, honest, and pure. And good. He knew how to deliver things. He had almost a preacher's kind of cadence."[9]

***

Observant Muslims will kneel forward and place their foreheads on the ground at least thirty-four times a day in prayer. This can callous the foreheads of long-practicing Muslims and create a "zebibah" (Arabic for raisin), which some believe will emanate light on the Day of Judgment. To his friend Michael Muhammad Knight, Wesley was "a 6'5", 350-pound Mercy to the Worlds," and the permanent head-butt-caused bump on Wesley's forehead was "the mark of a genuine saint."[10] "That was the human contact he had," Winterbottom says. "He was kind of childlike otherwise ... so this was his human touch and his intimacy. It was really important to him to have those headbutts."[11]

Baba describes masts as being "very sensitive to the spiritual needs of those who come in touch with them ... [and they] can give to aspirants just that type of occult help that is necessary."[12] With Wesley, that sensitive awareness revealed itself through charisma. Winterbottom says flying with Wesley was fascinating because "people would look on in horror initially, then eventually be charmed [and] buying CDs."[13]

Dale Meiners, Wesley's friend and guitarist in The Wesley Willis Fiasco, saw the charisma work wonders with his hustle. They'd go to concerts together, and Wesley would bring his trusty carrying case full of CDs to sell in the front lobby.[14] He remembers the sales-driven Wesley once telling a distributor who tried buying albums on a standard consignment deal: "You're not taking my record—you're paying for my records." Meiners bets it's "the only deal in history where they paid full price in advance."[15]

And once Wesley began banking, Winterbottom says it all "got put back into existing," listing Wesley's existence-essentials as:

- eating
- having a place to sleep ("He looked pretty disheveled and some people might have jumped to the conclusion that he was homeless, but he never lived on the streets")
- making more art or music ("It was really that fundamental to his identity and his coping with everything").[16]

"Without that music, I'd be in a demon hell ride forever," Wesley said. "That demon would kill me."[17]

Meiners says one of the first songs the Fiasco recorded was "He's Doing Time in Jail," just days after what inspired the lyrics: "He goes, 'I was having a fight with a demon on the bus, and this guy thought I was yelling at him. He sliced me in the face with a boxcutter.' It was really grotesque and fresh when we recorded that. To experience that kind of energy in a room was just unbelievable [and] emotional."[18]

Wesley's albums are loaded with raw glimpses of internal torment … right alongside heartfelt hilarity, with inspired similes, turns of phrase, and other wordplay sprinkled throughout hundreds (thousands?) of songs. He may be infamous for issuing fauna-focused oral ultimatums, but as he says in *Wesley Willis's Joy Rides*, "I write songs about bestiality and real life."[19]

And it is in real life's portrayal of intoxicating music that this album is particularly powerful.

***

Rock 'N' Roll Will Never Die is a 1996 compilation[20] of songs almost entirely from self-released recordings, mostly about shows Wesley attended. "If he goes and sees a band he likes, he writes a song about how much he likes them," writes Jello Biafra.[21] "Since he has an erratic short term memory, it matters not at all whether it's the same song he wrote about the last band. Or the last fifty bands."

Most opening verses of the twenty-four songs here begin "This band played at," followed by the venue name, attendance estimate, and a recognition that the show whipped some animal's ass. The band in question is triumphantly revealed in the chorus and, over the course of these accounts, props are paid to how the band "got down" (often like a Magikist, a defunct Chicago rug-cleaning company), how the crowd "roared like a lion," and just how awesome the "jam session" was. (Songs that don't follow that concert motif here pay tribute to individual musicians such as Biafra, Meiners, Liz Phair, Dave Grohl, and KRS-One.)

Wesley not being the awestruck type—"he would think the Rolling Stones would want to meet him," says Meiners[22]—these tributes come from a purer place of a larger love. They are to those creating the intoxicating music, real names be proof, and as Wesley fulfills his own DIY rock-star prophecy, that intoxicating experience could be your life, a prophecy fulfilled with the last track, playing out like so many others and titled "The Wesley Willis Fiasco."

Throughout his mast missions, Baba would reiterate that he wasn't teaching new truths, but that those truths had already been revealed by "great Ones";[23] it's humanity's job to realize those truths, and Baba's job to awaken humanity to that realization. On *Rock 'N' Roll Will Never Die*, Wesley's mission is strikingly quixotic (Don, being a *book*-intoxicated traveler and suspected schizophrenia-sufferer, endeavored to pay tribute to literary heroes through adventures which "being once happily achieved, might gain him eternal renown"[24]), and definitely Baba-esque.

Wesley isn't playing covers; he's alerting listeners to what music *does*, with wake-up calls about every two minutes and fifty seconds. A concert as Wesley celebrates it is an experience where a roused crowd is crucial. ("Spin Doctors," track eight, not only begins with crowd noise, but has the occasional "rah"—begging for a "raow" reply—mixed in as well.) So, while "jam session" works anywhere in describing a band locking into a groove, Wesley repeatedly makes the phrase soar by incorporating—almost *requiring*—the audience response capable of unlocking all.

Wesley's idealized show whips one animal, and the crowd responds roaring like another. Barbara Ehrenreich, in *Dancing in the Streets*, writes of animals being conjured up by early hominids as they stamped and waved sticks in defensive unison ("the predator might be tricked by this synchronous behavior into thinking that it faced—not a group of individually weak and defenseless humans—but a single, very large animal"[25]), which likely led to "communal hunting" and on to dance rituals that re-enacted and celebrated those successes. "When we speak of transcendent experience in terms of 'feeling part of something larger than ourselves,'" she writes, "it may be this ancient many-headed pseudocreature that we unconsciously invoke."[26]

While music gets credit for soothing savage beasts (and muzzling mean suckers), a whip/roaring "jam session" connecting those on both sides of the artist/audience split creates a harmony grander than any pleasant-sounding note combo; it reveals a higher communal truth. Ehrenreich writes that religion today provides people with their sense of community, but that faiths are "pallid affairs—if only by virtue of the very fact that they *are* 'faiths,' dependent on, and requiring, belief as opposed to direct knowledge."[27] In prehistoric rituals, our celebrating ancestor *knew* her god/gods because "at the height of group ecstasy, they filled her with their presence."

To those in love with, intoxicated by, and striving to be an ecstatic force for music, that harmonious jam-session presence is an almighty joy ride, and it will never die.

"Wes was deeply religious," Biafra said after Wesley's death in 2003.[28] "He was afraid that if he died he would no longer get to go see bands play. If there is a hereafter, I hope he's right up front as Jimi Hendrix, Stevie Ray Vaughan, his beloved Otis Redding, and his dear friend Bradley from Sublime 'storm the stage' as the crowd 'roars like a sea monster.'"

"All opening for Wesley, of course."[29]

Phillip Crandall is the author of *I Get Wet* (#89). Find him at phillipcrandall.com.

CHAPTER 48

NINE INCH NAILS' *THE FRAGILE* (1999)

Luis Sanchez

The Fragile debuted at number one on the *Billboard 200* in the week of October 9, 1999. Whatever labels could be used to describe Nine Inch Nails before—industrial, alternative, sacrilegious—achievements like this aren't explainable in terms of genre. It was music blatantly staked out in opposition to the music of the moment, but at the same time an instance of it. "I like the challenges of flirting with the mainstream with Nine Inch Nails,"[1] Trent Reznor said in a *Rolling Stone* interview at the time. "You know, let Fred Durst surf a piece of plywood up my ass."[2] The week after it was released, *The Fragile* dropped fifteen spots. Notwithstanding the plywood trash talk, Reznor's words registered an ambition that only a few years earlier would've discredited any punk-rock politics in his music, if it ever had any. What made the moment *The Fragile* arrived matter is the way it embodied one of the great thrills of popular music. In full view of the mainstream, it broke apart and reassembled the pieces that previously held Reznor and his music together.

You only have to think back to the mainstream music of 1999 to remember how benign its creative nerve had become. *The Downward Spiral*, Nine Inch Nails' previous album—a staggering work of synthesized histrionics—was released in March 1994, about one month before Kurt Cobain ended his life with a shotgun: a warning against the collapsing of popular art under its own success. Over the next few years, Reznor outpaced Cobain. After turning Nine Inch Nails from a modest-sized alternative music act into a headliner of festivals, making soundtracks for Oliver Stone and David Lynch, even licensing songs for commercials, it seemed the only thing left was how to keep a line like "I want to fuck you like an animal" from sounding hokey. It wasn't that Reznor's growls about self-destruction and provocative music videos had lost their capacity to excite; it was that, once Cobain's suicide settled into a shared consciousness, Nine Inch Nails' trashy industrial BDSM stylings started wearing a bit tacky. And yet, by the end of the decade, as boy bands and teen singers resurged as if to make everyone forget that popular music could draw any lines, Reznor emerged as the only star capable of arousing any sense of fright in a mainstream that desperately needed it.

Art, success, expectations—all of this felt at hand when Nine Inch Nails performed on the 1999 MTV Video Music Awards. The live September broadcast featured a procession of performances by acts like Britney Spears, the Backstreet Boys, Kid Rock, Eminem, and Ricky Martin. The drift of their performances was little more than acknowledging for their audiences what those audiences already knew: to be a successful pop star in 1999 meant being good at drawing excitement out of camp and honing an image out of flamboyant stage gimmickry. Nine Inch Nails pulled off something else entirely.

Going against glam and ostentation, Reznor and his band performed "The Fragile," an unreleased piece from *The Fragile*, the first Nine Inch Nails album in five years, which wouldn't be released for another couple of weeks. What unfolded over the next several minutes was a drama of dissolution and reinvention. Gone was the ceaseless fury that defined the band's earlier performance style, when Reznor used his keyboards, his bandmates, and the stage itself as objects to thrash against. Here, the fury had given way to what one suspected was always behind it: stark, anchored beauty.

Reznor, like all the best performers, understands the language of gesticulation, of the body as spectacle. No longer the wispy figure from the "Closer" video, he now looked a more solid man, every physical movement and flourish indicative of well-conditioned muscle and bone. It wasn't in spite of this new image, but because of it, that the new music had an immediate and staggering effect. Lyrically, "The Fragile" is stock love song. But what was striking wasn't that you were hearing Reznor singing something as all-mawkish as "She shines in a world full of ugliness," but how the determination in the way he sang that line went beyond any sort of pop sentimentalism. Against the romanticism of the lyrics, Reznor's steady physicality registered a different sort of masculine vulnerability—the possibility of his virility being misread. "I won't let you fall apart," he vamped over and over, each repetition more forceful than before. The music expanded and swirled until it felt like the stage might actually burst open. The band summoned a torrent of sound, and Reznor, howling from the center of the stage, was the only force keeping it all together. Then it wasn't a love song anymore; Reznor wasn't singing to someone else. He was confronting a sense of himself. And he was more than just asserting his existence, he was insisting on it. The performance was about as masterful and free-floating as a musical gesture can be.

Even though as record-making *The Fragile* may be a feat of brilliance, as a double album that tries very hard to dramatize the pathos only hinted at on *The Downward Spiral*, it's a facile masterwork. This is what makes the record a B-side, why I can't stop listening to it. There's not much artistic profundity in it, and the harder you try to find any, the more you'll question the nerve of what you're hearing. *The Fragile* isn't an album of ideas or messages, it's an album of sensations.

Not one but two discs at first suggest that Reznor has broadened the scope of his rage and taste for luridness. What you actually hear isn't a wider range of those things but the sound of a person hurling himself into the fear and trembling that stir beneath them. If the concept of *The Downward Spiral* had something to do with one man's (semi-autobiographical?) descent into madness, Reznor trades plot for ambiguity here. Lyrics about betrayal, despair, and desolation float and collide through towering arrangements that veer abruptly from chaos to delicate murmur, usually within the same track. Reznor often sings about being haunted, not by specters somewhere out there but by the internal horror that he might himself be a ghost. Much of the adventure of *The Fragile* comes from hearing Reznor use the materiality of his voice to push that horror to the edge of dread, rendering the sense of self implied by the lyrics all but a figment of being. And then a line or musical phrase will break through to remind you what's at stake isn't some significance at the center of disquietude but the singer's—and by implication, the listener's—response to it. Most of these moments are passing, but when they occur, it's as if the music's entire architecture was erected just to give them their impact.

My favorite cut from the album, "Into the Void," suspends one of these moments into an entire song, and then goes one step further. Reznor's sense of the possibilities of rhythm has always been his signature strength. The best Reznor productions are marked by the way beat patterns, syncopations, and percussive textures pulse and swerve not as gestures of production virtuosity but as rhythmic articulations, as ways into the music by listening with your whole body. So it's no coincidence that "Into the Void" is the album's most danceable cut and, I think, the funkiest record Reznor has ever released. "Tried to save myself but myself keeps slipping away," runs the central line of the song. It's bleak, a little sardonic. Reznor sings it as if existential dread were nothing more than an attitude, a mood registered as style. Synthesized funk lines, guitar, and vocal tracks take shape and bear down hard. Everything is surface groove. Until it isn't. Three minutes in, the rhythms and textures start to sink, resurface, and fragment all at once. Suddenly Reznor is singing as if the dread were gushing from a laceration across his throat. What you're hearing is the sound of a man breaking apart and coming into being at the same time. And because "Into the Void" presents itself as a dance record, what really matters as a listener isn't the losing of yourself in the music but feeling more present—*more conscious*—in your body because of it. For an album that concerns itself with depths and voids, it's remarkable, then, just how well *The Fragile* gives form and dimension to the act of creation out of fragmentation. Taking on nothingness, Reznor says yes to existence.

Luis Sanchez is the author of *Smile* (#94). Find him on Twitter @LouieSanchezz.

CHAPTER 49
BOB DYLAN'S *LOVE AND THEFT* (2001)
Pete Astor

A is for abecedarium or abecedary. This is a way of addressing a subject alphabetically, apparently very popular in medieval times when the alphabet was thought to possess magic powers. This kind of stricture is also a useful way of limiting, and thus enriching, ways of understanding a record as layered and potent as Bob Dylan's 2001 album, *Love and Theft*.

B is for B-side. Taste is relative. With an artist as monumental as Bob Dylan, sometimes you need to go small to make sense of someone so big. So, I know *Love and Theft* is not the best Bob Dylan album, but it's *my* best Bob Dylan album. So there!

C is for clothes. Dylan has (mostly) covered this area excellently, but after some woeful sartorial mishaps, particularly in the 1980s, the clothes he sports on the sleeve photos reach an apotheosis—they are clothes that exactly mirror the mythic and timeless quality of the music within. Look at David Gahr's inner sleeve photos taken around Brooklyn, picturing Dylan standing in the pavilion on the Coney Island boardwalk: the piping on those trousers!

D is for Dylan. Just like the clothes he wears, *Love and Theft* shows an artist who has reached an understanding, a rapprochement, with who he really is. He's in step, in tune with himself.

E is for *Empire Burlesque*, a 1986 Dylan album that provides a neat mirror companion to *Love and Theft*, the former being pretty much everything that the latter is not. The jacket on the sleeve says it all—a timeless artist in high-end 1980s designer trash, worn because he doesn't realize his value exists beyond the contemporary Album-oriented Rock (AOR) market. Of course, on *Empire Burlesque* the songs are good but the band is made up of jobbing session players, the production is 1980s pop out-of-a-packet and Bob is just a lonely interloper in his own identity.

F is for flow. This is a theory, a way of living developed by Hungarian-American psychologist Mihaly Csikszentmihalyi. In essence, one achieves flow when one forgets oneself in the act of doing something. While this is not specific to *Love and Theft*, there is a sense that here Dylan achieves a kind of simple immersion in what he does, for the sake of doing it, which makes the record so comfortable in its skin.

G is for Grateful Dead. After his 1987 tour with the quintessential American road band, Dylan learned an important lesson; he discovered, or rediscovered, the value of making music for its own sake and foregrounding the act of performing it live. The live album that resulted from his collaboration with the Dead may be forgettable, but after this Dylan had a new faith and focus in his work.

H is for home; in this case, home on the road. After his tours with The Dead, Dylan located himself in the world of live performance, getting fully in step with his famous observation that he was "just a song and dance man."[1]

I is for inverted commas. The use of these in the album title creates a distance, putting the creator at one remove from the reader and presenting the phrase as something to be reflected upon.

J is for Jack Frost, the moniker that Dylan decided to give the "producer." Chris Shaw recorded, engineered, and mixed the record at Clinton Recording in Manhattan. Jack Frost would seem to be a moniker for the "producer" Dylan wanted, who made a recording that sounded like a recording rather than a production, capturing the sound of the musicians and creating the illusion of a "transparent" recording, albeit one that is effectively situated, sonically, in the 1950s and 1960s, using the sounds of tape, spring reverbs, and live takes. Listen to the 1960s-style hard left and right panning on the twin lead guitars on "Summer Days."

K is for knowledge. For all his eccentricities, for all the ways in which Dylan's singing and guitar-playing seem to get "worse" over the decades, let's not forget his huge, encompassing, and containing knowledge of his field. This is why, approximately thirty-nine years into his career, *Love and Theft* is so good.

L is for *Love and Theft* the book, or, more accurately, *Love & Theft: Blackface Minstrelsy and the American Working Class*. Eric Lott's study explores an often-overlooked part of America's musical history, mining more nuanced understandings of America's relationship with black culture, which would probably have struck a chord with Dylan and is likely to be the source of the album title, perhaps accounting for those inverted commas.

M is for musicianship. This is sometimes a contested area, the idea of virtuosic musicianship being fallaciously predicated on an encyclopedic knowledge of musical theory or playing music in complex time signatures. In fact, one of the best examples of true musicianship is demonstrated by the musicians on this album, who deliver sensitivity, restraint, groove, a lightness of touch, and understanding of the form; it's something like magic, I'd say. The players were Dylan's core live musicians at the time: Larry Campbell and Charlie Sexton on guitars, David Kempner on drums, and the perennial Tony Garnier on bass. These players, unlike the musicians on most of Dylan's previous records, had long been the nucleus of his touring show. Even so, Dylan maintained his sometimes-distant relationship with his band. When recording songs for the album, according to engineer Chris Shaw: "If the band wasn't grasping what he wanted, he was frustrated and would kick them in the ass by listening to the last take and saying, 'I guess I don't have the manpower to make this song work—I'll just go out there myself with my guitar.'"[2] In the end, the musicians would get to play on the song, but, as always, with no guarantees. As Larry Campbell remembers: "When we went on to the next tune, I guess that's when you knew we had got it in one form or another."[3]

N is for the so-called "never ending tour." Since 1988, after his epiphany playing with The Grateful Dead, apart from an enforced gap caused by a life-threatening illness in 1997, Dylan has been almost consistently on the road. He himself is somewhat dismissive of the name and the concept; in 2009, he made his point: "Does anybody call Henry Ford a Never Ending Car Builder? Anybody ever say that Duke Ellington was on a Never Ending Bandstand Tour?"[4] He knows it's a job like any other, he knows he has, like his heroes, become the aforementioned "song and dance man" he always aspired to be.

O is for old. *Love and Theft* was made as Dylan reached his 60th year, arguably finding a balance in his life and work, living his music and inhabiting his world, joining it all up, squaring the circle, also an "O" …

P is for photos. The front cover shot, along with a group shot, is by Kevin Mazur, booklet photos in Los Angeles are by Danny Clinch, and those around Brooklyn are by David Gahr. In each picture, Dylan embodies his persona: look at those black and white patent leather shoes, look at the leather coat he's wearing in Los Angeles, look at the gloves! The photos show someone inhabiting a parallel, self-created world. And one where only Dylan could be sporting a pencil moustache and it makes perfect stylistic sense.

Q is for quotation. Both musically and lyrically, Dylan uses quotation as part of the creative process. Remember, before the locking down of copyright law in the 1930s, the antecedents of Dylan's work operated in what was a basically copyright-free zone. On *Love and Theft* he carries the tradition on. There was some controversy regarding the discovery of lines that Dylan used; for example, some were lifted almost verbatim from Junichi Saga's book *Confessions of a Yakuza*, among other sources, highlighting the misunderstandings of how popular music was and is made. In 2012, Dylan explained it very clearly: "I'm working within my artform. It's that simple … it's called songwriting. It has to do with melody and rhythm, and then after that, anything goes. You make everything yours."[5]

R is for reception theory. Aesthetic value used to be thought to reside in a canonical hierarchy decided upon by the so-called "great and good"; that is to say, actually the powerful and influential, the critics, the business people, the cultural gatekeepers of any given time. Now we know that our estimations of works of art are largely personal and idiosyncratic and, therefore, relative. So, in my world, *Love and Theft* is the best Dylan album …

S is for style. Dylan has always understood how important style is: from his "authentic" tousled folkie look in Greenwich Village at the start of his career to the full-on Carnaby Street modishness of 1966. By the time of *Love and Theft* Dylan was the mythical dandy wearing clothes that looked like they came from an imaginary tailor who'd been making clothes for Hank Williams et al. since the 1950s.

T is for Theme Time Radio Hour, the name of Dylan's own satellite radio show that was broadcast between 2006 and 2009. Dylan as DJ raised eyebrows initially; it felt like a step sideways, down, even. But, of course, he proved us very wrong; his seductive tones and the exemplary choice of cross-era popular music were spot on and provided a perfect set of reference points for his recently invigorated music and muse.

U is for the United States of America. Non-native Americans, lacking their own King Arthur or Shakespeare's house in Stratford-upon-Avon even, had to make their own myths and legends, and the self-generated myth of the United States—a panoply of twentieth-century characters and places—suffuses the album.

V is for voice. By *Love and Theft*, Dylan's voice possesses a grain that would have made Roland Barthes proud (not withstanding Barthes's disregard for popular music). Dylan's 2001 voice has a line to all the great singers in Dylan's world—from Charley Patton to Hank Williams to Louis Armstrong—that is, the world of popular music.

W is for words. I'd say that no one really *listens* to the words on a record, we *hear* them. It's an important distinction. If we read back the lyrics on the album, they are remarkable: swerving, elliptical, wise, and funny distillations of an imagined idea of American song. When "Summer Days" swings, the words become performed language, existing way beyond the page.

X is for The Cross. God has always inhabited Dylan's work and world, sometimes overtly, as is the case here. He is a presence throughout *Love and Theft* and appears by name in the first and last songs on the album, partly benign, partly threatening, but always potent and omnipresent.

Y is for youth, specifically the music of Dylan's own past. There are theories that the music we hear in adolescence forms us and stays as a kind of spiritual and emotional bedrock to our musical worlds. There is some inconclusive evidence that it has something to do with synapse formation, but what's much more likely is that it is simply to do with social factors and the importance of identity formation during puberty. So, the album inhabits a musical world of Bob at, say, age 13 or 14, the era of jump blues, western swing, rhythm and blues, and pop, just before the idea of "rock 'n' roll" as a musical style solidified. And, sure enough, Dylan was looking to a specific pre-rock past for inspiration. "All my songs, the styles I work in, were all developed before I was born," he said at the time. "When I came into the world, that spirit of things was still very strong. Billie Holiday was still alive. Duke Ellington. All those old blues singers were still alive. And that was the music that was dear to me. I was never really interested in pop music."[6]

Z is for Zimmerman. Around 1959, a young Bob made the move to become "Dylan." In so doing, he was looking to the future, putting on the style, inventing himself, and stepping into show business. *Love and Theft* is the embodiment of that.

Pete Astor is the author of *Blank Generation* (#92). Find him at peteastor.com.

CHAPTER 50
SILVER JEWS' *BRIGHT FLIGHT* (2001)
Hayden Childs

There is no more seductive liar than depression. It's a voice that knows you better than anyone—hell, it's been with you for so long that you don't even know it's not you—but it is not your friend. If you let it, depression will wrap itself around you like a toxic cloud, obscuring the world with its haze. Or perhaps it'll tell you that you're alone in a diving bell, only able to access the world through its lens. You'll find yourself gazing out at the improbable miracle of existence and, when the voice whispers "all of this is better off without you," what can you do but believe it? This is how it seduces you, with words that say you are special, you are a mistake, you alone can see this, everyone knows, and the contradictions make it true.

These are depressing times. *Bright Flight* was written and recorded in 2000 and 2001, back when Bush 43 was relitigating the 1960s, and as awful as those times were, they seem quaint now. We have actual Nazis killing people in the streets and a government led by people who don't mind. But it wasn't just the outside world feeding the darkness on *Bright Flight*. David Berman was at his lowest here and, like other artifacts of pain (let's say *Blood on the Tracks*, *Pink Moon*, and *Shoot Out the Lights* for context), his art renders his suffering transcendent. These songs are co-written with that voice of depression; Berman is deep inside his own fog, lost in his own dark woods, lonely at the bottom of the coldest, darkest place in the ocean. The only defense he offers against whatever is encroaching is how fucking funny he finds it all.

That sense of pain is what makes *Bright Flight* a B-side, even among those who love the Silver Jews. It is easy to reach for 1998's *American Water*, with its Stephen Malkmus-influenced sense of fun. It is easy to reach for 2005's *Tanglewood Numbers*, which is as thorough a refutation of depression as one could imagine ("There is a place beyond the blues I never want to see again," as Berman sings on the final song). But *Bright Flight* is a hard album, a tough dive into Berman's psyche even for the tiny fraction of indie-rock fans who love the Silver Jews. When I chatted with other Jews fans at a surprise cover band event in January 2018, every single one recoiled when I told them I was writing about this album. Why not *American Water*? they asked, or why not *The Natural Bridge*? I love those albums, but they are easy to love. I love *Bright Flight* because it hurts.

Bright Flight opens with a creation myth. In the first lines of "Slow Education," a young god makes the world and sun. "And since then," sings Berman, "it's been a slow education." The idea Berman keeps returning to is the one about dying. How do you stop time when the times are falling apart? The only way to step off the inexorable march is to just stop experiencing it.

Bright Flight came out in 2001. Two years later, Berman attempted suicide through the old-school musician's exit, cocaine and booze. The voice does a lot of things well—it's witty and ruthlessly efficient in backing people into a corner—but the only thing it really cares about is being there when you're ready to give in to its one idea. That's what the voice needs: to invert your experience, turn your triumphs into proof of your failures. It's the only way to make it shut up. "I am the trick my mother played on the world," he sings in *American Water's* "Send in the Clouds." "I'm not the same," he says here, and while this raises the question "as what?" he doesn't offer any answers.

If "Slow Education" was the time-shattering manifesto, with the next song, Berman offers his own Little Red Book for living with the voice. "Room Games and Diamond Rain" starts out with an amazingly backhanded declaration of love, as the singer announces that he will love his object for *"a hundred years / through suffering and celebration, dear / 'cause only you can make my lies come true."* He ends his verse with a barbed comparison: this love makes him feel like drinking in the shade throughout the afternoon. Does he mean he feels relaxed and happy, like a person who's been getting drunk in the shade on a hot day? Or does it remind him that she's embracing his lies, leaving him so depressed that he needs to drink all afternoon to dull the pain? We don't know and it doesn't matter.

The chorus rips the dream out from under our feet. We get the mystery of the song title, the room games and diamond rain, but then Berman sings that this thing, this feeling, is a) a fox hunt, b) an f-stop, and c) a ten-acre wood. The specificity of these things elides any easy interpretation. One can imagine a Venn diagram overlapping slightly but impractically with fox hunts and the small wood, but the camera's f-stops sit in an untouched bubble. These things sound beautiful together, though, and whatever Berman's calling up with this imagery is so slippery that, although they make no logical sense, there's some truth in the pure sound of these words that cannot be ignored. Maybe his muse has just made his lies real. The weird magic of these things puts Berman on a cheap train out to the mystic borderlands, where he can dance, like the Judge in *Blood Meridian*, writing his violent dreams on the world. The second verse ends on the voice's one idea again, promising a ride in the dirt.

I chose to talk about this record because the voice wanted me to listen and despair, too. I'd lived with it all my life, whispering in my ear, but the last few years were the worst. I was unemployed for some time, and crushed under debts when the market collapsed. Close friends got sick. I was bullied in my new job, which is surprising when dealing with adults. I desperately needed the work, so, instead of standing up for myself, I just took it. The voice told me—I told myself—that I deserved it. I saw the darkness not as personal, but systemic. Monstrous people brought old cruelties into the political realm and ran amok. People I loved and thought rational were swept up in this madness while the madness swept the world, which brings us to today.

When my bandmate John died suddenly, the voice was always in my ears, telling me that it would be brave to let my family let me go. They would be better off, it said, like a virus blooming in my imagination. I was afraid to get help, but when I felt lucid, I was afraid not to. I had heard horror stories about antidepressants: how you could end up feeling nothing and wanting nothing, your appetite for life a dim spark. On the other side, there were Richard Manuel, Vic Chesnutt, and Mark Linkous. There was my friend Tom, the greatest writer I have ever known, at that point far along in the process of dying in a hospice. I was doing very little creatively, anyway. The time had come.

Berman told the *New York Sun* about his own use of antidepressants in 2008. "People who have ethics about nothing else start having moral qualms when it comes to antidepressants," he said. "People don't understand. It's not going to change them. It's just going to give them the ability to change in a natural way. It's like the rabbinical saying: 'Change your opinion and you might change your life.'"[1] Change your opinion and you might change your life. You can't improve on that.

Although I want to, I don't have the time or space to talk about all of *Bright Flight*. "Time Will Break the World" is a devastating chorus tied to a Victorian haunted-house fantasia. Oddly, it features the appearance of a DeLorean, which, in context, suggests time travel. "I Remember Me" is a contender for the saddest song ever written, telling the story of a happy, wild romance struck down by a sudden accident on the cusp of popping the question. In "He Stopped Loving Her Today"—the previous contender for the saddest song title—the subject of the song at least gets to die. In "I Remember Me," the singer, horrifyingly, persists. There's some element of a Raymond Carver epiphany when the song reveals that it is being sung while he looks at the spot on the truck that took his whole life away.

"Horseleg Swastikas" is an ode to the depression that was destroying Berman. His narrator starts off wasted, down and out in the Nashville suburbs. He's on the wrong side of Sunday morning: awake, drunk, with terrible light pouring in the windows. He wryly notes that this is also the wrong side of Saturday night. The song doesn't come out and say that his existence is destroying him, but it doesn't have to. His very shape, his inability to melt away, and the fact that he has to feel and care are all causing him pain. He sings:

I wanna be like water if I can
'Cause water doesn't give a damn

Beautiful, both the sentiment and the silly pun. Against this madness, Berman imagines a holy place dedicated to the Kantian notion of noumenal reality—"things in themselves as they are." He yearns for the reality behind the beholder's perception. Stripped of the illusions projected by conscious minds, there is no time, no lens, and no voice.

His holy place is also dedicated to the triumph of the obstacle, the inverse of the triumph of the will (because, helpful reminder here, Nazis are terrible people). Together, these two images push the notion that reality—that experienced without blinders trying to sway us, if there is such a thing—is bound by conflict that no one can quell, despite how strong we believe ourselves. Finally, his holy place calls up the titular horseleg swastikas, which track the Nazis' corruption of an ancient image of peace while also pushing the idea of escape. A horse's legs would only make such a shape while in full run. He describes a very specific take on depression: the reality we experience is forever distorted by our perceptions, forever bound by obstacles, forever taking innocent beauty and corrupting it. Berman's singer wants to escape. He wants to be like water. He wants to be free of all of this messy existence.

The second side of the album has the instrumental "Transylvania Blues," the barroom rollicker "Let's Not and Say We Did," and then "Tennessee," where Berman asks his wife to move to Nashville and save their lives. The chorus of "Tennessee" has two parts, with Berman singing the pun of the title ("you're the only ten I see," he tells her, as brave in emotion as it is in sheer silliness). His then-girlfriend, now-wife Cassie engages in some excellent wordplay in her part of the chorus. Where so much of this album is eaten up with depression, "Tennessee" is unafraid, happy, and loose.

The penultimate "Friday Night Fever" documents domestic bliss; however, the album ends with "Death of an Heir of Sorrows," as quietly devastating as "Slow Education." While I'd rather quote the lyrics here, among Berman's best, instead I'll point out that the one idea—that one about dying—has its moment, and nothing will ever be alright again.

My friend Tom finally died early this year. I can't think of any higher praise than Laurie Anderson's epitaph for her father: "it was like a whole library burned down." ("World Without End," from *Bright Red* by Laurie Anderson [1994]). With so many friends in the ground, I long to stop time. Time spent together is a luxury, never more apparent than in hindsight. When I chose this album at the end of last year—deeply depressed, not yet on medication—all I could hear in *Bright Flight* were the bleak, funny truths throughout. I raged against how unloved it was.

The spare beauty of this album is hard on me now. It is everything I thought it was, but it is so full of the voice that I can barely breathe. It is letters to yourself from the bottom of the ocean. It is the warm embrace of an untruth that you abandoned but still love. It remains the most seductive liar, but it is also a perfect artwork too harrowing to live in and numbingly difficult to visit. When I listen, I wonder if I have the light to find my way back through the fog.

Hayden Childs is the author of *Shoot Out the Lights* (#58). He occasionally updates his blog at fater.blogspot.com.

CHAPTER 51
GREEN DAY'S *AMERICAN IDIOT:*
THE ORIGINAL BROADWAY CAST
RECORDING (2010)
Cyrus R. K. Patell

I'm warning you now: this little chapter is doomed to fail. If its goal is to make you understand why sometimes, when I'm listening to the *American Idiot: The Original Broadway Cast Recording*, I get all teary and choked up, while at other times the music makes me want to pump my fists or play air guitar or—worse—air drums, and why sometimes those moments are the same moments—well, I'm not sure I'm going to find the words to express the tangle of emotions and thoughts that this record conjures up for me. And I'm a literature professor by trade, so usually I'm pretty good with words.

But sometimes—and I think that this is one of the lessons of this album and of most great rock albums and of most great song performances from any genre—words alone aren't enough. Nevertheless, as I routinely tell my students, you shouldn't be afraid to fail: if you adopt the right attitude toward failure, trying and failing and then trying again is a crucial part of what it means to become good at something, whether that something is education, sports, a career, or life itself.

The *American Idiot* Broadway cast album is a classic B-side: it offers an alternative version of a big hit and adds bonus content. My affection for it grows out of my affection for its predecessor. I spent the late 1970s listening to the Stones, the Clash, punk, and new wave. Naturally, I was later drawn to Green Day's late-punk sound, but I didn't become a devoted *fan* until *American Idiot.* Perhaps the side of me that also used to listen to Led Zeppelin and Queen liked the extended structures of songs like "Jesus of Suburbia" and "Homecoming." I loved *American Idiot*'s massive chords, its vocal melodies and soaring leads, and singer Billie Joe Armstrong's distinctive growl. But the album also resonated with me thematically: my doctoral work in the mid-1980s had been motivated in large part by a desire to understand the cultural mythologies that led so many Americans to adopt Reaganism as their creed, and I identified with the album's rage against the America that Reagan and the Bushes and their ilk had created, "the land of make-believe that don't believe in me," as Armstrong put it in "Jesus of Suburbia."

That political underpinning made *American Idiot* different from Green Day's earlier work. The documentary[1] which recounts the making of the record, makes it clear that the band knew from the start that it was doing something different, although its members weren't sure what to call it, using the terms "punk rock opera" and "punk rock concept record" interchangeably. Whatever it was, *American Idiot* was bigger, grander, and quite simply more meaningful than the band's earlier albums.

The cast album transforms *American Idiot* from a concept album into a full-blown rock opera. The presiding genius for that transformation was director Michael Mayer, who had won a Tony Award in 2007 for his direction of *Spring Awakening*. When Mayer approached Armstrong about doing a theatrical version, the singer was interested. In an interview with *Theater Talk*, Mayer later recalled:

> The more I listened to the whole record I started to really parse out a narrative that was very compelling to me about this kid, the Jesus of Suburbia, waking up one day and realizing that this world he has inherited isn't really where he wants to be and he makes this journey to the city and meets St. Jimmy, and this girl, and there's this triangle, and an eventual homecoming.[2]

Green Day's album, however, consisted of only nine songs with a running time of just over fifty-seven minutes (although some of those songs were quite long and multi-sectioned—epic, in rock 'n' roll terms). To transform the album into a theatrical production, Mayer needed more material.

Mayer had "the little shred of an idea" that he wasn't willing to share with Armstrong just yet for fear that Armstrong would think, "Eh, that's not so interesting." That shred was "that it would be three friends who all, sort of at the same time, recognized the pointlessness of their existence at that moment and recognized that they had a bad-faith relationship to their country and that they wanted to change that. They would go into the world, and somehow they would be separated and come back together".[3] That is, in fact, the show's story in a nutshell, though in addition to the experiences of the three friends—Johnny (the "Jesus of Suburbia"), Will, and Tunny—Mayer would devote significant attention to the experiences of the women in their lives.

Determined to keep the original structure of the album, opening with the iconic song "American Idiot" and closing with the reflective "Whatsername," Mayer interpolated additional Green Day material: the band's contribution to the *Rock Against Bush* compilation album ("Favorite Son"), a B-side from the *American Idiot* European release ("Too Much Too Soon"), new songs that would appear on the next Green Day studio album *21st Century Breakdown* (2009) ("Last of the American Girls," "Last Night on Earth," "Before the Lobotomy," "Know Your Enemy," "21 Guns"), an outtake from the *American Idiot* sessions ("When It's Time"), and text notes that Armstrong had written for a special edition CD of the original album (which were spoken between several songs on stage, but omitted from the cast album). Mayer had good taste: all of the songs enrich the narrative arc of the show, and "Last Night on Earth" and "21 Guns" would become vocal high points of both the stage production and the cast album.

I saw the production for the first time in January 2010 with members of the first group of students from New York University's campus in Abu Dhabi (NYUAD), a start-up international liberal arts college with which I'd been involved since 2008. The students came from all over the world, not just the United States or the United Arab Emirates: the class I was teaching had students from Canada, Jordan, Korea, Pakistan, Russia, and Westchester. NYUAD's ethos was resolutely cosmopolitan, by which I mean it had a perspective from which difference represents an opportunity to be embraced rather than a problem to be solved. A truly cosmopolitan venture will, of course, include a variety of different attitudes and belief systems, not all of which are going to embrace cosmopolitan values fully. Most of the kids loved the show—and loved the fact that we'd been able to arrange for Mayer to talk with the group about the show. But not all the students were enamored. "That was totally inappropriate," said one student, from a rural community in the American South. "We should not have been taken to see that."

My reaction was rather different. I saw the show three more times—once in the balcony with a group of New York-based students, when Melissa Etheridge was playing the role of St. Jimmy; once in the fourth row of the orchestra with my wife, after Billie Joe Armstrong had taken over the role; and by myself on the last day of Armstrong's initial run in the role.

Don't worry, though: you don't have to have seen the show to love this album. Just like the original record, the cast album rocks. Why shouldn't it? After all, Armstrong, bassist Mike Dirnt, and drummer Tré Cool play on every track. What makes the cast album even richer than the original to my ear are the contributions made by Tom Kitt, who arranged the songs for multiple voices and orchestrated them to include string parts. In the *Heart* documentary, Dirnt pooh-poohed the idea that a rock opera would necessarily include such things: "you say 'punk rock opera,' people think Pavarotti and strings, a lot of melodies, a lot of singing—all this other stuff, but really it's almost like playing a Ramones set: no break. It's like shifting gears five times and playing five different punk songs".[4]

But I think Dirnt might have been selling the original album a little short. *American Idiot* already had a lot of (great) melodies and a lot of singing, although the singing was almost all done by Armstrong. Kitt figured out ways to arrange the songs for different voices in order to embody the multiple perspectives that Mayer had brought to the story, and he used the dreaded "strings" as a tonal counterpoint to the punk guitar and bass, thereby expanding the emotional range of the piece. In an interview that took place before the opening of the show's Toronto production, Mayer said: "What Tom has done so brilliantly is really taken a single voice and turned it into the voice of an entire huge community, or series of communities: there's suburbia, there's the city, and then there's the Middle East … this multitude of people".[5]

One of the most moving moments in *Broadway Idiot*, Doug Hamilton's documentary about the making of the show, comes when Mayer and Kitt's working group presents Kitt's arrangement of "Last Night on Earth," which Mayer is using to dramatize a scene in which Johnny and his girlfriend ("Whatsername") take heroin. To convey the idea of a "trippy love ballad," Kitt creates a "wall-of-sound, beautiful vocal arrangement, kind of in the style of the Beach Boys—these beautiful falsetto harmonies just raining down on them".[6] Not, in other words, what one normally associates with a Green Day song. It works. Dirnt, like the rest of the band, is visibly moved by the performance, and I find myself a little teary every time I watch the moment when Armstrong's wife, Adrienne, leans forward to give him a kiss as the song unfolds.

After that session, Mayer says, the band not only gave him and Kitt permission to do the show, but also had a real "appetite to hear their songs in a really different way".[7] It's that difference that is one of the joys of the cast album. If you're a Green Day fan listening to the album without having seen the show, I suspect that it's a little disconcerting at first to hear Armstrong's lyrics sung by a male voice other than his and then amplified by a Broadway-style chorus of voices, but the real sonic revelation comes when Mary Faber sings the "Dearly Beloved" section of "Jesus of Suburbia."

For me, the new elements come together most powerfully in the anthemic "21 Guns." Driven by Rebecca Naomi Jones's powerful lead vocal, the song builds slowly. Jones opens the song, accompanied only by clean guitar notes with digital delay, to which are then added bass, piano, and vocals from the full cast. The first chorus suddenly becomes sparer, with Jones and the other female leads—Christina Sajous and Mary Faber—accompanied only by strings. The second verse adds drums and the male voices of Stark Sands, John Gallagher Jr., and Michael Esper. With the second chorus, Kitt's arrangement magnifies the choral power hinted at in Green Day's original version, and the song builds to its anthemic climax. Before the show went to Broadway, Green Day and the cast recorded a version of "21 Guns" with Armstrong singing the male lead parts, and he commented afterward: "The new arrangement of '21 Guns' made me sort of re-fall in love with the song. I think some of these versions are better than what we recorded".[8]

It may be heresy, but if I could only have one of them, I'd choose the cast album over the original. I wouldn't even be giving up Armstrong's singing, not entirely: the album concludes with the band's version of the redemptive love song "When It's Time." It's a fitting way for the album to end: as mad as Green Day are about the state of America— and they're even madder about Donald Trump's America than they were about George Bush's—ultimately, they are making music about the power of love to help us survive our failures.

Cyrus R. K. Patell is the author of *Some Girls* (#81). Find him at patell.org.

CHAPTER 52
PERFUME'S *LEVEL3* (2013)
Jordan Ferguson

The summer after she left me, I moved to a tiny bachelor pad in one of Toronto's more "authentic" neighborhoods, on a block alternating between vegan restaurants and methadone clinics. Sitting alone in the swelter of late July, encouraged by the advent of legal streaming and eager to retreat to the simpler pleasures of the past, I started watching anime again. The pastel-tinged battle royales and adolescent melodramas provided the perfect distraction from all the decisions that had led me to that point.

Searching out theme songs and soundtracks from *Madoka Magica* or *Michiko and Hatchin* likely skewed my YouTube algorithms into filling my Suggested sidebar with the videos of Harajuku weirdo Kyary Pamyu Pamyu. Pamyu, a former street fashion model, had been invited to collaborate with producer Yasutaka Nakata, despite her total lack of musical experience. Those early songs and their accompanying videos went viral locally and abroad in 2011, on the strength of Pamyu's *kawaii* grotesqueries and Nakata's slick, bouncy electropop accompaniment.

I was never much of an electronic music enthusiast. I'd bought a couple of albums in the late 1990s (Chemical Brothers, the *Trainspotting* soundtrack), but it was never anything more than a passing interest. Yet something in Nakata's production, especially on Pamyu's debut EP *Moshi Moshi Harajuku*, tempered the cutesy toy piano tinkles with more sophisticated pop songcraft: bass melodies would descend into minor keys unpredictably, bringing jarring and darker tones to the music, tempos snugly strolling along at 125 BPM. It wasn't EDM for nightclubs at 3:00 a.m., it was headphone music for navigating Tokyo's dense pedestrian pathways on a weekend afternoon. It felt more … *human*. When it turned out some of my favorite Kyary songs were actually covers of Nakata's older work with his group Capsule, I started searching out his discography, including ten years' worth of material he'd made for a Hiroshima trio called Perfume.

Perfume had everything that drew me to Kyary's music, without the more puerile elements I had started to find alienating. Nakata's use of genre sounded like nothing I'd come across in Japanese music to that point, and the presentation of the group sidestepped much of what I found saccharine and insincere about the country's manufactured pop music.

Developing the sort of irrational devotion people typically reserve for artists like Beyoncé was not something I was prepared or equipped for at that stage of my life. I had spent my youth immersed in hip-hop and drumming in arty rock bands. I considered myself as open-minded a poptimist as one could find, but JPop was a disposable trifle I dabbled in occasionally, not my primary avenue of fandom. This was not something I *did*.

That was in 2014. Since then I've imported Perfume's entire catalog on vinyl, made custom T-shirts to declare my love to the world, driven nine hours to attend two of their rare North American concerts, and annoyed or alienated every person in my life evangelizing for them.

Such investment in a Japanese pop group required me to develop a new vocabulary, because the act of consumption as a fan is entirely different. To love Perfume is to recognize and accept that the women on the album cover have everything and nothing to do with the product in your hands. They aren't artists per se, they're sales people. Every Perfume single is tied to a fizzy drink or an automobile or a line of supplements, because in Japan "selling out" isn't something to be avoided, it's necessary for survival. The trio themselves are just one cog in the machine that is Perfume, a vehicle to deliver the combined elements of the team around them: Nakata's music, the dance routines by their long-time choreographer Mikiko Mizuno, and the forward-looking visuals and technical effects from computer artist Daito Manabe and his firm Rhizomatiks. Those elements were present in part or in sum on previous works, but their fourth album *LEVEL3* is the moment when they coalesced most seamlessly.

Albums from JPop groups are rarely cohesive artistic statements. They typically serve to collect previously released singles with a handful of new songs and some extras to entice fans into buying music they've already purchased (twice if they go in on the standard *and* limited editions). But *LEVEL3* is an album of intention. Perfume's first album after signing to an international label, it is aggressively designed to reach out globally and fill stadiums. It's the perfection and elevation of a formula tested on previous efforts pushed to a euphoric maximalism; the J-Pop equivalent of Kanye West's *Graduation*.

The design is apparent from the first note of track one. Since their sophomore effort *Triangle* in 2009, Perfume albums have always opened with short introductions, brief instrumental *aperitifs* to set the mood before the album starts properly. *LEVEL3* starts with something like a swarm of wasps for eight full seconds before the kick drum slams into your chest and begins its syncopated march countered by off-time zips and bleeps. The prelude pauses, briefly teasing the listener into thinking the old rules might still apply, when the march begins again, pushed along by rolling bass tones. Nearly a minute in, the trio appears, riding along a corresponding triplet of synth stabs:

Walking out from within the light,
If you focus your eye …

Then the cycle repeats, with a short detour into the sounds of a robot carnival. "Enter the Sphere" is not a place setter, it's an invitation and an imperative. As the track ends, that wasp buzz hangs and sustains for another *ten seconds*, pushing itself into the listener's face forehead-to-forehead. *If you're coming*, it says, *this is where we're going*. There's barely any time to respond before the throb of "Spring of Life" kicks into gear.

"Spring of Life" is the first of three album mixes that appear on the track list. Nakata had made liberal use of them on Perfume's earlier albums, as another means to make buying the same songs twice more palatable. But they've never been used to the extent they are on *LEVEL3*. "Spring of Life" keeps the buoyant joy of the original but gets an extended intro and outro, perfect for club DJs mixing in a set. "Magic of Love" and "Spending All My Time" both get a bass boost and additional rearrangements. When given the chance to alter a previously released A-side, Nakata's answer is almost always the same: *go bigger*.

The album design feels even more obvious when "Mirai no Museum" threatens to derail the entire proceedings. Tradition dictates that every single goes on the album, even one commissioned for a children's animated movie starring the robot cat Doraemon. But following a flawless five-track run from "Enter the Sphere" to "1mm," the twee bounce of "Mirai" is an unwelcome throwback to more traditional JPop sounds. Why it wasn't buried near the end of the album (or swapped for popular B-side "Hurly Burly") remains a mystery, but it was a mistake, possibly one Nakata realized given how hard the album course corrects with what follows.

"Party Maker" is the single greatest Perfume song ever released. Other songs are better written—with stronger melodies and more memorable vocal performances—but no song in their catalog accomplishes what "Party Maker" does so emphatically. It is the gravitational center of *LEVEL3*, every other song revolves around it. A seven-minute trance epic, largely instrumental, with little traditional song structure, it is a rave in miniature. The women's vocals and ascending notes push the momentum upward before the bottom drops out with a saw-toothed snarl and the inexorable four on the floor pound of the kick. This isn't J-pop, this is the relentless techno piping through Detroit airwaves in 1989. There are a handful of moments that bound my heart to this fandom, the beat drop on "Party Maker" is one of them. Subsequent work reached for similar levels of grandeur, but nothing this audacious.

It wasn't just the music that elevated, the visual components did as well. Mizuno, who had worked with the group since they were teenagers, needed to take music made for fist pumping and design movements appropriate for the group's exuberant live shows. Her work during this era incorporates everything from sassy hair flips, dizzying finger puzzles, and pop and locks, doubling down on the "twitchy android discovers love" motif the group previously flirted with but never fully committed to. Mizuno's dances often suffer from a sense of muchness. Movements don't punch exactly on beat, or feel rushed into a measure they don't naturally fit. It can seem oddly amateurish until you watch one of the many dance covers performed by fans online, and see how difficult it is to make something that seems easy look fluid and effortless.

Arguably, the true star of the era is the full incorporation of Manabe and Rhizomatiks into the machine. Fans of the group who first worked on Perfume's ten-year anniversary concerts, *LEVEL3* marked the first time Manabe and his team were present from concept to completion. Their increased use of technology in their presentation and performance is perhaps what's continued to turn heads and allowed the group to thrive in the years since. Things like the lighted costumes in "Spring of Life," programed to flash on the beat of the song; the digital projection mapping for "Magic of Love," tracking the group's movements while never hitting the stage behind them; or the use of holograms and geometric displays on televised appearances; all added new layers of cool to their image at the precise moment the group was best aligned for it.

But none of it works without A-Chan, Kashiyuka, and Nocchi holding it together. As teenagers, they struggled in the ruthless indie scene, running the streets of Akihabara, 800 km from home, handing out show flyers to a disinterested public. When a commercial director heard them on the radio, he took a chance on casting them in a national recycling campaign in 2007. That appearance cemented their position in the industry, and established them as fixtures on the Jpop landscape for the next decade. They are a miracle success story who not only have never forgotten it, but *appreciate* it, with a sincerity unlike anything I've ever seen in pop music. They don't write their own music or lyrics. Their concerts are more of a dance recital than what we think of as a live performance, lip-synced or accompanied by a generous backing track. Yet when they break down in tears bowing deeply to a rapturous crowd, I feel a closer human connection to these women than I ever have with any artist who speaks my own language. My relationship with them is uncomplicated and empathic. It is rooted in the pride I take in their accomplishments and the giddiness I feel watching them succeed, for coming through the other side of their Campbellian Heroes' Journey intact. Despite the heavy commercialization of the music, the only things they're really selling are happiness and hope. Of *course* I was going to buy in.

In hindsight, the actual story of *LEVEL3* might be one of failure. Despite the album's creative successes, the grand global experiment didn't yield the desired results. A Western distribution deal made no impact. A four-stop American tour in 2016 was beset by technical glitches and failed to sell out its second New York date. In 2018's *Future Pop* felt like Perfume retreating to Japan, content to settle into their role as a senior group prioritizing performance over studio recording.

But for two years at the start of the decade, three women from Hiroshima stood on a precipice at the edge of their world, breath held in hope and expectation. The story of their albums, and of them, is one of escalating growth and expansion. *LEVEL3* remains their longest album, their biggest, and their loudest. It remains the sound of a balloon bursting, of stadium status, of arms reaching around the world, and the story of girls becoming Queens.

Jordan Ferguson is the author of *Donuts* (#93). Find him online @jordan_ferguson.

CHAPTER 53
DAWN OF MIDI'S *DYSNOMIA* (2015)
Charles Fairchild

Being an aging academic teaching popular music always presents a few conundrums that can often threaten to become a series of potentially dispiriting tasks. Trawling through some pop star's Twitter feed with my students or trying to identify the signifiers of authenticity without attributing that benighted quality to the inherent qualities of a piece of music present challenges to both my ability and sometimes my professional sense of self. But this is not due to some untoward denialist nostalgia for my past or "the past." There were plenty of overwrought, self-important musical celebrities when I was 20. They aren't really all that different from the ones we are saddled with today. I certainly don't hark back to some better, vanished age.

Instead, I try to pay as close attention as I can to the broadly construed "culture." I try to teach about things that predominate our world right now in order to create threads linking the present to a past that often appears to be as misty and distant to my students as seventeenth-century French court music. But sometimes I am simply bewildered and these struggles are not mine and mine alone. The stark uncomfortable fact is that none of us—old, young, or indifferent—can keep up any more. I spend a lot of time trying to help students respond critically and consciously to the digital deluge and, believe me, despite their age and comparative agility, they are overwhelmed, too; most of them just think it is normal.

In teaching, I try to create a place outside of the flood, a little patch of dry land, for an hour or two, once a week, in which we do not check our notifications or allow ourselves to be distracted by the micro-events of the comparatively few lives that dominate so many wider macro-social-media networks. I do this because what is pressing down on all of us all the time is an economic and cultural ecology that can't abide allowing us too much time for extended thought, especially when that thought appears "unproductive," that is, producing nothing immediately apparent or tangible. Popular culture under neoliberalism is intensely limiting and directing despite its astounding breadth, bulk, and constant availability.

This has experiential corollaries. As with so much of our shared experience of music, there is a constant and palpable sense of slipping—slipping away, slipping under, or slipping past the materials of the wider culture. This doesn't just happen to me in aggregate, it often happens inside one thing, one video, or one album. The seemingly constant ratcheting up of the intensity of the color, movement, editing, cuts, and jumps on our screens, not to mention the vivacity of the multitude of sounds that surround us, are an insistent and continual grab at the most valuable of commodities in our increasingly chaotic, yet rationalized, worlds: our attention.

Dysnomia by Dawn of Midi is the opposite of all that. It is austere, specific, and limited. It is a "B-side" because of how it was made and what it does. It is the work of a jazz trio, but it was not improvised. It was scored and fixed into a firm set of very precisely-realized boundaries. And yet, it is somehow expansive, flowing, and penetrative. In fact, it was so captivating to me that, when I first listened to it, it felt so crystalline a sound that I deliberately didn't talk to anybody about it or even read anything about it for months. It was this reduction, this gut-level not knowing, that shaped my experience and understanding of this mere forty-seven minutes of music. I wanted to be alone with this music. I honestly can't remember the last time that happened. While the quarantine was impossible (and probably foolish) to maintain, that initial feeling was strange and right. This is not to say that I thought *Dysnomia* was pure or perfect. I wasn't afraid I would "ruin" it somehow if it were admitted into a more social world. But this feeling of care and segregation came from somewhere else, somewhere that was not preciousness. It came from the intense focus this music made me practice, however briefly, when I listened to it. Unexpectedly, the more I listened to this music, the more that focus was fed, and the more it was sustained.

Dysnomia was posted on Bandcamp in 2015, but was apparently released earlier. I was told about it by a friend and ordered it on CD without much thought or exploration. I was not aware of its constellation of anchor points: the Erased Tapes label that sponsored it, the jazz trio tradition these musicians were consciously extending, and the work that had preceded it. One of the key facts about *Dysnomia* that I did not learn until much later was that it was a departure, in some ways a radical departure, from Dawn of Midi's previous work.

The trio's first album, *First*, is easily recognizable as the product of a jazz trio. There are ten tracks that all act as distinctly individual pieces, linked by a common style, technique, and aesthetic purpose. It is lush, complex, improvised music fitted into the long tradition of the jazz trio. *First* had moods, transitions, and complex, intensely improvisatory, interactions between the three musicians. These ebbed and flowed in intriguing ways. There was a lot of space on this album for each member to fit themselves into, often in ways that surprised and impressed. *First* was expressive in the way jazz trio works are expressive. It was momentary and alive from second to second in the way jazz trio works have always been.

Dysnomia is almost none of these things. It is a scored piece broken into nine movements each with a separate title. But these divisions have had little effect on my understanding or experience of this album. When I listen to this album it is as one piece of music. It works as a continuous flow from start to finish. The entire work consists of a gradually mutating set of interlocking rhythmic phrases. The piano, bass, and drums gently peck and thump percussively, constantly coupling and uncoupling from meters and tempos that merge, mesh, overlap, and contest the pulse over and over again. The capabilities of the instruments and their operators are not explored in the ways jazz trios have done before them. There is no improvisation on *Dysnomia*. The instrumental timbres are stark and almost brutally constrained. There is nothing really resembling a melody or a chord progression. And it is beautiful.

When I did start reading more about this album, I disagreed with almost everything. I don't mean that all these other writers are wrong. Instead, I simply didn't recognize my experience in anything they wrote. This obviously has very little to do with their writing. It springs from the fact that I couldn't incorporate *Dysnomia* into my listening habits or experiences and I didn't want to; they could, and they did.

Most writers did so by linking this album to other works, not unreasonably. The guiding stars were minimalism, especially Steve Reich, as well as music that was often simply referred to as "African" polyrhythms, and the more spare, "intelligent" corners of DJ culture. One central rhetorical move was to place these musicians in an obscure, marginal box and call it "jazz," and then explain that this seemingly disinterested work was actually a link to a wider world of far more friendly kinds of music. Instead of hearing these three people exercising astounding feats of interlinked restraint, these writers instead heard the loops and breaks straight off the dance floor. But I didn't hear any of the endlessly looping breaks and hooks or beats and horns that always draw me back to hip-hop and house. I still don't. While this album is defined by repetition, to me it produces an entirely different species of the thing. It does not circle back on itself in the way that DJs deliberately do in order to allow us to catch that one set of gestures over and over and over again, to our bodily benefit and joy. *Dysnomia* just keeps moving almost heedlessly towards a distant horizon that never gets any closer.

Others tried to affix this work down to the floor of historical inevitability. They saw it as part of a musical tradition that was increasingly reduced in scale and complexity, winnowed down to a steadily beating heart of endlessly repeated passages of electronically-mediated gestural and stylistic familiarity. Because we so often hear the vivid echoes of obscure disco, soul, and funk in our music now, this distance, this remove, is thought to be innate to our musical worlds. If music had become synthetic and made at a considered reserve from the material world, *Dysnomia* must have reflected this immaterial turn.

Yet I continue to find *Dysnomia* an insistently material experience. The reduced means enhance my focus on each sound. Each strike becomes an event, each metric modulation an evasion of my pattern recognition. When I started to learn more about the album and its makers this feeling was only furthered. I had not known just from listening how the pianist played both the inside and the outside of the piano to modulate and reduce the otherwise potentially expansive resonance of the instrument. The piano became a percussive string instrument in the process. I could hear each strike on the strings in a way that is rarely evident in most piano playing. This fact tied the piano to the bass in direct and immutable ways. All those fingers on the strings kept the natural reverberations at bay. The drums were similarly kept tight and dry. But they were not simply backing the other two, not just keeping a beat. On this album, each of this trio sounds equal. No one carries the tune or gives it off to someone else. The endlessly twisting strips of rhythm they produce meld into each other, always precariously balanced between being three things and being one. In the same way, this music resists becoming one thing or another;

it's not "African" or minimal or looped. It is in a constant state of evoking and becoming all of these things that it never actually becomes.

What this album did for me was give me a sense of agency as a listener that I don't feel I am allowed very often. It made me feel like I was making something with my hearing and my attention and that, without me, it would be nothing. Multiple times throughout this album I simply lost the beat. The tempo, the pulse, the center eluded me. It shook me off ever so slightly. It never quite left me behind, but it did move out ahead in the direction of wherever we were going. This music asked me to do something. I had to run to catch up and the only way I could do that was to listen more intently, to pay even closer attention. I didn't need to have any specialist knowledge or technique to do so. I didn't need a secret code for the magic to be revealed. It didn't demand the right contacts or networks. It just asked me to focus. That still seems to me to be a radical circumstance.

Charles Fairchild is the author of *The Grey Album* (#98).

PERMISSIONS

NOTES

Preface

1   Austin Scaggs, "Q&A: Alicia Keys," *Rolling Stone*, February 24, 2005. (Web).

Introduction

1   Robert Christgau, "Review: *Chaos and Disorder*." (Web).

2   Ernest Hardy, "Review: *Chaos and Disorder*," *Rolling Stone*, August 22, 1996. (Web).

3   If the metaphor of enslavement and liberation, darkness and the dawn, struck the press as particularly heavy handed, especially for a black artist, it was not unprecedented. In his chapter on The Dells' *There Is* for this collection, Joe Bucciero points to the Association for the Advancement of Creative Musicians, formed in Chicago in 1965 for the purpose of supporting black musicianship against the "oppressive forces which prevent Black people from reaching the goals attained by other Americans." Prince's performative opposition to label "oppression" drew on this long tradition of black artists positioning themselves against an appropriative, thieving industry.

4   My knowledge of Prince history owes much to Ben Greenman, *Funk, Sex, God, & Genius in the Music of Prince* (New York: Henry Holt and Co., 2017); Matt Thorne, *Prince: The Man and His Music* (Chicago: Bolden, 2016); and Ronin Ro, *Prince: Inside the Music and the Masks* (New York: St. Martin's Press, 2011).

5   Hardy, "Review: *Chaos and Disorder*."

6   The truth is somewhat more complicated. Prince took a break from recording *Emancipation* to compile *Chaos and Disorder*. Most of the songs he included were a couple of years old. But, aiming to capture something more spontaneous, Prince finished the record during a ten-day session in Miami (Ro, *Prince: Inside the Music*, 276).

7   Quoted in Ro, *Prince: Inside the Music*, 284.

8   Christgau, "Review: *Chaos and Disorder*."

9   Stephen Thompson, "Review: *Emancipation*," A.V. Club, March 29, 2002. (Web).

10 Dan Weiss, "Prince's 20-Year-Old Emancipation Wasn't Just an Industry Kiss-Off, It Was a Going-Away Party," *Billboard*, November 11, 2016. (Web).

11 "Top 10 Best-Selling Prince Albums," CBS Minnesota, April 20, 2017. (Web).

12 Beyond the biographies cited above, see Ann Powers, *Good Booty: Love and Sex, Black and White, Body and Soul in American Music* (New York: Dey St., 2017), 274–9; and Touré, *I Would Die 4 U: Why Prince Became an Icon* (New York: Simon & Schuster, 2013).

13 The point actually seems to be that Warner Brothers is a ravenous whore. "Delores" eats food and men "like a brontosaurus." Her doorbell's been "broken since 1984," the year of *Purple Rain*'s release. It's not hard to hear a diss of the label, as Nick Deriso argues in "Prince's 'Dinner with Delores' Takes a Swipe at His Label (or Madonna?)," *Diffuser*, June 10, 2017. (Web).

Notes

Reintroduction

1 Lela Cobo, "Rudy Pérez Tops Hot Latin Tracks Producers List for 2000," *Billboard*, December 30, 2000: 17.

2 George Steiner, *After Babel: Aspects of Language and Translation* (Oxford: Oxford University Press, 1998), 66.

3 Matthew 6:31–33.

4 Allie Jones, "Christina Aguilera on 'Longing for Freedom' & Her Hip-Hop-Inspired Return to Music," *Billboard*, May 3, 2018. (Web).

Chapter 1

1 Josh Terry, "Ryley Walker Listens to Leonard Cohen for the First Time: 'Fuck This Guy,'" *Noisey*, August 29, 2018. (Web).

2 "Avalanche" and "Dress Rehearsal Rag" by Leonard Cohen. Copyright © 1966 and 1971 by Leonard Cohen, used by permission of The Wylie Agency LLC.

Chapter 3

1 Mark Paytress, *The Rolling Stones—Off The Record* (London: Omnibus Press, 2005), 239.

2 Albert Murray, *Stomping the Blues* (McGraw-Hill, 1976).

Chapter 4

1 Vini Reilly interview with Steve Taylor, "Convalescing with the Durutti Column," *Melody Maker*, February 2, 1980: 12.

2 The phrase, which became something of a mantra for McLaren, is used in the chorus of the Sex Pistols' song "The Great Rock 'n' Roll Swindle" from the album *The Great Rock 'n' Roll Swindle* (Virgin, 1979).

3 Quotation from William Blake, "The Tiger," line 4. *Blake: The Complete Poems*, ed. W. H. Stevenson (London: Longman, 1971), 214–15.

4 On the Durutti Column's second album, *LC* (Factory, 1981), Vini Reilly paid lyrical tribute to Curtis in a song called "The Missing Boy."

Chapter 5

1 B. Berry, P. Buck, M. Mills, and M. Stipe, *Wolves, Lower* [LP] (I.R.S. Records, 1982).

2 Ibid.

3 The reason it was so short was because it was an EP (extended play) rather than LP (long play) recording. This outdated promotional concept refers to recordings, like this one, which contained just a few songs. These less-costly, less whole, artifacts were intended to introduce a new artist or "extend" their commercial life. I consider it a B-side rather than an apotheosis, because it was intended as a preview, rather than a masterwork, like the band's official first record *Murmur*, which was released in 1983.

Chapter 6

1 This entry is for the group's eponymous debut LP as it was released in 1985. The album was re-released on CD with additional tracks in 1991 as *End on End*.

2 Guy Picciotto, interview with the author, June 2015.

3 Ian MacKaye, interview with the author, July 2017.

4 Picciotto interview.

5 Ibid.

6 Brendan Canty, interview with the author, July 2015.

7 Picciotto interview.

8 Ibid.

9 Ibid.

10 MacKaye interview.

11 Picciotto interview.

12 Canty interview.

13 MacKaye interview.

14 Picciotto interview.

Chapter 8

1 Robert Bolano, *2666* (London: Picador, 2009).

Chapter 9

1 Robert Hilburn, "O'Connor Pulls Out of Grammys: Irish Singer Attacks Music Industry for 'False, Materialistic Values,'" *Los Angeles Times*, February 2, 1991. (Web).

2 Mikal Gilmore, "I Do Not Want What I Haven't Got," *Rolling Stone*, January 22, 1997. (Web).

3 Michael Agresta, "The Redemption of Sinéad O'Connor," *Atlantic*, October 3, 2012. (Web).

4 Bob Guccione Jr., "Special Child," *Spin*, November 1991.

5 Harriet Sherwood, "Pope on Sexual Abuse: 'We Showed No Care for the Little Ones,'" *Guardian*, August 20, 2018. (Web).

Notes

Chapter 11

1 Digable Planets, "Rebirth of Slick (Cool Like Dat)," *Reachin' (A New Refutation of Time and Space)* (Pendulum/Elektra, 1993).

2 Digable Planets, "It's Good to Be Here," *Reachin' (A New Refutation of Time and Space)* (Pendulum/Elektra, 1993).

3 Ibid.

4 Digable Planets, "The May 4th Movement Starring Doodlebug," *Blowout Comb* (Pendulum/EMI, 1994).

Chapter 12

1 All section titles pulled from the *Cyberpunk* six-panel photo-collage cover.

2 Chuck Eddy, "Billy Idol, Cyberpunk," *Spin*, August 1993.

Chapter 14

1 "Readers' Poll: The Best Smashing Pumpkins Songs," *Rolling Stone*, June 13, 2012.

2 Ryan Leas, "The 10 Best Smashing Pumpkins Songs," *Stereogum*, February 15, 2018.

3 Joe Coscarelli, "Smashing Pumpkins Say They're Happy Now. Can They Keep It Together?" *New York Times*, March 22, 2018.

4 Ann Powers, "Smashing Pumpkins, *Mellon Collie and the Infinite Sadness*," *SPIN*, December 1995.

5 Jim Derogatis, "Mellon Collie and the Infinite Sadness," *Rolling Stone*, November 30, 1995.

6 Douglas Wolk, "*Smashing Pumpkins, Adore*," *SPIN*, July 1998.

7 Greg Kot, "Adore," *Rolling Stone*, May 18, 1998.

8 Sam Kelton, "Smashing Pumpkins' Billy Corgan Refuses to Indulge Fans' Nostalgia for Past Hits," *News.com.au*, April 26, 2012.

Chapter 15

1 Griffin Kelly, "Sometimes I'm Surprised: An Interview with John K. Samson," *All Things Go*, January 12, 2017. (Web).

2 The Weakerthans, "Aside," *Left and Leaving* [CD] (Sub City SC011-2, 2000).

3 The Weakerthans, "Left and Leaving," *Left and Leaving* [CD] (Sub City SC011-2, 2000).

4 The Weakerthans, "Watermark," *Left and Leaving* [CD] (Sub City SC011-2, 2000).

Chapter 19

1   Much of this information comes from the NBC TV documentary *Oh What a Night*, Robert Pruter's *Chicago Soul*, and Pruter's liner notes to the *There Is* CD reissue.

2   *There Is* stayed on *Billboard*'s R&B charts for thirty-nine weeks, peaking at number four, and the pop charts for twenty-nine weeks, peaking at twenty-nine.

3   George E. Lewis, "Improvised Music after 1950: Afrological and Eurological Perspectives," *Black Music Research Journal*, vol. 16, no. 1 (Spring 1996): 111.

4   Muhal Richard Abrams and John Shenoy Jackson, "Association for the Advancement of Creative Musicians," *Black World*, vol. 23, no. 1 (November 1973): 72.

5   Lewis, "Improvised Music after 1950," 117.

6   LeRoi Jones (Amiri Baraka), "The Changing Same (R&B and New Black Music)," in *Black Music* (New York: William Morrow & Company, 1968), 203.

7   Brian Ward, *Just My Soul Responding* (Berkeley, CA: UC Press, 1998), 204.

8   "Mainly, I think [R&B] songs are about what is known as 'love,' requited and un," Baraka writes. "But the most popular songs are always a little sad, in tune with the temper of the people's lives. The extremes. Wild Joy—Deep Hurt." Jones, "The Changing Same," 182.

Chapter 20

1   Sam Inglis, "Shirley Collins: Shirley Collins, Ian Kearey & Ossian Brown: Recording Lodestar," *Sound on Sound*, December 2016. (Web).

Chapter 22

1   Quoted in Matthew Specktor, booklet essay for the CD reissue of *Paris 1919* (Reprise, 2006), 7.

2   Victor Bockris and John Cale, *What's Welsh for Zen: The Autobiography of John Cale* (New York: Bloomsbury, 1999), 141, 153.

3   Ibid., 20.

4   Ibid.

5   Ibid., 141.

6   Stephen Holden, review of *Paris 1919*, *Rolling Stone*, May 10, 1973. (Web).

Chapter 23

1   Colin Harper, *Dazzling Stranger: Bert Jansch and the British Folk and Blues Revival* (New York: Bloomsbury, 2000), 59.

Notes

2 Jansch's arrangement uses "Drop D"—not, as popularly supposed the "DADGAD" tuning Davey Graham derived from the Moroccan Oud.

3 Harper, *Dazzling Stranger*, 87.

4 "Bert's Blues" and "House of Jansch."

5 Harper, *Dazzling Stranger*, 287.

6 With a capo at the second fret, Jansch plays the *shapes* E minor and A7 but they sound a tone higher.

7 Paul Simmons, "Interview with Bert Jansch," *The Ptolemaic Terrascope Magazine*, 1996.

8 Simmons interview.

9 Author interview with Stephenson.

Chapter 24

1 As Cateforis reports, Elvis Costello and Patti Smith had albums in the Top 40 and Top 20, respectively, and Blondie charted in the Top 100, but these were album, not singles, charts and the records were not specifically marketed as "new wave." Theo Cateforis, *Are We Not New Wave?: Modern Pop at the Turn of the 1980s* (University of Michigan Press, 2011), 28. In his review of *Candy-O* for *Rolling Stone*, Tom Carson wrote: "It's almost inevitable that *Candy-O*, the Cars' second album, doesn't seem nearly as exciting as their first. The element of surprise is gone, and the band hasn't been able to come up with anything new to replace it." The *All-Music Guide* calls *Candy-O* "a carbon copy" of the debut. Reviews reprinted at: https://www.superseventies.com/spcars.html.

2 Cateforis, *Are We Not New Wave?*, 28.

3 Maria Elena Buszek, *Pin-Up Grrrls: Feminism, Sexuality, Popular Culture* (Duke University Press, 2006), loc. 3408 of 7470.

4 Ibid., loc. 220 of 7470.

5 As Buszek notes: "in keeping with the Playboy template [i.e., Playmates should reflect the compliant and accessible girl next door] … Vargas's women from his *Playboy* years lost the style, aggression, and the clothes of his *Esquire* pin-ups. Now nude and accompanied by gag-caption one-liners … Vargas's *Playboy* illustrations generally lacked the references to women's culture and clear reverence for his subjects that had made his World War II work subversive." Ibid., loc. 3466 of 7470.

6 Ibid., loc. 3466 of 7470.

7 Ibid., loc. 3494 of 7470.

8 Alfred Soto, "The Cars: *Shake It Up*," *Pitchfork*, March 31, 2018.

Chapter 25

1 Jemima Dury (ed.), *"Hallo Sausages": The Lyrics of Ian Dury* (London: Bloomsbury, 2012), 158.

Chapter 26

1 See Ben Harker, *Class Act: The Cultural and Political Life of Ewan MacColl* (London: Pluto, 2007); and Dave Arthur, *Bert: The Life and Times of A. L. Lloyd* (London: Pluto, 2012).

2 Plant Life, a venture which lasted perhaps ten years, run by then Steeleye Span drummer Nigel Pegrum.

3 "Tam Lin," *Mainly Norfolk: English Folk and Other Good Music.* (Web).

Chapter 27

1 Bob Last, tape-recording of telephone interview with the author, July 17, 2018.

2 Green Gartside, tape-recording of interview with the author, New York City, July 17, 2006.

3 Ibid.

4 David Gamson, interview with Pete Phillips, "Heart to Art: Scritti Politti," *Electronic Soundmaker & Computer Music*, July 1985; archived on mu:zines.

5 David Gamson, email transcript of interview with the author, August 25, 2018.

6 Fred Maher, tape-recording of telephone interview with the author, August 3, 2018.

7 Ibid.

8 Geoff Travis, tape-recording of telephone interview with the author, August 28, 2018.

9 Green Gartside, interview by Simon Reynolds, "Hearts and Flowers," *The Guardian*, May 26, 2006.

10 Gartside interview, July 17, 2006.

Chapter 28

1 Negativland. *Fair use: The Story of the Letter U and the Numeral 2* (Concord, CA: Seeland, 1995), 72.

2 All unattributed quotes come from personal interviews.

3 Personal Interview.

4 Personal Interview.

5 Personal Interview.

6 https://www.facebook.com/Negativlandland/posts/1098963353464741

7 Personal Interview.

8 Personal Interview.

9 Negativland (1989) *Helter Stupid* [LP] (Los Angeles, SST).

10 See above. The interview is included on the LP.

11 Negativland, *Helter Stupid*.

12 Personal Interview.

Notes

13 Personal Interview.

14 Negativland (1991) *U2* [LP] (Los Angeles, SST).

15 Personal Interview.

Chapter 29

1 Jonathan Perry, "Guided By Voices Founder Sounds Off," Rolling Stone, July 10, 1998.

Chapter 30

1 It's worth mentioning that this curtain of obscurity has been pushed back in recent years. Scott Tennent's excellent 33 1/3 installment on *Spiderland* offers the most comprehensive look at the band to date; Lance Bangs's documentary *Breadcrumb Trail*—whose release coincided with the reissue of *Spiderland*—sheds light on the members of the band. Both are well worth your time.

2 The "I MISS YOU" bit in Slint's opus "Good Morning, Captain" remains one of the most perfectly developed and executed heavy moments in Louisville music history. Go listen if you don't believe me.

3 Foreshadowing Jason Noble's time in the chamber ensemble Rachel's, whose album *The Sea and the Bells* is the full evolution of the ideas found in "Bible Silver Corner."

4 Damon Krukowski, *The New Analog: Listening and Reconnecting in a Digital World* (New York: New Press, 2017).

5 Ibid.

6 Michael T. Fournier, "Jason Noble Interview Part II: 2/9/2009," *Cabildo Quarterly Online*, June 26, 2013. (Web).

7 Ibid.

8 Such as the one recently re-released on the *Fifteen Quiet Years* compilation.

9 Michael T. Fournier, "Interview with Jason Noble Part I: 1/26/2009," *Cabildo Quarterly Online*, June 12, 2013. (Web).

10 Including the absolutely crucial and astonishing "Before the Train," which gestures towards the work Jeff Mueller would later do in June of 1994. Track down the live version recorded at Chicago's Lounge Ax, which adds vocals (and crowd reaction).

Chapter 31

1 (*"1991: The Year Punk Broke*, directed by Dave Markey, distributed by Tara Films, released on 24 December 1992.")

2 Lauren Gofton, "10 Point Introduction," *Fast Connection*, vol. 1, no. 1 (1995): 15.

3 Everett True, "Singles," *Melody Maker*, May 27, 1995: 34.

4 Simon Williams, "Singles," *NME*, May 27, 1995: 44.

5 *Slamptumentary* [Film], Dir. Nick Allott and Deby Dukes (UK, 1995).

6 Rachel Holborow, "Viva La Punka," *Fast Connection*, volume 1 (1995): 4.

7   Author interview, July 23, 2018.

8   Author interview, July 30, 2018.

9   Author interview, August 21, 2018.

10 Ian Harrison, "We're Clever. Deal With It," *Select*, February 1997: 18.

11 Steven Wells, "Socialist Smirkers Party," *NME*, May 10, 1997: 21.

12 Simon Price, "To Hell With Teen Spirit," *Melody Maker*, January 11, 1997: 8.

Chapter 32

1   Loren Kajikawa, "'Bringin' '88 Back': Historicizing Rap Music's Greatest Year," in *The Cambridge Companion to Hip-Hop*, ed. Justin A. Williams (Cambridge, MA: Cambridge University Press, 2015), 301–13.

2   See "Hip-Hop's Greatest Year: Fifteen Albums That Made Rap Explode," *RollingStone.com*, February 12, 2008. (Web); and Christopher Weingarten's "Best of '88" series for *RollingStone.com*.

3   Stereo Williams, "New Jack Summer: In June '88, Bobby Brown, Teddy Riley & New Edition Announced the Arrival of R&B's New School," *Billboard.com*, June 20, 2018. (Web).

4   Stereo Williams, "The Year That Changed Hip-Hop Forever," *thedailybeast.com*, February 26, 2018. (Web).

5   Teddy Riley and Peder "Lido" Losnegård, "Teddy Riley and Lido in Conversation with Jeff Weiss," *native-instruments.com*, July 18, 2018. (Web).

6   Timmy Gatling, "Timmy Gatling Interview—Part 1," YouTube video, posted by Knyte77, October 15, 2007. (Web).

7   Robert "Bob" Celestin, interview with author, May 2016.

8   Ibid.

9   Joseph "Jojo" Brim, interview with author, June 2015.

10 Riley only produced the one single on Kemp's debut and "I Want Her" was the only up-tempo song Riley produced on Sweat's slow-jam-laden debut album. As such, while Sweat and Kemp's releases from that time are remembered as New Jack Swing, it was only the individual singles that pushed the new sound of R&B.

11 Much of *Guy* was mixed at Greene Street and Chung King studios, where numerous late-1980s rap records were mixed.

Chapter 35

1   Tristan Bath, "'Noise Is Japanese Blues': An Interview With Boris," *The Quietus*, June 19, 2014.

2   "Top 50 Albums of 2006," *Pitchfork*, December 19, 2006.

3   Vicente Gutierrez and Mizuho Ota, "Boris," *Pitchfork*, April 28, 2008.

4   Nina Corcoran, "Review of Boris – *Pink* (Deluxe Edition)," *Consequence of Sound*, July 21, 2016.

5   John Wray, "Heady Metal," *The New York Times*, May 28, 2006.

Chapter 37

1 Fred Cole in *Unknown Passage: The Dead Moon Story* [DVD], Dir. Jason Summers and Kate Fix (Magic Umbrella Films and Tombstone Records, 2006).
2 Ibid.
3 Ibid.
4 Ibid.
5 Les Paul and Mary Ford, "Vaya Con Dios" (Los Angeles: Capitol Records, 1953).
6 The Range Rats, "Vaya Con Dios," *The Range Rats* (Portland, OR: Mississippi Records, 2010).

Chapter 38

1 Simon Reynolds, *Retromania: Pop Culture's Addiction to Its Own Past* (New York: Faber and Faber Ltd., 2011).
2 Daniel Lopatin, "I Am Musician Oneohtrix Point Never, Currently Importing SysEx Files into FM8—AMA: Indieheads," *Reddit*. (Web).

Chapter 40

1 ("Bruce Springsteen." Interviewed by Kirsty Young on BBC Radio 4 on 18 December 2016.)

Chapter 41

1 (Author interview with artist, 2006).
2 (Author interview with artist, 2006).
3 (Author interview with artist, 2006).

Chapter 42

1 Steve Guttenberg, *Can't Stop the Music* [Amazon Prime streaming], dir. Nancy Walker (Los Angeles: Associated Film Distribution, 1980).
2 J. D. Bratt, J. Worst, L. Zuidervaart, Q. J. Schultze, R. M. Anker, and W. D. Romanowski, *Dancing in the Dark: Youth, Popular Culture and the Electronic Media* (Grand Rapids, MI: Wm. B. Eerdmans Publishing Co., 1990).

Chapter 43

1 Clive Bell, "Sayonara Cruel World: Haruomi Hosono," *The Wire*, August 1997: 35.

2   Paul Roquet, *Ambient Media: Japanese Atmospheres of Self* (Minneapolis: University of Minnesota Press, 2016), 12, 55.

3   Quoted in ibid., 179.

4   Bell, "Sayonara Cruel World," 35.

5   Yuji Tanaka, "Interview with Haruomi Hosono," liner notes to Haruomi Hosono, *Philharmony* [33 1/3 rpm] (Light in the Attic Records [LITA], 2018), 170.

6   David Toop, *Exotica: Fabricated Soundscapes in a Real World* (London: Serpent's Tail, 1999), 222; Roquet, *Ambient Media*, 58, citing a 1984 conversation between Hosono and science-writer Yoshinari Mayumi.

7   Mark Derry, "Ryuichi Sakamoto: The Noise from Nippon," *Elle*, September 1988. (Web).

8   Toop, *Exotica*, 223.

Chapter 44

1   *Metroid* was released one year earlier in Japan on the Famicom disc system—the Japanese equivalent of the NES.

2   Alexander Brandon, "Shooting from the Hip: An Interview with Hip Tanaka," *Gamasutra*, September 25, 2002. (Web).

3   Brad Shoemaker, "History of *Metroid*," *Gamespot*. (Web).

4   Jonti Davies, "The Making of *Super Metroid*," *NowGamer*. (Web).

5   Brandon, "Shooting from the Hip." Tanaka later reworded this same idea, noting his love for the idea of a game "whose audio [would be] composed of sound effects"; see Tomohisa Kuramitsu, "GameSetBaiyon: An Audience with Hirokazu Hip Tanaka," *GameSetWatch*, December 10, 2009. (Web).

6   William Gibbons argues that Tanaka's functionally ambiguous score to *Metroid* highlights the simultaneous diegetic and non-diegetic nature of game sound—"we are not able to separate what Samus [the game's protagonist] hears from what we hear." In doing so, "Tanaka's soundscape becomes an experimental reflection of how we interact with games—the fine line between human and machine, or between player and avatar" (357); see William Gibbons, "The Sounds in the Machine: Hirokazu Tanaka's Cybernetic Soundscape for *Metroid*," in *The Palgrave Handbook of Sound Design and Music in Screen Media*, ed. Liz Greene and Danijela Kulezic-Wilson (London: Palgrave Macmillan, 2016), 347–60.

7   William Cheng, *Sound Play: Video Games and the Musical Imagination* (New York: Oxford University Press, 2014), 97–103.

8   William Gibbons, "Wandering Tonalities: Silence, Sound, and Morality in the Shadow of the Colossus," in *Music in Video Games: Studying Play*, ed. K. J. Donnelly, William Gibbons, and Neil Lerner (New York: Routledge, 2014), 122–37.

Chapter 46

1   Bradley Bambarger, "'Shutter Island' Soundtrack Casts Eerie Spell," *The Star-Ledger*, March 12, 2010.

2   Paul Coates, *The Story of the Lost Reflection* (London: Verso, 1985).

Chapter 47

1 *Wesley Willis's Joy Rides* [DVD], dir. Chris Bagley (Eyeosaur Productions, 2008).

2 Meher Baba, *Discourses* (Myrtle Beach, S.C.: Sheriar Press, 1995), xiii.

3 *Wesley Willis's Joy Rides.*

4 Ibid.

5 Ibid.

6 Carla Winterbottom, telephone interview, 2018.

7 Ibid.

8 Ibid.

9 Ibid.

10 Michael Muhammad Knight, *Blue-Eyed Devil: A Road Odyssey Through Islamic America* (New York: Autonomedia, 2006), 8–9.

11 Winterbottom, telephone interview.

12 William Donkin, *The Wayfarers* (Myrtle Beach, S.C.: Sheriar Press, 1988), 8.

13 Winterbottom, telephone interview.

14 Dale Meiners, telephone interview, 2018.

15 Ibid.

16 Winterbottom, telephone interview.

17 *Wesley Willis's Joy Rides.*

18 Meiners, telephone interview.

19 *Wesley Willis's Joy Rides.*

20 Carl Caprioglio (Executive Producer, Oglio Records) and Jonathan Rosner (Publishing, The Bicycle Music Company), telephone interviews in 2017 and 2018, respectively.

21 Jello Biafra, "Why I Love Wesley Willis," in *Greatest Hits*, vol. 2 [Vinyl] (San Franciso, C.A.: Alternative Tentacles Records, 1999).

22 Meiners, telephone interview.

23 Baba, *Discourses*, xv.

24 Miguel de Cervantes, *Don Quixote*, trans. Thomas Shelton (New York: P. F. Collier & Son Corp., 1970), 19–20.

25 Barbara Ehrenreich, *Dancing in the Streets: A History of Collective Joy* (New York: Metropolitan Books, 2006), 28.

26 Ibid., 30.

27 Ibid., 256.

28 Scott Heisel, "Wesley Willis: 1963–2003," *Punknews.org.* (Web).

29 Ibid.

Chapter 48

1 Trent Reznor, interview by Anthony Bozza, "The Fragile World of Trent Reznor," *Rolling Stone*, October 14, 1999.

2 Ibid.

Chapter 49

1 R. J. Gleason, "Bob Dylan Gives Press Conference in San Francisco," *Rolling Stone*, December 14, 1967). (Web).

2 D. Browne, "How Bob Dylan Made a Pre-Rock Masterpiece with 'Love and Theft,'" *Rolling Stone*, September 11, 2016. (Web).

3 Ibid.

4 D. Brinkley, "Bob Dylan's Late-Era, Old-Style American Individualism," *Rolling Stone*, May 14, 2009. (Web).

5 M. Gilmore, "Bob Dylan Unleashed," *Rolling Stone*, September 27, 2012. (Web).

6 Browne, "How Bob Dylan Made a Pre-Rock Masterpiece."

Chapter 50

1 Steve Dollar, "David Berman Finds Comfort in His Own Head," *New York Sun*, June 17, 2008. (Web).

Chapter 51

1 *Heart Like a Hand Grenade*, (*Heart Like a Hand Grenade*: Roecker, John, dir. 2015. [https://www.imdb.com/title/tt1018728/]).

2 ("Billie Joe Armstrong, Michael Mayer on 'American Idiot,'" interview with *TheaterTalk*, CUNY TV, 8 May 2010. [https://youtu.be/deEg-M6fEWE]).

3 ("Billie Joe Armstrong, Michael Mayer on 'American Idiot,'" interview with *TheaterTalk*, CUNY TV, 8 May 2010. [https://youtu.be/deEg-M6fEWE]).

4 (*Heart Like a Hand Grenade*: Roecker, John, dir. *Heart Like a Hand Grenade*, 2015. [https://www.imdb.com/title/tt1018728/]).

5 ("Interview with Michael Mayer & Tom Kitt - Green Day's American Idiot: The Musical," *The Arts Guild*, 29 December 2011. [https://youtu.be/-Z83SvsGVJY]).

6 (Hamilton, Doug, dir. *Broadway Idiot*, 2013. [https://www.imdb.com/title/tt2689966]).

7 (Hamilton, Doug, dir. *Broadway Idiot*, 2013. [https://www.imdb.com/title/tt2689966]).

8 (Hamilton, Doug, dir. *Broadway Idiot*, 2013. [https://www.imdb.com/title/tt2689966]).

ALSO AVAILABLE

65. Big Star's *Radio City* by Bruce Eaton

66. Madness's *One Step Beyond ...* by Terry Edwards

67. Brian Eno's *Another Green World* by Geeta Dayal

68. The Flaming Lips' *Zaireeka* by Mark Richardson

69. The Magnetic Fields' *69 Love Songs* by L. D. Beghtol

70. Israel Kamakawiwo'ole's *Facing Future* by Dan Kois

71. Public Enemy's *It Takes a Nation of Millions to Hold Us Back* by Christopher R. Weingarten

72. Pavement's *Wowee Zowee* by Bryan Charles

73. AC/DC's *Highway to Hell* by Joe Bonomo

74. Van Dyke Parks' *Song Cycle* by Richard Henderson

75. Slint's *Spiderland* by Scott Tennent

76. Radiohead's *Kid A* by Marvin Lin

77. Fleetwood Mac's *Tusk* by Rob Trucks

78. Nine Inch Nails' *Pretty Hate Machine* by Daphne Carr

79. Ween's *Chocolate and Cheese* by Hank Shteamer

80. Johnny Cash's *American Recordings* by Tony Tost

81. The Rolling Stones' *Some Girls* by Cyrus R. K. Patell

82. Dinosaur Jr.'s *You're Living All Over Me* by Nick Attfield

83. Television's *Marquee Moon* by Bryan Waterman

84. Aretha Franklin's *Amazing Grace* by Aaron Cohen

85. Portishead's *Dummy* by R. J. Wheaton

86. Talking Heads' *Fear of Music* by Jonathan Lethem

87. Serge Gainsbourg's *Histoire de Melody Nelson* by Darran Anderson

88. They Might Be Giants' *Flood* by S. Alexander Reed and Philip Sandifer

89. Andrew W.K.'s *I Get Wet* by Phillip Crandall

90. Aphex Twin's *Selected Ambient Works Volume II* by Marc Weidenbaum

91. Gang of Four's *Entertainment* by Kevin J. H. Dettmar

92. Richard Hell and the Voidoids' *Blank Generation* by Pete Astor

93. J. Dilla's *Donuts* by Jordan Ferguson

94. The Beach Boys' *Smile* by Luis Sanchez

95. Oasis's *Definitely Maybe* by Alex Niven

96. Liz Phair's *Exile in Guyville* by Gina Arnold

97. Kanye West's *My Beautiful Dark Twisted Fantasy* by Kirk Walker Graves

98. Danger Mouse's *The Grey Album* by Charles Fairchild

99. Sigur Rós's *()* by Ethan Hayden
100. Michael Jackson's *Dangerous* by Susan Fast
101. Can's *Tago Mago* by Alan Warner
102. Bobbie Gentry's *Ode to Billie Joe* by Tara Murtha
103. Hole's *Live Through This* by Anwen Crawford
104. Devo's *Freedom of Choice* by Evie Nagy
105. Dead Kennedys' *Fresh Fruit for Rotting Vegetables* by Michael Stewart Foley
106. Koji Kondo's *Super Mario Bros. Soundtrack* by Andrew Schartmann
107. Beat Happening's *Beat Happening* by Bryan C. Parker
108. Metallica's *Metallica* by David Masciotra
109. Phish's *A Live One* by Walter Holland
110. Miles Davis's *Bitches Brew* by George Grella Jr.
111. Blondie's *Parallel Lines* by Kembrew McLeod
112. Grateful Dead's *Workingman's Dead* by Buzz Poole
113. New Kids on the Block's *Hangin' Tough* by Rebecca Wallwork
114. The Geto Boys' *The Geto Boys* by Rolf Potts
115. Sleater-Kinney's *Dig Me Out* by Jovana Babovic
116. LCD Soundsystem's *Sound of Silver* by Ryan Leas
117. Donny Hathaway's *Donny Hathaway Live* by Emily J. Lordi
118. The Jesus and Mary Chain's *Psychocandy* by Paula Mejía
119. The Modern Lovers' *The Modern Lovers* by Sean L. Maloney
120. Angelo Badalamenti's *Soundtrack from Twin Peaks* by Clare Nina Norelli
121. Young Marble Giants' *Colossal Youth* by Michael Blair and Joe Bucciero
122. The Pharcyde's *Bizarre Ride II the Pharcyde* by Andrew Barker
123. Arcade Fire's *The Suburbs* by Eric Eidelstein
124. Bob Mould's *Workbook* by Walter Biggins and Daniel Couch
125. Camp Lo's *Uptown Saturday Night* by Patrick Rivers and Will Fulton
126. The Raincoats' *The Raincoats* by Jenn Pelly
127. Björk's *Homogenic* by Emily Mackay
128. Merle Haggard's *Okie from Muskogee* by Rachel Lee Rubin
129. Fugazi's *In on the Kill Taker* by Joe Gross
130. Jawbreaker's *24 Hour Revenge Therapy* by Ronen Givony
131. Lou Reed's *Transformer* by Ezra Furman
132. Drive-By Truckers' *Southern Rock Opera* by Rien Fertel
133. Siouxsie and the Banshees' *Peepshow* by Samantha Bennett

134. dc Talk's *Jesus Freak* by Will Stockton and D. Gilson
135. Tori Amos's *Boys for Pele* by Amy Gentry
136. Odetta's *One Grain of Sand* by Matthew Frye Jacobson
137. Manic Street Preachers' *The Holy Bible* by David Evans
138. The Shangri-Las' *Golden Hits of the Shangri-Las* by Ada Wolin
139. Tom Petty's *Southern Accents* by Michael Washburn

Which essay should become a new ?

You've read *The 33 1/3 B-sides*, now we want to know which album
you'd like to know more about!

If you could see one of these authors expand on their essay and write a new
volume for the 33 1/3 series, who would you vote for?

Please visit https://333sound.com/vote-for-the-next-33-1-3!/
to vote for your favorite.

- ☐ Prince's *Emancipation* (1996)
- ☐ Christina Aguilera's *Mi Reflejo* (2000)
- ☐ Leonard Cohen's *Songs of Love and Hate* (1971)
- ☐ The New York Dolls' *Too Much, Too Soon* (1974)
- ☐ The Rolling Stones' *It's Only Rock 'n Roll* (1974)
- ☐ The Durutti Column's *The Return of the Durutti Column* (1980)
- ☐ R.E.M.'s *Chronic Town* (1982)
- ☐ Rites of Spring's *Rites of Spring* (1985)
- ☐ Jane's Addiction's *Nothing's Shocking* (1988)
- ☐ Del Amitri's *Waking Hours* (1989)
- ☐ Sinéad O'Connor's *I Do Not Want What I Haven't Got* (1990)
- ☐ De La Soul's *De La Soul Is Dead* (1991)
- ☐ Digable Planets' *Reachin' (A New Refutation of Time and Space)* (1993)
- ☐ Billy Idol's *Cyberpunk* (1993)
- ☐ Guided by Voices' *Mag Earwhig!* (1997)
- ☐ The Smashing Pumpkins' *Adore* (1998)
- ☐ The Weakerthans' *Left and Leaving* (2000)
- ☐ Hank Thompson's *Smoky the Bar* (1969)
- ☐ Robert Johnson's *King of the Delta Blues Singers* (1961)
- ☐ The Doors' *Strange Days* (1967)
- ☐ The Dells' *There Is* (1968)
- ☐ Shirley and Dolly Collins' *Anthems in Eden* (1969)
- ☐ Von Freeman's *Doin' It Right Now* (1972)
- ☐ John Cale's *Paris 1919* (1973)
- ☐ Bert Jansch's *L.A. Turnaround* (1974)
- ☐ The Cars' *Candy-O* (1979)
- ☐ Ian Dury and The Blockheads' *Laughter* (1980)
- ☐ Frankie Armstrong, Brian Pearson, Blowzabella, and Jon Gillaspie's *Tam Lin* (1984)
- ☐ Scritti Politti's *Cupid & Psyche 85* (1985)
- ☐ Negativland's *Escape From Noise* (1987)
- ☐ Frank Black's *Frank Black* (1993)
- ☐ Rodan's *Rusty* (1994)
- ☐ Kenickie's *At the Club* (1997)

- [ ] Guy's *Guy* (1988)
- [ ] Sleep's *Dopesmoker* (2003)
- [ ] The Blood Brothers' *Crimes* (2004)
- [ ] Boris's *Pink* (2006)
- [ ] Stars of Lid's *And Their Refinement of the Decline* (2007)
- [ ] The Range Rats' *The Range Rats* (2010)
- [ ] Daniel Lopatin's *Chuck Person's Eccojams Vol. 1* (2010)
- [ ] The Band's *Rock of Ages* (1972)
- [ ] Bruce Springsteen's *Bruce Springsteen and the E Street Band Live at the Geneva Theater* (1974)
- [ ] Talisker's *Dreaming of Glenisla* (1975)
- [ ] The Village People's *Can't Stop the Music: The Original Motion Picture Soundtrack* (1980)
- [ ] Haruomi Hosono's *Philharmony* (1982)
- [ ] Hirokazu Tanaka's *Metroid* (1986)
- [ ] Various Artists' *Music from the Motion Picture Pulp Fiction* (1994)
- [ ] Various Artists' *Casino Soundtrack* (1995)
- [ ] Wesley Willis's *Rock 'n' Roll Will Never Die* (1996)
- [ ] Nine Inch Nails' *The Fragile* (1999)
- [ ] Bob Dylan's *Love and Theft* (2001)
- [ ] Silver Jews' *Bright Flight* (2001)
- [ ] *The Original Broadway Cast Recording Featuring Green Day's American Idiot* (2010)
- [ ] Perfume's *LEVEL3* (2013)
- [ ] Dawn of Midi's *Dysnomia* (2015)